ISLAM AND MUSLIM COMMUNITIES IN SOUTH ASIA

ISLAM AND MUSLIM COMMUNITIES IN SOUTH ASIA

Edited by
NADEEM HASNAIN

SERIALS PUBLICATIONS
NEW DELHI (INDIA)

First Published-2006

ISBN: 81-8387-014-7

Published by

SERIALS PUBLICATIONS
4830/24, Prahlad Street, Ansari Road
Darya Ganj, New Delhi-110002 (India)
Phone : 23245225
Fax : 91-11-23272135
E-mail: serials@satyam.net.in
www.serialspub.com

CONTENTS

PREFACE

Islam and Muslim Communities of South Asia is still a deficient area of study within the domain of social sciences. Though academicians of history have been contributing to this area of investigation, sociologists and social anthropologists have turned any serious attention to it only during the last decade. TN Madan's *Muslim Communities of South Asia* (1976) with two revised editions is a notable contribution to this field followed by Imtiaz Ahmed's works and now Ahmed & Refield's *Lived Islam in South Asia (2004).*

When we acknowledge the fact that 'Textual Islam' and 'Lived Islam' are not one and the same thing, we acknowledge the empirical validity of Islam as practiced by its followers, the different Muslim communities living within their respective cultural-ecological zones. The dichotomy between the 'Great Tradition' and 'Little Traditions' of Hindus have already established the empirical validity of Hinduism with reference to the Textual Hinduism and there is a variety of studies done by sociologists and social anthropologists.

The present volume is also an attempt to understand Islam and its derived socio-cultural practices and their concomitant economic and political dimensions through empirical investigation in different parts of India, Pakistan and Bangladesh. The volume does not carry any study from Nepal and Srilanka and admittedly this is a glaring deficiency but it has been compensated through a variety of studies ranging from caste and social stratification, family and kinship structure, Islamic movements, rites and rituals, Islamic mysticism, saint worship, Hindu-Muslim relations and rise of communalism, papers on fringe communities such as Bohras and Shias, plight of the descendants of the erstwhile Awadhs ruling dynasty to impact of Gulf migration and 'ecology and social organization.' Thus, it is hoped that this volume will be able to present so many different dimensions and aspects of Islam and Muslim communities.

Some of the papers appearing in this volume were published in a special issue of the internationally renowned journal *The Eastern Anthropologist* guest edited by the editor of the present volume in 2001. Some of the papers had already been published by this journal even before this special issue was published while the remaining were especially invited for this volume. The editor is thankful to the *Ethnographic and Folk Culture Society* for allowing the inclusion of all these papers from its journal in the present volume. At the same time the editor also expresses his gratitude to the authors especially invited to contribute to this volume and thank them for bearing with him the unavoidable delay in the publication of this volume. Mr. S.K. Jha and his able son Mr. Vijay Kumar deserve special thanks for undertaking the actual production of the volume within the shortest possible time.

Nadeem Hasnain

CONTRIBUTORS

Jonah Blank is Senior Editor (Anthropology), US News & World Report, Washington, DC.

Hafeezur Rehman Chowdhry teaches in the Department of Anthropology, Quaid-i-Azam University, Islamabad.

Frank S. Fanselow teaches Anthropology at the University of Brunei, Darusslam, Gadong, Brunei.

Nasreen Fazalbhoy teaches in the Department of Sociology, Mumbai University, Mumbai.

Amir Hasan (late) was an administrator turned anthropologist in Uttar Pradesh.

Qamar Hasan teaches in the Department of Psychology, Aligarh Muslim University, Aligarh.

Nadeem Hasnain teaches in the Department of Anthropology, University of Lucknow, Lucknow.

Monirul Husain teaches in the Department of Political Science, University of Gauhati, Guwahati.

Laura D. Jenkins is on the faculty of Political Science, University of Cincinnati, Ohio.

Mohd. Shairul Mashrique teaches in the Department of Public Administration, University of Chittgong, Chittagong.

Haider Mehdi is on the faculty of Sociology, Shia PG College, Lucknow.

Sekh Rahim Mondal teaches at the Centre for Himalayan Studies and Department of Anthropology, University of North Bengal, Darjeeling.

M.H. Sidkey is on the faculty of Anthropology, The Ohio State University, Columbus, Ohio.

Yoginder Sikand, till recently, was teaching in the Faculty of Islamic Studies, Jamia Hamdard, New Delhi.

Ifrah Zilberman teaches social anthropology at Beit Berl College, Beit Berl, Israel.

Theodore P. Wright Jr., is Emeritus Professor of Political Science, State University of New York at Albany, USA.

INTRODUCTION

There are more Muslims in South Asia than any other region of the world. South Asia is also a compact geographical region which is the meeting place of three major world religions. The majority populations in the four most important South Asian countries, India, Pakistan, Bangladesh and Srilanka, profess Hinduism, Islam and Buddhism.

But South Asia also presents a unique facet of life. As Donald E. Smith (1966) rightly points out, one is impressed by the essential unity of South Asia in various important respects. Racially, linguistically, historically and to a considerable extent culturally, the region has a distinctive identity which can not be readily merged with either Southeast Asia or West Asia. At the same time there are strikingly different social values, institutions and patterns of behaviour rooted in the three great religious traditions. He further says that it is important to recognize that there are indeed *three* traditions. While Buddhism originated as a sectarian movement within Hinduism and accepted certain basic Hindu concepts with little modification, its social and political implications and manifestations have been very different. As we shall see, at several important points, the differences between Buddhism and Hinduism are fundamental. Hinduism and Islam share certain assumptions about the role of religion in society which find no parallel in Buddhist thought and practice.

As this volume endeavours to show Islam can not and should not be understood through the works of theologians alone, for whom it is a formal, uniform and rigid system of beliefs and practices. As Imitiaz Ahmed and Helmut Reifeld (2004) rightly points out 'Popular Islam', or Islam as it is practiced by millions of Muslims in South Asia, has an empirical validity and is a dynamic process of adjustment and accommodation as well as conflict with other religions, with which it coexists. "There are many Islams". Incidentally but unfortunately Islam in South Asia has not received its due attention. The present volume, through its twenty one papers, endeavours to gain an understanding of how Muslim communities live with non-Muslim populations and practice Islam in their own ways. Historically, there has been multi-cultural and multi-religious co-existence because nowhere in South Asia did Islam develop in a religiously isolated and exclusively Islamic environment. The togetherness and the overlapping spheres of life with other religions has been common pattern. "South Asia is probably the largest area in the world where Islam exists within a mixed, composite culture, overlapping with several other religions. No matter how many origins of political conflicts one may find in the domain of culture and religion, there are, at the same time, elements of peaceful co-existence as well" (ibid).

This 'Islam in practice', or 'real existing Islam' may guide the students of Islam to understand Muslim communities. That is why one gets amused by the soaring sales of the *Qoran* in the West after 9/11, as non-Muslim world especially the Christian west rushed to find out what is said about this or that. Oliver Roy (2004) sounds very convincing when he writes that "the key question is not what the Koran says, but what Muslims say the Koran says. The issue is not Islam as a theological corpus, but the discourses and practices of Muslims." Roy knocks the idea that the problems of the contemporary Muslim world can be explained in terms of Islam. He further points out that most of the world's Muslims are not Arabs hence the main reason for the political backwardness of the Arab world may be Arab culture rather than Islam. Nor it is true that secularization always leads to democracy. In west Asia secularization is associated with dictatorship, whether you take Shah of Iran, Saddam Husain, President Ben Ali in Tunisia or the cancellation of Algeria's parliamentary elections in 1992 on the grounds that the Islamists would have won. We may deplore the relative absence of liberal reformist thinkers in Islam, but that is also a problem with global protestantism.

Muslim communities in South Asia, with a few exceptions such as some Muslim communities of Gujarat, are living under conditions of extreme poverty and, perhaps with the exception of Muslims of Kerala, under high rates of illiteracy and dropouts. In case of India redundancy of traditional arts and crafts, in which they once excelled, due to introduction of new technologies and the socalled globalization has led to largescale unemployment. With the cost of education going up and the growing communalization of course content, the poor Muslims, particularly artisans and peasants, prefer to send their children to *Madrasas*, where they get outdated and irrelevant education. Neglect and sometimes opposition to the education of the girl child is a serious problem, further accentuated by the *purdah* system. Obscurantist and regressive outlook of the socalled religious leaders is also a big hurdle in the modernization of Muslim communities. The above state of affairs has led to stagnation of the majority segments of Muslim communities. Instigation of communal riots, communalization of education, especially at the primary and secondary school level, discrimination in employment in government, public and private sectors and prejudices against Muslims in residential areas of cities leading to segregation of Muslims promotes 'ghettoization'. All such factors contribute to creating a mindset among the Muslims leading to opposition to any reform and secularization.

The present volume does not have a precisely defined theme. It should be seen as a book of readings consisting of diverse facets of Islam and Muslim communities but most of the papers deal with modes of social organization, religiosity and spiritualism/mysticism, and attributes of social-cultural identity. On the whole it tries to portray various aspects of Adaptation, Accommodation and Conflict on the canvas of Muslim communities of South Asia.

II

Despite the ideological and doctrinaire posture of Islam, Muslim societies of the South Asia are highly stratified. The first three papers–by Laura Jenkins, Monirul Husain and Amir Hasan deal with the empirical aspect of social stratification among the Muslims. Jenkins has taken up a virtually invisible area of investigation with Muslim stratification by talking about 'boundaries of social backwardness' in terms of Muslim OBCs. There is constitutional support for special policies for the weaker sections of Indian society and it included, besides the Scheduled Castes and Scheduled Tribes, Other Backward Classes (OBCs). The socially and educationally backward Muslim 'castes' or 'caste like groups' (occupational categories) have also been brought under the protective umbrella of Constitution of India. It has also sharpened the divide between the *Ashraf* (higher castes/status groups) Muslims and *Ajlaf* (lower castes). Significantly the Muslim OBCs are bitterly opposed to any demand of reservation of jobs for Muslims as a category because in that case the more 'advanced' groups among them shall grab all the opportunities. Jenkins, tracing the historical roots of Muslim stratification, makes an objective analysis of the economics and politics of 'backwardness' among the Indian Muslims. Monirul Hasan in his paper has analysed caste based stratification among the Muslims of Assam on the basis of Assam's history and contemporary Assamese society. He categorises Assamese Muslims into Assamese Muslims, Neo-Assamese Muslims, Muslims of Barrack valley and North Indian Muslims settled in Assam and takes up only the first category. Amir Hasan in his paper takes up the case of the Muslims of the larger Gujjar community, an important pastoral group of North India. The way elements of caste are brought forward by the neo-converts to Islam reminds us of an empirically established fact–a number of Hindu populations changed their religion but not the caste.

In every social group or community kinship is considered to be a vehicle for understanding the internal mechanism of social structure. Some scholars have described the system of kinship itself as a 'sub-structure'. Shairul Mashreque in his paper has analysed the structure of kinship relations in a peasant community of Bangladesh. The objective of this paper is to identify kinship grouping, description of the concepts involving kinship relations and an analysis of the terminological features in the context of the exiting network of relations. He shows in his paper that to recognize the structure of kinship relations one may look at it from three dimensions–consanguinity, affinity and fiction. His field work demonstrates that the kinship structure appears to combine all these three dimensions.

Manu Bhaskar's paper takes a look at the family law and customary practices of Moplah/Mappila Muslims of Kerala. The paper seeks to argue that one cannot understand the legal process of formulation of the law, divine or otherwise, without understanding the dynamics of social transformation, i.e. even divine law which is believed to be immutable cannot escape the effect of social transformation. An attempt has been made in this paper to show the prevalent customary practices of the Muslims and to compare them with the Mohammadan Law with regard to family law.

The next nine papers present, in some way or the other, different aspects of religious system. Yoginder Sikand's paper presents a narration and analysis of the *Tablighi Jamaat*, the most widespread, yet least studied, Islamic movement in the contemporary world. Sikand's paper takes a close analytical view of this movement in post-1947 Mewat, the region where the movement originated in the 1920s. The author is of the view that the post-Babri Masjid demolition situation has convinced many Meos of the pressing need to consolidate their ranks and push towards the economic and educational development of the community, if it is to withstand the growing challenge and threat of Hindutva militancy. This would almost certainly also entail a growing stress on their Muslim identity.

The annual rites of the Daudi Bohras, a fringe community among the Muslims of South Asia, is the theme of Jonah Blank's paper. The author has analysed the annual rites with reference to the Islamic identity as universal and unique. For Indian Muslims, the question of identity permeates all aspects of life. The issue of identity, of how to relate both the universal Islamic *ummah* and to the land of their birth, is one with which all Muslims of the subcontinent wrestle. Unlike Muslims of almost all other denominations, the Bohras have a rigidly centralized clergy under the hegemonic guidance of a single apex cleric known as the *dai al-mutlaq*. In the Bohra world view, there is no inherent conflict between their identity as Muslims and their identity as Gujarati Indians.

Another fringe community, the Kutchi Memons, is the population studied by Nasreen Fazalbhoy with reference to two of their rituals of protection, *Niyaz* and *Sadqa*. Mohd. Shairul Mashreque in his paper on religion and religiosity in rural Bangladesh has demonstrated that socio-religious institutions shape the peasant's world view and orientation about community power and about their own limited good and predicament. This study shows the range of activities coupled with the instruments of social action that are oriented toward sacred values within the fold of Islam. It also indicates the dynamics of community organization at the micro-level with reference to various manifestations of religiosity and their constructive and dysfunctional aspects.

Shia Muslims are one of the least studied religious minorities of the Indian sub-continent though Shiaism as a part of the religious ideology of Islam has got a fair share in social science literature. Nadeem Hasnain in this paper has discussed the religious system of the Shias focusing on the exclusive Shiite concepts viz. *Ahle-e-Bait, Imamate, Ismah, Taqqiyah* and *Taqleed*. Then he goes on to relate their religious world view, especially mourning over the 'martyr dom of Kerbala', with their day to day life.

Two papers of Hafeezur Rehman Chowdhry dealing with Islamic mysticism, saint worship and relationship between *Pir* and *Murid* have been included in this volume to understand an important dimension of spiritualism in Pakistan. The symbiotic relationship between a devotee and a shrine is maintained through regular rituals confirming their mutual dependence. Shrines are complex social institutions with a number of characteristics distinctive to their role in the life and culture of Pakistan. In the rural areas of Pakistan the majority of the people believe in a system popularly known as *Piri-Muridi*. If some one does not believe in *Piri-Muridi* he is labeled as *Beypira* or *BeyMurshida* i.e. without an elder and religious guide. *Bay'at* is a system of spiritual allegiance to a spiritual leader. All these come under mystical dimensions of Islam. Kumkum Srivastava's paper reveals the secret of the Sufi, Abu Bakr Tusi, and explains some of his more startling achievements. Drawing from a wide selection of the Sufi teachings and classical writings she offers an introduction to a body of thought widely relevent to the contemporary world.

The domain of the grave is an important area of investigation in a religious system. Ifrah Zilberman in her paper has analysed the domain of the grave among the Muslims of North India and compared it to the same domain among the Palestinian Muslim. Exploration of the social and religious notions of death and burial is a journey into the core of the systems of belief of a society. The main argument in this paper is that the core of rituals and belief in the domain of Muslim burial in India is similar to that of Muslim burial in Palestinian society, and indeed, among the Muslims of the Middle East. However, the envelope of rituals surrounding the acts of burial and visiting graves among the Muslims of North India was largely influenced by Hinduism.

Communal riots between Hindus and Muslims have been a familiar feature of North and Western India. Its spread into South India is a recent phenomenon. The two papers by Theodore P. Wright Jr. and Frank Fanselow deal with the phenomenon of communalism and communal riots in South India especially Tamil Nadu. As Fanselow details, the communalization of the South began with the sudden conversion to Islam of several villages inhabited by the Scheduled Castes in Tamil Nadu in 1981. It was largely a reaction to the continuing atrocities and humiliation of the Scheduled Castes in day to day social life of the local society. With the help of the primary data the authors have analysed the role of Hindu organizations in keeping the communal cauldron boiling to help the Pro-Hindu political parties through polarization of people along religious/communal lines.

The word 'life-space' is a key concept in the field theory proposed by Lewin. Lewin made use of a picture of circle enclosed by but not touching an ellipse to represent life space. Qamar Hasan in his paper demonstrates that life space of Indian Muslims can not be understood without the behaviour of the members of the community which can not be considered independent of psychological environment in which they find themselves. He has taken a close look at the Muslims in post-partition era which he divides into the periods of 1947-59, 1960-69, 1970-79, 1980-89 and 1990-1999. Through the periods social and political attitude of Muslims, their educational-economic backwardness, quality of life and sense of deprivation, minority complexes, assimilation and identity etc. have been analysed and discussed.

One of the largest Muslim populations have inhabited the undivided Bengal and even West Bengal, now coming under India. Sekh Rahim Mondal in his paper has discussed culture change among the Muslim society in West Bengal. Like the Muslims of the other parts of the country, Bengali Muslisms, too, adhere to basic principles of Islam and at the same time share the local traditions of Bengal. There is no conflict between the two spheres, although both the boundaries are sharply defined by their respective ideology and practice. In this paper, the author has analysed the traditional social organization of Muslims and the trends of change coming into it through the process of modernization.

The Awadh dynasty of Nawabs has been one of the few Shia ruling dynasties in South Asia. Haider Mehdi in his paper has undertaken a socio-historical study of *wasiqa* and *wasiqa* holders of Awadh. *Wasiqa* in Arabic language means a document or bond or obligation. The East India Company in the 19th century borrowed a huge amounts of money from the then ruler of Awadh and under this treaty the fixed interest (*wasiqa*) was to be disbursed among the royal descendants by the East India Company. The practice is still in vogue. Interestingly with the division of the *wasiqa* in successive generations, the amount being received by some families has shrunk to ridiculous amounts of money – as low as rupee one only per month. Ironically a person is seen spending twenty rupees or more on conveyance to collect this amount from the *wasiqa* office. With the passage of time the socio-economic plight of the *wasiqa* holders kept on deteriorating to the extent of pauperization and many of them are now eking out their livelihood through odd jobs such as rickshaw pulling, vendors, labourers, etc. Of course, some of the enterprising and educated among them are glaring exceptions.

The identity of a community is not only a conscious construct of the group members but is perpetually influenced and redefined through the mediation of various historical and socio-political circumstances. Contemporary social-identity studies have broadened the scope of the concept of identity from individual role conflict to a larger socio-political issue. For the Muslims in South Asia, religious beliefs and practices are an important part of their ethnicity. Shareena Banu in her paper on the Muslims of Kerala has discussed the influence of gulf migration on identity assertion patterns. It is to be noted that the Muslims in contemporary Kerala are categorized among the backward communities. This paper attempts to delineate some of the recent trends emerging in the process of construction and reconstruction of identity in the changing socio-political scenario. In comparison to other communities, Muslims in Kerala have witnessed rapid enrichment of the lower classes by Gulf remittances. For them material prosperity has not led to inculcation of motivation toward higher education or professional qualifications. But the author contends that migration may also lead to change in socio-religious identity and status of the migrants in society and even spiritual relationship with God may be reformulated in the process.

The Hunzakut, the people of Hunza, live in the Western Karokoram mountains (now part of northern Pakistan), in what has been called one of the most formidable upland regions on earth. These agri-pastoral people have been studied by M.H. Sidkey with reference to subsistence, ecology and social organization. The paper focuses on production strategies and their influences on the socio-economic organization of Hunzakut society. Each Hunzakut production strategy entails different social arrangements, as well as different land-use patterns that have certain implications for the social organization of Hunzakut households, villages and larger inter-village units.

REFERENCES

Ahmed, Imtiaz (2004), *'Lived Islam' in South Asia,* New Delhi: Social Science & Helmut Reifeld (eds.) Press.

Madan, T.N. (ed.) (1976), *Muslim Communities of South Asia,* New Delhi: Vikas Publishing House.

Roy, Oliver (2004), *Globalized Islam,* London: Hurst & Co.

Smith, Donald E. (ed.) (1966), *South Asian Politics and Religion,* Princeton: Princeton University Press.

CASTE, CLASS AND ISLAM: BOUNDARIES OF BACKWARDNESS IN INDIA

Laura D. Jenkins

Introduction

Muslims in South Asia are part of a global religion, yet local variations among Muslim identities persist. One aspect of this local variety is continuing class and even caste distinctions among Muslims. Almost forty years ago, *Eastern Anthropologist* published a classic work on caste and Islam, Ghaus Ansari's 'Muslim Caste in Uttar Pradesh' (1960). Building on Ansari's insights, in this article I will discuss the issue of Muslim caste in India in the 1990s. My focus is on contemporary debates over whether the Indian government should, for the purposes of compensatory discrimination policies, categorize Muslims as a whole together or retain the distinction between backward and forward members of the community. India's longstanding efforts to uplift its disadvantaged or backward sections through group based policies offers many lessons from which the rest of the world might learn. Since the United States and many other countries are trying to deal with issues of race and gender based disparities through affirmative action policies targeted at such groups, we find India's much longer history of group based policies instructive.

Caste inequalities within Islam is puzzling, for as Ghaus Ansari points out :

> "The philosophy of caste as a superstructure of social discrimination is quite contradictory to the basic beliefs of Islam which implicitly emphasizes quantity and universal Muslim brotherhood' (1960: 27)".

Many are surprised to learn of caste among Muslims in part because the creed is egalitarian and in part because caste has become so strongly associated with Hinduism. Caste, class and religious categories in India are so contingent and complex that the official categories used for group based policies are constantly thrown into question. Indian Muslims themselves are divided over who should benefit from reservations, or quotas in public employment and, in some cases, higher education. This issue highlights the variety among South Asian Muslims in two ways. First, the debate over who should fall into the officially 'backward' categories and benefit from affirmative action schemes forces us to consider the presence of class- and even caste- in Muslim society. Second, Muslims in India are at odds over the issue of reservations, some arguing for reservations for Muslims as a whole and other defending the subcategory of backward Muslims. Whether caste exists in Muslim society is not only an anthropological question but also become a legal and political one. Drawing on interviews, organizational literature, media accounts, and speeches, this article uses the issue of reservations to highlight both anthropological and political variety among Muslims in India.

Various compensatory discrimination policies in India are directed at Scheduled Castes (SCs), Scheduled Tribes (STs) and Other Backward Classes (OBCs). One form of these policies, reservations, have included reserved seats in university as well as reserved government jobs. Some Muslim groups currently benefit from reservations because they are included in the ST and OBC categories, but they are not supposed to be included in the Scheduled Castes, which are restricted to Hindus, Sikhs and Buddhists. As complicated as these categories may seem, they inevitably oversimplify society; yet society does not simply allow itself to be boxed up by the state. A common critique of compensatory discrimination on the basis of caste or racial categories, whether in India or the United States, is that the official classifications will reinforce caste or race. Yet social groups challenge state categories, both reacting to and exploiting the inherent complexity of overlapping identities. One example of this is the increasing number of groups in India contesting what it means to be backward. Constant claims and counter claims keep the official categories from stagnating, as the government adjust the categories in response to various demands.

Demands about reservations for Muslims are a case in point. There is such variety in the current demands that it seems we have little to fear about the reification of either the Muslim community or the Backwards category. Some Muslim organizations are trying to have Muslims as a whole declared backward, by advocating a simple religion based category. Since some Muslim groups are already Other Backward Classes or OBCs, a Muslim OBC group is opposing reservations for all Muslims on the grounds that class, or even caste, not just religion, must be taken into account. A Muslim SC association would prefer to be allowed to be included within the category. Still other Muslims are opposed to accepting affirmative action at all due to a reluctance to associate their religious group with the backward category. Thus it is not just the mostly Hindu beneficiaries of current policies that are worried about Muslim reservations, but also factions within Muslim society itself. Many state policies, as James Scott has pointed out, result in state simplifications of complex realities (Scott 1998). With any group based policy there is tension between state simplifications and social complications, the latter seem to be holding their own in India.

Religious Challenges to Caste or Class Categories

The current demand for a group based policy benefiting Muslims as a whole has some historical basis. During the colonial period, Muslims benefited from reserved legislative seats, provided in 1909, and separate electorates and a quota of 25% of positions in the civil service, introduced in 1926. Due to their generally lower socio-economic status in the Presidency towns of Madras, Bombay and Calcutta, and, except in the latter city, lower relative numbers, Muslims tended to lag behind Hindus in taking advantage of the new opportunities for western education, government service and other professional employment concentrated in these places. As British influence spread to other areas such as the North-Western Provinces and Oudh, however, Muslims in these regions were in a position to enjoy more advantages than their Hindu counterparts, particularly in the educational sphere (Ahmad 1981: 1460). These inconsistencies in the relative sizes of the Muslim and Hindu middle classes muddled the debates over the need for affirmative action.

In 1947, when longer term affirmative action for Muslims came under consideration by the Indian Constituent Assembly's Advisory Committee on Minorities and Fundamental Rights, the committee recommended the continuation of the first type of affirmative action granted to Muslims, namely, the reservation of legislative seats. The Partition of India and Pakistan shortly thereafter changed the political outlook for such policies. As Theodore P. Wright describes, 'after the communal carnage following independence, neither were Hindu representatives willing to continue this concession nor were the remaining Muslim committee members ... prepared to press for it' (Wright 1997: 853). That spelled the end of Muslim reservations, for the time being. The political death of such policies for Muslims coincided, however, with a renewed need for measures to uplift the now decreased Muslim minority. Although statistical data is not available, it is widely and reasonably assumed that the heaviest migration of Muslims to Pakistan from India during partition was from the middle and upper social strata that had the means to move (Ahmad 1981; Syed Hamid's interview, 2 September 1996). This left the remaining Muslim population in India more disadvantaged on average than before.

There is constitutional support for special policies for Scheduled Castes, Scheduled Tribes as well as the vague category of Other Backward Classes. To date, SCs cannot be Muslims; STs can be Muslims, but Muslim STs are relatively rare. Only the category of OBCs seems open to Muslims, but since lists or even criteria for inclusion in this category were not specified in the Constitution, reservations for OBCs were relegated to a back burner. Although some states implemented reservations for OBCs over the years, it was not until 1990, when V.P. Singh implemented portions of the 1980 Mandal Commission Report on backward classes, that reservations for this category were put into practice at the national level for government jobs. The Mandal Commission had declared 82 Muslim groups to be backward. According to the data they used, these backward Muslims made up 8.4% out of the total 11.2% of the Indian population that was Muslim (*Times of India*, 18 January 1996). Those specified as backward include groups such as weavers, oil crushers, carpenters, and *dhobis*–washerman (Syed Hamid's interview 9-2-96). Some southern states have proposed or implemented reservations for Muslims as a group, classifying them as backward for the purposes of state-level reservations. The current demand for national reservations for Muslims was jump started in 1994, although rumblings of such a demand had occurred from time to time in previous years (Ahmad 1980, Khan 1996).

Contemporary Demands for Muslim Reservations

'In my view, the entire Muslim community in the country forms a backward class,' writes Syed Shahabuddin, an M.P. and a leader of the demand for affirmative action for all Indian Muslims, in a letter to the Welfare Minister in 1995 (*Muslim India* February 1996: 78). In the previous year, he was one of the founders of the Association for Promoting Eduication and Employment of Muslims (hereafter referred to as the Association) and a convenor of the First Conference on Reservation for Muslims, that the entire Muslim community in India is depressed and discriminated (Syed Hamid interview September 1996). Other groups have made similar demands, such as the Islamic Council of India as well as the All-India Milli Council, which formally 'demanded the Government to declare the entire community as economically backward and grant 'reservations to it accordingly' (*The Hindu* Saturday 13 April 1996; 10; quotation from *Indian Express* 22 July 1996: 9). In two more conferences in 1996; in Delhi and Hyderabad, the Association reiterated its major demand :

> The recognition of the Muslim community, as a community, as a Backward Class, in the Constitutional meaning of the term, both in the country, as a whole, and in various States/UTs (Union Territories) for the consequent extension of reservation to the community, in *proportion of its population and level of backwardness,* both in higher and professional education as well as in public employment, at the central and state levels and in all job categories, subject to decennial review (*Resolution on Promotion of Employment, Reservation in Public Employment and Management of Wakf Properties* 1996: 1, emphasis theirs).

This resolution touches on a theme of the movement for reservations for all Muslims, a reluctance to divide the 'Muslim community' due to preoccupation with their own unity and the relative numbers of the religious groups in India.

The Association is challenging current affirmative action categories, but at the same time adopting other categories that have historically been equally problematic. The constant numerical comparison of Hindus and Muslims, the tendency to treat them as 'enumerated communities' is a case in a point:

> The process by which separate Hindu and Muslim identities were constructed at a macro-level, and transformed not just into imagined communities but also into *enumerated communities*, is only the most visible pathology of the transfer of the politics of numerical representation to a society in which representation and group-identity had no special numerical relation to the polity (Appadurai 1993: 332).

Shahabuddin (1996-97) uses relative numbers to argue that:

> 'Theoretically, they [Muslims] may be entitled (at the central level) to 4.2% out of 27% quota for the OBCs, 2% out of 15% for the SCs and 1% out of 7.5% for STS. And a fourth subquota in the quota for High Castes.'

Shahabuddin stresses the importance of proportional numerical representation through these figures, but ultimately critiques subquotas for Muslims within each existing quota. Such subquotas, like those advocating affirmative action only for OBC or SC Muslims, subdivide Muslims and hurt their unity, so Shahabuddin ultimately proposes a single Muslim quota on the basis of the total Muslim population.

Shahabuddin is particularly adamant in his claims that a policy differentiating Muslims would be detrimental to Muslim unity. To return to his 1995 letter to the Welfare Minister, in which he argues that 'the entire Muslim community in the country forms a backward class,' Shahabuddin writes:

> I feel that the Muslim community is not going to benefit either by being bracketed with the SC or with the OBC, who are educationally and economically much more advanced and politically far more influential, any more than being bracketed with the High Castes in the General List ... Moreover, I do not think you would like your Government and Party .. accused of dividing the Muslim community (1995; 78, *sic*).

Ironically, those advocating Muslim reservations through these accusations of government plots to 'divide and rule' the Muslim minority are echoing *critiques* of the original reservations for Muslims, which have often been portrayed as a colonial effort to divide and rule Indian society as a whole along religious lines

(Wright 1997: 852). As one advocate of reinstating Muslim reservations on the basis of religion argues, 'by giving reservation to certain classes among Muslims the government will be creating casteism among Muslims to divide their strength' (Khan 1996: 226). In short the Association pays attention to relative numbers and opportunities available to Hindus and Muslims, but draws the line at similar comparisons between classes or castes within the Muslim community, in the name of preserving Muslim unity. Arguments about both relative numbers and group unity–although at times in tension with each other are the main themes of the Association's demands.

Together these themes underlie the Association's arguments for reservations in order to ensure Muslim representation in government jobs. The Association's claims are reinforced by fears about Muslims as a group not getting a proportionate piece of a rapidly disappearing cake. In an interview, Shahabuddin repeatedly pointed out the necessity of 'cutting the cake' not just horizontally by caste and class, as is currently done, but also vertically, by religion, in order to evenly distribute opportunities (Shahabuddin interview 11 September 1996). Such a concern is not unusual in the context of reservations. Political Scientist Theodore Wright, referring to the leades of the renewed demand for Muslim reservations, writes, ;'they feared that if Muslims did not get on the backwardness bandwagon, they would be left competing for an ever diminishing proportion of open (unreserved) seats with an ever larger pool of Forward (twice-born Hindu) rivals' (Wright 1997: 854). The concern over getting a proportionate piece of the cake is evident in another resolution of the Association, which prefers categorizing religious communities rather than bracketing groups together. The Association :

> Demands a separate quota for the Muslim community, as it does for each identifiable community, so that each of them may enjoy the full benefit of their rightful measure of reservation, free of all apprehensions of any encroachment by other relatively advanced communities if bracketed with them (*Resolution on Promotion of Employment, Reservation in Public Employment and Management of Walf Properties* 1996: 1).

The goals of Muslim empowerment through unity and numerical representation in the government services are reflected in the religious category advocated by the Association, class or caste based boundaries being less crucial to this agenda. Although Shahabuddin recognizes that caste is a factor in Muslim society, his Association continues to press for reservations for Muslims as a whole. He, like the Association in its official resolution, notes that those Muslims already declared backward shall have 'first claim' to benefits, but is this enough to protect them? OBC and *Dalit* or 'Scheduled Caste" Muslim groups are skeptical. They have their own ideas on how the cake should be sliced.

Caste and Class Counter-challenges to a Religious Category: Historical Background

There is a social stratification among Muslims in India, which some have even characterized as a sort of caste system (Ahmad 1966 and 1978, Ansari 1960). These categories within Muslim society in India are described and named in various ways. Contrasting the *ashraf*, or gentry, and *ajlaf*, or non-gentry, is one distinction (Ahmad 1966, Wright's lecture). In her work on Muslims in Aligarh, entitled *Boundaries and Identities*, E.A. Mann describes this dichotomy as the distinction between Muslims who are descended from immigrants and those who are converts' descendants, who are considered lower. She writes about other class rankings and a 'hierarchy of status' among Indian Muslims using the term *zat*, or status category, and *biradari*, or status group (Mann 1992: 38). Others have described a '3-way caste based division in Muslim society-Ashraf, Ajlaf and Arzal': The Ashraf include Syeds, Sheikhs, Pathans, etc.; those currently on the OBC lists are largely from the Ajlaf and Arzal categories (*Muslim India* February 1996).

This stratification is ironic, given Islam's professed egalitarianism. Moreover, it has some caste-like qualities, as can be seen in the following description of Indian Islam.

The conception of equality and brotherhood was an ideal and as an idal it exists even today, yet in practice some social grades emerged within the Muslim society. At the beginning there were three distinct grades of Muslims which consisted of the priestly section, the rulers and nobles and all others i.e. the commoners. The religious elites (*ulema* or *sufis*) .... constituted the uppermost segment in Muslim society. They did not come from the indigenous converts, but were of foreign descent and belonged to the hierarchy of Ashraf (Mondal 1996: 105-126).

The association of these groups with various occupations, the higher ones more closely associated with religious or 'priestly' duties, explains why some consider this a 'caste' system. In short, the status distinctions between immigrants' and converts' descendants, the occupational hierarchies, and the pre-existing caste distinctions of those who became converts have resulted in a complex system of categories internal to the 'Muslim community'. Many from lower social strata object to reservations for Muslims as a undifferentiated group on these grounds. Some organizations take the intersection of caste or class and religion as their starting point, arguing that neither the existing OBC and SC categories nor the proposed Muslim category adequately address their identities or problems. The following review of caste and class based counter challenges to the demand for udifferentiated Muslim reservations will focus on OBC Muslims, with briefer references to some "SC Muslims" (currently not a legally recognized category) and upper class Muslims.

Contemporary Caste and Class Based Challenges

'While Islam may be casteless, our society is divided on the basis of castes,' started Shabbir Ansari, President of the All India Muslim OBC Organization or *Sangathan,* at their first national convention (*The Hindu* August 30, 1996: 3). The All India Muslim OBC Sangathan has only recently entered the political scene to demand reservations and other benefits for Muslim OBCs (Bidwai: 1996). It emerged out of a progressive Marathi literary organization, the Muslim Marathi Sahitya Parishad, started in 1989, although it is now attempting to live up to its 'All India' claims and appeal to non-Marathi speaking Muslim OBCs. Their first, national convention on August 29, 1996 was held in New Delhi, an example of such outreach efforts.

The All India Muslim OBC Sangathan (hereafter referred to as the Sangathan) has several demands, including various other educational and economic opportunities for OBC Muslims, such as scholarships, land, housing and loans, but the primary demand is to 'include all backward communities among Muslims in the OBC lists at the State and Central Level' (From 'Demands' included in a Memorandum from Shabbir Ansari, President of All India Muslim OBC Organization to Welfare Minister B.S. Ramoowalia, delivered at a meeting on 16 September 1996, hereafter referred to as 'Memorandum'). Although some Muslims are currently included in the OBC category, they want to expand the boundaries to include other Muslim subcommunities not currently on the lists. In part due to a lack of data, many arguably backward Muslim communities are not currently identified on the OBC lists.

The Sangathan was spurred on by the implementation of the Mandal Commissions' recommendations to extend affirmative action to OBCs and by the Supreme Court's 1992 decision on the legality of the Mandal recommendations. To aid its efforts on behalf of listed and unlisted Muslim OBCs, the Sangathan, in response to OBC lists made by the various national and sate level backward Classes Commissions, has done its own surveys and compiled lists of Muslim backward casts, including OBCs, SCs and STs. In Maharashtra they have demanded the addition of 42 Muslim groups to these lists, mostly OBCs (Sonavane's interview 2 December 1996). According to their estimates over 90 percent of Muslims should be considered members of these officially backward lists–but not *all* Muslims. 'This "self-discovery" has inspired an awareness that transcends religious identities,' notes scholar and journalist Praful Bidwai. In contrast to those demanding that all Muslims should be taken as the unit to be categorized as backward, the Sangathan 'takes the stand that secular social structures and class/caste hierarchies transcend and come prior to religious identities' (Bidwai 1996: 12).

An activist in the Sangathan, Vilas Sonavane argues that 'Religion has been used to suppress basic contradictions in Indian society, which is caste' (Sonavane's interview 12 December 1996). In contrast to the Association for Promoting Education and Employment of Muslims, which he says has accused him of 'dividing Muslims', Sonavane argues that reservations should be an OBC issue not a Muslim issue. Using class/caste categories to undermine arguments for reservation categories based on religion, he describes this movement as 'deconstructing' the myth of religion in India, namely the perennial polarization of majority versus minority religions. Because it is focusing on other axes of identity, he describes his organization as the 'first postmodernist movement in India' (Sonavane interview 12 December 1996).

This reorganization of categories puts the emphasis on backwardness rather than Islam : 'There is a conscious effort to relate Dalit Muslims and Hindu OBCs and to create bonds of solidarity across religious divides' (Bidwai 1996: 12). There is also a pan-religious effort to hitch their wagon to the arguments of the more organized and active movement to allow 'Christian SCs' to receive affirmative action. President of the Sangathan, Shabbir Ahmed Ansari, asks, 'When Hindu Sikh and Buddhist categories have been given these facilities then why the Christians and Muslims Categories have not been provided?' (Memorandum 1996, sic). The Sangathan is also pan-backward in nature, meaning that they are not only submitting arguments before the government on behalf of Muslim OBCs but also Muslim SCs and STs as well.

The Sangathan has called for an end to 'discrimination' against 'Muslim Dalits only on grounds of Scheduled Castes categories of India' (Memorandum 1996). Since SC reservations, unlike those for STs and OBCs, are closed to Muslims, the 'SC Mulsim' demands may be the most controversial. There have been successful demands for including Sikhs (in 1956) and Buddhists (in 1990) among the SCs and a growing demand for including Christian SCs. These developments have inspired 'similarly situated groups among Muslims,' such as *Halal Khors*, to also seek official SC status (*Times of India* 18 January 1996: 10). In addition to the Sangathan, other groups have taken up this demand. For example, the All India Backward Muslim Morcha (AIBMM) has likewise demanded that Muslims be included within the SC categories. Led by Ajaz Ali, they are opposed to the demand for a religiously based quota for all Muslims, preferring to press for the claims of the 'Dalits' within the religion. Shahabudin and those in his Association are critical of these attempts to prioritize an alliance with the 'backwards' rather than with Muslims.

A third class based critique of Muslim reservations is worth mentioning, although they are not an organization actively pressing their point of view. Some upper class Muslims are opposed to religious based reservations for Muslims, particularly the proposal for Muslims as a whole to be declared backward. They are posing a different sort of class/caste challenge to religious reservations, generally from the opposite end of the class spectrum from the backward groups just discussed. Rather than arguing against religious affirmative action categories on category, they object to their entire religion being categorized with India's lower classes. Two motivations for this objection emerge. One is community pride, which results in reluctance to jump on the backwardness bandwagon. This opinion was expressed to me most strongly in Hyderabad, where the third convention this issue, sponsored by the Association for Promoting Education and Employment of Muslims, was held. In discussions of reservations for Muslims, some people referred to the princely history of the area and pride in the community, which led to their reluctance to lump themselves in with 'backward' groups. In the conference's more informal afternoon discussion, audience members raised the following objections and comments : [Hindu] Dalits and Brahmins will definitely put their own person forward, but our approach is altogether different. We don't want to be treated as backward, like SCs and STs. A Hindu tailor may be treated as backward, but a Muslim tailor is not backward (audience members at Hyderabad conference, afternoon discussion, 18 August 1996).

In short, there are a variety of caste and class based counter-challenges to the proposed reservations for Muslims. These critiques are coming from across the Muslim social spectrum, ranging from those who argue that they should be categorized with the lowest, scheduled caste to those who blanch at the idea of being considered backward. Of the Muslim groups discussed here, the OBC Muslims, already an officially recognized category, pose the most organized caste and class based challenge to those demanding reservations based on religion alone.

Conclusion

The reservations debate in India seems to be shifting away from the pros and cons of a quota system toward demands and critiques relating to the boundaries of the categories used. Is the rush to be declared backward and the increased clamouring over categories reinforcing these categories? This is common assumption, voiced in the following newspaper article:

> "The result is that with more and more clamouring to be categorized as backward or put in the schedule of castes and tribes needing special protection, the quota system has come to acquire a self-perpetuating character...widening the scope to cover communities that hardly need such props is nothing but the height of inequity, which will only aggravate social tension by deepening caste division" (*Hindustan Times* 9 March 1996).

The debates over reservations involving various Muslim organizations in India do suggest that such fights provide fuel for groups to criticize and antagonize each other, arguably adding to tensions. Yet the very crosscutting nature of identities in India makes it impossible for any religious organization to present a united front on the issue of affirmative action categories. Those that do demand revisions in the current official categories, such as those waiting affirmative action for all Muslims, continuously problematize the official lists and keep them from becoming cemented into the public consciousness. Those that engage in counter demands, such as OBC or Dalit Muslims, in turn prevent the reification of a notion of a unified 'Muslim community'. In short, although these movements challenging the current reservation schemes undeniably contribute to some social and political tensions, taken as whole they are not simply reinforcing community fault lines, but rather proposing many alternative and often conflicting categorizations of Indian society.

Robert Horowitz has written about several ways to alleviate or avoid ethnic conflict. One way he addresses is the 'dispersal of conflict' or the creation of 'a new lower layer of conflict laden issues'. He discusses this in the context of federal systems that geographically disperse national level ethnic bifurcations into the more complicated context of many states, resulting in 'a more complex-and therefore less tense–politics at the center' (Horowitz 1985: 604-605). The cases examined in this article illustrate a variation of this principle. Rather than dispersing the polarized politics of Hindu versus Muslim or of upper versus lower caste in a geographic sense, the above debates over affirmative action categories shatter dichotomized conflicts by constantly questioning the boundaries of 'caste' and 'Islam' and their relationship to each other. In this sense, intergroup tensions do not disappear but become certainly more complex and arguably less tense than conflicts between clear cut and unambiguous groups. The trend toward nitpicking over who is in which category, and where and when, rather than nationwide fighting between unified sides, signals a lower, and generally less explosive, form of conflict over reservations.

By recognizing the agency of disadvantaged groups, we can appreciate their ability to put fourth their own self-definitions rather than simply absorbing state definitions of their identities. The standard categories used for reservations in India face varied Muslim challenges and counter-challenges, which reshuffle notions of religious, caste, and national identity, challenging state identifications with dynamic self identifications. The lively contemporary debate over the future of reservations in India illustrates the continuing variety–both anthropological and political–within the Muslim community.

Acknowledgement

This project benefited greatly from my year as a Fulbright scholar working on issues of categories and groups in India. I am extremely grateful to the Government of India for their permission to do this research as well as the staff of the United States Educational Foundation in India and the faculty of Jawaharlal Nehru University who helped make this research possible.

REFERENCES

Ahmad, Imtiaz (1996), Ashraf-Ajlaf Dichotomy in Muslim Social Structure in India, *Indian Economic and Social History Review* 32, 344-50.

——(1978), (ed.) *Caste and Social Stratification Among Muslims in India.* Delhi: Manohar.

——(1980), "Job reservation for Muslims", *The Hindustan Times* 25 January.

——(1981), "Muslim educational backwardness: An inferential analysis," *Economic and Political Weekly* 16 (36), 1457-1465.

Ansari, Ghaus (1960), *Muslim Caste in Uttar Pradesh,* Lucknow: Ethnographic and Folk Culture Society.

Appadurai, Arjun (1993), "Number in the Colonial Imagination". In Breckenridge, Carol A and Peter Van der Veer (eds.) *Orientalism and the Post-Colonial Predicament.* Philadelphia: University of Pennsylvania Press.

Bakshi, P.M. (1996), *The Constitution of India with Comments and Subject Index.* Delhi: Universal Law Publishing Co. Pvt. Ltd.

Bidwai, Praful (1996), "Age of empowerment: Muslim OBCs discover Mandal". *The Times of India* (12 September), 12.

Dasgupta, Swapan (1997), "Madness Unreserved: Caste, gender, religion: Where will it stop?" *India Today* (9 June), 27.

Davis, Adrienne D. (1996), "Identity Notes Part One : Playing in the Light." *The American University Law Review* 45 (3), 695-720.

Frykenberg, Robert Eric. (1993), "Constructions of Hinduism at the Nexus of History and Religion," *Journal of InterdisciplinaryHistory* 23(3), 523-550.

Galanter, Marc (1991), *Competing Equalities : Law and the Backward Classes in India*. Delhi: Oxford University Press.

Ghosh, S.K. (1996), *Reservation in Services: A Manual for Government and Public Sector*. New Delhi : Akshar Publications.

Hamid, Navaid (1996), "Association for Promoting Education and Employment of Muslims : A Brief Note". Press Release at Conference in Hyderabad, 18 August.

Horowitz, Donald L. (1985), *Ethnic Groups in Conflict*. Berkeley : University of California Press.

Khalidi, Omar (1999), "Other Backward Classes (OBC) Among Muslims : Who are they: What do they want?". Conference Paper, Association for Asian Studies Annual Meeting.

Khan, Masood Ali (1996), "Masood Ali Khan on Reservation of Muslims," *Muslim India* 161 (May), 225-226.

Mann, E.A. (1992), *Boundaries and Identities : Muslims, Work and Status in Aligarh*. New Delhi : Sage.

Metcalf, Barbara (1995), Presidential Address : "Too Little and Too Much : Reflections on Muslims in the History of India." *Journal of Asian Studies* 54(4), 951-967.

Mondal, Sekh Rahim (1996), "Tradition Versus Modernity in Muslim Society : An Analysis of Social Movements Among Muslims in India" *Islam and the Modern Age* 27(2), 105-126.

APEEM (1996), "*Resolution on Promotion of Employment, Reservation in Public Employment and Management of Wakf Properties*, Third National Conference of the Association for Promoting Education and Employment of Muslims, Hyderabad – 18 August.

Rudolph, Lloyd I and Susanne Hoeber Rudolph (1996), "Occidentalism and Orientalism: Perspectives on Legal Pluralism." In Sally Humphreys (ed.) *Cultures of Scholarship*. Ann Arbor: Michigan: University of Michigan Press.

Scott, James C. (1998), *Seeing Like a State: How Certain Schemes to Improve the Human Condition Have Failed*. New Haven : Yale University Press.

Shatrugna, M. (1999), "All Kapus as BCs: Reducing Reservation to a farce", *Economic and Political Weekly* 29(37), 2397-2400.

Wright, Theodore P. (1997), "A New Demand for Muslim Reservations in India", *Asian Survey* 37 (9), 852-858.

CASTE AMONG NON-HINDU INDIANS: AN EXPLORATORY STUDY OF ASSAMESE MUSLIMS

Monirul Hussain

Introduction

One of the strikingly peculiar features of the Indian society is the existence and continuity of the caste system among the Hindus. This institutionalized expression of social inequality among the Hindus based on unchangeable ascriptive criteria of superiority and inferiority, superordination and subordination, purity and impurity, touchability and untouchability has been operating pervicaciously in India with the approval of both religion and society. The caste system is so pervasive that Louis Dumont observes that caste in India is a primordial loyality and everything in Indian Society springs from it (Dumont 1970), though I have some reservations (Hussain 1986) about Dumont's thesis. Studies on various facets of the caste system are not new to the Indian sociology. In fact, such studies have shown gradual growth alongwith the growth of sociology and social anthropology in India. The caste system has been occupying a substantial majority of the empirical studies of the Indian subcontinent. Today, we have a huge number of studies related to the various theoretical and empirical dimensions of the caste system. A critic even feels that the subject of Hindu caste has been overtreated and now it deserves a holiday (Swarup 1987: VI). However, systematic studies on the existence of case/caste-like elements among other non-Hindu segments of multi-religious Indian Society emerged at a relatively later stage and developed further only recently. Perhaps, it was Ghaus Ansari, who for the first time attempted a full scale study of the caste system among the Indian Muslims (Ansari 1959). However, during the seventies, studies on caste and social stratification among the Indian Muslims have been impressive. A volume on caste and stratification among the Muslims edited by Imtiaz Ahmed (Ahmed 1973), has succeeded in drawing attention from academic circles both in India and abroad. This volume has considerably filled the gap of our knowledge about the structure and functioning of the caste-based stratification among the Muslims in India. It includes ten empirical studies carried out by sociologists and social anthropologists in different cultural and geographical milieu during the late sixties and early seventies. This volume however, does not cover the Muslims of Jammu and Kashmir and Assam, which have the largest and second largest concentration of Muslim population respectively in terms of percentage of total population among the 24 Indian States.

In this paper, an attempt has been made to describe and analyse caste-based stratification among the Assamese Muslims. The analysis of mainly based on my understanding and observation of Assam's history and contemporary Assamese society and is not based on a rigorous field investigation. Therefore, this paper is preliminary and exploratory in nature and has limitation and inadequacies. Inspite of these limitations, I feel that this study would help us to start comprehending atleast some aspects of the realities related to the existence and extent of caste-based stratification among the Assamese Muslims.

Before going into the substantive theme it is necessary that certain sociologically pertinent historical, demographic and cultural aspects of the Muslim population of Assam be noted. Assam, at present, would be having atleast 6 million Muslims out of a population of nearly 25 million people.[1] The Muslims constitute 24 per cent of total population of Assam (Census of India, 1971). The Muslims of Assam, contrary to popular notice, though belonging to the same religious faith, reflect significant observable, differentiations and unevenness in terms of caste, class, language, culture, occupation, education, geographical distribution, political participation and ideology (Hussain 1987 A: 21). Besides, in terms of exclusion and assimilation with their immediate Assamese Hindu population, the various Muslim communities of Assam at the present stage of social, economic and political development, are standing at uneven level (ibid: 21). In short the Muslim of

Assam are not a single homogeneous community but are divided into several distinctive historical, economic, political and cultural communities having evolved through different historical situations. Broadly, I have categorized the Muslims of Assam (ibid: 22) into 4 groups i.e.,

1. the Assamese Muslims,
2. the Neo-Assamese Muslims,
3. the Muslims of Barrack Valley and finally,
4. the North Indian Muslims.

This categorization is necessary in order to comprehend systematically any contemporary social, political, economic or cultural issue related to the Muslims of Assam.[2]

In this paper, I propose to cover only the first category of the Muslims of Assam, i.e. the Assamese Muslims. They are also known in Assamese as *Asomiya Musalman* meaning the Assamese Muslim, *Thalua Musalman* meaning the local Mulsims, and *Goria*.[3] This community which has evolved gradually over a long period of time covering several centuries, includes the descendents of :-

1. Muslims/Mughal/Pathan/Turk soldiers who were left behind as prisoners of wars and those who decided to stay back in Assam after the wars were over,
2. Medieval technicians and artisans brought by Ahom Kings to engage them in various state and economic activities for which perhaps the local skills were inadequate,
3. Preachers of Islam, and finally,
4. the local converts to Islam during the Ahom period.[4]

Historical records have pointed out that Assam came into contact with the Muslims for the first time in 1198 A.D. (Bhuyan 1975: 173; Gait 1905: 36).[5] This demonstrates explicitly that the Muslims had established contact with Assam much earlier than any other Aryan/caste groups and even Ahoms who ruled Assam for long 600 years, i.e. 1128 to 1826 A.D. Because of this deeper historical roots in a relatively isolated region, the Muslims had become an inseparable part of the medieval Assamese society and polity. They together with other sections of the non-Brahmin Assamese, fought against the might Mughals in several battles including the famous battle of Saraighat in 1671.[6]

At present, the population of the Assamese Mulsims would be roughly between 5 per cent to 7 per cent of the total population of the state. Numerically, their demographic status would be roughly above 1.5 million out of Assam's total Muslim population of 6 million. A considerable number of their population lives in urban Assam. Assamese (Asomiya) is their mother tongue. Except for religion and rituals, the Assamese Muslims are linguistically, culturally, economically and socially highly similar and close the Assamese Hindus. Their dress pattern, food habits, day-to-day behaviour, housing and settlement pattern, even most of the interior arrangements are nearly indistinguishable from the Assamese Hindus. This group of Muslims is fully assimilated, well accepted and largely well treated in the larger Assamese society, and nationality.

II

Numerical empirical studies have demonstrated that the Indian Muslims have classed themselves into endogamous hereditary groups and sub-groups which are hierarchically ranked in relation to one another (Ansari 1959; Misra 1964; Kudryavtsev 1965; Ahmad 1973, etc.). This is mainly because alongwith the Hindus, the Indian Muslims share some of the basic characteristics of the civilization and they also share characteristics of region in which they live and the socio-economic level to which they belong (Mandelbaum 1984: 548). The Assamese Muslims are also no exception to this kind of social development. The Assamese Muslims like their Assamese Hindu neighbours, have explicitly demonstrated the existence of loose kind of caste-like elements in their social structure. It would be necessary to state here that the caste system that evolved among the Assamese Hindus is qualitatively somewhat different from that of north and south India. The caste among the Assamese Hindus was even less rigid than neighbouring Bengali Hindus. It seems that the caste system in Assam was never as strong as in the rest of the sub-continent. This may be due to certain historical reasons viz.

1. Until the British colonization, by and large, Assam stood in the periphery of Indian society, polity and history,
2. different material conditions,
3. relatively later immigration of the Aryans to Assam,

4. the non-caste Ahom rulers ruled Assam for long 600 years from 1228 to 1826.[8]
5. prior to the Ahoms, Assam was ruled non-Aryan rulers,
6. large majority of Assam's population belonged to the non-caste categories,
7. the Muslims also became an inseparable part of the medieval Assamese society,
8. impact of the *vasnava* movement in Assam led by the saint Sankardeva[9], and finally,
9. multiplicity of racial and ethnic elements in Assam. Interactions and influences of all these factors decisively contributed towards relative looseness of the caste structure in Assam.

Though there is a general looseness of the caste structure among the Assamese Hindus, the Assamese Brahmins have been, by and large, very conscious about their caste background and ritual status. Besides, the Assamese Brahmins, other twice-born castes like *Ganakas*, a section of the Assamese *Kalitas* and Kayasthas who claim their ancestry from Kanauj in northern India (now in U.P.), are also largely very conscious about their caste and ritual status in the hierarchy. The population belonging to all these high castes together would not roughly be more than 8 per cent of the total population of Assam. The caste system that evolved in Assam was thus qualitatively somewhat different from northern and southern India. However, that does not necessarily mean that there exists no caste or casteism in Assam. It perpetuated among the socially, economically, culturally, and politically dominant high castes. And obviously, they were the reference group for some other sections looking for social mobility within the traditional structure including the Assamese Muslims. It would be important to recall that the Assamese Muslims had the similar north Indian and ethnic connections. Besides, the Assamese Muslims alongwith the caste Hindus experienced the similar historical developments in the mutual closeness of two religious communities and penetration of influences of the Assamese Hindu caste structure and its resultant ideology and practices into the Assamese Muslim community.[10] Both these communities have been historically closer to one another without any trace of Hindu communalism or Muslim communalism in the medieval Assamese society and state.

III

Caste among the Hindus is generally defined in terms of a list of cultural characteristics which are supposed to form a syndrome (Leach 1969: 2). From a large number of sociological and anthropological materials available, it is not very difficult to locate certain fundamental characteristics which are, by and large, found with some variations in linguistic, sub-caste, urban, rural and regional levels in caste among the Hindus (Hutton 1945; Ghurye 1950; Dumont 1970, Weber 1958; Srinivas 1962 and 1959, etc.) These characteristics are :

1. caste is an endogamous group,
2. traditional specialization of occupation or hereditary division of labour,
3. a hierarchal order among the castes and sub-castes and,
4. a set of religio-caste ideology involving –
   (a) restrictions on social intercourse and commensality,
   (b) belief in the concept of *Dharma* and *Karma,* which helps reinforcement and perpetuation of caste as an irreversible and innate system of social relationship.

In order to comprehend the question of existence of caste structure and practices among any religious, racial, linguistic or regional group of people, it would be pertinent to look into the groups in terms of characteristics as stated earlier. An analyhsis of operation of these characteristics among the Assamese Muslims can help us to explain the existence (or non-existence) of caste among them. The Assamese Muslims are an inseparable part of the larger Assamese society which is fundamentally a unilingual composite society.[11] The Assamese Muslims like the Assamese Hindus, are also divided into three distinct caste-like groups i.e. (1) The Syeds or the *Dawans* in local language, (2) the Shaiks or the *Goria* and (3) the *Morias.*

Economically both the Syeds and the Shaiks have been better off than the *Morias* since the Ahom days. Occupationally, the Syeds and the Shaiks had no direct or specific link with traditional or hereditary occupations. The occupations of both of these two groups are overlapping. However, the *Morias* have a link with traditional occupation of making household utensils from brass and bell-metal. Even the word *'Moria'* has a reference to the way in which they make utensils by beating. *'Moria'* in Assamese language means 'to beat' (Gait 1905: 95). The Syeds, though they claim their descent from the prophet of Islam, are not a priestly class or caste. Islam as a religion does not permit or recognize any institutionalized role of priests. Of course, there are certain controversies about the role of *Ulema*. However, Smith has rightly pointed out that "the *Ulemas* are in no sense priests, rather they correspond to the 'scribe' in Judaism, strictly speaking Islam has no clergy as any Muslim can lead a congregation of prayer" (Smith 1963: 38). The priest as a class or caste also did not emerge among the Assamese Muslims. The *Imams* and the *Mouazzins* of mosques are drawn from all sections of the Assamese Muslims besides from Cachar and Karimganj districts of Assam in the predominantly Bengali speaking Barrack valley, Manipur and northern India, particularly from Bihar and Uttar Pradesh. Their status among the Assamese Muslims, at present, is not as high as that of the Brahmin priests among the Assamese Hindus. As these occupations are neither economically rewarding nor prestigious, people from even traditional elites are reluctant to prepare themselves for such an occupation. Besides the *Imams* and the *Mouazzins* have almost no power in the affairs of mosque and conduct only their assigned religious duties because most of the mosques in Assam are controlled by a management committee elected by the *Zamat* of the respective mosque. Though, there is no visible priestly caste or class among the Assamese Muslims, the Syeds, in their certain behavioural aspects demonstrate their similarity with the Brahmins. Like the Assamese Brahmins, the Assamese Syeds do not traditionally involve themselves in any job that demands serious physical labour which was considered as the job of lower castes. Particularly they refrain from ploughing land, as if it is a taboo for them like it is for the Brahmins. The occupational restrictions, that too in a predominantly agrarian society, have been meticulously observed by the Assamese Syeds.

The Syeds are also an endogamous group like the Assamese Brahmins. They do generally tend to resist marriage outside their own group. As this group is numerically not very large their tendency to maintain endogamy strictly within a limited group seriously restricts their matrimonial choice. Therefore, they are very often involved in the practice of marriage between cousins including the first cousins.[12] This enables them to maintain their exclusiveness and distance from other Assamese Muslims whom they consider is a lower in the presumed caste-like hierarchy. From this point of observance of endogamy among the Assamese Syeds, it would be safe to assume that this fundamentally reflect the implicit existence of non-Islamic belief of purity, perhaps more in the sense of blood than ritual.[13]

The Assamese Shaiks are numerically the largest group among the Assamese Muslims. Their position in the caste-like hierarchy comes next and very close to the Syeds and much above the *Morias*. The Assamese Saikhs are also largely an endogamous group. However, unlike the Assamese Syeds, their matrimonial choices are much wider because their community is larger than of the Syeds. But like Syeds, they also try to maintain distance from the *Morias* whom they both consider much lower to them in the hierarchy. They too avoid marriages with the *Morias*. However, the Assamese Shaiks accept marriages with the Assamese Syeds, which the latter resist. This signifies the desire of the Assamese Syeds to maintain their assumed purity of blood and higher position within the Assamese Muslim community.

Occupationally, the Assamese Shaikhs are involved in innumerable occupations. However, the dominant occupation among them at present is mainly related to agriculture. During the Ahom days, they were engaged in :-

1. Gun and gun power making, 2. cannon making, 3. engraving, 4. minting, 5. Persian reading and interpreting documents/letters sent by the Mughal/Muslim emperors of Indian to the Ahom kings, 6. sword making, 7. rope making, 8. taking care of birds and elements, 9. dying and garment making, 10. as carpenters and masons, 11. Hindu temple workers and 12. soldiers and officers in the Ahom army and court (Bhuyan 1975: 165-71). With the decline of the Ahoms and consolidation of the British, the entire Assamese society gradually faced a qualitatively different social transformation under colonial limitations. The traditional occupations of the Assamese Shaikhs also changed under the changed colonial situation. They generally emerged as cultivating classes with different amounts of land holdings. They slowly alongwith the Assamese Syeds responded to the process of middle class formation in the Assamese society. Many of them try to maintain distance not only from the *Morias* but also from the relatively less assimilated Neo-Assamese Muslims (see Guha 1977: 210-II).

The *Morias* not only economically but also socially and culturally stand at the bottom of the caste-like hierarchy among the Assamese Muslims. They too, like the Assamese Syeds and the Shaikhs, are an endogbamous group. Occupationally, they have been engaged in making household utensils from brass and bell-metal since early Ahom days. A British administrator wrote in 1841 that "the *Morias* are generally employed as braziers. They are looked upon as a very impure tribe (robinson 1841: 264)". Bhorali too has observed that the *Morias* were regarded as an inferior caste (Bhorali 1982: 21). The utensils made by the *Morias* found acceptance not only in the Assamese households irrespective of caste and religion but also significantly found acceptance in Hindu places of worships and religious rituals (Barua 1957: 51). Though both the Assamese Syeds and Shaikhs have been maintaining interactional distance from the *Morias*, they are not regarded as untouchables in ideological and empirical sense. However, there still exists some stereotypes against the *Morias* which have stigmatized the entire community as dirty and unreliable in the eyes of the upper groups.

Besides the *Morias*, there is still another small caste-like group known as *Julahas*. They occupy a lower position in the hierarchy among the Assamese Muslims. It is very difficult to identify their exact position in relation to the *Morias* but their position is definitely much below the Shaikhs. The *Julahas*, unlike the Assamese Syeds and the Shaikhs have a traditional link with a hereditary occupation, i.e. weaving. The Julahas had migrated from the Hazaribagh region of Bihar during the Ahom Period (Sattar 1967: 50). The Assamese Syeds and the Shaikhs have been maintaining distance from the lowly placed Assamese *Julahas*. However, no most of the *Julahas* have gradually become a part of the Assamese Shaikhs by giving up their traditional occupations and traditional surnames besides opting the ways of life of the Shaikhs. The smallness of the group and changed economic situation wherein weaving became a non-subsistence occupation, helped them in becoming Shaikhs gradually.

Among the Assamese Muslims, the Shaikhs have emerged as the largest group. The number of the Assamese Syeds, *Morias* and *Julahas* are much smaller. It would be pertinent to state that besides the vertical division, the Assamese Muslims are also divided horizontally. Like the Assamese Hindus, the Assamese Muslims are also divided on the regional basis within the state i.e. upper Assam and lower Assam.[14]

IV

From our descriptions we have seen that a caste-like structure exists among the Assamese Muslims. Similar to the traditional Hindu caste system, certain fundamental characteristics are also found among the Assamese Muslims. Firstly, a caste-like hierarchy operates among the Assamese Muslims though their religion does not permit such hierarchy and inequality. Secondly, the various groups in the hierarchy are endogamous. Thirdly, though, there is no strict adherence to traditional occupation among the highly placed Assamese Syeds and the Shaikhs, the lowly placed *Morias* and *Julahas* have traditional links with hereditary occupations. Fourthly, though the Islam as a religion does not permit belief in the religio-case ideology of purity and pollution and the concept of *Dharma* and *Karma,* the Assamese Muslims as a community; particularly the Syeds and the Shaikhs by and large, believe in and dry to maintain their assumed purity of blood. However, this tendency is limited to the practice of endogamy and certain restriction in social intercourse. One may therefore, infer that social stratification, quite similar to the Hindu Caste System, is present among the Assamese Muslims. This shows the profound influence of the Assamese Hindu caste system on the Assamese Muslims.

Acknowledgement

The author thanks Prof. R.K. Bhadra, Dr. Mita Bhadra and Prof. B.P. Misra of North Bengal University, Prof. S.M. Dubey of Dibrugarh University, Prof. Partha N. Mukherji of the Indian Statistical Institute, Prof. K.L. Sharma and Prof. Imtiaz Ahmad of Jawaharlal Nehru University, New Delhi for their comments on an earlier draft of this paper. However, the author alone is responsible for inadequacies and errors that still remain in the paper.

NOTES

1. It is very difficult to ascertain the exact number of population of Assam because the census was not conducted in Assam in 1981, in view of disturbed political situation and opposition from the All Assam Students Union and All Assam Ganasangram Parishad, two

organizations which led the Assam movement. This estimate has been arrived at on the basis of earlier census and their corresponding growth rate and the statistics provided by the Government of Assam (1986).

2. Even to comprehend the complex issues related to Assam movement, Assamese society and nationality, one needs to know about the diversities and differentiations among the Muslims of Assam. I have also written elsewhere in a little more details about the Muslim of Assam (Hussain 1987- a & b).
3. Goria, this term is very often used to denote the entire Assamese Muslims. According to Gait, the word *Goria,* is an indication of their claim to have come from Gour the Mohammadan capital of Bengal (1905: 95). In addition it should be remembered that the Muslims had entered Assam obviously through Gour or Bengal. There may be some controversy, but, by and large, *Goria* refers to the Assamese Shaikh Muslims.
4. Historian Bhuyan has described 8 groups, however, which are by and large similar to the 4 groups that we have stipulated (Bhuyan 1975: 171-172).
5. A distinguished Assamese scholar has stated that the Muslim religious preachers and *pirs,* etc. came to Assam much earlier than 1198 AD i.e. 11th and 12th centuries (Barua 1957: 51).
6. One of the reasons behind the successful resistance against the mighty Mughal army was that the Ahom army had many sincere Muslims as soldiers and officers who had the knowledge of Mughal ware.
7. See note–1.
8. Though the Ahom who racially belonged to the Mongoloid stock, accepted Hinduism latter they have been conspicuously maintaining some of their cultural, social and ritual practices of pre-Hindu stage. It is very difficult to determine their position in the traditional Assamese Hindu caste structure. At present, atleast their position is lower in terms of ritual purity. It seems that their position in the Hindu caste structure stands between the intermediate and the lower castes. Officially, of course, they are included among the Other Backward Classes (OBC).
9. However, caste elements emerged among the Assamese Vaisnavites at a later stage. The position of the priests among the Vaisanavites is quite similar to the Brahmins among the Assamese *Shaikhs.*
10. This is however, not to deny the influences and the contributions made by Islam and by Muslims to the Assamese society which is fundamentally composite in nature. For details are Barua 1957; Sattar 1972; Choudhury 1982; etc.

11. In Assam, the Marwaris, the plantation labour, the tribals and even most of the Bengalis in the Brahmaputra valley are, by and large, bilingual. Besides their mother-tongue they can communicated well in Assamese language. This point has been perniciously ignored not only by the followers of intransigent nativist ideology but also by our journalists and even social scientists working on Assam or north-eastern India.
12. Though the religion approves the marriage between cousins and even first cousins, the Assamese Muslims, except the Syeds, do not encourage such marriages mainly because of influence and proximity of the Assamese Hindus. As a result, if marriage between two first cousins takes place, there is a tendency to look down upon such marriages and in many cases such type of marriage also face boycott even from the close relatives.
13. Leela Dube (1977: 27) has also observed 'even among Muslims and Christians there is some consciousness of purity and pollution, if not in terms of organic food, atleast in terms of blood purity.'
14. This division has emerged not because of caste, but because of relatively earlier social transformation under the colonial constraints in Upper Assam which gave the people, both Hindus and Muslims, a sense of false consciousness of superiority over the people of Lower Assam.

REFERENCES

Ahmad, Imtiaz, (ed.) (1973), *Caste and Social Stratification Among the Muslims.* Delhi : Manohar Books.

Ansari, Ghaus, (1957), *Muslim Caste in Uttar Pradesh: A Study of Culture Contact.* Lucknow: Ethnographic and Folk Culture Society.

Barua, Birnchi Kumar, (1957), *Asamiya Bhasa Aru Sanskriti.* Nalbari: Journal Emporium (Reprint edition, 1985).

Bhorali,Devdas, (1982), *Occupational Diversion: A Caste Study of Moriya Community of Guwahati: Its Past, Present and Future.* Guwahati: Handique College Teachers Unit.

Bhuyan, S.K., (1975), *Swargadeo Rajeswar Sinha.* Gauhati: Assam Publication Board.

Choudhury, Medini, (1982), *Luit, Barak Aru Islam.* Gauhati: Rhino Books.

Dube, Leela, (1977), Discussion in S.C. Malik (ed.) *Criteria of Status Evaluation in India.* Simla : Indian Institute of Advanced Study.

Dumont, Louis, (1957), For a Sociology of India: *Contribution to Indian Society.* 1970 *Homo Hierarchus.* London: Paldin.

Gait, Edward, (1905), *A History of Assam.* Gauhati : LBS Publications (Reprint edition 1984).

Ghurye, G.S., (1960), *Caste and Races in India.* Bombay : Popular Prakashan.

Government of Asam (1986), *Important Statistics 1986.* Gauhati : Directorate of Economics and Statistics.

Government of India (1972), *Census of India 1971, Religion Series I, Paper II of 1972.* New Delhi: Registrar General and Census Commissioner.

Guha, Amalendu, (1977), *Planter-Raj to Swaraj: Freedom Struggle and Electoral Politics in Assam, 1826 – 1947.* New Delhi : Indian Council of Historical Research.

Hussain, Monirul, (1986) , 'Interaction Between Caste and Politics,' *Indian Journal of Politics,* Vol. XX, Nos. 3-4, July–December 1986.

———(1987a), 'The Muslims of Contemporary Assam: A Sociological Introduction,' *Journal :North East India Council for Social Science Research,* vol. XI, No.2, October 1987.

———(1987b), 'Muslim of the Indian State of Assam: A Note,' *Journal: Institute of Muslim Minority Affairs,* Vol. VIII, No. 2, July 1987.

Hutton, J. (1946), *Caste in India.* Cambridge : Cambridge University Press.

Kudryavtsev, M.K. (1965), 'Musual mankie Kasty (Muslim *Kastya V. India.* G.G. Kotovski ed. pp. 214-232. Mosco : Akademic Nauk, S.S.S.R., Institute Nordov Azii.

Leach, E.R.(1969), *Aspects of Caste in South India, Ceylon and North West Pakistan.* Cambridge : Cambridge University Press.

Levy, R., (1962), *Social Strucutre of Islam.* Cambridge: Cambridge University Press.

Mandelbaum, David G., (1984), *Study in India.* Bombay: Popular Prakashan.

Misra, Satish G., (1964), *Muslim Communities of Gujarat.* Bombay: Asia Publishing House.

Robinson, William (1841), *A Descriptive Account of Assam.* Guwahati: Government Seminary, Reprinted. 1975, Delhi : Sanskaran Prakashan.

Sattar, Abdus (1972), *Sangmisranat Asamiya Sanskriti.* Jorhat : granthapeeth.

Smith, D.A. (1963), *India As a Secular State.* Princeton: Princeton University Press.

Srinivas, M.N. (1959), 'Caste': A Trend Report and Bibliography,' *Current Sociology* (3), 135-185.

———(1962), *Religion and Society Among the Coorg of South India.* New Delhi: Oxford Univesity Press.

Swarup, Ram, (1987), 'Purity and Pollution,' *Sunday Review,* New Delhi, Times of India, 15 March 1987.

Weber, Max (1958), *The Religion of India: The Sociology of Hinduism and Buddhisms,* Translated and edited by Gerth and Martindale. Chicago, Free Press.

ELEMENTS OF CASTE AMONG THE HINDU CONVERTS TO ISLAM: A CASE OF MUSLIM GUJARS OF UTTAR PRADESH

Amir Hasan

Introduction

The Caste System is the *sine qua non* of the Hindu socio-economic order. It is perhaps the most prominent feature of the Hindu way of life. It is, therefore, not surprising that Hindu converts to another religion, strove hard to retain some features of the caste to which they belonged as Hindus. They usually retained their caste profession because of economic compulsions. If they belonged to higher caste, they usually found a way to retain or exhibit their caste names to acquire a higher status among the converts. However, the Hindus who embraced Islam were also attracted by *Masawaat* (Islamic principle of equality) and therefore, made conscious efforts to discard the Caste System, not oddly enough the Muslim society itself could not keep itself completely aloof from its influence.

The following are considered essential features of the Hindu Caste System (Ghurye 1979).

1. It divides the society in segments on the basis of birth;
2. the hierarchal position of each caste is well defined;
3. it enjoins restrictions on feeding and social inter-course;
4. the system imposes civil and religious disabilities on certain castes and provides privileges to certain others;
5. members of a caste have no unrestricted choice of occupation; and
6. it imposes certain restrictions on marriage.

A caste is further divided into subcastes which are endogamous. The rigidity with which the sub-caste follows the principle of endogamy has led many scholars to hold this feature as the essence of the Caste System and many scholars recognize sub-castes as real castes (Ghurye 1979). The sub-castes are further divided into exogamous sub groups called *gotra*. The Hindu Gujars of Western U.P. are known for their large number (1178) of *gotras* (Ghurye 1979).

Majority of Indian Muslims are converts from Hinduism. To distinguish between these converts and descendants of the Muslims of foreign origin, who had migrated and settled in India, the terms *ajlaf* and *ashraf* respectively have been coined. As the *ashraf* have acquired a higher status, there is a tendency among the *ajlaf* to identify themselves with *ashraf* status groups by making determined efforts to discard their Hindu origin and by undergoing through a process of Islamization.

This paper tries to show that the Muslim Gujars, one of the *ajlaf* groups are an exceptional group among the Muslims because they have not only made little efforts to *ashrafize*[2] themselves but have so far guarded their separate identity.

The Gujars

The Gujars are an important pastoral tribe of the Indian sub-continent. Although they are followers of three different religions, Hinduism, Islam and Sikhism, they have retained their name irrespective of their religious affiliations. According to the Census of 1981, the Gujars numbered over two million which included nearly one million Muslim Gujars in undivided India. The exact population of Gujars in India is not known as they have never been enumerated after 1932 Census. Their present population in India should be around 2.5 million. The Muslim Gujars are now live mainly in Jammu and Kashmir, Himachal Pradesh and Uttar Pradesh and their number is roughly estimated at one third of a million.

Most probably the early Gujars were foreign immigrants belonging to White Huns (Ephalites) who entered India in large numbers in the fifth Century A.D. We have evidence of their having ruled parts of India till seventh century. Gradually they were absorbed into Hinduism. Many hold the view that Gujars, Jats, Ahirs and Goallas come from the same ethnic stock (Crooke 1896).

The tribe derives its name either from the Sanskrit word Gujar, the original name of their earliest habitat, Gujrat (now one of the states in India) or from Gochar i.e. cow-grazier (Crooke 1896), the later term showing that originally they were cow-keepers and not buffalo-keepers as they are at present.

As reported by Crooke, the Gujars embraced Islam at various times. But according to a legend current among the Gujars of Avadh in U.P. it was Taimur who carried out the mass conversion of Gujars to Islam when he attacked Delhi (Crooke 1896).

Uttar Pradesh has a sizeable population of both Hindu and Muslim Gujars. They numbered around one tenth of a million by the turn of nineteenth century. They should have doubled their numbers by now. The Muslim Gujars also include what we will term as Jammu Gujars who form the subject matter of this case study. The Jammu Gujars are a recent arrival in U.P. It appears that they entered the north western portion of Uttar Pradesh through Himachal Pradesh about 85 years ago.

Most of Hindu and Muslim Gujars lead a settled life. A large number of the Gujars still stick to their ancestral profession of buffalo-keeping and selling of milk and milk products.

Table 1
District-wise Population of Jammu Gujars

Name of District	*Population*
Nainital (non-hill portion)	1418
Garhwal (non-hill portion)	626
Sahranpur	1556
Bijnor	1749
Dehradun (non-hill portion)	1939
Total	7278

As in case of other Gujars, we do not have any census of Jammu Gujars. According to the forest officials, there are 7278 Jammu Gujars in U.P. and the districtwise break-up in their winter resorts as in Table 1. According to forest department survey, only 2813 of these Gujars migrate to the hill areas of U.P. and neighbouring Himachal Pradesh during summers. The remaining Gujars either do not shift at all or shift alongwith their cattle to other foreset areas in the Tarai Bhaber region of U.P.

Ambit of the Study

A study of this tribe was made by me in the early eighties. Out of the entire population of 7278, 221 families with 1309 members spread over twelve forest ranges in the districts of Saharanpur, Dehradun, Bijnor and Pauri Garhwal were covered. Thus Gujars of Nainital district only did not come within the ambit of the study. This paper covers a part of the study dealing with certain aspects of their social organization, religion and ritual with a view to examining elements of Hindu Caste System in the Gujar socio-religious system.

Socio-Economic Life, Religion and Ritual

It is considered relevant to present here a few facts about Gujar economy. Buffalo keeping still remains their main occupation. Our survey showed that only 7.7 percent families possessed land, the average holding being 6.2 acers per family whereas all the surveyed families possessed buffaloes, the average number of buffalos per family being 11.5. Because of poor yield and exploitation by middleman in the marketing of milk products, the majority of Gujars were found to be quite. It was found that 85% of the surveyed families were indebted.

The Gujars profess the Sunni form of Islam. Although they do not possess much knowledge of Islam, the Gujars are very sincere and devout Muslims. A large number of men and women offer prayers five times a day and fast during the month of Ramzan. The men invariably keep beards, Muslim teachers (*maulvis*) are employed in many Gujar habitations to teach Urdu and Arabic alphabets, recitation of Koran and religious principles to the children. It was found that nearly half the men and 20 percent women above the age of 15, have read the Koran.

The *maulvis* also, function as their witch doctors and perform *Jhar Phoonk* on sick persons believed to be possessed by *jinn*. Obviously, the *maulvis*, themselves little educated and interest only in earning money, are not only incompetent to impart a proper education but in a way increase Gujars' ignorance and help them to adhere to their age old beliefs, rituals and superstitions.

It was found that many families owe allegiance to the Deobandi Jamaat, a puritan movement with the centre at Deoband in Saharanpur district and the Barelvi Jamaat, a reformist movement. However the two movements are not at all active among the Gujars and their workers do not visit their area. The Gujars, however make contribution of money to the organizations off and on these movements in the course of their visit to towns. The only evidence to show that the Deobandis had started influencing the Gujars is that some Gujars have stopped offering *nazr-o-neyaz* (sanctified food) to the dead during *Shabe-barat* festival as this is discouraged by the puritans on the ground that it is un-Islamic.

Marriage Regulations

Like the Hindus, the Gujars too stick to certain principles of endogamny and exogamy in their marriages. The Gujars of Jammu constitute an endogamous group. They have a system of *gotras* on the pattern of the Hindus. The Gujars do not marry within the same *gotra*. As such the Gujar *gotras* are exogamous.

A survey of the *gotras* of 140 Gujar families living in eight elected forest ranges, was conducted. The results are seen in Table 2. This table shows that the predominant *gotras* were Kasana, Lodha and Padhana.

The Gujars themselves are not always clear about the genesis of their *gotras*, except that these refer to their Hindu ancestry. According to Haji Kalu of Bijnor district, the Gujars of Kasana *gotra* were followers of Kansa and he narrated the well-known the well-known story of Raja Kansa with reference to the birth of Krishna. The names of these *gotras* clearly establish the Jammu Gujars Hindu origin, but many of the *gotra* names, I came across in the course of this study are not identical with Hindu *gotras*. Some are clearly be identified as Hindu castes or sub-castes., For instance, Chauhan is a well-known Kshatriya sub-caste, baniya a Vaishya Caste, Chopra a sub-caste of Khatri (a Vaishya caste) and Lodha or Lodh another well-known Hindu caste. Bhainsi, however, most probably originates from *bhains* (buffalo).

It has been found that there is a role for the *gotras* in some of the rituals connected with marriage. In the engagement ceremony, called *Kurmai* held at the house of the bride, the boy's side is treated with a special dish of hot milk mixed with butter. If in the boy's party, there is a member having the *gotra* of the bride, he cannot touch this dish. The ceremonial bath of the bridegroom can be performed only by men having the same *gotra* as the groom.

There is no evidence to show that one *gotra* is superior to another. In fact all *gotras* are considered equal and barring one's

Table 2
Gujar *Gotras*

Name of the forest range	*Gotras & number of families in each*													
	Kasana	*Lodha*	*Padhana*	*Bagri*	*Dinda*	*Bhainsi*	*Chauhan*	*Baniya*	*Pessuwal*	*Chechi*	*Katana*	*Chopra*	*Kalas*	*Total*
Mohand	21	14	8	1	5	1	1	1	-	-	-	-	-	52
Dhaul-khand	5	3	2	-	-	-	1	-	-	-	-	-	-	11
Ranipur	2	1	2	-	-	-	1	1	-	-	-	-	-	7
Asarori	1	1	-	-	-	-	-	3	-	-	-	-	-	5
Mouchur	4	-	1	-	-	-	3	-	-	2	-	-	2	12
Chandi	-	4	10	-	-	-	6	4	4	3	-	-	-	31
Sabalgarh	4	3	2	-	-	-	-	5	1	-	2	1	1	19
Laldhang	2	-	-	-	-	-	-	-	-	-	1	-	-	3
	39	26	25	1	5	1	12	14	5	5	3	1	3	140
	27.9	18.6	17.9	0.7	3.6	0.7	8.5	10.0	3.6	3.6	2.1	0.7	2.1	100.0

own *gotra*, one can marry a girl from any other *gotra*. Except for regulating endogamy and a few marriage rituals, the *gotras* do not appear to play any further significant role, in the social-religious life of the Gujars. The Gujar society, as a matter of fact is based more on *masawaat* (principle of equality) and is more socialistic than many other Muslim communities in India, which have in-built stratification in their social orders.

Discussion

The above would show that the Gujars still follow a 'caste profession' i.e. buffalo keeping and their society prescribes certain restrictions and regulations on marriage. They have a system of *gotras* which like Hindu *gotras* are exogamous. The Jammu Gujars, as a whole, form an endogamous unit and do not allow their boys and girls to marry the Muslims outside their brotherhood. A study of *gotras*, however, shows that they are not analogous to Hindu *gotras*. These are most probably Hindu castes and sub-castes to which the Gujars belonged before embracing Islam. If this is so, the process has resulted into the transformation of an endogamous unit into an exogamous unit. It is not difficult to explain this. In the hoary past, when the Gujars of different castes/sub-castes became Muslims, they found that the number of families of the same caste/sub-caste was so small among the converted Gujars that a marriage alliance within the caste/sub-caste was an extremely difficult proposition. They were, therefore, compelled to seek matrimonial ties outside their caste/sub-caste among other Jammu Gujars. This having become a popular and accepted practice, the *gotras* became redundant and the caste/sub-caste became, for all practical purposes, exogamous units and were renamed *gotras* in course of time.

There are a large number of Muslim groups in India which follow 'Caste occupations'. We have Muslim *darzi* (tailor), *nai* (barber), *dhobi* (washerman), *bhangi* (sweeper), etc. As such adhering to buffalo keeping as a caste occupation by the Jammu Gujars, is not a subject or characteristic feature of their society. So is the position with regard to presence of some Hindu traits in the Gujar rituals and ceremonies as many other Muslim groups too have retained and even adopted Hindu rituals and ceremonies in one form or another (Ansari, 1959).

The evidence of *gotras* among the Muslims, is, however, not easily detectable. Most of the *ajlafs* have made persistent efforts to get rid of the remnants of Caste System among them in an effort to delink themselves from their Hindu ancestry and to bridge the social gap between themselves and *ashrafs*. The principle of *masawaat* advocated by Islam which is, in fact, anti-thesis of the principles on which the Caste System is based, accelerated this process with the result, that there are not many Muslim groups who have retained their *gotras* or castes or sub-castes or make use of them in marriage. However, there are a few Muslim groups like the Meos, who still possess a *gotra* system. But the Gujars are exceptional in as much as no other Muslim group seems to have so jealously guarded its *gotra* system and entity. They do not have any links either with Hindu or Muslim Gujars (of one-Jammu origin) or with the other Gujars of Jammu and Kashmir. They do not have any social intercourse with the other Muslims in their neighbourhood or anywhere else in U.P. The Gujars are thus one of the most exclusive groups in U.P.

The reasons are not far to seek. The Gujars are a recent arrival, their presence in U.P. not being more than 30 yeas. They hve been nomadic and like to live in the interior of the forests. While the women have hardly any chance to come in contact with non-Gujars, the men have only occasional contacts with others when they visit markets or forest range offices. No wonder, they have not been affected by the process of *ashrafization.*

NOTES

1. Islamization is a process of purification from non-Islamic practices.
2. *Ashrafization* is a process of upward social mobility within the Muslim fold.

REFERENCES

Ansari, G. (1959), 'Muslim Caste in Uttar Pradesh : A Study of Culture Contact' in Eastern Anthropologist, Vol. XIII, No. 2 (special number).

Ghurye, G.S. (1979), Caste and Race in India, Bombay :

Crooke, W. (1896), Castes and Tribes of North Western Province and Oudh, Vol. III, Calcuta.

STRUCTURE OF KINSHIP RELATIONS IN A PEASANT COMMUNITY OF BANGLADESH

Md. Shairul Mashreque

Introduction

In every community kinship is considered to be a vehicle for understanding the internal mechanism of social structure. The system of kinship is itself a 'sub-structure' (Alavi 1971) or an internal structure within the social structure. Kinship relations are streamlined through 'cultural mechanism' which give expression to multidimensional social institutions. They are patterned through culturally defined sets of customs dictated by religion and are inherent in language.

So far as the communities of Bangladesh are concerned kinship systems may vary at various socio-cultural levels. They do not follow a uniform pattern; there are, of course, differences in forms of kinship organization, kinship relations specified by kinship concepts, and their terminological features.

In search of identifying a uniform pattern I would like in this article to examine kinship relations found in Ratanpur[1] - a study village. The selection of Ratanpur is justified on the ground that a Muslim dominated village would present a structure of relationship that may exist in other Muslim villages of Bangladesh. In this sense the study of one village may be representative – reflecting the cultural pattern of Bengali Muslim villages, of course, there may exist some localized customs regulating behavioural pattern by which Ratanpur may claim some distinction in respect of kinship system.

More specifically the purpose of this article is three-fold: identification of kinship groupings, description of the concepts involving kinship relations and analysis of the terminological features in the context of the existing network of relations.

Kinship Grouping

The study of kinship groups is important for determining the social contous and the nature of the 'compartmentalised' and 'segmented' rural social structure. In this context we may refer to Oscar Lewis (1958: 22) who writes of a village near Delhi: "to understand the social organization of Rampur we must understand the meaning of four basic terms used by the villagers, viz., *kunba, gotra, tholla* and *pana*"[2]. His study of the nature of the 'compartmentalised' and 'segmented' rural social organisation deals with the composition, the location and the size of the small groups that have much influence on the housing and settlement pattern of the village.

The 'segmented' and 'compartmentalised' nature of peasant social organizations has been reflected in other micro-anthropological studies made by Zaman (1977), Aminul Islam (1974), Profulla Sarker (1980), Eglar (1960), Zaidi (1970), Ellickson (1972) and Bertocci (1970). These peasant studies have emphasized on small groups recognizing their significance in all spheres of life such as economic, political and cultural. For understanding the kinship system which is itself a 'sub-structure' within the social structure, it is necessary to categorise the small groups.

Aminul Islam (1974), in his discussion of social organisation of Badarpur, speaks of four important compartments such as *ghar, bari, paribar* and *gushti*. His identification of different types of groupings seems confusing so far as the kinship groupings of the study village are concerned, for he termed *bari* as extended family consisting of the eldest member and his wife and unmarried children, and wives of the married and unmarried grand children. He considers *ghar* as consisting of a husband and wife and their children. In Ratanpur a number of households which differ typologically make up a *bari* that tends to occupy a definite area, so a *bari* bearing a title or named after is founding father may have different types of *ghar* or *duars*.[3]

Distinction Between Bari, Gushti and Bangsa

The villagers use the terms *bari, gushti,* and *bangsa* interchangeably to refer to their lineages. Although it is possible to draw a line of demarcation among these three terms, they are in essence synonymous. *Gushti* may be identified with *bari,* for the villagers frequently mix it with *bari* by saying – the *gushti* of of this *bari,* e.g., the *gythi* of mulla *bari.* But the term *gushti* more inclusive than *bari.* In the village *bari* members are united by the bond of *gushti* relation, thus indicating the concentration of the *gushti* people in a compound.

Gushti sometimes may develop into a wider network of kinship relations transcending the *bari* boundary to include within its bounds those living elsewhere in other villages or towns, so the boundary of the *gushti* may stretch to other villages and towns wherein live the fellows of the same. "in the wider sense it is a term that means that the relationship is somehow more intimate, more demanding of fellowship and special privilege than other relationships" (Aminul Islam 1974:67).

In Ratanpur all the kin who can trace their relationship to near or distant ancestors, no matter how deep the lineage is, belong to the same *gushti.* So the identification of a *gushti* emanates from having a common ancestor. Daughters belong to the *gushti* of their father, but are included in that of their husband after marriage. Therefore, after marriage they are identified with another *gushti* but do not shun their fellowship of the *gushti* of their parental home. The size of the *gushti* is indicated by the level of upward generations its members can recall. If a *gushti* member can trace their relationship to one or two ascending generations, then it is a small one. Of course, the size of the *gushti* also influenced by the number of household and their members.

Social scientists differentiate between *gushti* and *bangsa.* Jean Ellickson (1972) gave a clear distinction between these two terms based on the data she generated. The term *bangsa* includes a group of kin tracing their agnatic connection back to an immediate ancestor, not going in most cases far beyond the grandfather (Zaman 1977: 64). Though the difference is recognized theoretically and is applied in practice, commonly the villagers use these terms synonymously. However, *bangsa* is used more by those belonging to the noble families. The people of these groups frequently use this term 'we are the member of *ucco bangsa*' (high lineage) while tracing their relationship to a common ancestor who may have been a landlord or a rich man, some two or three generations ago. They try to maintain their aristocratic background (*khandan*). The poor families or families of lower status do not have such sentiments. They do not use the term *bangsa*, hyaving no *ucco bangsa garba* (pride). Making frequent reference to *bagsa* is an expression of high status. A rising family having lower family background, tries to hide its connection with its ancestors. On the other hand, a poor family with higher lineage may boast of its hereditary background, and may refer to its *bangs* frequently. Inden and Nicholas (1977:5) used *bangsa* synonymously with the term *kula* to refer to a lineage. In the study village the Muslim do not use the term *kula*.

Concepts Involving Kinship Relations

The concept involving kinship in Ratanpur are *atmiya, kutum* and *sariik*. The term *atmiya* is pervastive throughout Bangladesh and, refers to all kinds of relatives–consanguinal, affinal and fictive. Bertocci (1970) used the concept of *atmiya* to indicate all consanguinal and affinal kinsmen. The term *kutum* has a special meaning. It is used by the villagers to indicate only the affinal kinsmen. The term *sarik* is used to include all the *bari* members particularly related, sharing the property of their ancestors. The kinsmen that are referred to as *sarik* fall within the bounds of *gushti*.

The villagers categorise two types of *atmiya, nikat atmiya* and *dursamparka atmiya*. The former includes all the kinsmen closely related through father's and mother's lines. The latter includes all the kinsmen distantly related, may be detached relatives of mother's line and the collaterals having marital ties. These two categories of relatives have been focused in the studies made by Ellickson (1972) and Ashraful Azis (1979). Ellickson used the term *ghanistha atmiya* to denote closely related kinsmen.

In Ratanpur some nuclear families comprising husband, wife and children have developed into wider families that include within their bounds all the relatives vertically and horizontally related, such as parents, children, grand parents and children and siblings of the spouses. There is a tendency to distinguish between primary and secondary kin. The primary kin included a person's parents and children, while any kin–cosanguinal or affinal–related to a person through primary kin is secondary kin to him; a person's father's brother for instance, or his step mother, etc. (Fuchs 1963:115).

It may be mentioned that the nuclear family includes the parents and their unmarried children who are united through the ties of primary kinship. The joint family includes both the primary and secondary kin. But *the atmiya* or the kin groups embody the widest circle of people including all relatives–primary, secondary, consanguinal and affinal.

Terminological Aspects

From our perusal a number of studies on kinship terminologies covering the subcontinent it appears that studies on terminological aspect of kinship in Bangladesh are at a premium. Inden and Nicholas (1977) analyse kinship terms that exist in West Bengal of India. For analysis of kin terms with special reference to Bangladesh village communities we have to fall back upon a few studies. Bessaignet (1958), Aziz (1979) and Khaleque (1983) present a detailed profile of kinship network by showing the structure of kinship terminologies. They seem to relate kin terms to the system of kinship. Among these scholars only Aziz offers peasant studies with emphasis on terminological features.

The confluence of Hindu culture and Islamic traditions affect the kinship terms embedded in Bengali culture. Therefore, it seems a challenging task to draw a sharp line of demarcation between Hindu and Muslim kinship so far as terms of address are concerned. Nevertheless, it is possible to emphasise the distinctiveness of Muslim kin relationship mirrored by some subtle difference in terminological setting that displays unique features of kinship in Bangladesh. The *atmiya* relationship is expressed in referential and addressing terms. The kinship terms that are inherent in Bengali culture give a clear distinction between two sets of relatives–paternal and maternal, i.e., relatives belonging to the patrilineage or *gushti* or those belonging to the matrilineage. For the study village I have analysed the kinship terms in accordance with the accepted practices. Nevertheless, there are some deviations from the accepted practices. They are embedded in the local usages and customs and correspond much to the kinship system itself. Here the explanations of various kinship terms are useful for understanding the web of social relations, the ascription of status and role of the individuals and the pattern of behaviour. The following analysis covers only some terms of address that are associated with these variables. All the kin terminologies are given in Chart I and Chart II[4]. I shall explain kin terms with the use of male ego.

In Ratanpur, most villagers use the term *bapjan* for address instead of using the term *baba* (accepted for Bangladesh) to denote the father. Father is the most important person to the ego, who abides by his instructions and gets to learn the values of kinship and society. As the relationship between the children address him as *bap* adding the suffix *jan*. The character of the father is reflected in his children who learn the way of behaving towards their kin. So, the resultant behaviour of the children is reflected in the manner they address the superior of their own *gushti* as well as of other families. Fathers of high status families are more aware of defects of status behaviour in their children and are quick to correct them. But in the low status families fathers seldom care about their children's faults and defects. The way they are being socialized in the family environment is reflected in their behaviour towards their fellows. Fathers are even addressed as *bap* and *tui* (the word usually used for a junior member). To address without adding suffix *jan* indicates either disrespect or extreme familiarity. Such behaviour is also shown to the senior agnates of identical status.

In Ratanpur some variations in addressing father's brother have been marked indicating fully the social and economic positions of these relatives. Within a *bari* different terms of address may express the same relationship, depending on the social and economic power of the heads of the individual households. If ego's father's brother is not economically solvent but socially inferior he addresses him as *caca* and in many cases adds this term of address to his nickname (nickname + *caca*). This term may be extended to some more people, other than relatives, such as servants and day-labourers, if they command respect due to age. The addition of suffix *jan* to *caca* (*caca* + *jan*) express respect. Usually ego says *caca jan* to those persons who have sufficient economic power and stronghold over the rural power structure. These people play leadership roles both in their respective *baris* and in the village. If they are contemporary to ego's father then he addresses them as *pradhancaca*. In some families the senior-most members are addressed as *cacajan* (if the person is senior to ego's father).

Different addressing terms have been used within the *gushtis* ranking high in the social rung. In a *gushti* of low social position people seldom use the term *cacajan* to designate their father's brother. But there may be some exceptional cases in which different terms of address do not necessarily denote different socio-economic positions. For example, in the case of special relationship between ego and his father's brother the terms of address, *caca* or nickname+ *caca*, may appear. This relationship indicates extreme familiarity.

Father's brother is differentiated from mother's brother, who is ego's *mama*. Mother's brother's wife is called *mami*. Father's sister is called *khala*, and mother's sister's husband is called *khalu*. Ego's relationship with his maternal-uncle is more intimate than that with his paternal uncle. *Mama* is a sweet word, full of love. Ego does not share paternal property with his *mama*. He cannot do harm to his *vagne* (sister's son). This dyadic relationship has featured in the recent kinship study of Ashraful Aziz (1979 : 115) of some village of Matlab near Comilla. A high degree of reciprocal cooperation between *mama* and *vagne* has been shown by Aziz. He also shows various dimensions of the dyadic relationship as prevalent in rural Bangladesh. On the other hand, as ego and his father's brother belong to a *sarik*, sharing the ancestor's property, the relationship between them is not so intimate and may turn worse if they are in perpetual conflict over the possession of paternal property, or if ego thinks that his father is mulcted of due share of paternal property by his *caca*. Since property consideration is a cardinal factor in the sarik relationship, relations between ego and his father's brother are hardly ever sincere, intimate and sweet. Even if they are on good terms the relationship between them is one of respect and obedience.

In ego's own generation, ego uses the terms *bhai* and *bon* to refer to all his brothers and sisters. The term *bhai* are used to refer to the siblings of ego's primary conjugal natal family and the relatives of his own generation. Mostly the villagers use the terms *bhai* and *bu* to address all their brothers and sisters. As kinship terms vary from place to place, in some places elder brothers and elder sisters are addressed as *dada* and *didi*. These two terms, used for senior brothers and sisters respectively, are considered to be Hindu terms by many Muslim families.

In ego's own natal family ego addresses his elder brothers using the words such as *barabhai, majabhai, sejabhai* and *noabhai,* according to relative age. In dominant *gushtis,* the guardians of the interacting households endeaveour to socialize their offspring in accordance with the norms and values of the groups. So the etiquette and discipline the children learn from the family environment generate these terms of respect. The younger siblings, thus, systematically apply kinship terms to their elder ones depending on their age, status and role in the household.[6] For example, ego addresses his eldest brother as *barabhai* or *miabhai* sometimes. *Barabhai* is an important person in the natal family who wields power and exacts respect from all his younger siblings. In some households in Ratanpur, the eldest brothers have been found to have adopted a paternal attitude towards their much junior siblings and assumed the roles of *de facto* heads of the households when the real heads are inactive because of old age. The younger brothers in such householdes abide by the advice of the eldest brothers with respect. In a joint family the male and female dependents, irrespective of age, sometimes refer to eldest brother as the head of the family if the father is dead or inactive. *Mejabhai,* the second eldest brother of ego, may be treated in the same manner if he has appreciable influence on the family and a strong voice in its decision-making process. The extent of exercising authority over the junior siblings by *sejabhai* (third eldest brother), and *noabhai* (fourth eldest brother) and other senior ones of a household depends on their personalities and self assertion. But in a wider setting, e.g., in *bari* the term *bhai* or nickname+*bhai* may be designated to refer to all the senior brothers.

It may be mentioned that within the bounds of *gushti* many elder brothers are addressed by their nicknames. Yet this behaviour of the juniors towards their senior ones may be changed if the latter raised their social placement. So, this changed behaviour leading to the change in the terms of address, corresponds to changes in the relationship among elder and younger brothers. For example, in many cases a younger brother who once addressed his older one by his nickname using the term *tui* (usually the term is used for the younger members), began calling him *bhai* realizing his raised status.

In a cor..plex joint household cousins may be treated as siblings through the application of the same kinship terms for brothers.

The dominance of a lineage rests on good familial relations among the members of the joint households. It is usual for the parents of the households to teach their children to behave properly towards their senior brothers. The cousins exchange kinship terms amongst themselves respective the person's age, position and personality. Usually the terms *miabhai* and *chotabhai* are universally accepted as terms of address. Normally such family norms are maintained in the complex joint households belonging to socially dominant kin groups. This indicates harmony in the joint residence and corporateness in the *gushti* relationship. Such a pattern of relationship is marked in the cohesive kinship groups, of course, with a little deviation.

The position of women in the kin groups is inferior to that of men. In most cases ego adderesses his elder sisters by their nicknames. Only the siters several years elder are addressed as *bujan, barabu, mejabu* and *chotabu*. Ego frequently uses the word *tui* while talking to his elder sisters. As a woman cannot play any authority over ego the relationship between an elder sister and him is one of love and affection. The elder sisters sometimes play, the same role towards their younger siblings far junior in respect of age, as does their mother.

As regards ego's descending generation the term *vaste* and *vasti* are used for ego's brother's son and daughter. *Vagne* and *vagni* are respectively used for sister's son and daughter. For addressing them ego may use their nicknames. Normally, ego addresses them as *abba* or *baba* or *beta* and *amma* or *ma* or *beti* as if they are his father and mother. Such terms are symbolic of love and affection. In the realm of *sarik*, this relationship expressed by the terms of address may be hyampered if there exists internal conflict between the interacting households. In such a situation these terms of address may not appear. In the village it is noticed that several cases of inter-household antagonism centering around disputed property engendered a situation in which the juniors and the seniors behaved toward one another quite differently. Tension may mount to an extent that there is scuffling between the members of the same *gushti*. In such a situation, they may pronounce abusive terms, irrespective of rank. But among the dominant and cohesive *gushti* this kind of behaviour is not noticed. The relationship between *caca* and *vaste* is one of obedience, respect and loyalty.

The term *nati* and *natin* refer to ego's grandson and grand-daughter. In the village the grand-father jokes with the grandchildren. Grand-father sometimes makes fun with grand daughter by calling her his wife. Likewise a grand-mother may make fun with her grandson by calling him her second husband. Joking relations mutually accepted, correspond to exchange of banter, making faces at or grimace that cause laughter, and teasing one another using erotic language.

Separate terms are used to indicate the affines. After marriage a man establishes relations with a host of people with whom he was not previously related. Thus, marriage generates a set of affinal kins and also a new set of terms like *sasur* (spouse's father), *sasuri* (spouse's mother), *vasur* (groom's elder brother), *debar* (groom's younger brother), *bhabi* (ego's elder brother's wife), *dulabhai* (ego's elder sister's husband), *sala, Sali, biai, bouma* and *mamandhi*. The terms *sala* and *sali* are referred to bride's younger brother and sister. The parents and all maternal and paternal uncles, as well as aunts of the groom address the bride *bauma*. The term *svamandi* refers to bride's elder brother. The ego is *svamandi* to his younger sister's husband he is addressed as *bhai* or *bhaisab*.

The word *vasur* is a compound of *bharatar* (brother) and *svasura* thus symbolizing the fact that the brother of the husband is like the father-in-law (Karve 1968: 112). The wife cannot develop any joking relations with him. It is expected of her to respect him like her father-in-law. She cannot utter her *vasur's* and cannot touch anything that he is touching. In this village where *parda* system is strictly followed, she is expected to cover her head with *ghomta* (veil) and follow a decorum while talking to her *vasur*. This behaviour expected of the wife towards her *vasur* and *sasur* corresponds to the ideal of the *parda* system.[6]

Marriages among kin are common in the village, people are often related to one another in more than one capacity. Such a marriage among the relatives strengthens ties, bringing them more close to each other. Under such circumstance the terms of address remain unaltered, because change of terms of address would lead to change in the long standing relationships. And this may not be acceptable by the other relatives within the kin group. The fathers of the bride and groom may be brothers and endeavour to maintain the earlier relationship. Their families use the term they previously used to address the bride and the groom. So, the affinal terms of relationship do not appear. The families of the bride and the groom use the terms of address that symbolize the previous rather than the present relationship. For example, a father-in-law is called *caca* (father's brother), because this was the earliest relationship of the person to the daughter-in-law. The relationship between the groom and the siblings of the bride remains unchanged . If he is elder than his wife's elder brother the groom would continue the previous relationship by calling his nickname as before. And the wife's elder brother would also try to respect him with the previous terms of address, *bhai*. The groom's younger brothers and sisters would not use the term *bhabi*.

Therefore, all these groups of people that I have mentioned terminologically6 make up the relatives. Discussing the terminological aspect of kinship relationship it may be said that there is a co-relation between the status and terms of address. That the kinship terms determines status and power is true but not always true, because sense of honour may not develop in many young boys and girls. And in some cases the terms applied by the juniors to their superiors not symbolizing respect and obedience, may indicate a special relationship marked by extreme intimacy and familiarity.

Fictive Kinship

Besides consanguinal and affinal kin, we may have another kind of *atmiya* that may be referred to as *dhanna-atmiya*. In certain circumstance, kinship behaviour provides a pattern of relations between people who are not relatives. Fictive relations are also stressed in the village. In the village where face-to-face relationships exist one may use kinship terms towards anyone in every day context. While coming in contact in the market place with persons with whom he has nodding acquaintance or even unknown persons he may exchange kinship terms with them. This exchange may even take place in the interaction between buyers and sellers. The terms such as *bhai* and *caca* are frequently used. Playing up of these relations among the interacting persons or group of persons is transitory and does not necessarily imply intimate bond of union. If a man makes personal and intimate contacts with anyone by uttering kinship terms considering age and status, it would eventually result in the formation of intimate bond of union. Such relationship may be referred to as fictive relations.

Fictive relations may be expressed in the address of friends and neighbours. If any friendly relations exist among the contemporaries of the village they use terms such as *dosta* and *bandhu*. The former is frequently used by the Muslims and thye latter by Hindus and the Muslims. They refer to a special kind of friendship. The term *mita* is used if there is a similarity in the names of two persons.

As the villagers are more or less gregarious, friendships frequently develop among them. Apart from institutionalized relationship, friendship is recognized as a personal relation (Sarma 1963: 195). It is usual for friendship to develop among people of equal status. In Ratanpur children of higher families feel reluctant to develop friendships with those of lower families. They are apt to make friends with the families of equal status. If under any circumstance friendships grow between the children of the families of unequal status the relationship may turn into one of superior and inferior. Between the families having strained relations friendships never develop.

Interestingly, fictive relationship relates the people of different socio-economic groups closely. In this context we may refer to Profulla Sarker (1980:55): "Poor will ask an influential person of the village to set up this fictive relation with them, and sometimes the influential will agree. The poor person will get financial and political benefits such as land for share-cropping and fertilizer from the agricultural officer". In the village it has been noticed that the patron-client relationship develops into fictive kinship as a result of prolonged association between the persons involved in such relationship. In case of fictive relationship between a large farmer and a poor farmer (between land owner and landless labhour), one giving economic support and another receiving it, kin terms may be used symbolizing the existing power relationship between them. In such a case the client may address his patron who may be a politically prominent figure as *bapjan, cacajan* or *pradhan caca*. He may address the wife or wives of his patron as *ammajan*, and expression of full allegiance and loyalty to the patron's family . The younger members of this dominant family by virtue of this intimate bond of relationship extend the terms *caca, dada* or *bhai* to them as they do to indicate their kinsmen.

Conclusion

In the light of the above, the implications of kinship system now in existence in the study village may be taken to demonstrate a pattern that would be found in most villages of Bangladesh with, of course, some variations. In fact the study presents a profile of kinship relations and thereby reflects the cultural pattern of Bengali Muslim villagers in general. The existing framework of kinship has been established through the metamorphosis of culture in which there is a happy combination of the two elements–language and religion.

To recognize the structure of kinship relations one potent way might be to look at it from three dimensions: consanguinity, affinity and fiction. In the village under study the under kinship structure appears to combine these three dimensions.

Another potent way might be to trace the nature of groupings. The kinship system observed here exhibits typological distinction in terms of groupings. Such distinctive features stem from the fact that the type of kinship organisation is visible in the position of the small groups–the household clusters and the lineage with referene to the empirical content to their definitions.

Kinship terms described in the context of the system discover kinship behaviour. The study of the terminological aspect suggests that the kinship system in Bengali culture is elaborate, descriptive, wide ranging and demanding of fellowship. The terms analysed symbolize position, rank, status, power relations and the extent of familiarity.

NOTES

1. The village selected for the study is given a pseudonym-Ratanpur. The village is located in the district of Pubna, Northern Bangladesh. Through participant observation the author endeavours to go deep into villagers' perceptions, the accentuated symbols expressing any striking relationship or behaviour and their orientation to kinship organization symbolized by existing structure of relations. The village was surveyed for collecting data for my M.Phil. thesis. 'Kinship and Power Structure in Rural Bangladesh: A Case Study'. This paper is a part of my thesis.
2. *Kunba* signifies a group of agnates tracing their relationships through the male line. The word *gotra* is designated to refer to non-localised, exogamous, patrilineal, and named kinship group that may be

regarded a clan. The terms *tholla* and *pana* indicate Jat lineages and clans that are grouped into units. Each *pana* includes one *tholla* with a *pana* name and another *tholla* with a different name.

3. Literally *duar* means door. Many villagers use it instead of using *ghar*, to denote their households that may be variant typologically. Each of the several *duars* within the boundary is referred to as *cula* (hearth).
4. Ashraful Aziz (1979:97-98) has shown the Muslim male ego kinship tree and Muslim married female ego kinship tree covering six generations along with terms of reference and classification of kin categories according to consanguinal relationship (*svajan*), relationship reference (*atmiya-svajan*) and affinal relationship (*atmiya*). Here the author has not included in his chart the terms of address. Copying the format used by him I present the terms of address prevalent in my study area.
5. Inden and Nicholas (1977:10-11) made mention of elder-younger relationship among the siblings as cousins of ego's generation. Here the authors did not categorically analyse these relationships, because they called all siblings *bhai* and *bon*. Their analysis, in this respect, did not emphasize power relations and status among the siblings.
6. Profulla Sarker (1980) has shown two aspects of the *parda* system as they are functioning in both Hindu and Muslim societies; one is physical aspect and other is behavioural aspect. For details see : "Institution of Purdah system between Hindu and Muslims in Bangladesh : A Cross Cultural Study" in *Spectra of Anthroplogical Progress*, 1980.

REFERNECES

Alavi, H. (1971), 'The Politics of Dependence : A Village in West Punjab' in *South Asian Review*. Vol. 4, No.2.

Aziz, K.M.A. (1979), *Kinship in Bangladesh*. Monograph Series No. 1, Dacca : International Centre for Diarroheal Disease Research, Bangladesh.

Berteocci, P.J. (1970), Elusive Village : Social Structure and Community Organization in Rural East Pakistan. Unpublished Ph.D. Dissertation, Michigan State University.

Bosaignet, P. (1958), *Tribesmen of Chittogang Hill Tracts*. Dacca : Asiatic Society of Pakistan.

Eglar, Z. (1960), *A Punjabi village in Pakistan*. New York : Columbia University Press.

Ellickson, J. (1972), A Believer among Believer : The Religious Belief, Practices and Meanings in a Village in Bangladesh. Unpublished Ph.D. Dissertation. Michigan State University.

Fochs, S. (1963), *Origin of Man and His Culture.* Bombay : Asia Publishing House.

Inden and Nicholas (1977), *Kinship in Bengali Culture.* Chicago : Chicago University Press.

Islam, A.K.M.A. (1974), *A Bangladesh Village : Conflict and Cohesion.* Cambridge Massachusetts Schenkman Publishing Company.

Khaleque, K. (1983), 'Garo Kinship Terminology : Idealisation and Reality' in *The Dhoka University Studies,* vol. XXXIX, Part A. Dec. 1983.

Lewis, O. (1958), *Village Life in Norther India.* Berkeley : University of California Press.

Sarker, P.C. (1980), 'Dharmo-Atmiyo : Fictive Kin Relationship in Rural Bangladesh' in *The Eastern Anthropoologist.* Vol. 33.

Sarma, J. (1963), 'A Village in West Bengal' in Srinivas (ed.). *India's Villages.* Bombay: Asia Publishing House.

Zaidi, S.M.H. (1970), *The Village Culture in Transition : A Study of East Pakistan Rural Society.* Honolulu : East West Press.

Zaman, M.Q. (1977), Social Conflict and Political Process in Rural Bangladesh–A Case Study Unpublished M.Phil. Dissertation, Institute of Bangladesh Studies, Rajshahi University.

FAMILY LAW AND CUSTOMARY PRACTICES OF MUSLIMS IN SOUTHERN KERALA

Manu Bhaskar

Introduction

The Muslims of Kerala originated in the 8th and 9th centuries through the settlement of Arab converts, trading with the Malabar coast and the community has grown by extensive proselytisation as well as natural increase. The arrival of the Portuguese in 1498 checked their progress. By the mid-18th century the majority among them had become landless labourers, poor fisherman and petty traders. Thus Kerala Muslims were in psychological retreat in the British age and at independence (Nossiter 1982). But Muslims and Syrian Christians have to some degree provided the trading and business community of Kerala. In Kerala money-lending was taken by the Konkani and Tamil Brahmins and entrepreneurship by Europeans and Gujaratis[1].

According to 1981 Census, Kerala has 58.14 per cent Hindus and in the only major State where two-fifths of the population is non-Hindu. Among the non-Hindus, Muslims comprise 21.25 per cent and Christians 20.56 per cent. The Scheduled Castes and Scheduled Tribes are 10.02 per cent and 1.03 per cent respectively of the total population.

In Kerala Nairs, Ezhavas, Muslims and Christians are the forces in making and unmaking of the State politics.

Muslims in Kerala

The Muslims are called the Moplahs or Mappilas in erstwhile Malabar and Jonaka or Jonaka Mappilas in the rest of Kerala

(Mathur 1978). They constitute the second largest religious group in the percentage of the total Kerala population. Various studies have shown that Mappilas[2] are of mixed ethnic origin. The honorific title Mappila is added even this day by the Christians of former Travancore to their names. The Muslims of Kerala are called Jonaka Mappila (people from Yavanak which refers to Ionian or Greek) to distinguish them from the Christians who go by the appellation 'Nazarani' Mappila (Thurston 1909: 459).

In 1981 Census Report it is noted that some Mappilas have been referred to as (Putiya Islam) meaning new converts to Islam (Ibid). According to Lewis Moore (1905) the word Mappila means:

1. the bride-groom or son-in-law
2. the name given to Mohammedan, Christian or Jewish Colonists in Malabar who have intermarried with the natives of the country. The name is now confined to Mohammedans.

The Mappilas are divided into several endogamous groups which are stratified into regional hierarchy. The Mappila fisher folk of Malabar, occupy the lowest social position in the hierarchy of the Muslim society in Kerala. Muslim society in Kerala is a segmented one. Muslims are divided into three main sects : Sunni, Shiah and Ahmadiyyah (Quadiyansi). The Shafia, one of the four-sects of Sunnis, forms the overwhelming majority of the Muslim population of Kerala. The Wahabis (an offshoot of Sunni sect), call themselves Mujahids in Kerala form one third of the Mappila (Mathur 1978). The vast majority of them are found in Malappuram and Kozhikode districts. The Ahmadiyyahs are distributed in Kozhikode, Malappuram districts and in Karunagappaly of the erstwhile Travancore region.

The Mappilas are a Sunni Muslim group, originated by 8th century Arab traders and indigenous converts to Islam (Gough 1972). They settled mainly in the ports of Central and North Kerala. Over the centuries, the Mappilas have been recruited largely from Mukkuvas, a coastal fishing caste form Tiyars and other polluting castes (Ibid). No doubt because of the historical origins, the Mappilas of Central Keala are patrilineal and those of North Kerala are matrilineal. The Muslims of South Kerala too are mainly partilineal.

Demographic Profile of Muslims in Kerala

According to 1981 Census Report, the Muslim population are 54,09687 (Table 1). They constitute 21.25 per cent of the total population of the State. The concentrations of the Muslims (74.47%) are mainly in the erstwhile Malabar region, viz. Malappuram, Kozhikode, Kannur, Palakkad, Trissur and Wayanad. 16.52 per cent of the Muslim population are in the erstwhile Travancore region, viz. Thiruvananthapuram, Kollam and Alappuzha districts. The rest (9.01%) are distributed in Kottayam, Indukki and Ernakulam district which are in the region of Central Kerala.

Table 1
Population of Muslims in Kerala
(District-wise population–1981)

Sl. No.	*District*	*Total population*	*Percentage*
1.	Malappuram	1573988	29.10
2.	Kozhikode	762207	14.09
3.	Kannur	720192	13.31
4.	Palakkad	472787	8.74
5.	Kollam	394353	7.28
6.	Trissur	363218	6.71
7.	Ernakulam	339737	6.28
8.	Thiruvanthapuram	324545	6.00
9.	Alappuzha	175021	3.24
10.	Wayanad	136091	2.52
11.	Kottayam	84217	1.56
12.	Idukki	63331	1.17
	Total	54,09,687	100.00

***Source:** Census of India 1981, Household Population.*

Sex-wise analysis of Muslim population shows that except for Ernakulam, Kollam, Wayanad, Kottayam and Idukki districts the female outnumber the male (Table 2).

Mohammedan Law in India

Muslims make up the second largest community in India. The two major schools among them are Sunni and Shiah. The Sunnis, by and large, follow the Hanafi school. The Shiah law in India is that of Ithna-Ashari School or of the Ismailis. The Personal Law of the Muslims is applied to marriage, dower (mehr or mahr), dissolution of marriage, percentage and legitimacy, guardianship and maintenance gifts, wakfs, pre-emption and wills and giftsw. It also includes intestate susccession, special property of females, personal property inherited or obtained under contract or gift. The sources of law are considered to be the Koran, the Sunnat and the Hadith (the words and precepts of the Prophet).

Table 2
Population of Muslims in Kerala
(District-wise population – 1981)

Sl. No.	*District*	*Total population*	*Male*		*Female*	
			Number	*Percentage*	*Number*	*Per-centage*
1.	Malappuram	1573988	765303	48.62	808686	51.38
2.	Kozhikode	762207	376778	49.43	385429	50.57
3.	Kannur	720192	350107	48.61	370085	51.39
4.	Palakkad	472787	233048	49.29	239739	50.71
5.	Kollam	394353	198004	50.21	196349	49.79
6.	Trissur	363218	170071	46.82	193147	53.18
7.	Ernakulam	339737	171809	50.57	167928	49.43
8.	Thiruvan-thapuram	324545	159583	49.17	164962	50.83
9.	Alappuzha	175021	87465	49.97	87556	50.03
10.	Wayanad	136091	69269	50.90	66822	49.10
11.	Kottayam	84217	43173	51.26	41044	48.74
12.	Idukki	63331	32617	51.50	30714	48.50
	Total	54,09,687	2657226		2752461	

Source: *Census of India 1981, Household Population.*

The Muslim Personal Law (Shariat Act of 1937) (MPLA) and the Dissolution of Muslim Marriage Act of 1939 (DMMA), which have been the crucial legislations of the Muslim family law, were both introduced during the British period. In addition, we now have the Muslim Women (Protection of Rights and Divorce)Act, 1986. MPLA abolished all customs like agnatic succession among North Indian Muslims, matrilineal succession among Mappilas in Kerala and succession according to Hindu Law among the Khojas, Memons, etc. This was an attempt to unify the Muslims somewhat along the same lines as unifying the Hindus through their personal laws.

A personal law be that part of the community laws that govern personal affairs like marriage, dower, divorce, legitimacy, custody, succession to property. It is different from non-personal law which govern all within the national boundaries like Criminal Law, Law of Torts, Constitutional Law, etc. It governs a person because he/she belongs to a particular religion, race, caste, sect or tribe.

Family Law and Customary Practice in Southern Kerala

The paper seeks to argue that one cannot understand the legal process of formulation of the Law, divine or otherwise, without understanding the dynamics of social transformation, i.e. even divine law which is believed to be immutable cannot escape the effect of social transformation. Accordingly, in analyzing the position of women in Muslim society, one has to take into account the rights granted by the Islamic doctrine and the actualities of the present condition. The Islamic doctrine embodying the teachings of Koran and traditions of the Prophet (Hadith) constitute an important source of the status and position of women. The Islamic doctrine therefore provides the legal normative postulates. However, a distinction should be made between the Islamic doctrine, and Islamic, i.e. those customs which are inherited by and not invented by the Muslim society. A number of customs now treated as Islamic have nothing to do with Islam. These customs and practices have been the features of the social life of people who did not abandon them after embracing Islam and have adopted certain cultural forms of the dominant. Hindu community in the process of capitalist development. In other words, religion, normative or popular, is not and should not be viewed as an autonomous and an independent phenomenon. It is a part of network of social and cultural relationships and linkages. Religion is one important factor but there are other equally important factors which determine the status of women in a society. Secondly, the legal postulates are the abstract expression of the actual existing relations which are not permanent but are historical and transitory. However, it is not the legal postulates alone that determine the position of women, since the position of women has creased to be social and has assumed political and economic forms.

Secondly, the issue of Muslim Personal Law is closely linked with Muslim urge for identity. Through Muslim community of India has its peculiarities, its urge for identity is part of more universal phenomenon. For it is now widely recognized that the process of capitalist development sharpens all ethnic and communal identity.

Thirdly, a religious tradition might become unjust in the changed context and its practice may lead to injustice to a section of society and yet that community might insist on its practice as the Constitution guaranteed freedom of religion. Hence, to the elites religion seems to be irrelevant in framing laws, even in the personal arena. But to the masses, religion is not irrelevant. Thus the elites would favour the enforcement of a common civil code but to the masses it is reform of the Personal Muslim Law.

Here, an attempt is made from the data collected from Thirvananthapuram district to show the prevalent customary practices of the Muslims and to compare them with the Mohammedan Law with regard to family law. The study is based on the data collected through in-depth interviews from Muslim women belonging to different classes, legal personalities, religious leaders, intellectuals and political personalities.

Marriage

Islam regards marriage as a most sacred institution and makes it incumbent on every Muslim man and woman, unless prevented by valid physical or economic incapacity, to lead a married life. Tradition of the Holy Prophet stresses the importance of marriage. "It is necessary for you to marry because, marriage is the most powerful shield against allurements of sight and protection of your private parts, if one of you cannot afford let him fast because fasting weakens the sexual impulse".

Muslim marriage is known by Arabic Word 'Nikah'. It is Sunnah (traditions elaborated by the Prophet) and is considered an obligation to be fulfilled. The three steps of a Muslim marriage are:

1. a proposal made by or on behalf of the parties,
2. an acceptance of the proposal in the presence and hearing of two male or one male and two female witnesses and,
3. settlement of dower.

The objective of Mohammedan Law regarding marriage or 'Nikah' is procreation and legal status of children consequently. Under the Mohammedan Law, a Muslim male can have four wives but a woman can have only one husband at a time.

Marriage has been considered something more than a means of producing progeny even by the Prophet. He is supposed to have said "marry to enjoy their (woman's) love and beget children". In order to ensure happy home and a really stable family life, Islam has assigned to marriage the status of a contract dissoluble, if one party develops grievances against the other leading to a final and irrevocable break in their mutual relations (Ibid: 44).

Preferred Age at Marriage

In India, early marriage prevailed among both in Hindus and the Muslims. Boys and girls were married off at a comparatively very early age. But with the passing of the Child Marriage Restraint Act of 1929, it is a punishable offence to permit the solemnization of the marriage of a bridegroom under 18 years of age and a bride under 15 years. In spite of this the early marriage has been widespread in the Muslim community.

In Islam no age limit is fixed for marriage. It was often seen that young girls may be legally married but a girl is handed over to the husband only after attaining puberty. In practice early marriage is still preferred among Muslims, i.e. between 16-20 years. Education has, however, raised the marriageable age. Now the acceptable age of marriage is 20-23 years.

Marriage Restrictions

The Islamic law provides certain restrictions and limitations where marriage is concerned. One such restriction is the law that a Muslim woman cannot marry a 'Kithabian' (non-Muslim) while a Muslim man can marry a Kithabia.[3]

Presently love marriage and intercaste marriage do occur. There is always an initial rejection and an eventual submission.

In practice, intercase and interreligious marriages are not accepted, unless he/she is converted to Islam. If their children should get access to the mosque, then both parents should be Muslim.

Arrangement of Marriage

The Muslim marriage or 'Nikah' is a contract and is essentially social in nature. In southern Kerala it is observed that the contract is mainly between the parents of the bridegroom himself and the father or brother of the bride. The marriage is usually arranged by the father. In cases where the father is incapacitated or dead, then mother's brother arranges the marriage. Marriage could be arranged through a common friend, through newspaper advertisement, sometimes between relations or through marriage brokers. The general practice is that when there is a proposal, the girl's family enquires about the prospective of groom. In the selection of bridegroom rational considerations like personality, occupation, character and other details regarding him are enquired. After this, bride's male relatives talk to the groom's family. Then the bridegroom's party come to see the girl. If they are impressed by the girl, they make negotiations for dowry.

Usually there is a mediator who talks to both bride's and groom's families and make negotiations for dowry. The mediator is normally a friend or a marriage broker. If it is a broker, he is given a percentage of dowry. In some rare cases parents negotiate directly the dowry. The negotiation generally takes place at the bridegroom's house. If dowry is agreed upon marriage is arranged. Most often the consent of the girl is not asked. Even it is asked it is only after the parents have confirmed that it is a good match. If her reply is against the parent's decision, they persuade her to conform.

With the spread of urban values, education and employment of women, a gradual change has taken place in the modern woman's notion about the kind of man she would like to have as her husband. Even though parents or guardians still take the initiative of arranging marriages, now-a-days the consensus of the boy and the girl are taken into consideration. They are allowed to meet each other and discuss their likes and dislikes and expectation about marriage. In earlier days, marriage negotiation was an one-sided affair with the girl having no voice at all. Today girls, especially the educated ones, insist on their consent being taken while negotiations are made about the marriage. The most popular pattern of marital choice in modern times as arrangement of wedding by parents with the const of daughter.

In rural and suburban areas girls often agree to the marriage because of parent's persuasion. Consent-seeking is just a formality. Most often even in an educated family this is the case. Thus it is varies from explicit 'yes' to nodding head. City-bred educated girls are more sure of their opinions and so they say 'yes' or 'no'. But in the orthodox Muslim families, the girls have absolutely no say in the marriage.

In fact in Islam, if a girl is given in marriage without her consent the marriage would be considered null and void and the girl has the right to have it annulled. But in the case of a widow, consent is not sought.

The main consideration during negotiation is education, occupation, economic status, income, character, etc. Once the marriage is fixed the bride is kept under strict seclusion. She would be prevented from interacting when even women from outside. Only after the marriage ceremony the bridegroom would be able to see the bride and *vice-versa*.

Thus, it can be seen that the arrangement of marriage is an all-male affair in which the bride does not have any voice. It is these provisions of the Muslim law that are used by many parents to "sell out" their female children in the guise of marriage to adults and in prostitution on monetary considerations.

Marriage Ceremony

Presently, the marriage ceremony has two parts, of which one is in accordance with the Mohammedan Law and the other is in accordance with practices prevalent among other communities. The formal 'Nikah' constitutes the first part. During the ceremony Khatib sits with the bride's father, groom along with the people from the local Jamaat, relatives and guests and the Khatib says some prayers and then formally would ask whether the bride's father and the groom agree for the marriage. In response to it the bride's father would formally state that he would give his daughter to the groom and the groom on his part formally accepts her has his wife along with the 'mehr'. After this, the bridegroom, the bride's father and two witnesses sign a register which is kept in the mosque. Women have no role in it as "Nikah" is to be seen only by men.

The second part is dominated by women. It is an informal part for conforming to the practices prevalent among other communities. The groom is brought in a by few close relatives to the place where the bride is sitting. The groom ties the 'thali' which is knotted by the sister of the boy. In some cases the boy has no role and the sister-in-law herself ties the 'thali'. They further exchange garlands and the boy would exchange golden necklace or golden right as is done in the case of marriage among Hindus. Next, the bride's mother give milk to the groom who drinks a little and gives the rest to the bride. While returning the glass Rs.101 is given by the groom to the mother-in-law. Mehr is also tied to the Pallav of the sari of the bride (Munthikettu). Also, the Hindu tradition of observing auspicious time and date (Rahukalam) has invaded Muslim marriage ceremony, i.e. Rahukalam is observed when the bride leaves the house and enters the groom's house. Tuesdays and Saturdays are not considered auspicious days for marriage, so also, 'nahaz time'[4] is not considered auspicious.

The marriage ceremony is generally performed in the place where the bride resides. Recently marriages in the urban centres are being conducted in halls. The formal marriage dress of a girl is sari withy a veil covering her head. In the case of bridegroom there is no formal dress. It may range from the traditional Mundu and Shirt to full suit depending on the economic background.

Dowry and Mehr

Under the Mohammedan Law, the bridegroom has to pay bride-price or mehr to the bride at the time of marriage. A Muslim woman has got right only over this amount and other than this she has no right. The amount of bride-price or dowry is dependent on the socio-economic status nof the families of the bridegroom. But in practice the 'mehr' is merely symbols. On the other hand, dowry is widely prevalent among Muslims though Mohammedan Law does not provide the same.

According to the Prophet such payment is taken off for man as a respect for his wife and was meant to protect women against the arbitrary powers of men regarding divorce. But in practice, it is merely a ritual and does not guarantee any financial security for a woman. It does not serve the purpose of protecting women against arbitrary powers of men regarding divorce. It is seen that both the ritualisation of 'mehr' and the unversalisation of dowry have had the effect of lowering the status of Muslim women. The practice of giving dowry once it became popular in Muslim community, drew 'mehr' to the back seat , making it look small and unnecessary. But since it is an integral part of Muslim marriage, 'mehr' is still continued as a ritual.

In practice 'mehr' is only nominal for conforming with provision of Mohammedan Law. Mehr varies from Rs 51 to Rs.101 and is paid fully during marriage. Among the affluent families sometimes it is given as gold, while in poor families the amount given is even as low as Rs. 20/-. Dowry also depends on the economic capacity of the families. It is usually in the form of gold, money, property and vehicles. The amount of money, quantum of gold, extent of property, etc. vary with the status of the bride and bridegroom. Dowry is given one or two weeks before marriage at the groom's place at a very elaborate function. Sometimes it is given on the day of the engagement and in some other cases the entire amount is given within 6 months to one year. Previously, a list of dowry items was kept at the Jamaat. But with the passing of the Dowry Prohibition Act of 1961 this was stopped. There are lots of marriages being held for want of adequate dowry. 2-5 per cent of the dowry should be given to the mosque.

Nikahnama is preprinted and woman cannot stipulate any conditions. In Nikahnama[5] the mehr is given in written. Hilala[6] marriages are rare.

Divorce

As said earlier, in Islam marriage is always regarded as a contract. Therefore, there are provisions under the Mohammedan Law for any breach in the marriage contact which included divorce. But all the provisions for divorce are loaded in favour of the husband. Under the Muslim Personal Law, a husband can divorce his wife at any time without giving any reason. A divorce can be made in any of the following three ways :

1. A husband can freely divorce his wife without giving any reason. This is the usual practice among Muslims and is a term termed 'talaq'.
2. Divorce can be made by mutual consent or agreement between husband and wife. This is termed as 'Khula' or 'Mubarat' but such divorces are rare.
3. Divorce can be by a usual decree either by the husband or wife through a civil code. Such divorces are frequent in cases where husband resorts to talaq.

Muslim women do not have right to divorce – 'Fasah'. If they want to divorce, they have to go to the court, which is a cumbersome affair as one has to wait for a very long period to get a decision. Moreover, only the affluent can afford it.

Though the Koran mentions about the possibility for a woman to her husband on account of her cruel treatment by forgoing her 'mehr'; there are no provisions for the same under the

Mohammedan Law. At the same time, the husband can freely divorce his wife by merely stating, that he is divorcing her, in front of two witnesses. He is expected to return the 'mehr' which, in any case, is only a negligible amount.

But in the case of woman, under the Dissolution of Muslim Marriage Act of 1939, they can initiate divorce proceeding only on the following grounds which makes it practically impossible.

1. Disappearance of the husband for a period of 4 years or more.
2. His failure to provide maintenance for 2 or more years.
3. His imprisonment for 7 years or more.
4. His failure to perform marital obligations for 3 years or more.
5. His impotency since marriage.
6. His insanity for 2 years, leprosy or virulent venereal diseases.
7. The wife's desire to observe "option of puberty" i.e. if she had been married off before the age of 15.
8. Cruelty on the part of the husband.

The following rights and obligations arise on the completion of divorce whatever may be the mode of divorce :

1. Right to contract another marriage.
2. Dower becomes immediately payable.
3. Mutual rights of inheritance cease.
4. Cohabitation becomes unlawful.
5. Remarriage of divorced couple (It is not lawful for him/her to marry each other again until she married another man and divorced him).

Under Islamic law a woman who divorces will have to wait for three menstrual periods before she can get remarried but there are no restrictions in the case of men. If a women is pregnant at the time of divorce he will have to look after her till the child is born and the till the suckling period of child which is two years. Also a man can resume at will the marital relationship with his divorced wife until she remarried. Further the husband can have the custody of children till the age of 17 in the case of boys and till the age of 11 in the case of girls.

In practice, the divorce is quite frequent among Muslims. It is always the men who make initiative in the divorce process. Though according to the Mohammedan Law, nearly a year is required to complete the formalities of 'talaq' this is not followed in actual practice. Often the husband says 'talaq' three times simultaneously and sometimes even without the knowledge of his wife. This generally happens when the husband is away at Gulf.

There are instances where the mosque leaders talk to the couples and make compromise. Girl's relatives talk to both the parties and try for reconciliation. If the talks of reconciliation do not succeed, then the husband sends a notice to the Jammat in which two witnesses also sign vouchsafing it has taken effect. The mosque committee on receipt of this notice, informs the woman and her family about the 'talaq'. Nearly one year is needed for divorce by uttering talaq. It should be said at intervals only. The second and third 'talaq' should be told at the gap of three months. It is a time for rethinking. Only after the third pronouncement of 'talaq' divorce is effected. The boy then sends a notice to the mosque which is signed by two witnesses. There is a document to register the divorce cases. The document 'talaqnama' contains return of dowry, maintenance during iddal, etc.

The mosque keeps a register in which all divorces are recorded. When the divorce takes place, the husband is expected to return the dowry but often the dowry is not returned. On divorce women get the custody of the children.

The major causes of divorce in the surveyed area are infidelity, extra-marital relationships (especially where the husbands are away in Gulf), alcoholism, wife-beating, incompatibility, prostitution, unfulfillment of dowry demands, economic reasons, illness, interventions of in-laws, irresponsibility of husband and in the cases of childless couples.

Polygamy

The Koran has sanctioned polygamy, but it has restricted the maximum number of contemporaneous wives to four. Husbands are expected to give equal treatment to all the wives. According to Siddiqui (1980: 110) Polygamy 'arose out of the circumstances that Islam found itself engaged in an almost unending series of wars with its deadly foes. This naturally led to the progressive reduction of the male population. The problem of surplus women left in such circumstances could not be solved except by permitting men to marry more than one wife in order to provide for helpless women and to save them from falling into the evil of prostitution.

Polygamy is an unspoken threat hanging over many a Muslim wife and daughter-in-law. Educated and modernized young women today, justly say, that if nothing else the sheer cost of living should dissuade people marriages in the modern world. Many women are of the opinion that polygamy is a barbarous institution, most unfair to a woman and that it should be changed. Others argue, that a woman is as much a victim of circumstances as is a man, and that there should be only one woman for every man. Some women wonder if polygamy is the only that exists in Islam. Others, justly ask, if I can't have two husbands why should our husbands be allowed to have two wives or more?

Presently, polygamy is prevalent among those Muslims who are not educated. Polygamous marriages are found more among the Muslims in the rural areas. Men usually enter into polygamous marriages for the sake of pleasure. Polygamy along with easy "talaq" have reduced Muslim women to pathetic conditions. Many victims of "talaq" and polygamy end up as prostitutes in metropolitan cities like Bombay or in Arab countries.

Polygamy, must be remembered, has always been an oriental institution continued to no particular religion or area. Polygamy thus was as much simple or upward mobility as purdah and was considered a natural state for man of means (Brij Bhushan 57).

Much harsh criticism has been leveled against polygamy. The Muslim Personal Law which sanctifies the right to four wives has been dubbed as a reactionary law even by Muslim scholars and jurists. A law that legalizes polygamy in this area needs to be reviewed and changed (Ghosh 1989: 43). A strong social and moral feeling against polygamy is on its way to rooting out this custom among the Indian Muslims. The Muslim women surveyed unanimously condemn the practice of polygamy. They asserted that they were against the law that allows a man to have upto four wives at a time.

A few women said polygamy in a way protects the women who would be otherwise subjected to divorce. It is another way of keeping a society clean off prostitution. Polygamy is detrimental to women in the sense she is not given the right to freedom of love, affection, self respect, etc. Polygamy is advocated by some because in Kerala, female outnumbered men. Also dowry is not demanded in polygamy. To some polygamy is detrimental to women because they are neglected and most of the times it is not possible to look after all the wives equally. The co-wives may live harmoniously only for a short period.

Maintenance

The Mohammedan Law provides for the following three types of maintenance:

1. Every Muslim has personal and absolute obligation to maintain his wife.
2. A Muslim has a personal obligation to maintain them only if they have no source of income or property.
3. A Muslim is also expected to maintain his parents if they have no source of income or property.

But the provisions for maintenance of wife operates only so long as the marriage is valid. In the case of divorce, a Muslim woman is not entitled for any maintenance from her husband. But the Supreme Court decision in Shahbanoo Begum Case altered this situation. Many Muslim women who initiated similar civil and criminal proceedings for getting maintenance could get favourable verdict from the court.

1. The husband is bound to maintain his wife (unless she is too young for matrimonial intercourse) so long as she is faithful to him and obeys his reasonable orders (S. 277).
2. If the husband neglects or refuses to maintain his wife without any lawful cause, the wife may sue him for maintenance but she is not entitled to a decree for past maintenance, unless the claim is based on a specific agreement or she apply for an order of maintenance under the provisions of the Code of Criminal Procedure, 1908 Section: 125 in which case the court may order the husband to make a monthly allowance in the whole for her maintenance not exceeding Rs. 500 (SS 278).
3. After divorce the wife is entitled to maintenance during the period of Iddat. If the divorce is not communicated to her until after the expiry of the period, she is entitled to maintenance until she is informed of the divorce (SS 279).
4. A widow is entitled to maintenance during the period of Iddat consequent upon her husband's death.
5. Where an order is made for maintenance of a wife under Section 125 of the Criminal Procedure Code and the wife

afterwards, divorced, the order ceases to operate on the expiry of the period of iddat.

With the Passing of Muslim Women's Protection Right on Divorce Act 1986, Muslim women had been brought within the purview of Ss : 125 of Criminal Procedure Code.

In Practice no maintenance is given to a divorced Muslim wife. Many religiously devout among the Muslims considered it immoral for a divorced woman to get maintenance from her former husband. The divorced woman is expected either to live with her relatives as dependents or sustain themselves by earning a livelihood. But there are many educated affluent Muslim women who go to the court for getting maintenance from the divorced husband.

Custody and Guardianship

According to Mohammedan Law in the even of divorce the mother is entitled the custody of minor children. But when the male child attains the age of 7 and the female child attains the age of 11 or puberty, the divorced husband the right for their custody. But in practice the divorced women have to look after the male and female children and the divorced husband never bother about either the custody or maintenance. But in this regard also many educated divorced Muslim women have approached the court for getting maintenance for them and their children and have succeeded in getting favourable verdict from the court.

Adoption

Under the Mohammedan Law there is no provision for adoption. Though the Muslim Adoption Bill was introduced in the Parliament in 1972, later in 1976 it was abandoned on account of the opposition from Muslim fundamentalists.

Even though there is no provision for adoption in the Muslim law there are some instances in which children of immediate kin are adopted in certain families. In other cases, the adoption is done in early infancy; so that the child is not initiated into any religion. The procedure for adoption is like in the normal civil code.

Inheritance–Heritable Property

There is no distinction in Mohammedan Law of inheritance between movable and immovable property and between ancestral and self-acquired property where the daughter's are excluded from inheritance either by custom or by statute. They should be treated as non-existent and the shares of the other heirs should be calculated as they would be in default of daughters.

There are three classes of heirs (for details see Subbamma 1988):

1. Shares – are those who are entitled to a prescribed share of the inheritance (see Table 1).
2. Residuaries–are those who take no prescribed share but succeed to the residue after the claims of the sharers are satisfied.
3. Distant kindred are those relations by blood who are neither sharers nor residuaries.

Residuaries in Order of Succession according to Sunni Law are as follows :

I. Descendents

1. Sun-Daughter takes as a residuary with the son, the son taking a double portion.
2. Son's son h/s – the nearer in degree excluding the more remote. Two or more son's son inherit in equal shares. Son's daughter h/s takes as a residuary with an equal son's son. If there be no equal son's son, but there is a lower son's son, she takes as a residuary with him, provided she cannot inherit as a sharer. In either case, each son's son h/s takes double the share of each son's daughter h/s.

   Note : When the son's daughter h/s becomes a residuary with a lower son's son, and there are son's daughters h/s equal in degree with the lower son's son, she shares equally with them, as if they were all of the same grade.

II. Ascendants

3. Father
4. True grand-father – the nearer in degree excluding the more remote.

III. Descendents of father

5. Full brother

   Full sister – takes as a residuary with full brother, the brother taking a double portion.

6. Full sister – in default of full brother and the other 'residuaries' named above, the full sister takes the residue, if any, if these be (1) a daughter or daughters, or (2) a son's daughter or daughter h/s or even if these be (3) on daughter and a son's daughter or daughter h/s.
7. Consanguine brothers.

   Consanguine sister – takes as residuary with consanguine brother, the brother taking a double portion.
8. Consanguine sister – in default a consanguine brother and the other residuaries names above, the consanguine sister takes the residue, if any, if there by (1) a daughter or daughters, or (2) a son's daughter or daughter h/s or even if there be (3) one daughter and a son's daughter or daughters h/s.
9. Full brother's son
10. Consanguine brother's son
11. Full brother's son's son.
12. Consanguine brother's son's son.

Then come remoter male descendants of no. 11 and 12, that is, the son of no. 11, then the son of no. 12, then the son's son of no.11, then the son's son of no. 12 and so on in like order.

IV. Descendants of true grand-father

13. Full paternal uncle
14. Consanguine paternal uncle
15. Full paternal uncle's son
16. Consanguine paternal uncle's son
17. Full paternal uncle's son's son
18. Consanguine paternal uncle's son's

Then come remoter male descendents of nos. 17 and 18 in like order and manner as descendents of no. 11 and 12. Male descendants of more remote true grand-fathers : in like order and manner as the deceased's paternal uncles and their son's and son's son.

The sharers are the father, true grand-father, husband, wife, mother, true grand-mother, daughter, son's daughter, son's son's daughter, uterine brother or sister, full sister and consanguine sister.[7]

In practice, the property is divided between the ratio of 1:3 or only a small part of property is given to daughter and bulk of it is given to the sons.

Issues Confronting Kerala Muslim Women

The major issues confronting the Kerala Muslim women today are illiteracy, early marriage, polygamy, lack of resources, lack of adequate support system, lack of motivation and awareness of their social, political and legal rights. Thus economic dependency, religious orthodoxy and subjugation result in the suppression of women. For the most part, Muslim women are economically dependent. Even when they take up employment they remain in low-paying and low-skill jobs. Although organizations like Muslim Women's Welfare Society have come forward in raising their awareness and providing employment, their activities have remained minimal. The women's Association has not been able to achieve success due to lack of participation by the Muslim women. Hence there is a need for strong leadership and adequate motivation. Due to the intervention of the fundamentalist, orthodox mentality and lack of education it is difficult to organize the Muslim women.

Trends in Muslim Law

Interviews with legal personalities reveal that the number or Muslim women litigants has increased and also their legal awareness. The major causes for women seeking legal redress are cruelty, adultery, abandonment, etc. Most often, women sought relief for maintenance and custody. A number of origanisations like Niyama Sahaya Board (NSB), People's Councils for Social Justice, etc. have helped the litigants to get some awareness.

Repeated misinterpretations of the Muslims Personal Law (MPL) have resulted in making the laws regressive. The MPL has not kept pace with the changes taking place in the larger society. The family laws are still in obsolete state. However, there are two opposed views for change, viz. the elites favouring the Uniform Civil Code; while for the masses it is reform within the Muslim Personal Law. Hence there is an urgent need to modify and update the existing Muslim Personal Law for a more gender just society.

NOTES

1. The absence of a Vaisya community coupled with the deep-rooted resistence of the upper castes to engage in (polluting) commercial or industrial activity has undoubtedly limited the State's development.
2. The term Mappila is combination of two Dravidian words, Maha(great) and Pillai(child). Pillai is a term endearment and intimacy used also as a suffix among Nairs. The title of Mappila was conferred by local rulers upon the Muslim immigrants in Malabar from Arab countries, particularly the Zamorians of Calicut. They had encouraged the Arab traders to enter into marital relations with the women of untouchable castes, especially those of the Mappilas has been attributed to the intermarriage of Arab traders and some local people of the Malabar coast.
3. Kithabia is a man/woman who believes in a religion revealed through a book (other than the Koran) but not in idolatry or fire worship.
4. Nahaz is the time observed for prayers.
5. Nikahanama is a certificate which the couple receives at the time of marriage.
6. Hilala is marriage with the former husband.
7. List of Sharers and Residuaries is taken from Subbamma.
8. Full sister is one born of the same parents and cosanguine sister is a sister brought into existence by the father through a women other than the Ego's mother. Uterine sister is one who is born to the Ego's mother through some other than the person's father.

REFERENCES

Ghosh, S.K.(1969), *Indian Women Through the Ages*. New Delhi: Ashish Publishing House.

Gough, Kathlene, (1972), *Matrilineal Kinship*. Allahabad: P.H. Wheeler.

Mathur, P.R.G. (1978), *The Mappila Fisher Folk of Kerala*. Trivandrum: Kerala Historical Society.

Menon, A. Sreedhara (1970), *A Survey of Kerala History*, Kottayam: Kerala Sahitya Pravarthaka Cooperative Society Ltd.

Moore, Lewis (1905), *Malabar Law and Customs* (3rd edition). Madras: Higginbothams and Company.

Nossiter, T.J. (1982), *Communism in Kerala*. Delhi: Oxford University Press.

Sudduqui, Mazheruddin (1980) *Women in Islam*. Delhi: Adam Publishers and Distributions.

Slubbamma, M. (1988), *Islam and Women*. Delhi : Sterling Publishers Pvt. Ltd.

Thurston, E. (1975), *Caste and Tribes of Southern India*. Delhi : Cosmos Publications.

Tisserant, Eugene (1957), *Eastern Christainity in India : A History of the Syro-Mrladar church from the Earliest Times to the Present day*. London: Longmans Green.

GLOSSARY

Hadith — "Tradition", savyings of Prophet Mohammed and his companions, one of the four sources of Islamic law; and the collectios of Hadith are vast.

Or

A report of a statement the Prophet is alleged to have made.

Hanafi — A member of the sect of Sunnis founded by the Imam Abu Hanifah.

Or

One of the four schools of Islamic jurisprudence founded by the Imam Abu 'Hanifa (699-766 A.D.; 80-150 A.H)., a characteristic of which is the use of the principal disciples were Gadi Abu Yusef and Imam Mohammed al-Shybani. The Hanafi School was introduced into the Sudan by the Ottoman administration in the 19th century and continued under the British colonial administration.

Iddat — The period during which a divorced woman or a widow must wait before remarrying according to Muslim Law. After a divorce the period is three months, and after the death of her husband, four months and ten days.

During the "iddat" period the wife is entitled to maintenance which is referred to as nafaqat al-iddea. Mo's tedah – woman undergoing 'iddat' period.

Imam — Leader or guide.

Jamaat — A company, body, party, assembly, or a congregation or Muslims assembled for prayers.

Khatib — One who delivers a sermon, a public speaker or orator.

Kitabiyya — 'A woman of the Book' referring to women from one of the great religious traditions other than Islam – Christianity6 or Judaism. For example; marriage to a 'Kitabiyya' is allowed in sharia.

Koran — The Holy Book of Islam revealed to Prophet Mohammed (may pleace be on Him).

Mahr/Mehr — A bridal gift made by the husband to the wife without which the marriage is not lawful or valid according to Islam. In

	the Shari'a the term Sadag is synonymous. Usually paid in a sum of money in prompt (Mu'ajjal) and deferred (Mu'ajjal) payments. It serves as a check on the capricious was of the unilateral right of divorce by the husband.
Maulanna/ Moulavi	A teacher of Muslim religious laws; or a title of respect. A religious leader.
Nikah	Marriage contract.
Nikahnama	Muslim marriage contract.
Shari'a	Literally 'the way', originally the road to the watering place; according to the holy laws, the path to be followed. The common law of Islam, the totality of Allah's commandments.
Shiah/Shia	Muslim sect of the followers of Hazrat-Ali. The Shiahs maintain that Ali (Cousin and son-in-law of Prophet Mohammed) was the first legitimate Imam or Khalifa or successor of Prophet Mohammed (Peace be on him).
Sunni	A term generally applied to the large sect of Muslims who accept the first four khalifa as rightful successors of Prophet Mohammad and who belong to one of the four schools of Sunni jurisprudence.
Talaq	Divorce, repudiation which is the unilateral right of the Muslim husband who is of sound mind.
Talaqnama	May only be the record of an oral talaq or it may be the deed by which the divorce is effected. The deed may be executed in the presence of the Kazi or the wive's father or other witnesses.

Table 1
List of Sharers According to Sunni Law[7]

Shares	*Normal share of one or two or more collectively (b)*		*Conditions under which normal share is inherited*	*(a) Sharers 3, 4,5,8 and 12 as varied by special circumstances* *(b) Conditions under which sharers 1,2,7,8, 11 & 12 succeeded as residuaries*
(1)	(2)		(3)	(4)
1. Father	1/6	-	Where there is a child or a child of a son (h/s)*	When there is no child or child of a son (h/s), the father inherits as a residuary
2. True grand-father	1/6	-	Where there is a child or a child a son h/s and no father or nearer true grand-father	When there is no child or child of a son (h/s), the true grand-father inherits as a residuary provided there is no father or true grand-father.
3. Husband	1.4	-	When there is a child or a child of a son, h/s.	½ when no child or a child of a son h/s.
4. Wife(c)	1/8	1/8	When there is a child or a child of a son, h/s.	¼ when child or child of a son h/s.
5. Mother	1/6	-	(a) when there is a child of a child of son h/s or (b) when there are two or more brothers or sisters or even brother and one sister whether full, consanguine or uterine.	¼ when no child or child of a son h/s and not more than one brother or sister (if any); but if there is also wife or husband and the father only. 1/3 of what remains after deducing the wife/s husband'sshare.
6. True grand-father	1/6	1/6	(a) Maternal – when no mother and no nearer true grandmother either paternal or maternal. (b) Paternal- when no mother, no father, no nearer true grand-mother either paternal or material and no immediate true grand-father.	

(1)	(2)		(3)	(4)
7. Daughter	1/2	2/3	When no son	(With the son she becomes a residuary)
8. Son's daughter h/s			When no (1) sons, (2) daughter (3) higher son's son (4) higher son's daughter or (5) equal son's son (cl)	When there is only one daughter, or higher son's daughter but no (1) son, (2) higher son's son or (3) equal son's son, the daughter or higher son's daughter will take 1/2 and the son's daughter h/s whether one or more will take 1/6 (i.e. 1/3-1/2) (with an equal son's son she becomes a residuary)
For example			When no (1) son (2) daughter, or (3) son's son	When there is only one daughter, the son's daughter (whether one or more) will take 1/6, if there be no son or son's son with the son's son she becomes a residuary).
(i) Son's daughter	1/2	2/3		
(ii) Son's son's daughter	1/2	2/3	When no (1) son (2) daughter, son's (3) son's son (4) son's daughter or (5) son's son's son.	When there is only one daughter or son's daughter, the son's son's daughter (whether one or more) will take 1/6, if there be no (1) son, (2) son's son or (3) son's son's son. (with the son's son or she becomes a residuary)
9. Uterine brother or	1/6	1/3	When no (1) child (2) child or a son his, (3) father or (4) true grand-father	
10. Sister	1/2	2/3		
11. Full sister	1/2	2/3	When no (1) child, (2) child or son h/s (3) father, (4) true grand-father or (5) full brother	With the full brother she becomes a residuary.
12. Consan-guiine sister	1/2	2/3	When no (1) child, (2) child of son h/s (3) father, (4) true grand father, (5) full brother (6) full sister of (7) consanguine brother	But if there is only full sister and the succeeds as a sharer, the consan-guine sister (whether one or more) will take 1/6, provided she is

Contd....

(1)	(2)	(3)	(4)
			not otherwise excluded from inheritance (with the consanguine brother she becomes a residuary).

(a) h/s stands for low low so ever, means and includes son's son, son's son's son, son's son' son's son and so on.+ (b) The collective share is always divided equally among those to whom it is allotted. (c) A Mulsim can has as many as four wives at a time. (d) If there be son's son and a son's son's daughter, the former is higher than son's son in relation to the latter.

If there be a son' son's son and a son's son's daughter, the former is lower than a son's son in relation to the latter.

And if there be a son's son and a son's daughter or a son's son's son and a son's son's daughter, the former is equal to son's son in relation to the latter, both being equally removed from the deceased.

Source: *Malladi Subbamma : Islam and Women, New Delhi: Sterling Publishers Pvt. Ltd. (1988), pp. 86-88.*

THE TABLIGHI JAMA'AT IN POST–1947 MEWAT

Yoginder Sikand

Introduction

The Tablighi Jama'at (TJ) is the most widespread, yet least studied, Islamic movement in the contemporary world. In 1992, Faruqui (1992: 43) noted that the movement was active in around 165 countries. The TJ had its origins in the 1920s in the villages of Mewat, a culturally distinct area south of Delhi, home to a tribe known as the Meos. While considerable literature (Sikand 1998) exists about the beginnings of the movement in Mewat, little is known about how the movement fares in the region in the post-1947 period. This paper looks at the state of the TJ in post-47 Mewat. It begins with a brief introduction to the TJ, followed by an overview of recent Mewat history that provides the context to understand the present state of the movement in the region. The activities of the TJ and the Meo response to it in the period from 1947 to date are then analysed in some detail.

The TJ : Beliefs and Principles

The TJ, as we know it today, was started in Mewat in the 1920s by a charismatic *Alim* or Islamic scholar, Maulana Muhammad Ilyas (1885-1994).[1] The immediate cause behind the launching of the movement was the *shuddhi* campaign of the Arya Samaj to reconvert to the Hindu fold numerous neo-Muslim groups (Sikand and Katjum 1994) in northern India, most notably the Malkana Rajputs of the western districts of the United Provinces.[2] In the wake of the *shuddhi* movement, it dawned on Ilyas that the only way that the neo-Muslims, who till then continued to practice many customs derived from their Hindu Past, could be saved from being absorbed into the Hindu fold was to instill in them a firm consciousness of being Muslim, along with teaching them the basics of Islam. The Meos, being, like the Malkanas, a neo-Muslim group, Ilyas chose them as his initial field for missionary efforts.

In the course of his work among the Meos in the early 1920s, Ilyas came to develop a set of techniques for missionary or *tabligh* work. These techniques are faithfully followed even today by Tablighi activists or *muballighin* (singular *mulballigh*) wherever they may go for missionary work throughout the world. Briefly, the focus is on teaching a set of principles known in TJ parlance as *chhe baten* or 'the six points'. These are : the *kalmia,* the Islamic creed of confession–"There is no god but Allah and Muhammad is his Prophet'; *namaz* or ritual prayer; *ilm,* or knowledge of the basics of Islam, and *zikr,* remembrance of God *ikam-i-muslim* or respect for [other] Muslims; *tashih-i-niyyat,* or the purification of intention; and, lastly *tafrigh-i-waqt* or devoting time for Tabligh work. Sometimes, a seventh point, *tark-i-layani* or giving up frivolities is also added (Bulandshahri n.d.). Ilyas saw the 'six points' as a means for the eventual ordering of all social affairs of the Muslims in accordance with the *shari'at* or Islamic law.

All Muslims, men as well as women, are exhorted to participate as *muballighin* in the work of the TJ. The *tabligh* group or *jama'at* may consist of both *ulama* or trained Islamic scholars as well as Muslims from humble backgrounds who may know but little about their faith. Groups of activists are dispatched under a leader or *amir* to visit Muslim localities and spend time there teaching the 'six points' to local Muslims as well as, in the process, improving their own understanding and practice of Islam by learning from their fellow *muballighin.*

The global headequarters or *'alami markaz'* of the TJ are located at a mosque known as the Banglewali Masjid, in Basti Nizamuddin Auliya in Delhi. In each country where the movement is active, it has its own headquarters. In India and elsewhere, provincial, district, town and village-level headquarters also exist, which are, in turn, linked to the Nizamuddin *markaz.* At the global level, the TJ is headed by a leader, or *amir,* but at present, owing to internal leadership problems the movement is headed by *shura,* a committee of elders or *zimmedaran.*

The TJ in Mewat

Extending southwards from the town of Sohna, some sixty kilometers south-west of Delhi, and covering tracts in the Gurgaon and Faridabad districts of Haryana, the Mathura district of Uttar Pradesh and the Bharatput and Alwar districts of Rajasthan, is the culturally distinct region known as Mewat. Mewat's principal community are the Meos, who, in 1983, were estimated to number some 800,000 (Aggarwal 1978: 338).

Most Meos claim 'high' caste Rajput Hindu descent, but although there is certainly a Rajput element among them, they are probably a mixture of Rajputs and tribes traditionally considered low in the social hierarchy such as the Minas, Jats and Gujjars (Mewati n.d.). Although little can be said about the process of the introduction of Islam into Mewat, Islamic influence seems to have exerted itself on the Meos from as early as the twelfth century A.D., primarily through contacts with invading armies from Delhi as well as the introduction of numerous Sufi orders into the region (Powlett 1878: 38). As elsewhere in India, the gradual process of Islamisation in Mewat resulted in the incorporation of Islamic beliefs and practices into the existing local tradition. Consequently, many of the pre-Islamic 'Hinduistic' customs and beliefs of the Meos continued to be held on to with great tenacity despite their nominal status of Muslims. Writing in the last quarter of the nineteenth century, Major Powlett, Settlement Officer of the Alwar State, observed:

> "The Meos are all Musalmans in name, but their village deities are the same as those of the Hindus and they keep several Hindu festivals. Thus, the *Holi* is with the Meos as a season of rough play and is considered as important a festival as *Muharram, Id* and *Shahibarat*, and they likewise observe the *Janamashtami, Dashera* and *Diwali*. They often keep Brahmin priests to write to note [*pilli-chitthi*] for fixing the date of marriage. They call themselves by Hindu names, with the exception of Ram; and Sinh [Singh] is a frequent affix, though not as common as Khan. On the *Amawas*, or monthly conjunction of the sun and moon, the Meos, in common with the Hindu Ahirs, Gujjars, etc. cease from labour; and when they make a well the first proceeding is to erect a platform to *Bairuji* or *Hanuman*. Meos, in their customs are half Hindu. In their villages there are hardly any mosques ...The Meo places of worship are similar to those of their Hindu neighbours,

as for example, *Panchpira, Bhaiya* and *Chahund. Chahund* or *Khera Deo* is dedicated to *Mahadevi* to whom sacrifices are made (1818: 38)."

Writing to the religious conditions in Mewat less than half a century later, a Muslim scholar–observer exclaimed (Falahi 1996: 303) that by the time of Ilyas' death in 1944, a 'veritable new revolution' had taken place among the Meos, with scores of Islamic schools and mosques being set up in the region, all a result of the untiring efforts of Ilyas and his movement. I have analyzed the factors behind the rapid expansion of the TJ in Mewat in the period till Ilyas' death elsewhere, (Sikand 1994) and so will not deal with the issue here, but suffice it to say that by 1947 the TJ had struck firm roots in Mewat.

Post-47 period: The Partition Experiences

The partition of India 1947 marked a major landmark in Meo history and a significant turning point in the process of the fashioning of Meo self-identity. In the months preceding the partition in August, 1947, fierce rioting broke out between Hindus and Muslims in Gurgaon. This was followed by the launching of well–planned attacks-what amounted to nothing less than a genocide–against the Meos by the rulers of Alwar and Bharatpur, leading patrons of Hindus chauvinist organizations such as the Rashtriya Swayamsewak Sangh (RSS) and the Hindu Mahasabha. N.B. Khare, one-time President of the Hindu Mahasabha, had by this time taken over as the Primer Minister of Alwar. In Bharatpur, the state militia worked in close collaboration with the RSS, providing it arms and training. At RSS meeting throughout Bharatpur, Hindus were exhorted to 'drive out the Muslims' and such bloodshed was predicted the like of which the country had 'not seen in the last two thousand years' (Mayaram 1996: 133-4).

In the wake of the attacks unleashed against them in 1947, almost the entire Meo population of the princely states of Alwar and Bharatpur was forced to flee their homes. An estimated 30,000 Meos were slaughters and many women raped (ibid: 139). Scores of Meos made their way to Pakistan, much against their will, and an even larger number sought safe refuge in Gurgaon and Faridabad. Several thousand Meos who chose not to flee Rajputana were forced to turn Hindu by undergoing the Arya Samaj *shudddhi* rite, to which was added a humiliating pork-eating test.

Following the upheavals of 1947, leading *ulama*, many affiliated to the TJ or to the Dar-ul 'Ulum Islami seminary at Deoband, such as Maulana Ibrahim, Mufti Jamaluddin Qasim and Maulana Hifzur Rahman, worked tirelessly to supply relief to the Meos, to get their lands that had been seized by Hindus returned to them and to bring them back to Islam (Miyan n.d.: 35). Besides these *ulama* the Meos had few others to the Meos, to get their lands that had been seized by Hindus returned to them and to bring them back to Islam (Miyan n.d.: 35). Besides these *ulama* the Meos had few others to turn to for help. Naturally, their involvement in providing relief to the panic-stricken Meos worked further to strengthen the growing Meo identification with Islam. It is generally accepted that although in Ilyas' time the TJ managed to establish strong roots in the Mewati countryside, it was only after the unprecedented violence of 1947 that the TJ actually took off as a mass movement in the region.

In times of acute social crisis, beleaguered communities need strong and effective leaders who can provide protection, promote their interests and negotiate with external forces. Muslim *ulama*, in general, and the TJ leaders, in particular, seem to have played this crucial role in the troubled days of 1947 and shortly after. In the wake of the partition violence, almost the entire fledgling Meo educated middle class, including several Muslim League leaders, fled to Pakistan, leaving behind what Rathee (1971: 23) calls a 'leadership lag'. The TJ now stepped in to fill their departure, and thousands of Meos began turning up at Tablighi rallies that began to be held in Mewat once a semblance of peace was restored. Heightened insecurity and persecution now drove the Meos towards consolidating their rank and, responding enthusiastically to the Tablighi message of Islamic solidarity and brotherhood. Adding to this pressure towards increasing Islamisation were memories of the bitter experiences of untold sufferings that the Meos had to undergo at the hands of Hindu attackers in the course of the partition-related violence which led to a conscious revulsion against many of the more glaring Hinduistic traditions that they had been following for centuries. Meos who had been forcibly converted to Hinduism thus quickly returned to Islam once the TJ leaders began their campaigning to bring back the apostates to the Muslim fold. Many of them were disillusioned despite having turned Hindu, because the Hindus still looked upon them with suspicion, refused to accept them as their co-religionists and seized much of their land. Moreover, as Aggarwal (1966: 160) remarks, 'the only groups outside Mewat which were willing to accept them socially were the Muslims' and, therefore, 'the Meos felt that they had no other choice than to turn to Islam'.

Developments in the economic sphere in the years after 1947 gave further impetus to the Meo drive for an Islamic identity. In the violence of partition, much Meo-owned land was seized by 'low' caste Hindus. Further, lands belonging to the Meos who had fled to Pakistan were allotted by the state to the incoming Hindu and Sikh refugees from West Punjab. While earlier the 'low' castes had hardly owned any land at all, being employed for the most part, as hereditary clients or *kamins* of the Meos and other land-owning castes, their usurping the lands of their former masters greatly weakened the traditional patron-client system in which the Meos had occupied a dominant position owing to their control over land and their claims to Rajput status. The *jajmani* system also began to disintegrate as a result of the growing monetisation of the village economy, greatly reducing the inter-dependence between the Meos and the 'low' castes. Because of this, the traditional privileges that the Meos had earlier enjoyed as a dominant caste were now increasingly curtailed. For their part, the 'low castes', in particular the Chamars, increasingly sought to stress a Hindu identity, seeking upward social mobility through '*sanskritisation*' and taking advantage of statutory reservations in educational institutions and government jobs that were now available to them. This translated into a growing conflict of interests between the Meos and the 'low castes', with the latter increasingly defying the low ascriptive status that they had been consigned to, and denying the Meos the exalted Rajput status that they claimed for themselves. According to Aggarwal, this 'low' caste assertion 'irks the Meos immensely', and they now realize that 'it is futile to try to regain their high rank in the Hindu caste hierarchy.' Consequently, he says, 'the Meos think it is better for them to become full Muslims' (1969: 1679).

Once the TJ had drawn most Meos into at least formal allegiance to it, Islamisation carried out on apace under the influence of new external factors. Improved means of communication resulted in the rapid promotion of Tabligh tours of Mewat by outside Muslims and by Meo *muballighin* both inside and outside the region. Young Meo men now increasingly went to leading Islamic seminaries in Delhi and Uttar Pradesh to train as *ulama* and then returned to Mewat to spread the Islamic reformist message. More generally, the spread of the education system in Mewat itself from the 1950s onwards, through both Islamic as well as secular schools, equipped growing numbers of Meos with reading skills that enabled them to gain greater access to Islamic literature.

Hurdles on the Path of Islamisation

In present-day Mewat, the Islamisation agenda of the TJ is increasingly coming to content with hurdles in its path, which have, in turn, provoked many commentators to remark that the movement has now lost its earlier momentum. One crucial factor is the growing ascendancy of the Gujarat-trader element in the top Tablighi leadership in the Nizamuddin *markaz*, and what, many Meos feel, is the gradual marginalization of Meos in the movement's decision-making structures. In recent years, numerous vocal Meos have voiced concern about what they perceive as unfair nepotism in top Tablighi circles to the detriment of the Meos[3]. Another reason for the stagnation of the TJ in Mewat today is the growing perception among young, educated Meos that the movement is far too other-worldly for their liking. A Meo writer strongly critiques the functioning of the Islamic schools (*maktab*) in Mewat that are being run by *ulema* associated with the TJ thus:

> The system of *maktab* education in Mewat presents a miserable picture today. Our 'lovers of (Islamic) education' are under no circumstances willing to emerge from the environment of the sixth century ... Their sort of education encourages asceticism and withdrawl from the world, which is forbidden I Islam. As regards the syllabus, the children are taught such things as might enable them to become *mullahs* and *pesh imams* (prayer leaders) in mosques and *madrasas* at best, but cannot succeed in setting off a revolution in their minds (Arya 194: 20).

Many Meos, particularly of the younger generation, also find that the TJ, in its concern with ritual minutiae, is completely neglectful of their existential concerns, in particular of their dire poverty, and see this attitude as not just wrong but un-Islamic as well. According to a Meo college student, many *muballighin,* who actually have little knowledge of Islam themselves, raise controversies about such relatively inconsequential issues as the length of one's beard or the prohibition on wearing trousers, but remain blissfully silent on the pathetic economic plight of the bulk of the community. Because of this, he says, many young Meos are beginning to drift, away from the TJ.[4] This is most strikingly illustrated in the decline of the prestige of *madrasa* education in Mewat today. *Madrasas* are now associated generally with young Meo men from poor, and often landless families, while better-off Meos all wish to send their sons to the numerous expensive, English-medium schools that have cropped up in Mewat in recent years.

It would be misleading, however, to give the impression that the TJ is fast disappearing in Mewat today. Many of Meos still display a strong emotional and ritualistic attachment to the TJ, and the movement still has many *muballighin,* more so in Haryana than in the remoter Meo inhabited villages in Rajasthan. What seems to be the case is that the Meos have managed to work out a creative, yet highly selective, adoption of the Tablighi message. Thus, it is customary for all Meo men to grow their beards and for Meo women to wear the *shalwar-qamiz,* which is seen as an 'Islamic' dress in contrast to the 'Hindu' skirt and blouse that they once used. These act as crucial external markers of Islamic identity, clearly and visibly setting off Meo Muslims from Hindu others. On the other hand, given Maulana Ilyas' insistence that the 'six points' of the TJ were merely a means for the complete Islamisation of Meo society so that all its social affairs could be run on the lines of the *shari'at,* the TJ has scored little success. The Meos today continue with many of their pre-Islamic traditions that the TJ would regard as un-Islamic and which are in direct contradiction of the *shari'at.* The most glaring case of this concerns Meo women or Meonis (Sikand 1997b). Thus, while the *shari'at* grants Muslim women considerable inheritance rights, almost no Meoni gets a share in her parental or decreased husband's property. Likewise, although the TJ sees women's roles as being limited to the four walls of the house, in Mewat almost all agricultural, in addition to household, work is undertaken by women. Since the Meonis are put to work in the fields they cannot wear the *burqa,* which, again, is quite at odds with the Tablighi position. Dowry is rampant in Mewat today, although this, too, is in gross violation of the *shari'at.* To take another insistence, *zakat,* the 'poor-due' incumbent upon every Muslim who can afford it, is hardly paid by any Meos who are eligible for it.

This resistance to the implementation of the *shari'at* on the part of the Meos has been ironically, facilitated by the Tablighi mode of Islamisation itself. Tabighi *muballighin* are warned not to raise any contentious issue (*ikhtilafi masa'il*) in their preaching that might cause unrest or resentment (*fitna*). Meo traditions that contravene the *shari'at* must not be directly challenged, for it is believed that once the Meos become firm in their faith in Islam they themselves would seek to lead their lives in accordance with the *shari'at*.

Tablighi authorities seem to have taken serious note of the consequence of efforts by some *muballighin* to encourage marriage between close relations in Mewat, which resulted in the *muballighin* being physically assaulted and some Meos threatening to even desert Islam if cross-cousin marriages were encouraged, for, like their Hindu neighbours, such marriages are strictly forbidden in Meo society.[5] As a result, Tablighi activists, in actual practice, turn a blind eye to what in Tablighi discourse would be seen as un-Islamic practices and institutions.Furthermore, the *muballighin* are taught that the focus of their missionary endeavours must only be to encourage a thirst for Islam by recounting the immense heavenly rewards (*faza'il* or *sawab*) for pious ritual acts such as prayer or fasting, and that they must strictly abstain from all 'worldly (*duniyavi*) matters. Hence their silence on not just the crushing poverty of the Meos but also on many of their patently un-Islamic practices, such as dowry or the denial of inheritance rights to women. This, of course, suits the interests of Meo men, who then do not see the TJ's agenda as threatending patriarchal structures. In other words, as Mayaram (1997: 209) suggests, despite seven decades of Tablighi efforts in Mewat, the Meos today continue to face an acute dilemma of reconciling their pre-Islamic 'Rajput' traditions and institutions and their 'sense of a new Islamic spirituality.'

Following the violence that greeted the exit of the British in 1947, inter-communal relations in Mewat were, on the whole, relatively peaceful, although the Meos continued to reel under the exploitation of the Bania traders and money-lenders. The events leading to December 1992, when *Hindutva* mobs stormed the Babri mosque in Ayodhya, however, had crucial consequences for the people of Mewat. Tension had been heightened when *Hindutva* leaders began touring Mewat whipping up hatred against the Muslims. When the Ayodhya mosque was torn down, bloody clashes between Meos and Banias broke out in a few towns in Mewat, some temples were damaged and four Meos lost their lives. Curfew was clamped throughout the region, and the Meos complained of considerable persecution by the police and discrimination at the hands, of the local administration. One redeeming consequence of the chain of events, however, was the decision by some Meos to set up their own little shops and businesses rather than patronize those run by Banias who were known *Hindutva* sympathizers.

The post-Babri situation has convinced many Meos of the pressing need to consolidate their ranks and push forward the economic and educational development of the community if it is to withstand the growing challenge and threat of *Hindutva* militancy. This would almost certainly also entail a growing stress on their Muslim identity. However, since the basic issues before the Meos today is not religion *per se* but community identity and the worldly interests of the community, this is unlikely to translate itself into greater commitment for the TJ's strictly other-worldly agenda. In the other words, the TJ may not be the major beneficiary of any heightened Islamic consciousness among the Meos, particularly the growing numbers of educated youth in the community, in the years to come.

NOTES

1. For biographical details of Ilyas, see Haq (1972) and Nadvi (1983).
2. For varied Muslim responses to the *shuddhi* movement, see Sikand (1997a).
3. See, for example, Bahotavi (1987), Ferozepuri (n.d.) also makes an oblique reference to this.
4. Interview with Rahim Khan Nuh 1 January 1996.
5. Interview with Hasan Khan Nuh, 23 November 1994.

REFERENCES

Aggarwal, P.C. (1969), "Islamic Revivalism in Modern India: The Case of the Meos", *Economic and Political Weekly*, IV: 42.

———(1978), 'Rajasthan' in Richard V.Weeks (ed.) *Muslim Peoples–A World Ethanographic Survey*. Connecticut: Greenwood Press.

Arya, Diwan Chand (1994), *Ithhas Ki Trasadi: Arthat Bhartiya Darpan Mein Mewat*. Punahava.

Bajhotvi, M. Sulaiman. n.d. *Dusra Khula Khat Banam Janab Emam-ul-Hasan Sahib, Amir-i-Tablighi Jamaat*. Delhi: Khadim Abdur Rabb.

Falahi, Ubaidullah Fahad (1966), "A Muslim sub-caste of Northern India– Problems of Cultural Integration", *Economic and Political Weekly*: 46.

———(1996), *Tarikh-i-Dawat-e-Jihad Barre Saghir Ke Tanazur Mein*. Delhi: Hindustan Publications.

Faruqui, Ziaur Rahman (1992), *Ulemai Deoband : Kaun Hai, Kahan Hai, Kya Hai*? Deoband: Darul Kitab.

Ferozepuri, Mohammad Isa. n.d. *Tabligh Ka Muqaim Kam*. Delhi: Rabbani Book Depot.

Haq, S. Anwarul (1972), *The Faith Movement of Maulana Mohammad Ilyas*. London: Allen & Unwin.

ANNUAL RITES OF THE DAUDI BOHRAS: ISLAMIC IDENTITY AS UNIVERSAL AND UNIQUE

Jonah Blank

Introduction

For Indian Muslims, the question of identity permeates all aspects of life. Sunni or Shia, from any part of the country, all are implicitly asked to define themselves every time they get dressed in the morning, prepare a meal for the family, or open their mouths to speak. Often, the question is explicitly posed by their neighbours. Do they make the Uniform Civil Code and the destruction of Babri Masjid the basis for voting? Which side do they cheer for in cricket match? How do they feel about India's nuclear weapons, of the insurgency in Kashmir, of new from any Muslim country from Morocco to Malaysia? Such question is proxies for the underlying query: are they Indians who happen to be Muslim, or Muslims who happen to be Indian?

The issue of identity, of how to relate both the universal Islamic *umma* and to the land of their birth, is one with which all Muslims of the subcontinent wrestle. Some veer towards assimilation, some towards Islamization, most (on both an individual and a communal level) try to accommodate both sides of their identity. This paper examines the annual rituals of one such group: the Daudi Bohra, a denomination of some one million Mustali Ismailis spread throughout the world but heavily concentrated in Maharashtra, Madhya Pradesh, and their ancestral province of Gujarat.

Unlike Muslims of almost all other denominations, Ismailis have a rigidly centralized clergy under the hegemonic guidance of a single apex cleric: for the Bohras, this cleric is the *dai al-multaq*, more commonly referred to simply as the *dai* or by the honorific term Syedna (for Khojahs and other Nizari Ismailis, the only other Major Branch of the faith to have survived since the Fatimid caliphate, the apex cleric as the Aga Khan). The *dai*'s authority is exercised through clerical network called the *dawat*, and for the past two decades this clergy has active propagated a communal identity that is both thoroughly modern and thoroughly Islamic. As I deal with the subject of this identity reification project elsewhere (Blank 1998; 199b), the current paper focuses less on the theoretical points raised by this programme than on a straightforward ethnography of the denomination. The annual rituals of the group, as these rites are currently observed, paint a picture of a community that is deeply committed to universal Islamic identity, but equality committed to its unique version of how this identity can best be expressed.

Methodology

Any attempt to conduct research in an orthodox Bohra community would be virtually impossible without the cooperation of the religious authorities, cooperation which prior to my fieldwork had never been granted to any outside scholar.[2] After receiving Syedna's permission, I was given full freedom to attend all community rituals and private access to many top *dawat* figures. The basis for most of the information contained in this paper is participant observation during 18 months of field work, primarily in Mumbai, but with significant portions of time spent in Surat, Karachi and other sites. My attendance at community functions was complemented by private interviews with scores of sources of varying degree of orthopraxy.

To create a statistical framework for my direct observations and the paradigmatic information provided my *dawat* sources and also as a means of measuring the clergy's success in maintaining common orthopraxic norms in communities far from the *dawat's* Mumbai headquarters, I obtained questionnaire responses from Bohras living in four disparate locations (Mumbai, Nagpur, Karachi and Calcutta). The universe for these surveys was 169 households containing a total of 1,068 individuals. Since my survey was distributed with the cooperation of the *dawat* and the participating families were those with children in *dawat madrasas* (religious schools), I present these findings solely to supplement and quantify my ethnographic observations. The survey figures represent the views and practices of the devotional elite of the community- I make no claim that a similar survey conducted among a different group of Bohras (for example, dissident families sympathetic to the views of *dawat* opponent Asghar Ai Engineer) might not produce quite different results. This paper presents ethnography of orthopraxic norms, which are followed by a great many members of the community–to one degree or another, by the vast majority–but not by all.

The Daudi Bohra Calendar

The Bohra's ritual calendar is based not on actual sightings of the new moon, but on astrological charts dating to the Fatimid caliphate. For this reason, Bohra observances of universal Islamic holidays do not correspond exactly with the observances of other groups: in recent years, they have generally preceded the Sunni and Ithana-Ashari dates by several days. The divergence of calendars serves as a reminder to the denomination's Fatimid heritage emphasizes the group's unique current identity, and implicitly helps prevent assimilation into the mainstream of Islam.

Of the most important Bohra rites, some are shared with all Muslims, some only with other Shia, and others (such as the *Urs* of Syedna Taher Saifuddin, and the birth date of Syedna Muhammad Burhanuddin) are uniquely Bohra. The primary rituals are (l) *Waaz* : a formal ceremony officiated by the *dai* or his local *amil* (priest)[3] . The sermon is delivered from a throne several steps above a raised platform known as a *tekhet.* (2) *Majlis*: less ceremonial than the *waaz,* it is presented on the evening preceding the holy day in question. Syedna (or his *amil*) sits on a small *gadi* (couch) rather than a throne. A *majlis* can be quite informal, sometimes without even the delivery of *khutba* (sermon).

Four types of commemoration practiced by the Bohras are given particular prominence : Birthdates of important religious figures; *Shehadat*–the date of a religious figure's martyrdom; *Urs,* an individual's death anniversary; and *Chhelum,* a Shia rite marking the end of the obligatory 40-day mourning period after an individual's death. The foremost annual rituals of the Daudi Bohras are as follows[4]:

1.	Muharram	1-10	:	Ashura
		27	:	Shehadet of Syed Fakhruddin
2.	Safar	20	:	Chhelum of Imam Husain
		26/27	:	Shehadet of Imam Hasan
3.	Rabiul Awwal	12	:	Birth date of Prophet Muhammad
4.	Rabiul Akher	4	:	Birth date of Imam Tayyib
		20	:	Birthday of Syedna Muhammad Burhanuddin
5.	Jamadi Awwal	10	:	Shehadet of Hazrat Faatima
6.	Jamadi Akher	27	:	Urs of Syedna Qutabuddin
		29	:	Pehli Rejib
7.	Rejib	13	:	Birth date of Wasi Ali[5].
		19	:	Urs of Syedna Taher Saifuddin
		27	:	Mebas (date of Muhammad's recognition as prophet)
8.	Shaban	1	:	Zikra (beginning of theological exam period)
		15	:	Shabb-e-Baraat
9.	Ramadan	17	:	Commemoration of Amina
		19	:	Shehadet of Wasi Ali
		21	:	Commemoration of Khadija
		23	:	Lailat ul-Qadr
10.	Shawwal	1	:	Eid-ul-fitr
11.	Ziquad	27	:	Birth date of Syedna Taher Saifuddin
12	Zyl-Hajj	9	:	Culmination of Hajj
		10	:	*Eid-ul-Adha* (Bakr Eid)
		18	:	*Eid Ghadir al-Khumum* (rite of *mithaq*)

In addition to these dates, the Urs of all past *dais* and many Syeds are observed at the sites of their shrines. At these times, such shrines become sites of devoted reverence not unlike the tombs of charismatic Sufi *Pirs*. *Ziyaret*, the act of pilgrimage to one of these sites, can occur at any time during the year, but is particularly auspicious on the *Urs* of the *dai* in question. Respondents to my survey ranked *ziyaret* third out of ten practices fundamental to orthopraxy, with 82.1% citing its central importance. *Musafirkhanas* (pilgrims' rest houses) at Bohra shrines, also were deemed highly significant. An overwhelming 86.6% of respondents said that they had personally made use of these hostels, with more than a fifth (21.7%) citing them as one of the top two *dawat* services. Of the services listed, *musafirkhanas* had a popularity second only to that of *madrasas*.[6]

Burial sites of *dais* and *imams* in Egypt and Yemen have become important sites for *ziyaret* in recent decades, but the tombs of the Indian *dais* have always been the most widely visited such shrines. The most important of these are located in the following cities and towns : Ahmedabad (tombs of *dais* 25-33); Jamnagar (tombs of *dais* 34-36 and 38); Mandvi (tomb of *dai* 37); Ujjain (tombs of *dais* 39, 40 and 47; Burhanpur-tombs of *dai* 41, Syed Abdul Qadir Hakimuddin, and Shaikh Jivanji); Surat (tombs of *dais* 42-46) and 48-50, and Mullah Wahidhai; Galiakot (tomb of Syedi Fakhruddin); and Mumbai (tombs of *dai* 51 and Seth Chandabhai).

Muharram

By far the most important annual ritual for Bohras, as for all orthodox Shia, is that of Ashura. As Keith Hjortshoj notes:

> "During Muharram the Shia's do not define themselves as members of a sect or religious community but rather as the followers and family of Husayn at Kerbala" (1987: 302).

The tenth of Muhraam had been a pre-Islamic fast-day, and for a time fasting on *Ashura* was obligatory for the early Musim community (*ahadith:* a-Bukhari 1986; vol. 3: 65, 124; vol.11, 38; al-Muslim 1978; 548, 569). Since at least the fourth Islamic century, however, *Ashura* has commemorated the martyrdom of the prophet's grandson Imam Husain. The earliest recorded observance of *Ashura* as a uniquely Shia ritual is in Abbasid Baghdad (AH 315/962 CE), and it soon became standard practice in Fatimid Egypt (Abbas 1991: 41).

The event commemorated is the one defining moment in Shia history: the date on which Imam Husain and 72 of his relatives and companions were slaughtered on the fields of Kerbala. It was at this battle, fought in the year 61/680, that hopes for Shia ascendancy throughout the unified Muslim *umma* were permanently dashed David Pinault (1992: 56, 106), characterizes *Ashura* observances as an opportunity for Shia to atone for all the moral failings of the world: their own, those of their ancestors, and those of all mankind. In Bohra theology, however, the atonement aspect of *Ashura* is individual rather than communal: a believer might reflect upon his or her personal guilt, but not that of the world?. The grief is overwhelming, and it serves to link humanity with transcendental spirituality. The faithful *mumineen* (faithful) wail and beat their breasts to remind themselves, and others, of the agonies suffered by the *ahl-e-bayt* (family of the Prophet): Imam Husain died for the sins of all mankind, and mankind can partake of his antirecessionary aid by voluntarily recalling, accepting and unifying with his pain. The parallels with central aspects of Christian doctrine are obvious, and have been commented upon by other scholars (see Asad 1993).

The various types of observance practiced throughout the Indian subcontinent (let alone throughout the Shia world) vary widely from place and community to community. Common rituals include women breaking of glass bangles, construction of elaborate replicas of the tomb of Husain in Kerbala (*tazia*), establishment of sequestered mourning-houses (generally called *Imambaras* in north of India and *Ashurkhanas* in the south), and a wide variety of emotionally charged parades or processions (Hasnain and Husain 1988: 145). Bohras occasionally participate in such rituals, but their primary observance is focused on the *waaz* and *majlis* of the *dai*. Here, as in all other aspects of Bohra life, the person of the *dai* is central to the spiritual life of the community.

During *Ashura*, more so than at any other time of year, the Bohra clergy solidifies the identity of the community. Its methods are modern as well as traditional: personal contact with the *dai*, facilitated by any technological means available. Each year Syedna personally leads *Ashura* observance in a different city, and tens of thousands of Bohras come from all parts of the world to participate. Despite his advanced age (Muhammad Burhanuddin is over 80 years old) the *dai* tries to spread the sites of Muharram observance as widely as possible. In recent years he has held *Ashura* rites in Mombasa, Jamnagar, Pune and Dar-es-Salaam (Davoodbhoy 1990: 4; 1993; 18). The site of each year's service is a secret not even revealed to Syedna's closest family members until a few weeks before the date. Wherever *Ashura* is held, the *Dawat* provides room and board free (or at nominal charge) for all who choose to attend. Transportation is paid for by the individuals themselves, but everything else is arranged by the clergy. When the 1994 ritual was held in Mumbai, over 200,000 Bohras from out of town had to be accommodated in *musafirkhanas*, *jamatkhanas* (community centres), hotels and private homes (Bekhud 1994: 4).

The *dawat* likewise uses a variety of technologies to reach Bohras who cannot attend Muharram rites in person. For the past two decades the clergy has circulated video-cassettes of the *dai's* *khutbas* and *waaz*, and encouraged believers to purchase VCRs for home viewing. Those who cannot afford VCRs are urged to watch the tapes at their local *jamatkhana* . In the 1990s the *dawat* began sending videos of Syedna's daily service by air-courier to most of the 700 *masjids* and 400 *jamatkhanas* around the world (Davoodhbhoy 1992a: 4) so that worshippers could follow the service the very next day. For the past decade Muharram services have been broadcast by radio relay to congregations in London, Paris, Singapore, Cairo, Karachi, Stockholm, Jerusalem, Sanaa, and several cities in the United States (Bekhud 1994a: 8). The large majority of my survey respondents owned at least one item of technology enabling them to observe rituals afar: 90.9% owned a television (96.6% in Mumbai, 94.7% in Calcutta), over half (54.4% in Karachi, 75.6%) owned a VCR and more than three-quarters (77.3%) owned a radio. Almost all respondents reported having observed Muharram rites either by videocassette or radio relay.

The use of audio tapes, videocassettes and other communications technology is not uncommon among Islamic revivalists groups (Esposito 1988: 177; Abbas 1991: 43; for radio *fatwas*, see Messick 1996). The unity of *Ithna-Ashariya* of India has been fostered by the broadcast of *Ashura majalis* on the national station of *Doordarshan* (television). As Mobarak Abbas notes, technology has spread a variety of traditional and neotraditional practices more quickly than would have been possible a few decades in the past:

> "Technological innovation, particularly that of audiovisual ... has induced some non-conventional methods of mourning observance, during long periods of Muharram, through cassettes on tape recorders and videocassettes" (1991: 43).

Days of Muharram

Each of the first ten days of the month of Muharram has special significance–often, several different significances. In addition to retelling the story of Kerbala, Bohras assign each day to a different devotional character.

1. *Muharram*: The start of the Islamic year. On the evening of this day Bohras break their daily fast with an epic feast: those who can afford it lay out an array of 52 different dishes (one for each of

the 52 *dais*). Families of more limited mean prepare 21 dishes (for the 21 *imams*), or seven (for the *imams* upto the period of occulation). All of the assorted curries, sweets, and various types, of dry or fresh fruit are squeezed onto one communal *thal*, and each family member must eat at least a small portion of every dish.

On the second through the ninth days, a *waaz* is offered each morning. Generally, it begins between ten and eleven am., and lasts between two and three hours, terminating at midday prayer (*zuhar* and *asr namaaz*)". On the tenth of Muharram, the rituals last for most of the day. There is the usual *waaz* in the morning, and another in the afternoon lasts until evening prayers (*maghrib* and *isha namaaz*)–more than eight hours in al. As the week goes on and the cumulative effect of daily fasting takes its toll, the emotional pitch of the observance becomes increasingly more intense. The dedication the daily waaz is as follows; second day of Muharram: Adam: third day: Nuh (Noah); fourth day: Ibrahim (Abraham); fifth day: Musa and Isa (Moses and Jesus); sixth day: Muhammad; seventh day; Fatima; eighth day: Ali; ninth day: Hasan; tenth day: Husain.

Regardless of which holy figure is celebrated, each day's *waaz* is devoted in large measure to the retelling of a portion of the Kerbala story. The tale is one thoroughly familiar to every Bohra long before he or she leaves childhood. The courage of Husain and his companions, the lamentations of Fatima over the death of her son, the execution of Husain's six-month-old infant Ali Asghar along with all the adult males, the decapitated corpses trampled underfoot. The heads of the martyrs paraded through the streets of Baghdad on the points of spears. Every Bohra child can conjure up the memory of the women f the Prophet's own family dragged away into slavery, along with Husain's successor Imam Ali Zain Al-Abidin, whose illness prevented him from fighting on the plain of Kerbala and thus saved the lineage of the Imams from destruction.

At particularly emotional points of the service, participants engage in prolonged chanting of the name of Husain or Ali, accompanied by ritualized self-flagellation (*matam*). This breast-beating can take many shapes: one handed or double-handed, open-palmed or closed-fisted, light tapping or hearty pounding. Bohras are technically forbidden to practice the more extreme forms of *matam* found among *Ithna-Ashari* Groups, but this 'bloody *matam'* is carried out in some Bora *majids* without great secrecy. Clerical authorities discourage such observances, viewing them as dangerous to body and spirit alike. For other Indian Shia, however, various types of bloody *matam* are central to *Ashura* rituals.

In Northern India, devotees cut themselves either with daggers or walk barefoot through fire while chanting the names of those martyred at Kerbala (Hasnain and Husain 1988: 146). Scourges made linked knives (the only implements I personally witnessed in use among the Bohras) are used from the seventh through the tenth day of Muharram at various places on the subcontinent (Abbas 199: 42). One of the most complete discussions of bloody *matam* Indian Shia is that of David Pinault (1992), who has examined *Ashura* customs in the city of Hyderabad. Pinault notes that matam is divided into *sineh-zani* (empty handed breast-beating) and 'with implements' (the English term is employed even by the Urdu speakers of the city, for reasons the author does not establish). Even empty-handed forms of *matam* are highly complex, varying in cadence and intensity; one-handed *matam*, the type prevalent among the Bohras, is here reserved for the infirm or elderly. As is true for the Bohras, woman do perform *matam*, but only empty handed and only in seclusion from the men. Implements used include the scourge, the *chaq-chaqi* (spiked implements held in the palm), razor blades, and knivew or short daggers used for jabbing the scalp and chest. Like the Bohra clergy, many Hyderabadi *ulma* frown upon displays of *matam* with implements: some consider it too close to the dancing and exuberance of Sufi devotion, others regard it as insincere competition (148-150). Abbas also notes that significant numbers of Imami Shia clerics disapprove of 'extreme reverence,' seeing it as an orgiastic distraction from the prayer and soul-searching that are proper *Ashura* pursuits (1991: 42).

Ashura Relations with other Communities

Muharram is a time when intercommunal relations are both strengthened and weakened, depending on local circumstance and on unpredictable luck. In any community with a significant Shia population *Ashura* is a major event–and major events can be both good and bad things (for a more general discussin of Hindu-Muslim sectarian conflict see Blank 1994; 1999a; xi-xiv, 6-26).

Throughout the subcontinent, Muharram is often marked by a high degree of intercommunnal unity. As Hjrtshoj notes "In many areas Shia's, Sunnis, and Hindus participate in Muharram observances, together or separately, and no doubt for a variety of reasons" (1987: 292). He further reports that in one procession in Lucknow, the blood *matam* was led by Sikh (302). Pinault notes synergetic practices in Hyderabadi Muharram, with Hindu influences readily discernible (1992: 61-62). A.R. Saiyid reports that among the Mahagir fishing communities of the Konkan region, 'some of the accretions surrounding the observance of Moharram are Hindu in origin, or at least are influenced by Hindu practices' (1981: 115). Such ecumenical practices include the seeking of *darshan* by Hindus at the *tazia* constructions, the playing of Hindi filmi music interspersed with Quranic verses, and even (amazingly!) the serving of alcohol to Hindu guest at fast-breaking *iftar* meals (121-123: Madan 1991: 250-155).

Among the Bohras such ecumenicalism is considerably more rare. During *Ashura*, as at all times, the Bohras tend to keep to themselves in religious matters, and in more than two years of fieldwork I observed virtually no other outsiders at any Bohra ritual. What syncretism might occur seems to be at a less obvious level: The rhythmic chanting of the names of Husain and Ali may bear certain similarities to Sufi practice or to yogic mantras, and the use of coconuts and candy as ritual symbols of bounty and sweetness appear to be holdovers from Hindu customs.

While Muharram can be an occasion for neighbourly amity, it is often the spark of civil strife. In Lucknow, for example, when violence between Sunni and Shia erupts it is generally during *Ashura* (Hjortshoj 1987: 29). Hyderabadi Muharram has seldom led to rioting in the post-colonial era, but in recent years the Vishwa Hindu Parishad had attempted to stir up conflict by scheduling provocative marches during the week when Ashura passions run high (Pinault 1992: 149-150).

Among the normally quietistic Bohras, Muharram is the time of year when intercommunal strife is mot likely to occur. Part of the Bohra service, as is the case for most Shia, is the ritual cursing of the Umayyad Caliph Yazid and other figures regarded as usurpers. In Mumbai several years ago, Mukasir Sahib (the third-ranking cleric and chief *amil* of Mumbai) led the worshippers in a ritual condemnation of Abu Bakr, Umar and Uthamn, three men regarded by the Sunni as Rightly Guided Caliphs but reviled by Shia as thieves of the rule properly belonging to Ali. The *waaz* was broadcast into the streets for the overflow crowds unable to squeeze into Fatimi Masjid; apart from the blocks immediately surrounding the mosque most of the neighbourhood's population is Sunni, so the incident led to violence. Some witnesses say that Sunni bystanders attacked the Bohras at prayer, others say small groups of teenaged Bohras became so enraged at the injustices inflicted upon Husain that they sought out street-fights with Sunni boys.

After *Ashura*

For the first nine evenings of Muharram, families visit each other's homes and make great display of hospitality. On the night of the tenth, however, all the entertaining ends, and the community rests from the excitement of the day. The morning of the eleventh, shops open again, and life returns to normality. The mourning period continues for 40 days, a time during which no marriages or other festivities should take place. Those who can afford to do so may keep their businesses closed for an additional days past *Ashura*, a practice which Syedna encourages.

Muharram to Ramadan

The second through the eighth months of Bohra calendar are of less ritual prominence than the months of Muharram, Ramadan and Zyl-Hajj. There are, however, three major events during this period: the birthdates of the Prophet Muhammad and of Syeda Muhammad Burhanuddin and the Urs of Syedna Taher Saifuddin. In addition, the examination period at the Jamea tus-Saifiya seminary in Surat-while not a religious ceremony per se, and not observed outside of Surat itself – is an important annual event. The significant holy days are as follows, with most observance taking place on the evening preceding the date in question.

Safar (the second month): 20: Chhelum for Imam Husain, observed with a *waaz* 26/27 Shehadet of Imam Husan, observed with a *majlis*.

Rabiul Awwal (*the third month*): 12: Birthdate of the Prophet Muhammad. A Joyous occasion, although Bohras observe this day also as the one on which he was born. The Prophet's birthdate is celebrated throughout the Muslim world, although not always on the same day. Some Ithna-Ashariya observe it on the 17th of the month, the same date that they mark the birth of Imam Jafar-Sadiq.

Rabiul Akher (the fourth month) : 4: Birthdate of Imam Tayyib, the 21st and last Imam before the period of occulation which lasts until the present day. A happy occasion, celebrated with a *waaz.* 20: Birthday of Syedna Muhammad Burhanuddin. Another festive holiday. On this day Bohras throughout the world thank God for the guidance of Syedna, and for the happiness and prosperity of the community. At *madrasas* in India and abroad the date is the occasion for awards ceremonies and athletic competitions.

Jamadi Awwal (the fifth month) : 10: Urs of Hazrat Fatima. The death-date of daughter of the prophet and progenitrix of the Fatimid line is marked with a *majlis* and a day of community mourning. Many Athna-Ashariya commemorate the Urs of Fatima on the third of the following month, and celebrate her birth on the 20th of that month.

Jamadi Akher (the sixth month): 2: Urs of Syedna Qutubddin, the 32nd who is buried in Ahmedabad, so this is often the primary site of observance rituals. The date is marked by a *majlis,* unless Syedna is in Ahmedabad, in which case he delivers a *waaz.* 29: Pehli Rejib, the eve of the first day of the month of Rejib. A special night-time *namaaz* is offered, consisting of twenty-four *rakats.* A *rakat* is the cycle of prayer while standing, kneeling, kissing the ground, sitting, kissing the ground, and standing, as practiced in daily *namaaz.* A break is taken between every two *rakats,* during which time the worshippers chant or call out devotional phrases while seated.

Rajib (the seventh month) : Fasting during Rejib is not obligatory but it is considered highly laudable. As in Ramadan, *sawm* consists of a dry fast during daylight hours. Those choosing to fast during Reijb are strongly encouraged to commit to doing so for an entire decade. 13: Birthdate of Wasi Ali. The date (which is also observed by Ithna-Ashariya) is marked by a *majlis.* Since this is a fasting month – whether or not all of the faithful actually undetake *sawm* – celebrations are somewhat muted. 15: Commemoration of an occasion on which Imam Hafar miraculously located a child who had been kidnapped. 19: Urs of Syedna Taher Saifuddin. Ever since the death of the 51st *dai* in 1965, the event has been marked with a *waaz* in Mumbai. For more than a decade, since the construction of a spectacular marble mausoleum there, Syedna Muhammad

Burhanuddin has also made a special *ziyaret* to the *rauzah* (tomb) of his father. Community devotion is intense, with 60,000 typically gathering to mourn the death anniversary. 27: *Mebas*, an event commemorated on the same date by Ithna-Ashariya. The holiday marks the date on which Muhammad was given the title of prophet. Bohra observane consists of a *waaz* in afternoon, followed by an evening service of 22 *rakats*. 27: *Moti-us-Soalite*: This date is training for the fast of Ramaman. All children over the age of six months (and most adults as well) undertake a one-day fast in order to learn the rules of *sawm* and build the self-discipline to follow them.

Shaban (the eighth month): 1. Eid. The breaking of the Rejib fast marks the beginning of Jamea tus-Saifiya examination in Surat. Wherever possible to Syedna presides over the oral and written tests, which last between ten and twelve days. The first day of the examination period, called *zikra*, is initiated by a *majlis* by the *dai*. 15: *Shabb--e-Baraat*: The longest individual namaaz of the year. It is a night-time prayer of only fourteen *rakats*, but each *rakat* takes almost twelve minutes to perform, so the entire ritual takes an hour and a half. By contrast, a typical *namaaz* of 24 *rakats* can be performed in about fifteen minutes.

Ramadan

The ninth month of the Islamic calendar is a period for fasting, spiritual self-examination, and the reinforcement of religious identity throughout the Muslim world. Like all Muslims, Bohras observe a day fast during daylight hours: from before daybreak until after sunset, not so much as a drop of water can enter their bodies. There are no half-measures for the young, or old or ill: one either fasts completely or puts the fast off until such time as it can be undertaken whole heartedly. There is no stigma attached to a sick or infirm person postponing the *sawm*, but avoidance for more comfort is strongly discouraged. The members as much as by members of the clergy, is stronger during Ramadan than at any other time of the year except Muharram.

The daily Ramadan schedule of most Bohras differs markedly from that of their Sunni neighbours (cf. al-Bukhari 1986: vol. 6, 28; al-Muslim 1978: 533). The Sunnis of Mumbai's Muhammad Ali Road often reverse their day and night time schedules: they stay awake until three or four in the morning, eat a large dinner before going to bed, then sleep until noon and keep their shops open from three p.m. until midnight, Bohras are under no special *dawat* instructions as to how to fit their Ramadan observances into the course of their lives, but most try to keep to their normal schedule as much as possible. A typical shopkeeper might get up before sunrise to start the day with a hearty meal, go to *masjid* form morning *namaaz* rather than saying it at home, and open his store at the customary time. He might say[6] his midday *namaaz* at the *masjid* as well, although there is no obligation to do so. The shopkeeper would close up about two hours earlier than usual in order to reach the *masjid* in time for evening *nammaz*–and *iftar* (breaking of the fast). He would arrive home not long after sunset, and spend an hour or so feasting with family and friends before retiring early for the night.

Ramadan is a time for financial obligations. Bohras, like other Muslims, typically pay *zakat* during Ramadan. In addition, Bohras pay a range of other community fees and voluntary contributions during this month. During Ramadan the rich are under special obligation to give money to the poor: beggars from all parts of Mumbai converge on Muhammad Ali Road during Ramadan, and business is exceptionally good. This is when Muslim employers typically give their employees an annual bonus, and therefore it is the only time of year when many of the less advantaged community members have much disposable income. Ramadan is a time for haircuts and new clothes, for long-delayed household purchases and Eid gifts for the children. Bazaars are particularly vibrant during the evenings of Ramadan, especially as the holy month winds to a close.

Ramadan Days of Special Ritual

During the entire month of Ramadan, the *dai* will say *namaaz* publicly three times every day. 'Imamate namaaz', prayer in which Syedna leads an–assembled congregation rather than merely saying *salat* in the privacy of Saifee Mahal (his personal residence), is more common during Ramadan than at any other time of year. Syedna Muhammad Burhanuddin has performed Imamat *namaaz* three times daily during Ramadan for over thirty years, while his father did so for 53 years. The dates of special observance (the first three each marked with special night prayers of 24 *rakats*) are as follows:

17: Commemorates Amina, the mother of the Prophet Muhammad.

19: Shehadet of Wasi Ali, marked with a *waaz*. This date also commemorates the mother of Ali.

21: Commemorates Khadija, the first wife of the Prophet and mother of Fatima.

23: Lailat at-Qadr: This ritual, the most important of Ramadan, marks the birthdate of Fatima.

Eve of Eid: A prayer of 24 *rakats,* following by one of ten *rakats.*

Lailat al-Qadr

If a Bohra observes only one Ramadan ritual, this is the one (cf. al-Muslim 1978: 570). Particularly devout Bohras spend the entire night in prayer at a *masjid,* while others stay awake all night in prayer at home. The date is often referred to by its Gujarati name of *Jagvanirat.* Typically Bohras say their *isha* prayers shortly after their *maghrib* ones, but on this night the isha namaaz begins around 10:30 p.m. The highlight of the night is the *waaz* delivered by Syedna beginning around two a.m.

Competition for a space in any of the *masjids* is fierce. Any Bohra is permitted to attend any *masjid* at any time, but in order to prevent overcrowding people are strongly encouraged to go to the mosque in their own neighbourhood. Even local *masjids,* however, become overstuffed on a night like Lailat at-Qadr : like Christians flocking to church on Christmas and Easter, many Bohras participate in community rituals only of Lailat al-Qadr and *Ashura.* Those who come to *masjid* week in and week out do not like to be displaced by part-timers, so there are informal rules about who has or has not earned the right to be present. At particularly crowded *masjids,* the rights of attendance during special days – sometimes even a particular spot in the chamber – are informally handed down from father to son.

Due to strict municipal limits on the construction of new *masjids* or expansion of existing ones, Muslims of all denominations (both in Mumbai and throughout India) spill out onto the street during particularly busy holidays. The devout lay prayer rugs, oil-cloths, or layers of newspaper down on ground, while beggars from all over the city congregate around the congregants. The ritual on Lailat al-Qadr is similar to those of other Bohra observances: *namaaz, matam,* chanting and hymns, building up to an emotional *waaz* delivered by the *dai*. Fasting and prayer on Lailat al-Qadr is said to be superior to the prayers and fasts of a thousand other days.

Shawwal

1. Eid-ul-Fitr: Like Muslims the world over, Bohras celebrate Eid-ul-Fitr as perhaps the most joyous festival of the year. The day begins with *fajr nammaz* at sunrise, followed by the breaking of the night's fast with a dried date. During the day Bohras will visit neighbours and relatives, and eat festive foods such as *kheer*, dried fruit and *darfi*.

Ziquad

27: The birthdate of Sydna Taher Saifuddin. The only two *dais* whose birthdays are celebrated are the current supreme pontiff and his predecessor: all other dais are commemorated only by Urs. Both birthdays are joyous occasions. At Fatimi Masjid, the central 'cathedral' of the Bohra community, the intricately carved dark wooden pillars of the main chamber are festooned with sweet-smelling wreaths of white jasmine petals and bright strings of white lights. The chamber is surrounded by second and third floor purdah galleries: women can watch and take part in all rituals, while maintaining a modest distance from the men packed in below.

Immediately after *maghrib namaz*, the sons of Taher Saifuddein and the sons of Syedna Muhammad Burhanuddin (in that order of seniority) stand before the *dai* and lead the congregation in signing hymns in honour of the previous *dai* and of all the *imamas*. Next, Syedna (as the representative of his father) has his head circled three times with a *thal* containing coconuts and sweets. This practice, displaying clear similarities to Hindu custom and hence a likely holdover of the Viashya traditions of the Bohras' ancestors, is common at the birthdays of laypeople throughout the community.

After the circling of the *thal*, a vessel of *sherbet* is passed around: first it is given to Syedna, then to his brothers and sons. Even on this joyous occasion the central aspect of ritual is commemoration of the martyrdom of Imam Husain. Syedna and other speakers retell episodes from the story of Kerbala, chunt humns and recite poems about it and read sermons about it. These (as at all Bohra rituals) remind their audience that the tale is the blueprint for all later human developments. This holiday is focused on Taher Saifuddin, featuring poems and hymns by or about him – but the commemoration never strays far from the topic of *Ashura*. Periodically the audience breaks into loud cries of 'Ya Husain!' and periods of hearty breast-beating. The *majlis* lasts about two hours, after which Syedna and some of his close relatives perform *ziyaret* at the mausoleum of Taher Saifuddin (located just across the street from Fatimi Masjid).

Zyl-Hajj

For Bohras, as for all Muslims, the pilgrimage of Hajj is obligatory at least once in the life of every believer who is to make such a trip. Respondents to my survey ranked this an aspect of orthopraxy second only to conduct with Syedna, and 89.4% cited it as a fundamental journey, for the faith. Whereas for many Muslims this is an individual journey; for Bohras it is group activity: a high-ranking cleric (generally one of Syedna's brothers or sons) leads all pilgrims through the usual cycle of observances at Mecca and Medina. Of any survey respondents who were questioned on the topic, 83.3% reported having made use of the *dawat's* services in arranging their *hajj* and pilgrimage to Kerbala. As Barbara Metcalf notes, the experience of *hajj* is perhaps the greatest unifying ritual in Islam:

> "If a person is 'finding himself' he is doing so in a crowd, following a ritual program of dress and behaviour meant precisely to obliterate the markers that make a believer distinct by class, race or religion" (1990: 101).

The fact that Bohras keep themselves strictly separate even on *hajj* -the one ritual which Muslims of nearly all denominations and all nations celebrate together–is both a marker of and a means of perpetuating their distinct identity.

Although the Bohra calendar (and therefore timing of rituals) differs from that of other Muslims, the rituals forming the pilgrimage experience are similar or (in most cases) identical. Almost all of the rituals in place for Sunni and *Ithna-Ashari* pilgrims are observed (cf. Al-Bukhari 1986; vol. 2, 344-475; Muslim 1978: vol. 2, 578-700; Peters 1994). The main differences are as follows:

1. While most Muslims are free to undertake *hajj* on either an individual or a group basis, Bohras always make their *hajj* in an organized group under the guidance of a *hajj amil* appointed by the *dawat*. Often during the course of this century the duty fell to Syedna's brother, the late Syed Saleh Bhaisaheb Safiyuddin; the Mukashir Saheb of the *dawat* and head *amil* of Bombay, until his death in 1994 Syedi Saleh Bhaisaheb performed *hajj* 37 times, pilgrimage to Kerbala more than 40 times, and *umra* over 100 times (Bekhud 1994b: 8).
2. The dates of observance differ slightly, so Sunnis would consider some Bohra *hajj* observances to be technically *umra.*
3. Unless they have relations or friends living in Saudi Arabia, Bohras stay in *musafirkhanas* rather than in the pilgrim hostels set up for the rest of the *hajj* pilgrims.
4. Bohras shave off all of the hair on their scalps after *hajj,* while some Sunni pilgrims interpret the direction more loosely.
5. A ritual in which pilgrims hop on one leg is performed by only men among Bohra pilgrims, and by both men and women among Sunnis.
6. In the 'Stoning of the Devil' ritual (cf. al-Muslim 1978: 652-654), each Sunni pilgrim bombards the symbolic boulder with a torrent of rocks, sticks, or even sandals. The Bohras consider this an undisciplined display of violence. By contrast, they honour the twenty-one imams by each throwing precisely seven stones per day for three days.

For these members of the community not traveling to Mecca, the month of *Zyl-Hajj* contains two important dates: Eid-ul-Adha and Eid Ghadir-e-Khum.

Eid-ul-Adha (Bakr Eid)

The Bohra observance of Bakr Eid is basically the same as that of Sunnis and other Muslims. All *hajjis* are required to sacrifice a goat[9] (hence the name of the festival) and use the meat to provide a feast for family members or alms for the poor. People who have not performed *hajj* are also welcome to sacrifice, and *hajjis* are free to pay a local butcher or some other proxy to sacrifice in their stead, but the symbolism of the rite is an annual reminder of religious and community obligations. As is the case for Sunnis, it is considered particularly appropriate (although hardly obligatory) to perform the sacrifice with one's hands (cf. al-Muslim 1978: 1087). It is customary, for all who can do so, to prepare a lavish dinner featuring *pettar ka ghosth* (as the name implies, meat cooked on stones) with stones brought from Mecca by a family member.

Bohras are free to decide the logistics of their goat-sacrifice in any way they see fit. Many perform the rite in their *chawl*, so that the entire family can watch and take part. In urban areas such as Mumbai, however, most fulfill their obligation at the local *jamatkhana* for convenience. Urban professionals are, unsurprisingly, generally inexperienced in the techniques of slaughter and butchery, so in the modern age they often require assistance of professionals with premodern expertise. These groups offer a sort of one-stop shopping for all of a person's sacrificial needs. Instead of finding and buying a goat, leading it to a decent slaughter-site, finding a few friends to help him kill it, finding a person who reads Arabic to recite the appropriate verses, getting a sufficient supply of sharp knives and buckets of water, dismembering the carcass, dividing it into parcels of meat for distribution to the poor, and cleaning the site afterwards – instead of performing all of these tasks himself, a *hajji* can simply go to the *jamatkhana* and purchase tickets to have all of them carried out by a proxy. Many Sunni and *Ithna-Ashari waqfs* perform a similar function.

Ritual slaughter–whether that of a *hajji* at Eid or that *a halal* butcher at any time of year-should be performed in accordance with a strict set of rules (cf. al-Bukhari 1986: vol. 7, 322-334). For a Bohra *hajji* during Bakr Eid, the main rules are as follows : (1) He should turn the animal's face toward *qiblah*, and recite the *bismillah* prayer. The purpose of the set phrase is to sanctify an action which would otherwise be profane: it is never right to kill any creature without a good purpose, so that butcher must not that he performs his duty out of obligation. (2) He must give the goat a final drink of water. This is to commemorate Imam Husain, who was denied even a sip of water as he lay dying on the field of Kerbala[10]; by giving the goat a last drink, the *hajji* is implicitly recognizing Husain's sacrifice by acknowledging that no living thing should be treated as cruelly as he was. (3) The knife used for the slaughter must be razor-sharp. This is out of concern for the goat, since a sharp knife is less painful than a dull, blunted blade. (4) The sacrifice should be performed on soil rather than stone or concrete.

If the rite takes place in a paved *chawl,* soil is brought in an spread on the ground. Afterwards, the blood-soaked dirt is dug up and thrown away. This requirement is a manifestation of *tahara,* cleanliness, one of the Seven Pillars of the Ismaili faith.[11]

Eid Ghadir al-Khumm

The 18th of Zyl-Hajj is the date on which (Shia tradition holds) the prophet Muhammad and his son-in-law Ali received the oath of allegiancerom 70,000 new Muslims at Ghadir al-Khumm on the road from Mecca to Medina. The oath is said to be taken back to a verse from the Quran:

> 'God purchase from all the faithful their souls and their property in consideration of Paradise.' (Shia view of Ghadir al-Khumm: Abdul Husain 1920:61; Ali, Z. 1954: 378-379; Schimmel 1980: 71. cf. Hollister 1953: 266; for Sunni ahadith: al-Bukhari 1986: vol. 4, 128; vol. 9, 236-242).

The commemoration of this even is the occasion of (*mithaq*-the central rite of passage for Bohras, and the only major ritual unique to the denomination. This ceremony, obligatory for every Bohra who wishes to be part of the community, is a covenant between the believer and God. In addition to spelling out the duties a believer owes to God, it includes an oath of allegiance: a vow to accept the spiritual guidance of Syedna wholeheartedly and without reservation (cf. Daftary 1990; 229; Hollister 1953: 282-295). Before *mithaq,* a Bohra is a child. After *mithaq,* he or she is an adult, with all the rights and responsibilities of any mature member of the community.

The *mithiaq* oath is first taken at whatever age a child is deemed to have reached maturity: most commonly, thirteen years old girls, fourteen or fifteen for boys. First *mithaq* can be administered individually or in a group, depending on how many adolescents a local community may have. In small towns it may be given for a single child, while oaths administered by Syedna himself typically draw thousands of inductees. Usually the *mithaq* is held at the local *masjid,* but it can also be held in a private home or a rented hall. Boys and girls go through the *mithaq* rite together, but for the first time in their lives they are segregated by gender.

Every year on the 18th of *Zyl-Hajj* every Bohra congregation renews its *mithaq* vows together. The *amil* asks the faithful to reaffirm their vows with a series of specific question, to each of which the congregation replies with a resounding, 'Nam': Arabic for 'yes'. This wording of the *mithaq* oath, it should be noted, is a source of great internal controversy: since the vows explicitly bind the inductees to obey all of *dai's* instructions in both spiritual and temporal matters, they are central to the issue of *dawat* hegemony. *Mithaq* is the foundation for the legitimacy of *dawat* control, so dissidents have challenged the authenticity of the oath itself. The only published texts of the *mithaq* oath are identical versions printed in a variety of dissident works, all of them ultimately traceable to a text of 1920. The *dawat* has not authorized publication of the modern-day text and does not allow the tape-recording of religious ceremonies without permission, so an outside observer such as me (even after attending the service) can offer no authoritative alternate wording. The substance of the oath, however, does not seem to be in dispute: orthodox and dissident Bohras disagree on the precise wording and the provenance of the *mithaq* oath, but agree that in its current form it requires inductees to swear unfettered obedience to God and to Syedna.

Dissidents view the oath of allegiance as an infringement on their rights: some Bohras refuse to take the oath, and some others take it unhappily. The vast majority of my informants, however, did not regard *mithaq* as oppressive. Some saw it merely as a symbolic gesture, while most viewed it as sacred covenant: slightly over half of my survey respondents cited it as a bedrock component of the faith. Whatever private reservations members of the community might have, *mithaq* remains a defining ritual. Not only is it the fundamental rite of passage from childhood to adulthood for boys and girls alike, it also continues to be a pledge renewed by observant Bohra adults every year.

Conclusion

In the preceding pages I have attempted to present a stratightforward ethnographic account of the annual rituals of the Daudi Bohra community, with a minimum of theorizing. While rites such as *mithaq* are a continuing source of friction between the orthodox and the dissident members of the community, most annuals ritual are a powerful means of solidifying communal cohesion and fostering a uniform identity for all members of the denomination.

What is perhaps most noteworthy about the annual rituals is the fact that they strongly emphasize the Daudi Bohras' tie to universal Islamic identity shared with one billion Muslims worldwide, yet simultaneously highlight the unique nature of the Bohra identity as the Mustali Ismailis. Every ritual, even such universal observances as pilgrimage during *Zyl-Hajj* and fasting during Ramadan, are given a flavour unique to the denomination: the focus of all rituals is squarely on Syedna as the visible representative of the hidden *imam*. Even the overwhelming prominence of devotion to Shia figures such as Husain and Ali is tinged with an aura not found in any other branch of Islam. *Ithna-Ashari* Shia might share such devotion, but not channel it through a single, unified clerical hierarchy represented in the person of a single charismatic apex cleric. Nizari Ismailis share this tight central hierarchical structure, but not the deth of adherence to traditional pan-Islamic standards of orthopraxy (Asani 1987).

When compared with the annual rites of other Muslim communities of the subcontinent, these rituals demonstrate the wide diversity of practices that constitute Islam in India. In the Bohra worldview, there is no inherent conflict between their identity as Muslims and their identity as Gujarati Indians. The Daudi Bohras have always treated *deen* and *dunya* (religious and temporal realms) as two halves of an integrated whole. For them, there is no paradox in a communal Islamic identity that is at once universal and unique.

NOTES

1. Throughout this article, the term *'Bohra'* and *'Daudi Bohra'* are used interchangeably. This is the usage employed throughout the Daudi Bohra community, and throughout Mumbai (in 1995 the city's name was officially changed from Bombay to reflect Marathi pronunciation). While non-Daudi groups of Bohras exist as the result of schisms over the past four centuries, they make up less than ten percent of the total population. In addition to the Sulaimanis and such splinter sects as the Alias, Medhibaghwalas and Artaliswalas, there is a sizeable group of Sunni 'Bohras' which broke away from the Shia community in the ninth/fifteen century and has had no significant contact with the Ismailis Bohras for at least three centuries (cf. Lambat, 1976).
2. One of the very few scholars to have made the attempt, Theodore P. Wright, Jr., was denied access despite vigorous efforts (personal

communication, 3/13/99); he nevertheless produced two important chapters in edited volumes dealing with competitive modernization (Wright 1975: 151-178) and kinship patterns among Indian Muslims (Wright 1976: 217-238). Some material on Bohras can be found in more general works devoted to Ismailis (Daftary 1990), Gujarati Muslims (Misra 1964), Indian Shia (Hollister 1953), or topics as far a field as Indian jurisprudence (Mansfield 1993). Of the handful of non-peer reviewed sources available, virtually all are directly linked to either the Bohra *dawat* or the dissidents, and must be viewed in this light. Clerical sources include texts published by the *Dawat-e-Hadiyah's* Department of Statistics and Information (many of them pamphlets written by Shaikh Tyebally A. Davoodbhoy and Shaikh Yusuf Bekhud) and officially-sanctioned texts such as Raik 1975 and Shaikh Yunus Mubarakpuri's *Bohrah dai-Yi mutlaq bare mulla ji ka naya Islam.* Dissident sources (explicit or de facto) include those authored by members of the reformist/dissident movement (Abdul Husain 1920; Contractor 1980; Engineer 1989; 1993, and other works), and those drawing their information directly from such sources (Nathwani 1979; Roy 1984). Historical sources are scarce, but not as scarce as works on the contemporary community. The most important source for Daudi Bofra historiography is *Mausim-e-bahar fi akhbar al-tahrin al-akhvar*, a nineteenth-century Gujarati text by the *dawat* official Mian Sahib Muhammad Ali ibn muallah Jiwabhai Rampuri (1884) for a more extensive discussion of sources, see Blank (1998: 594-607).

3. An *amil* is the local representative of Syedna. The term is commonly translated by the Bohras themselves as 'priest'; while such terminology would be highly inaccurate in almost any Islamic context, for Ismailis it is not wholly inappropriate.
4. My personal observation of contemporary practice and the explication of *dawat* representatives such as Shaikh Dr. Mustafa Abdulhussein and Mullah Shabbir Muhammad Mansoorbhai Jamai bear out the calendar highlights recorded by sources earlier in the century (Abdul Husain 1920; 109-111' Fyzee 193: 9; Hollister 193: 303).
5. In Bohra (as opposed to *Ithna-Ashari*) tradition, Ali ibn abi Tabib, the son-in-law of the Prophet, is regarded as a *wasi* rather an *imam*.
6. Since the questionnaire was distributed to families with children in *madrasas*, the popularity of this service ranked an unrepresentative first.
7. Shaikh Dr. Mustafa Abdulhussein, personal communicationj, 5/11/98. Shaikh Mustafa is the liaison appointed by the Bohra *dawat* to facilitate my research and provide authoritative explanations for any points of ritual or theology. His help has been invaluable in collecting the information contained in this paper.

8. Like other Shia, Bohras say their *zuhr* and *asr namaaz* with only a brief separation, and do the same for their *maghrib* and *isha nammaz.* In this manner they maintain the universally-mandated five daily prayers, but say them at three intervals.
9. Often sheep are substituted for goats. Bohras living outside of India sometimes substitute cows or camels if they can afford do so. A desire to avoid tension with Hindus severely limits Bohra cow-slaughter, and expense keeps camel-slaughter to a minimum (although informants say it is practiced more often in the deserts of Rajasthan).
10. For Sunnis this drink is an act of ritualized kindness rather than a reminder of Kerbala.
11. The Bohras (and other Shias) observe seven pillars instead of the five recognized by Sunnis: *salat, zakat, sawm* and *hajj* are the same, but to these are added *jihad* (struggle, both spiritual and physical), *tahara* (cleanliness) and *walaya* (devotion to the line of imams); the Sunni pillar of *shahada* (witness to the unity of God) is incorporated into salat (al-Muslim 1978: vol. 1-9; Abdulhussein 1995: 225).
12. Nearly identical versions of the oath: Abdul Husain 1920: 125-138; Ali 1954: 326-329; Bhamgarhwala 1931: 50-53; Hollister 1953: 282-284; Nathwani 1979: 21-25. The text was provided by dissident plaintiffs in the Burhanpur Duirgah case initiated shortly after the First World War and stalled in litigation for many years (Judgment in Civil Suit # 32 of 1925 in the court of First Class Sub-Judge, Burhanpur) which in turn relied on the version of Abdul Husain. The Nathwani Commission cites the dissident journal *New Quest* (issue #7: Jan-Feb. 1978, Pune) as its source, and *New Quest* in turn cites both the court records and Abdul Husain. In the Burhanpur Durgah case, the dissident plaintiffs alleged that Syedna Taher Saifuddin imposed this version of *mithaq* in the early 20th century, replacing a less restrictive version that they claimed had been instituted around the year 560/ 1182 by the third dai, Syedna Hatim, in the book *Tuhfat al-Qulab.* Modern dissident author Asghar Ali Engineer cites what he says is the text of this from the *Tuhfat al-Qulab,* as entered into the book of exhibits of the case in the Privy Council on Appeal from the High Court of Judicature at Nagpur, pp. 835, part II (engineer 1993: 158). Not having personally seen the documents in question, I can offer no independent assessment of the validity of these competing claims.

REFERENCES

Abbas, S. Mobarak (1991), "Sociocultural Implications of Muharram Observance: A study in Rural North Bihar", *South Asian Anthropologist* 12 (1-2), 39-44.

Abdul Husain, Mian Bhai Mullah (1920), *Gulzare Daudi for the Bohras of India*. Ahmedabad [1997 Reprint] Surat: Progressive Publications.

Abdulhussein, Shaikh Dr. Mustafa (1995), "Bohras." In John Esposito (ed.) *Oxford Encyclopedia of the Modern Islamic World*. New York: Oxford University Press.

Ali, Zahid (1954), *Hamare Ismaili Madhhab Ki Haqiqat Aur Uska Nizam*. Hyderabad: Academcy of Islamic Studies.

Asad, Talal (1986), *The Idea of an Anthropology of Islam*. Washington: Center for Contemporary Arab Studies.

Asani, Ali Sultaan Ali (1987), "The Khojahs of Indo-Pakistan: The quest for an Islamic identity", *Journal of the Institute of Muslim Minority Affairs* 8(1), 31-41.

Bekhud, Shaikh Yusuf (1994a), *Tragedy at Kerbala : The Days of Sorrow and Revival (pamphlet)*. Mumbai : Dawat-e-Hadiyah.

———(1994b), *Mukasir-e-Dawat Syedi Salehbhaisahyeb Safiyuddin S.D.T.: An Appreciation*. (Pamphlet). Mumbai: Dawat-e-Hadiyah.

Bhamgarhwala, Tayebali Mahomedai (ed.) (1931) *Judgment in Civil Suit #32 of 1925 in the Court of First Class sub-Judge, Burhanpur*. Burhanpur: Tayebali Mahomedali Bhamgarhwala.

Blank, Jonah, (1994), "Ram and Ram Rajya : The Babri Masjid/ Ramjanambhumi Dispute and the Politicization of a Divinity", *Journal of Vaisana Studies* 2(4), 159-174.

———(1988), *Mullah on the Mainframe: Islamization of Modernity Among the Daudi Bohras*. (Ph.D. Thesis, University of Anthropology), Cambridge (USA): Harvard University.

———(1999a), *Arrow of the Blue-Skinned God: Retracing the Ramayana Throuigh India*. New Delhi: Penguin Books India [Revised Edition of 1992 Hardcover. Houghton Mifflin (Boston), 1993 Paper Back: Doubleday/Image (New York)].

———(1999b), "Identity, Innovation and Islam: Tradition and Modernity Among the Daudi Bohras." Under Submission to *the Journal of Asian Studies*.

Al-Bukhari, Muhammad ibn Ismail (1986), *Sahih al-Bukhari* (Arabic and English). Muhammad Muhsin, ed. And Trans. Medina: Islamic University Press.

Contractor, Noman L. (1980) *The Dawoodi Bohras*. Pune: New Quest Books.

Daftary, Farhad. (1990), *The Ismailis: Their History and Doctrines*. Cambridge (UK): Cambridge University Press.

Davoodhboy, Shaikh Tyebally A. (1990), *In the Footsteps of a Glorious Tradition*. (pamphlet). Mumbai: Dawat-e-Hadiyah.

———(1992), *Faith of the Dawoodi Bohras.* (pamphlet) Mumbai: Dawat-e-Hadiyah.

———(1993), *Barakate Azae Moulanal Imam Husain (AS) 1414 AD: The Mombasa Experience.* (pamphlet). Mumbai: Dawat-e- Hadiyah.

Engineer, Asghar Ali (1989), *The Muslim Communities of Gujarat: An Exploratory Study of Bohras, Khojas and Memons.* Delhi: Ajanta.

———(1994), *The Bohras.* New Delhi: Vikas.

Esposito, John (1988), *Islam: the Straight Path.* New York: Oxford University Press.

Fyzee, Asaf Ali Ashar (1934), "A chronological list of the Imams and Dais of the Mustalian Ismailis," *Journal of the Bombay Branch of the Royal Asiatic Society,* New Series, 10: 8-16.

Hasnain, Nadeem and Sheikh Abrar Husain (1988), *Shias and Shia Islam in India: A Study in Society and Culture.* New Delhi: Harnam.

Hjortshoj, Keith (1987), "Shi'i Identity and the Significance of Muharram in Lucknow, India." In Martin Kramer (ed.) Shi'ism, *Resistance and Revolution.* Boulder : Westview Press.

Hollister, John Norman (1953), *The Shia of India,* London: Luzac & Co.

Lambat, Ismail (1976), "Marriage among the Sunni Surati Vohras of South Gujarat". In Imtiaz Ahmad (ed.) *Family, Kinship and Marriage Among Muslims in India.* Columbia : South Asia Press.

Madan, T.N. (ed.) (1991), *Religion in India.* Delhi : Oxford University Press.

Mansfield, John H. (1993), "The Personal Lawsw or a Uniform Civil Code?" In R. Baird (ed.) *Religion and Law in Independent India.* Delhi: Manohar Books.

Messick, Brinkley, (1996), "Media Muftis: Radiio *Fatwas* of Yemen." In Muhammad Khalid Masud, Brinkley Messick and David Powers (eds.) *Islamic Legal Interpretation : Muftis and their Fatwas.* Cambridge (USA) : Harward University Press.

Metcalf, Barbara Daly (1990), "The Pilgrimages Remembered: South Asian Accounts of the Hajj". In Dale F. Eickelman and James Piscatori (eds.) *Muslim Travellers: Pilgrimage, Migration and the Religious Imagination.* Berkeley: University of California Press.

Misra, Satish Chandra (1964), *The Muslim Communities of Gujarat.* Baroda: Asia Publishing House.

Mubarakpuri, Shaikh Yunus (1978), *Bohrah dai-yi mutlaq Bare Mulla Ji ka naya Islam.* Delhi: Kitabvala.

Al-Muslim, ibn al Hajjaj (1978), *Al-Jami-us-Sahih.* Abdul Hamid Siddiqui, trans. New Delhi: Kitab Bhavan.

Nathwai, N.P., et al. (1979), *Dawoodi Bohra Commission: Report of Investigation Conducted by the Commission Appointed by the Citizens for*

Democracy into the Alleged Infringement of Human rights of Reformist Members of the Dawoodi Bohras in the Name of the High Priest. Ahmedabad: Nathwani Commission.

Peters, E.E. (1994), *The Hajj: The Muslim Pilgrimage to Mecca and the Holy Places.* Princeton : Princeton University Press.

Pinault, David, (1992), *The Shiites : Ritual and Popular Piety in a Muslim Community.* New York: St. Martin's Press.

Raik, S. Kikabhai (ed.) (1975), *Gulshan-e-Malumat.* Ujjain: Kalim Kutubkhana.

Rampuri, Mian Sahib Muhammad Ali ibn Mullah Jiwabhai *Mausim-e bahar fiakhbar al-tahirin al-akhyar.* Mumbai : Hyderi Press.

Roy, Shibani (1984), *The Dawoodi Bohras.* Delhi: B.R. Publishing.

Saiyid, A.R. (1981), "Ideal and Reality in the Observance of Moharram : A behavioral Interpretation." In Imtiaz Ahmad (ed.) *Ritual and Religion Among Muslims in India.* New Delhi: Manohar Books.

Schimmel, Annemarie (1980), *Islam in the Indian Subcontinent.* Leiden : E.J. Brill.

Wright, Theodore P., Jr. (1975), "Competitive Modernization within the Daudi Bohra sect of Muslims and its Significance for Indian Political Development." In Helen Ullrich (ed.) *Competition and Modernization in South Asia.* Delhi : Abhinav.

———(1976), "Muslim kinship and Modernization : The Tyabji Clan of Bombay" In Imtiaz Ahmd (ed.) *Family, Kinship and Marriage among Muslims in India.* Columbia: South Asia Books.

RITUALS OF PROTECTION IN A MUSLIM COMMUNITY

Nasreen Fazalbhoy

Introduction

This paper will raise some issues in the analysis of rituals in a Muslim community and use this as a means to discuss some general issues in the society of Islam in India. Though in recent years there has been a greater interest than was the case earlier, in exploring into the study of Muslim communities, the area of ritual is still little explored. Hence this paper can only be an initial exploration, pointing toward some of the issues, and suggesting the lines along which interpretation may proceed.

One of the major anthropological issues in the society of Islam has been the problem of reconciling the textually prescribed practices that are considered obligatory for a Muslim, with the variety of practices that are found along with the textual practices in the field situation. Early ways of formulating the issue identified aspects of practice as the 'great' and 'little' tradition or 'normative' and 'popular' or 'universal' and 'local' Islam. The problems with this way of formulating the issue are well known and I shall not expand on them further here. Suffice it to say that one of the major problems in these approaches was that of essentialisation. Scholars using these concepts often derived their notion of the core beliefs of Islam (or the great tradition) from the works of Islamist scholars, and treated these beliefs as if they were understood in the same way everywhere regardless of time and space. The little tradition was seen as 'syncretic' or as a 'survival' from the local culture, which again implied that these elements persisted over time with little modification. Recent writings have recognized the complexity of the issue, and have moved away from defining the problem in the dualistic form as above. This issue however remains a challenge for anthropologists writing about Islam.

A second issue in the anthropological study of Islam is the question of the text. What place should a religious text have in sociological analysis, or in the interpretation of ritual ? One approach to this issue is the approach adopted by Clifford Geertz (1960) in his study entitled "Religion of Java". As Eicklman (1982) points out, Geertz made a specific theoretical assumption when he chose to call his book "Religion of Java" rather than "Islam in Java" or by some other name that would indicate that the people he was study were Muslims. He treated Islam as practiced by the Javanese as unique to Java and with no connection with a work community. While Geertz's effort to avoid taking on the Islamist approach (which looked at the text normatively, and the practices in different societies in terms of their conformity or deviance from the prescriptions) can be appreciated, on the other hand, it is through the text and the idea that the text is normative, that Muslim societies consider themselves part of a world community. For the anthropologist the question becomes one of working out a way to read the text so as to allow for the multiple interpretations and expressions that are present in any society.

A third issue that also emerged in the writings on Muslim ritual, was the recognition that by and large the rituals that have been identified as belonging to the 'Great Tradition' of Islam, (the statement of faith, fasting, charity, pilgrimage and prayer) have been little studied sociologically. These practices being textually based, have by and large, been assumed to be the same everywhere, and therefore not of sociological interest. Consequently one finds in the literature discussions and analyses of rituals that are seen to be outside the 'mainstream' such as those associated with charismatic figures such as Sufi saints, or which have a plethora of symbols that make for a plurality of meanings, but virtually nothing on the rituals that are considered classical.

In this paper, I would like to discuss the issues with reference to two practices that I observed among the Kutchi Memon community of Mumbai in the course of field work. The Kutchi Memons are Sunni Muslims. The persons whom I interviewed had been settled in Mumbai for a generation or more. In terms of occupation, my informants ranged from hawkers, taxi drivers, to school teachers and those who had small business enterprises. The two practices that I will discuss are the ritual of *niyaz* and *Sadqa* - the practice of giving charity. Though both these are performed on several occasions, a specific situation that calls for their performance is a crisis or problem situation. They could also be performed with the general desire to meet the exigencies and problems of day to day life such as the need to promote general well being, or to ward off calamities. Both these practices involve some form of transaction such as the giving of good, grain, money or prayer. An intrinsic element in both is the *dua* or supplicatory prayer.

Niyaz

Hughes (182) translates the term *niyaz* as 'offering' though it can also mean desire or supplication (Haq n.d.). The term can refer both to the ritual as well as to the food associated with it, the context of usage providing the meaning of the terms.

The *niyaz* is a simple rituation in which verses of the Quran are recited and a supplication is made to God that the merit which accrues from reading these verses be shared with the person in whose name the *niyaz* is being done. The ritual builds on the idea that the merit from reading the Quran can be transferred or shared with the dead. It is therefore typically done on the occasion of a death anniversary, most often of a *wali* or holy person from the Sufi tradition[2]. Typically the merit is shared with the Prophet, and the Prophet's family, the *wali* (sometimes one in particular may be mentioned, such as Piran-e-Pir-the Pir of Pirs-Shaikh Abdul Qadir Jilani), all pious Muslims (referred to as the believing men and the believing women, and finally one or more specific for whom the ritual is being done). The verses may be recited by a *Maulana* (person learned in the Quran) if the family so desires, or it may be done by any pious person (man or woman) who is considered well versed in Quran.

The procedure for performing the *niyaz* is the same whatever the purpose for which it is undertaken. Since the ritual is connected with the dead some incense is always burnt since it has a good perfume and is supposed is to be pleasing to the dead. The person doing the *niyaz* keeps some water and some food, usually something sweet, while reciting the Quran. By association with the recitation of the Quran the food is considered to be sacred and is shared with the members of the household or those present, and depending on the occasion, may even be sent to relatives and friends. This sacred food *niyaz* is subjected to some prohibitions and prescriptions. It is always treated with great care, and always kept away from anything that is polluting. For instance, menstruating women (who are in the state of ritual impurity) will not eat *niyaz*, and it is never simply thrown away. Whoever eats *niyaz* is considered fortunate since *niyaz* is associated with *barakat* blessing. Since this is not a textually prescribed ritual, there are no stated recommendations or prohibitions regarding the foods that can be used for *niyaz*. By convention, however, my informants usually did a *niyaz* with something sweet, or something made of milk, since it is believed that the Prophet liked milk. Usually no meat or vegetable were used, unless it was made into a *polao* (a cuisine in fried rice), that is, not regular everyday food items were considered appropriate and usually nothing was in a raw or uncooked or unprocessed state. Even the milk was prepared into *kheer* or *halwa* (sweet dishes).

Typically the *niyaz* is performed on a number of calendrical occasions. Among the Kutchi Memons, doing a *niyaz* was a regular and important activity. Different women (or families) followed different cycles of *niyaz*. Practically every month was associated with a *niyaz*. In the first month of the year, *Muharram*, (as per Islamic lunar Calender) *niyaz* is done for the family of the Prophet who were martyred at Karbala. In the month of *Rabi-ul-Awwal*, the day of the Prophet's birth (said to also be the day of his death) a *niyaz* is done for the Prophet, usually of something made of milk. *In Rabiul-Akhir* the *niyaz* of Ghaus Pak or Abdul Qadir Jilani is performed. In *Rajab* the *niyaz* of Imam Jafar Sadiq, and in *Shaban* the *niyaz* for deceased kins is done on the occasion of *Shab-i-Baraat*. During the month of Ramadan a *niyaz* is done for Ali, the son-in-law of the Prophet. The two Ids were also observed with a *Fatima* in the name of the Prophet. The months of *Jumadal Awwal* and *Jumadal Akhir* were called 'empty months' since there was no fixed *niyaz* or festival during called 'empty months' since there was no fixed *niyaz* or festival during these months. I was told that at one time marriages did not take place during these months. Mondays were especially associated with the *niyaz* of Haji Pir of Kutch, and Thursdays with a *niyaz* which could be for the Prophet and *wali* in general, or specifically or Shaikh Abdul Qadir Jilani. The procedure of *niyaz* for *wali* sometimes involved special additional features apart from the core ritual described above. The *niyaz* for Shaikh Abdul Qadir Jilani for instance, employed the number 11 in diverse ways. The *niyaz* from the Quran 11 times each, others put aside 11 coins every day so that they would collect money throughout the year or during the month, and do the *niyaz* with the money that had been collected.

Since the *niyaz* is done on a number of different types of occasions, it is difficult to classify it definitively in any standard classification of rituals such as that described by Durkheim (1976). It is partly a commemorative ritual for it is done on death anniversaries of *wali*, as a means of remembering them and sending them merit. However, a major idea expressed regarding the *niyaz* was that doing *niyaz* regularly helped to maintain a state of well being in the household. As a general rule *niyaz* are domestic rituals done by an individual, though some or all members of the family may also be present. Since a *niyaz* essentially brings in the system of ideas relating to pious and holy persons, these are sometimes performed at *dargahs* (shrines of holy persons) especially on Thursdays.

Apart from these calendrical occasions, *niyaz* is also done on special occasions that call for thanksgiving, such as when a child takes it's first step, or sometime in the family recovers from an illness, or when a circumcision was successfully completed. A special type of *niyaz* calls for mention here. One of the common ways in which people dealt with the exgenesis of everyday life, was to make a vow (*mannat*) to do a *niyaz* and read a *niyaz namah* if some problem was solved, as for instance, an examination passed, or something that was lost, was located. The *niyaz namah* are short booklets of about 10-15 pages which have a story relating to some holy person. The booklets are easily available in predominantly Muslim areas. They cost between Rs. 3 and Rs. 5 which suggests that they are easily accessible to masses. They are generally available with hawkers in small stalls and handcrafts, which crop up around dargahs on Thursdays. Big bookshops do not stock these, since they do not count as religious literature in their eyes. The booklets are decorated with pictures of the Kaaba and the grave of the Prophet. The *niyaz namah* that were read by my informants were in Urdu. The language was simple and easy to read. Sometimes the *niyaz namah* gave special instruments regarding the procedure to be followed, such as that the story must be heard, and not read, or that some special food is required. These instructions were scrupulously followed.

By and large only women read *niyaz namahs*. While it was considered important that anyone participating in the *niyaz* should be in a state of ritual purity, there were some *niyaz* in which this was an important and essential requirement. For instance, a popular *niyaz*, which was conducted with the *niyaz namah*, was the *Kunda ki niyaz* dedicated to Islam Jafar Sadiq. In this *niyaz* menstruating women may even leave the house and go away so as to maintain a state of ritual purity in the house. In addition to this, garlic, onion and non-vegetarian foods are not cooked in the house the day the *niyaz* is being performed.

Sadqa

The giving of alms or charity which is normatively a recommended duty, was often spoken of by my informants as one of the most potent ways of preserving wellbeing and avoiding misfortune. There are three terms that are typically used for the kind of charity associated with protection: *khairat, sadaqa* and *utara*. These can be distinguished from the *zakat* which is a compulsory tax on wealth.

Underlying the giving of all alms is the idea that it is a pious act which is liked by God. *Khairat* for instance is a generic term for charity, which is done in many contexts as a pious act for the sake of God. While acts of charity are not necessarily linked to any specific situation or problem, they were often seen as having performed a protective function, when some calamity was averted, or when there was some unexpected positive turn of events. For instance, when the daughter of one of my informants escaped unhurt in a serious accident, she said that what had helped her was the regular feeding of the poor that she did in her daughter's name every Thursday. As an expression of gratitude she immediately arranged to feel a number of people at a *dargah* the very day that she heard of the accident.

Sadqa fits into the general category of peculiar rites or rites done at times of deep distress, or associated with warding off evil. In the Quran the term *sadqa* which originates from the root *sadaq* (to be righteous or truthful) is translated as almsgiving (Hughes 1982). In the Indian situation the term *sadqa* has some additional connotations. Platts (1984) translates it as 'an alms, a gift, a donation, a propitiatory offering, a sacrifice (to avert misfortune or sickness, etc.)'. The Encyclopaedia of Islam (1961) while pointing to the interchangeability of *zakat* and *sadqa* in the Quran adds that *sadqa* is connected with the atonement of sins. In general people said that the giving of *sadqa* and *khairat* remove *bala*. The term *'bala'* can be roughly translated as misfortune, but also includes the idea of evil spirit or fiend (Abdul Haq, n.d.). The *bala* is spoken of as some external misfortunes, whose cause is unknown.

When we compare *sadqa* and *khairat*, the context of giving *sadqa* is more delimited than the giving of *khairat*. For my informants the context of giving *sadqa* was always that of a crisis situation. *Sadqa* was regularly given on occasions of illness, at the start of a journey, or when one escaped some unexpected disaster such as a serious accident. One of them said that even if she had a bad dream, or a feeling of uneasiness as if something is weighing down on her, or a sene of foreboding one can take out money to be given away as *sadqa*. When giving it away they said in their minds *'Sadqe rad bala, qaul-i-Mustapha'* (*sadqa* removes bala, this is the assurance of the Prophet).

The items used in *khairat* and for *sadqa* are also different and suggest that the two forms of giving reflect somewhat different underlying notions. While *khairat* could be of any number of things – clothes money, food, festive or ordinary, virtually anything that a poor person might need, *sadqa* typically was restricted to a few items: money, wheat in the form of grain or cooked as bread or *chappatis*. Sometimes lentils were also given. Clothes, fruits, or foods associated with festive occasions were never associated with *sadqa*.

Sometimes the term *sadqa* was used interchangeably with the term *utara* (literally taking down) often used in conjunction with the idea of removing the effects of the evil eye. In such a case, the victim was encircled with a chicken or an egg or a sheep's lung which were then given away. The egg would be thrown away. These forms of giving were referred to as *jan ka sadqa* (*sadqa* of a life) which could involve even the sacrifice of a goat the problem was sufficiently grave. Interestingly the term *utara* was never used for the sacrifice of a goat, perhaps because of the association of a goat with the sacred sacrifice done on the occasion of *Bakri Idd* or the sacrifice at the *aqiqa* (ritual shaving of hair of an infant). It is also to be marked that money could be substituted for goat, but not for a chicken or an egg. While people said there was no question of transferring the evil, on the other hand they felt uncomfortable about the idea of eating it, or even having it in their house once the *utara* had been done.

Informants stressed that *sadqa* should be given as soon as possible to someone who is in great need. A common explanation for searching out such a person was that when a really needy person gets timely help, that person will spontaneously and from the heart cry out in gratitude, and supplicate God that such a generous person should be rewarded. My informants felt that such sincere prayers are sure to be answered.

Apart from the crisis situations that were experienced personally by individuals and which then motivated the giving of *sadqa*, some people also give sadqa during the first thirteen days of the month of Safar, when the Prophet had been ill. Tuesdays and Thursdays were also sometimes associated with days that are dangerous, and some people said they like to give something away at these times also, as a protection from the evil of these days.

One can contrast the *sadqa* with *zakat*, the compulsory poor tax, which is required of every individual who have any surplus left after attending to their needs. The ideas associated with *zakat* are not the same as the ideas associated with *sadqa*. For one thing, the *zakat* was considered a way in which one purifies one's wealth, so that there is *barakat* (blessing which causes abundance) in it. While it was understood in a general way that *zakat* should be given to needy person, it was not mentioned as specifically as it was with *sadqa* that the person should be in dire need. In fact, *zakat* could also be given to one's own family members if they were less well off, and this was mentioned as a primary duty, to help one's own before helping others.

Interpreting the Rituals

One can view these rituals from several different viewpoints and analytic frameworks. A straight functional interpretation enables us to see how people deal with the exigencies of the everyday world and the problems over which they have no control through the two practices described above. The *niyaz* brings in a system of ideas relating to the holy person or *wali*. The Sufi stream in Islam was always been able to accommodate people of a variety of persuasions and levels of spiritual development, from the most simple to the most learned. Many have deplored the decline of the Sufi centres which historically provided sanctuaries and centres of learning, and have commented on the fact that they have become centers of miracle and magic. Be that as it may, we can still see that this simple ritual can give us many insights into the way Islam is understood and practiced in the Indian setting.

At the most obvious level, we can see that the individuals who perform these rituals periodically, and at moments of crisis, remind themselves of the holy persons whose spiritual attainments have made them extraordinary in the history of Islam. Time or space does not limit approaching these persons. The people I interviewed said that it is said in the Quran that the *walis* do not die so that can be approached at any time since they are still alive. The transferring of merit which is an intrinsic part of the ritual, links the individual to the community of Muslims, starting from the Prophet, who is the fountainhead of the religion, to Shaikh Abdul Qadir Jilani who is buried in Baghdad, the believing men and women in the whole world over time and Haji Pir who links them to their origin in Kutch. The performance of *niyaz* in this way locates the individual in terms of his or her own local history and also connects the individual to the larger community of Muslims. The presence of food items, are reminiscent of the Prophet's preference (milk and sweet items) remind people that he was a human being with simple tastes. At the same time, the consecration of the food can be seen as the bringing together of the spiritual and the material through the mediatin of the Quran, the very means through which the Revelatin brought the message of God to human beings So also, in the faith that the *wali* can supplicate God for help in solving mundane this-worldy problems, we could infer there there is a paradox in that a persn who is recognized for his highly spiritual attainments, can play a role in helping to overturn the most material and mundane events.

The *sadqa* reveals interesting interplays between local factors and the ideas emanating from classica texts While there is little research on the different ways in which charity is done among Muslims, an interesting point of comparison can be seen with *dan* among the Hindus. Raheja (1988) discusses, the *warpher* as a form of derived from two wards *'warna'*, to make an offering to ward off inauspiciousness; and *'pherna'* 'to circle'. *Warpher* occurs most frequently during the course of wedding rites, but als in connectin with rituals of childhood, and it consists in the circling of small dishes of grain or other items over the head of the subject of the ritual, from whom the inauspiciousness is sought to be removed Through the actin hindrances are said to be removed from the body; the grain or other item is then given to the appropriate recipient as *carhapa*" (ibid). From Raheja's study there appears to be a striking similarity between her findings regarding the use of certain items as appropriate for situatins when misfortune is to be removed, and these same food items in the context of the Kutchi Memons. The giving of *dan* for instance in the measure of one and a quarter amount, the choice of grain and oil, are all items which Raheja has described as being appropriate for the transferring of evil. They are all given in situations where there is a problem which needs to be removed. The situations in which the giving of *sadqa* was in the form of kind (wheat, bread, oil, grain) are by and large linked with similar contexts. This aspect of *sadqa* therefore appears to be part of the wider culture in which this community of Kutchi Memons also participate. The sense of uneasiness that some persons felt with reference to the giving of some of the items of food and grain are also further indicative of this. We can also see a striking similarly between the *niyaz namahs* and the *vrat kathas* that Hindu women read for much the same purpose. It is the identification of such kinds of similarities that has often led to the statement that Islam in India is synergetic, combining elements from the local culture, with the normative or classical prescribed practices. However, while these correspondences and similarities can be noted, I would like to suggest that we can see different dimensions if we explore another feature of the rituals.

In much of the literature on Islam there is a tendency to emphasise the classically recommended practices of five pillars (the statement of faith, the ritual prayer, the poor tax, the pilgrimage and the fasting of Ramadan). These requirements which identify the practice of Islam, are sometimes seen as unbending and ritualistic, giving rise to statements such as that Islam is 'orthoprax' rather than 'orthodox'. However, it must also be noted that apart from the ritualized prayer in which the words, actins and timings are fixed, there is also *dua* or supplicatory prayer, which is also an intrinsic part of the prayer. In the *dua* the individual is able to move away from the fixed ritual, and speak to God from the heart. It is this institution that I would like to explore in a little more detail as it is common to both the forms of protection described above.

Izutsu (1964) in his structural study of the Quranic world view, points out that communications with God is a two-way process. God has communicated to humans through the Quran, and humans in turn can communicate to God through the *dua*, or supplicatory prayer. The Quran itself distinguishes between the two. The former is fixed, ritualized and unchanging, to be said in the sacred language, while the *dua* is spontaneous prayer that comes from the heart. An especially salient aspect of *dua* is that in *dua* the believer calls on God with the idea of expecting a response. Izutsu (ibid) discusses *dua* as corresponding structurally to Revelation in that while Revelation is direct verbal communication in the descending direction from God to man, *dua* is direct verbal communication in the ascending direction from man to God. He points out the like Revelation this can only occur in a very special form under unusual situations. "Only in an extraordinary situation, when man finds himself in an unusual state of mind, when for some reason or the other his mind has been strained almost to a breaking point, is he in a position to address words directly to God. In such a situation, man can no longer be man in an ordinary sense: he is .... Necessarily transformed into something above himself." (ibid).

The virtues of *dua* are often elaborated in booklets that are available in small stalls and bookshops These take the help of the traditions in explaining the basic tenets of the religion. They also elaborate on the theme of *dua*, seeking to bring to the attention of people the importance of calling on God for even the most insignificant and ordinary needs. They elaborate on the virtues of *dua* and illustrate how to enhance its effectiveness. For example, the Book "Etiquette of Life in Islam" (a book commonly available in Islamic bookshops) stresses that humility, sincereity, righteous disposition and faith are important in *dua*. Sacrifice, alms feeding the poor and hungry or offering superogatory worship or fasting are also recommended as enhancing the possibility of the fulfillment of petitions Traditions describe the significance of *dua* in fostering a sense of humility before God, since the believer in asking God for help expresses his own helplessness Traditions also give certain times and places as being especially efficacious for *dua*, such as *dua* recited at the Kaaba, or on the night of the *Lailat ul Qadar* (a mysterious night in the month of Ramazan when, it is believed, the whole of the animal and vegetable creation down in humble adoration to Allah).

The *niyaz* and the *sadqa* can be considered structurally similar in that in former case, the merit from reading the Quran is sent to the *wali*, and in the latter some material objects, like money or grain is given to the needy person. In both cases, it was a kind of expectation that the *dua* of these people would be heard by God, and answered Is there a significance in the choice of recipient? Is there any link between the choice of recipient of *sadqa* of the needy person, and the recipient of merit of the Quran by the *wali*? If we compare Raheja's findings (ibid) regarding the recipients of *dan*, we find that despite the superficial similarities in the occasions for giving *dan*, and the items that are considered appropriate for giving *dan*, there is a clear difference between the two situations as regards the ideas pertaining to the appropriate recipient. In Raheja's case the recipients were guided by a 'we/other' dichotomy since the idea of transferring evil had to g to someone who was not one's own. In the case of my informants the recipients were persons, who were described as being extremely '*mohtaj*' or 'needy'.

The recipient of the merit of reciting the Quran were the *wali*. I would like to suggest that there is a certain correspondence between the recipient of *sadqa* and the *wali* in that both are considered to be in a state that brings them close to God. The *wali* is a transformed person. He is no longer as distant from God as the ordinary human being who commits sins and misdemeanors at every point. The power of his *dua* relates to this. Similarly, the needy person (*mohtaj*) is in a state of great despair. He too, we can say, is transformed by his extreme misfortunes, such that when he calls out to God, God listens. The choice of recipient for the merit from prayer and the *sadqa* appears to me to be related to these considerations. The ordinary person, who considers himself a *gunahgar* (sinner) because of all the misdemeanors of everyday life, is not in a state where he has come close enough to God to approach God directly.

We could ask an additional question. Why are alms given in a state of distress and why does the afflicted person not simply do a *dua* himself and consider that adequate? To get a clue to this we can look at the ideas of why crises come in the first place, and the significance of charity.

Some of my informants who were well read regarding the Islamic Traditions said that one should not be unhappy over small illnesses and misfortunes, since they are a substitute for the more severe punishment that may await one in the grave. If such illnesses strike, it means that one is paying for some sins here in life itself. In other words, there is a connection, not perhaps uppermost in everyone's mind, that misfortunes are a result of some sinful deeds.[3] We must not lose sight of this when we look at the significance of almsgiving. *Sadqa* too is associated with the expiation of sins. If illness is seen as a result, in part from having been sinful, then the giving of charity may be seen as a rite of passage through which the individual tries to purify himself, and in so doing to change the external circumstances also.[4]

Concluding Comments

The analysis of Islamic ritual in the context of different societies and cultures has often been hindered by an opposition made between the normative rituals versus the variety of rituals that may be found in any particular community or society at any given time. As mentioned in the beginning of this paper,. The place to be given to the text, or to classical Islamic ideas in anthropological investigations, is also an issue that has provided a challenge to anthropologists. Many times anthropologists have not been sufficiently conversant with the texts to be able to take help from them in interpreting the observations in the field. I have tried to illustrate that no simple opposition can be made between the 'classical' and the 'local'. In the Indian situation, many Muslim communities have practices that are common to the practices of the local population. These perhaps provide a link of empathy and understanding between the communities at one level. The existence of such practices, outside the textually prescribed practices, has sometimes led the orthodoxy to zealous attempts to 'reform' the population by removing all such 'accretions'. A closer look at the rituals, however, can provide insights which do not allow for such a simple formulation. It is necessary and important to develop an anthropological approach in the Indian situation, which allows us to see the interplay of the various factors at work in the practice of ritual. I have tried to suggest that looking at the practices closely, and taking the help of classical ideas, the ground situation can better be approached in all complexity.

NOTES

1. This has been discussed in several articles A review of the problems can be seen in Tambiah (1970), among others.
2. The same recitation of verses, when done on the occasion of a death anniversary or for remembrance of the dead of one's own family is usually referred to as a *Fatiha* (after the first verse of the Quran which is always recited on these occasions, and whose recitation is considered to be equal to the merit derived from reading the entire Quran). The terms are fairly interchangeable for the ritual, since the procedure is exactly the same for both.
3. The following Traditions of the Prophet support this idea "This is God's rebuke of His servant by means of fever or misfortune with which He afflicts him, even such a matter as something He puts in his sleeve and grieves for when he loses it. The result is that the servant comes pure out of his sins as the pure gold comes out of the crucible." Tirmidhi (Robeson 1963: 325).
4. This line of thinking was suggested by the analysis in Abu Zahra (1988).

REFERENCES

Abu Zahra, N. (1988), "The Rain Rituals as Rites of Spiritual Passage". *Internatina Journa of Middle East Studies*, Vol. 20, No. 4: 507-529.

Durkheim, E. (1976), *The Elementary Forms of the Religius Life*. Great Britain: George Allen and Unwin (first published 1915).

Eicklman, D. (1982), "The Study of Isam in Loca Contexts", *Contributins to Asian Studies*, Vol. 17: 1-16.

Encyclopedia of Islam (1961), Leiden: E.J. Brill.

Geertz, C. (1960), *The Religion of Jawa*. New York : The Free Press of Glencoe.

Haq, A. n.d. The *Standard of Urdu Dictionary*. Delhi: J.S. Sant Singh and Sons.

Izutsu, T. (1964), *God and Men in the Koran*. Tokyo: Kei Institute of Philological Studies.

Khan, A.W. (1982), *Etiquettes of Life in Islam*. Delhi: Markazi Maktaba Islami.

Platts, J. (1984), *A Directionary of Urdu, Classical Hindu and English*. Delhi (first published 1822).

Tambiah, S. (1970), *Buddhism and the Spirit Cults in North-East Thailand*. Cambridge: Cambridge University Press.

RELIGION AND RELIGIOSITY IN RURAL BANGLADESH: ISLAMIC INSTITUTIONS IN REALITY

Md. Shairul Mashreque

Introduction

Sacred values continue to provide a nexus within which various segments of peasant population are organized into a unified community. Religious organizations in Muslim dominated villages crave for peaceful co-existence within a pattern of unification based on such values. Islamic institutions as embodiment of *Shariat*–based sacred value orientation provide a moral basis of community organization that is poised for regulating individual and social action of the Muslim society.

The community organization at the rural base is relatively stable and as such a functional entity with pre-existing religious values, precepts and meanings. Islamic institutions contributes to ideological indoctrination of the Muslim peasants crating a cluster of operative values that are instruments of maintaining stable equilibrium among divisive forces of development . Operative values tend to promote participation of the ordinary mass of peasants in rituals and festivals on the basis of equality and fraternity. On the rural communities are beset with some sort of confrontation as controversies crop up over interpretation of religious values and because dogmatic outlook of the dominant religious personalities militate against institution building and distinctive social movements. Even then the villages in general find genuine peace process in pre-existing socio-religious institutions and rituals that are forces of social integration. In fact socio-cultural institutions in traditional peasant communities have religious contents.

The present paper is based on both primary and secondary sources. The primary sources have been tapped from the available ethnographic accounts contained in villages studies. Besides, a large part of the qualitative treatment is drawn upon the author's empirical insights about social formation in a number of rural areas in Bangladesh.

Institutional Significance

The very nature of institutional perspective in Muslim communities shows an inherent impulse to put emphasis on the methods from the *Holy Quran* and *Sunnah*[1]. From times immemorial the believers look to the institutions like mosques, *mazars* (saint's graveyard), shrines, etc. for moral and spiritual development. They have seemingly generated value premises that regulate man's orientation to socio-cultural life. The 'valuative' and 'normative' framework of religious institutions are directed at divine unity, humanism, enlightment, universal complementaries and interactive network of relations conductive to wide-ranging cooperation and equity participation.

Empirical conditions in terms of the functioning of the Islamic institutions may help us to take cognizance of the social forces controlling human relationship and interaction. In other words, a careful study of functional relation within the institution itself may explore many things about the practice of Islam and also about dysfunctional features of traditional societies – we mean positive and negative implications of religion. Lewis (1958: 249), who writes of a village near Delhi, has aptly stated :

> "The Indians are essentially religious as the Europeans are essential secular, Religion is the alpha and omega of Indian life."

This statement holds good in so far as rural Bangladesh is concerned. Religiosity rituals and beliefs sufficiently echo the influence of Islamic institutions in binding the villagers into a district community.

Of the ceremonies observed by the villages every year as auspicious moments, many testify to religious significance. For example, *Ramzan*[2], *Eid-ul-Fitr* and *Eid-ul-Ahza*[3], *Shab-I-Meraj*[4], *Shab-I-Barat* and *Shab-I-Kadar*[5], *Muharam*[6], *Ziafar*[7], *Vishaistema*[8] and *Idd-E-Miladunnabi*[9] are observed in a befitting manner every year. The

Muslim also attach importance to the rituals connected with life cycle or rites-of-passage, for example : birth, naming, circumcision, marriage and funerals (Mashreque 1995, Sarkar 1997). These are the occasions for observing the nature of interaction among various persons or groups. Roles are well defined according to ritual status for organizing religious activities and arrangement of rituals.

"Muslim believe in one God and follow the way of life laid down for them by the Prophet" (Sarkar 1997: 11). Such a belief is an expression of deep respect for the *Tawhid* (Divine Unity) as the 'primal epistemology of the Islamic world view' (Chowdhury 1997). The Quranic commdants are by and large followed by the *Momin* (staunch believers). They are devotees following the rituals prescribed by the *Holy Quran* praying five times a day and attending weekly and periodic religious congregations. Those who are not practicing *Shariat*[10] are concerned about maintaining holy social atmosphere and the piety and purity of the religious institutions. The believers are deeply moved by the realization that there is a life after death; the sinners will be cast in the hell for misdeeds and the good souls will live in peace in heaven for pious life and merit. The Muslims believe that those who have gone astray from the right path will be severely punished even in the grave until the *Qiamant* (doomsday); for righteous persons the grave will be turned into an abode of peace similar to heaven. "Muslim expect to remain in their grave until the resurrection, when on the day of judgement, they will be sent to *Janant* (heaven) or *Jahannam* (hell) according to their deeds" (Sarkar 1997: 11).

Sacred values are intended to humanize community organization with all the necessity attributes of humbleness, sublimity, humanity, self-restraint, honesty, sense of ju8stice, gracious conduct proper desire and perfect human nature. They serve as an axis for moral, spiritual and humanitarian development to bring about well being to the generality of the community. For example the institution of *Zakat* (a redistributive mechanism). *Maroof* (good deeds) and *Waqf* (religious endowments) purport to facilitate fair distribution of wealth, charitable contribution in the form of cash or kind, micro-enterprise development and poverty alleviation in rural communities. They may pave way for proper utilization of resources and co-operative through a perfect receiving system and broadway participation.

Studies on Peasant Societies

The studies on peasant societies (Lewis 1958; Zaidi 1970; Ellickson 1972; Maloney *et al.* 1981; Zaidi 1988; Mashreque 1995; Sarker 1997) present the dimension of religiosity and its institutional role in regulating peasant's orientation to cultural style, individual and collective action, individual judgement, ethics, rationality, power, leadership and governance. Drawing upon empirical insights from these ethnographic accounts we are given to understand that a cluster of customs and practices dictated by religion is a 'fixed idealized category' that make up cognitive orientation of the peasants.

Peasant communities in Bangladesh are typically rural with pre-existing customs and practices of quasi-religious significance (little traditions) that allow for wider community participation in the significant events on the basis of equality thus creating the condition of unification and cooperation rather than disintegration and confrontation in strictly ideal settings. Traditional peasant communities in Bangladesh characterized by subsistence economy, inadequate socio-economic infrastructures, obsolete technology and mass illiteracy continue to nurture little traditions that are an amalgam of Islamic precepts and local practices.

The villages have been socalised in a traditional environment to show respect to Islamic institutions although many cannot practice Islamic tenets in a ritualistic manner. They have deep regards for the religious personalities like *Imam* (officiating priest), *Momin* (strong believer) and *Pir* (spiritual leader/saint). Many aspects of social organisation at the rural base are moulded by the religious personalities in the spirit of religious ideas. In the continuing process of socialization under the impact of socio-religious institution the Muslims have developed a common cultural background. Aziz (1979: 17-18), spelled out some featuers of Muslim cultural background that constitute prescription and proscription syndrome[11].

Spiritual in Islam institutionalized by syncretistic values has permeated rural life in Bangladesh. Here religiosity in a spiritual environment is manifest in the marked inclination of the villagers to the institutions like *Pabitrasthan* (holy places), shrines, and *Mazars* (saint's graveyard). The villagers strongly believe in the efficacies or *tabiz* (arms), *jharfuk* (charms and incantation), *mannat* (sacred pledge to make offering) an *parapam* (blessed water) for curing diseases.

Saint worship is believed to bestow immense divine blessings for material and spiritual benediction. Institutionalised relationship finds expression in a dyadic contract between *pir* and *murid* (follower). The *pir* personified as a path-finder and *murshid* an embodiment of *marifat* (highest form of spiritualism) as such. He moulds the perception of his followers in the spirit of syncretistic ideas. The villagers hold out the impression that the institution of *pir* representing the highest form of spiritual development is a vehicle of communication between the Almighty and the people. It is widely believed that proximity to Allah is obtained only through spiritual guidance from the *pir*. Syncretism obtains alimentation from the penetrating influence of Sufism that spread far and wide in Southeast Asia. Sufism proclaims 'highest working of mind' to stimulate profundity of perception about organic and superorganic phenomena. It developed a powerful proseletysing thrust through the formation of missionary orders (Aziz 1979:209).

The sufi saints carried the messages of universal love for mankind, communication between mind and soul and establishment of direct link to God. They came forward with spiritual mooring, lofty ideas, humanitarian appeals and popular movements that created sensation among the downtrodden masses.

In rural scenario mystical and devotional sons like *jari, sari, marami*, etc. are a clear pointer to orientation to syncretistic institutions. Some marks of this orientation are found in periodic *Urs mubark*[12].

Scores of villagers belonging to two religious communities – Muslim and Hindus – share esoteric traditions as legacies of the past. This is perhaps due to the fact that the sufi spiritual preceptors in the course of their efforts at influencing the ordinary masses under their fold came in contact with the Hindu spiritual personalities[13], Folk songs with indigenous musical instruments, folk literature, the daily movements of *boul* (roving mendicant) and *vaisnav*, visiting holy places and divine offerings are a reminiscent of such interaction pattern. Popular belief in ghosts, demons *jin*, cursed ponds and other supernatural forces and in the mysteries associated withy all inexplicable events has led the villages to take recourse to syncretistic institutions. Although 'materialistic idealism' or spiritualism facilitates superstition and fatalism it contributes to harmonious social construction, communal peace, development of broader vision about religiosity and wider community sentiment irrespective of caste creed and sect.

Description of the institutional significance of religion is incomplete without reference to the institutions like *Tabligh* and *Imam*. *Tabligh* stands out as the sacred continuum of associational significance that tends to prod and believes of all sects and subsects in common action. The *Momins* identified with this association are preachers moving from one place to another to call the attention of the people to the values of *Shariat*. Most of them wear *jubbah* (a long loose outer garment) symbolizing strongly fidelity and modeled behaviour of pious Muslims in traditional attire.

Persons involved in this institution are orthodox religious practitioners going out to visit many places with a purely religious mission. They would prefer to stay inside the mosque wherever they go. They, in several groups, sit around to mark food participation. As a matter of fact *Tabligh* is a non-profit voluntary organization consisting of believers with firm commitment who share more or less similar views on religious issues. Persons associated with *Tabligh* party render services in various institutions and public bodies. Of course many are retired officers, academicians and technocrafts.

The volunteers in a *Tabligh* party are organized into small groups for the purpose with deep-seated conviction. Some go out to visit rural areas to guide the villagers in a face to face situation with simple approach. The objective is to inspire them to get to learn the meaning and significance of *Namaz* (prayer). Visits by a *Tabligh* party as outsider with sacred purposes and the warmth with which the villagers receive them indicate villagers' social association with the persons who find delight in fulfilling sacred obligations.

With its static missionary orientation the institution of *Tabligh* does not seem to have much to contribute to social development. Several small groupos in this institution are not progressives in outlook being influenced by traditional orthodoxies. They do not have any dynamic programme to approach the poverty stricken villagers with humanitarian components of participatory social development.

In rural Bangladesh the administration of religious affairs is likely to be the function of the mosque committee consisting of village headman, the *Imam* land a few prominent figures. The *Imam* is thought to be the interpreter of Islamic precepts. As an officiating Muslim priest he is fully preoccupied with purely religious functions. His prime duty is to upkeep sanctity of the institution like mosque. He is supposed to do his normal routine job – leading prayer five times a day and weekly *Juma* congregation inside the mosque. In a big religious gathering like *Juma-tul-bida*[14] and two *Idds*, he has to deliver sermons.

The *Imam* has a privileged position as social value is placed on sacred institutions in peasant communities. He preserves a modicum of control over socio-cultural affairs. Among other distinguished guests in any ceremonial feasts the *Imam* is invited. Even the village headman discusses with him matters relating to social development in recognition to his advisory role. Realizing *Imam's* institutional role the present government led by the Prime Minister Shaikh Hasina has planned to convert *Imam* Training Academy into a national academy. The government also stresses upon mosque based poverty alleviation programmes involving the well trained *Imam* in poverty alleviation and social development projects like conscientization, mass education, moral teachings, human service, income generation and nation building.

Mechanism as Social Control: The Role of Religion

Internal village administration endogenous to socio-cultural system is largely one of social control. In many a rural community in Bangladesh the religious status of some persons have put them in a position to exercise their influence on every aspect of community organization. The internal administration is designed to manage affairs relating to social control through mediation council, life cycle ceremonies, religious institutions and rituals. The social space of peasant society is defined by old order and social sanctions. The concern of internal administration is to ensure proper application of religious customs and hierarchical values. In fact the social actors are careful about cleansing the ideological community through 'rigorous rituals'. During holy *Ramazan* the mosque committee passed orders for regulating social life into a prescribed pattern of what ought to be done during this auspicious month. It is expected of the committee to stop any process repugnant to the values of *Ramzan*.

The mosque committee has the obligation to decide upon matters relating to *Zakat*, one of the five pillars of Islam[15]. The monetary contribution of the affluents in favour of the poor is deemed a compulsory obligation. It is binding upon them to give one fortieth of their income to charity. An important aspect of social control is connected with funeral. The internal village administration sees to it that every part of this ritual is well attended to in a rigorous manner. It is customary on the part of a dead person's family to pay *Kaffara* (expiatory money) if he is considered sinner for his misdeeds or if he never attached weekly congregration during his life time.

It seems that all ritual functions are strictly regulated by a cluster of social sanctions. The judicial function of the internal administration is intended to punish offences against ritual customs. Any body found grossly violating the codes of religiosity in diverse rituals is liable to punishment. The forms of punishment include, among other things, paying fine, shoe strokes, lashes and social ostracism. Sometimes the judicial administration tries to prevent those activities that may create social degeneration, sometimes it may take decision on the spot to punish those guilty of violating sexual norms and of indulging in anti-social activities like gambling, attending opera at midnight and taking harmful drugs.

Hence, internal administration has become a functional entity involved in regulating individual and collective life according to *Shariat*. It imposes certain prohibitions and restrictions so that each individual lives as pure as possible. The function of the mosque is to:

> "Read religious doctrines, to exhort its members to obedience to and practice of its precepts, to provide the physical facilities, to counsel members on personal problems and to serve as an agency of social control" (Bertrand 1958: 240).

The mosque committee is to make necessary arrangement for holding *Idd* prayer with physical facilities. The committee members are expected to pass information to villagers regarding public announcement about the appearance of new moon if the sky is not scanned and the moon is not visible to herald the day of *Idd*. In the past announcement over electronic media on this behalf created resentment among the villagers as it was made late at night. However the villagers rely on the information of the village headman and officiating priest about public announcement so far as this matter is concerned.

Social sanctions intended to regulate human behaviour restricts women's participation and mobility. The conservatives in internal administration embark upon status behaviour in women, virtues of women's dignity and *Izaat* (honour). Being stranded in a close arena women follow the *purdah* system ordained by traditional leadership in Muslim villages (Mashreque and Amin 1993:86). Sarker (1950) refers to two aspects of the *purdah* operative in the Hindu and Muslim societies alike : physical and behavioural. The *purdah* system demands a complete seclusion of the women-folk and proper maintenance of virginity of the unmarried girls and chastity of married women. After attaining puberty a girl is expected to cover her head with veil and behave in a proper decorum. She is required to keep away from the company the male youth.

Negative Impact of Religious Institutions

In backward rural communities religious institutions are used as instruments of domination and exploitation. As the most ruralites are illiterate, quite unaware of the latest happening in remote placed the real message of Islam are far beyond their comprehension. Wrong interpretation of Islamic precepts promotes violation of human rights. On the one hand, it is wittingly done by the exploiters who trade on religion and on the other, orthodox fundamentalists untouched by the light of modern secular education, do it out of sheer ignorance about humanitarian content of Islamic tenets.

In the situational context of rural Bangladesh socio-religious institutions shape the peasants' world view and orientation about community power and about their own limited good and predicament. The impact of such institutional stereotypes on the peasant communities are number, reinforcing superstitions and fatalistic belief system other worldliness, non-material bias and uncritical acceptance of social explanation based on faith.

More participatory social development is plagued by the stubborn resistance of the orthodox *ulema* class. Basking in traditional prestige and prerogatives, *ulema* play advocacy role for notable power points and happen to react upon progressive social movement. In the backward peasant community characterized by low level of literacy and numerosity they indulge in village policies to reign supreme as mind elites. The militant *ulemas* are found agitating against development intervention of the NGO sector. A phenomenal growth of conflict between fundamentalists and the NGO activists presents an alarming situation. In many rural areas the *ulemas* in an attempt to resist doggedly against NGO activities sometimes hold militant rallies pressing home demand for the trial of so-called anti-Islamic elements and enactment of law against blasphemy and imposition of ban on NGO social movement.

Conflicts hovering around minor differences in religious matter threaten to weaken social foundation of the community. More often that not formation of two separate mosques divides a united village community. Differing interpretation of religious matters and conflicting views between two schools of thought: *Shariat* and *Marifat* (spiritualism) have led the believers to a state of utter confusion. On one side of the coin traditional orthodoxies are found on a strictly *Shariat* line prevent understanding of moral basis and human values of Islam. On the other side syncretistic values in the *Marifat* line distorted by the fraudulence of fake spiritual leaders and social touts are resented by the pious Muslims who want to rid Muslim community of all 'anti-Islamic' practices.

The prevalence of conflictual relationships with the Muslim community is because of marked differences among sects and sub-sects. There are two sects – *Sunni* and *Shia*. Besides, there is another group, *Qadiani*, which is a movement rather than a sect. The *Sunnies* are divided into five sub-sects : *Hanafi, Shafi, Hamboli, Malike* and *Ahlettadis* (Sarker 1997: 12). In the rural terrain of Bangladesh segmentation fermented by conflict, latent or manifest, has been found to be a common phenomenon. We have reports of sectarian conflict between *Shia* and *Sunni* and between *Sunni* and *Qadiani, Qadianis* are being treated as non-Muslims by some religious organizations. A celebrated English daily reported a fierce clash between the two rival *ulema* groups in a village in the district of Comilla, that left a man dead and 35 others injured. The local administration had to impose restrictions on gatherings to normalize the situation (*The Bangladesh Obsever*, Sept. 11: 1997).

Conclusion

This study shows the range of activities coupled with the instruments of social action that are oriented toward sacred values within the fold of Islam. The picture is thus straight forward about orthodox tendencies, moral basis and human values of religious institutions in peasant communities. The analysis helps our understanding of the significance of Islamic value framework in shaping the orientation of the rural masses. It also indicates the dynamics of community organization at the micro level with reference to various manifestations of religiosity and their constructive and dysfunctional aspects. It thus goes without saying that human conduct in any society is influenced by context rooted deeply in ideological framework and value system.

NOTES

1. Sunnah symbolize the ways of life of the Prophet accepted as valuative instruction and code of conduct.
2. During the lunar Arabic month of *Ramzan* every year the Muslims are supposed to do fasting, breaking it at sunset with *iftar* (special food prepared on the occasion).
3. *Eid-ul-Fitr* is observed on the first day of *Shawwal* (Arabic month) following the month of fasting. *Eid-ul-Azha* is observed on the tenth day of *Zilhaj* (Arabic month). In the Eids the Muslims go to the mosque or *maidan* (field) for offering special prayers, the only exception found in *Eid-ul-Azha* is the slaughtering of sacrificial animal according to prescribed religious customs.
4. *Shab-I-Meraj* is celebrated in observance of the remarkable arrival of the Prophet the *Meraj* (Space).
5. These two important religious festivals are observed by offering prayer for whole night at home or in the mosque. The former is observed on the night of the fourteenth day of *Shaban* (Arabic month) and the latter on the night of the twenty-sixty day of Ramzan.
6. *Moharam* is observed in commemoration of great *Karbla* tragedy with special street procession.
7. *Ziafat* means ritual feast usually offered by the solvent families after the death of family member.
8. *Visha Istema* is a special occasion for the staunch believers to join a large gathering. Pious Muslims all over the world arrive in Tongri near the capital of Bangladesh staying their for a couple of days to observe rituals in a large religious gathering until *Akheri Munajat* (last day of prayer with supplication) that concludes the occasion.

9. *Eid-e-Miladunnabi* is celebrated in commemoration of the birth of the Prophet with a profound honour. *Milad Mahfil* religious gatherings and special discussion makes the significance of the day.
10. *Shariat* is the basic and first stage of establishing communication with the God following the rigorous rituals set by Islamic precepts. It also denotes codes of conduct to regulate ways of life.
11. (i) Muslims eat beef, (ii) do not separate the head of a sacrifical animal from its body (iii) may wash hand on the eating plate after finishing a meal, (iv) may not defecate in an east-west (i.e. towards Macca) sitting position, (v) do not urinate in a western direction, (vi) circumcise male children, (vii) do not wear *dhoti* while praying, (viii) wear *topi* (cap) at the time of prayer (most elderly males wear it as an ordinary party dress), (ix) encouraged to wear a beard, (x) do not sleep or lie in bed with his or her feet in a westerly direction, (xi) need not change cloth used overnight by married men and women, (xii) women do not use vermilion or conchshell bangles, (xiii) widow may use luxurious clothing and ornaments, (xiv) music and drum beating in the mosque compound is prohibited, (xv) Muslims do not spread cow-dung mixed with water in a room or courtyard, (xvi) may do anything on their birth date day, (xvii) women are encouraged by religious leaders to observe seclusion from strangers, (xvii) Muslims choose most names from the Arabic and Persian languages, (xix) great by raising the right hand, (xx) prefer to use perso-arabic words, (xxi) do not prefer to breathe the last outside the dwelling house, (xxii) bury the dead, (xxiii) believe that the house of God is in the west, (xxiv) contract marriage and formally divorce (xxv) may change a marriage date and time.
12. People from all walks of life would like to join *Ursmubark.* The villagers –especially the poor – are found to be enthusiastic participants when all necessary preparations are made for the purpose. They trek to shrine to show deep reverence to Maizabhandan(great sand and soul) with devotional songs and *Jilair* (including *Allah Ho Allah Ha ....* to gain spiritual strength) Money thus collected from the well-to-do persons used to defray the cost of preparation including the feast.
13. Under the impact of this interactional pattern the Hindu spiritual personalities created a new movement – *vaisnavism.* They were the follower of Chaithnya the great Hindu spiritual leader and a religious reformers (Shahidullah 1963: 5).
14. It is a special weekly congregation attended by the Muslims as the last Friday during the month of Ramzan.
15. Five pillars of Islam are : *Kalema* (the faith that there is no God but Allah and Mohammed is His Prophet), *Namaz* (prayer), *Roza* (fasting), *Zakat* and *Haz* (pilgrimate to Mecca).

REFERENCES

Aziz, K.M.A. (1979), *Kinship in Bangladesh.* Monograph Series No.1 Dhaka: International Centre for Disease Research.

Betrand, A.L.(1958), *Rural Sociology: An Analysis of Contemporary Rural Life.* New York : Mc Graw Hill Book Company.

Chowdhury, M.A. *Lecture Series: Islamic Political Economy. Chittagong* : The International Centre for Islamic Political Economy.

Elickson, J. (1972), *A Believer Among Believers: The Religious Belief. Practices and Meaning of a Village in Bangladesh.* Unpublished Ph.D. Dissertation, Michigan State University.

Lewis, O. (1958),*Village Life in Northern India.* Berkeley: University of California Press.

Maloney, C. et al. (1981), *Beliefs and Fertility in Bangladesh.* Dhaka: International Centre for Disease Research. Bangladesh.

Mashreque, S. and R. Amin (1993), "Socio-cultural aspects of rural Development in Bangladesh", *Administrative Change, vol.XX* Nos. 1-2, July 1992 and June 1993.

Mashreque, S. (1995), *Kinship and Power Structure in Rural Bangladesh: A Case Study.* Chittagong: Homeland Press and Publications.

Sarker, P.C. (1980), 'Institution of Purdah between Hindus and Muslims in Bangladesh: A cross-cultural study', *The Spectra of Anthropological Progress.* Delhi: University of Delhi.

———(1997), *Social Structure and Fertility Behaviour.* Dhaka-Central Development Services (CDS).

Shadidullah, M. (1993), "Introduction," In M. Shahidullah and M.A. Hai (eds.) *Traditional Culture in East Pakistan* Dacca : University of Dacca.

Zaidi, S.M.H. (1970), *The Village Culture in Transition: A Study of East Pakistan Research Society,* Honolulu : East West Press.

Zaidi, S.M.I.A. (1988), *Politics, Power and Leadership in Rural India.* New Delhi: Commonwealth Publishers.

RELIGION AND SOCIETY AMONG THE SHIAS

Nadeem Hasnain

Introduction

Shias are one of the least studied religious minorities of the Indian subcontinent though Shiasim as a part of the religious ideology of Islam has got a fair share in social science literature. The present paper is largely an impressionistic account of the *Isna ashari* (twelver) Shias of Lucknow, one of the important seats of Shia culture in the world. I am presenting it as an 'impressionistic account' mainly because of the reason that it is not based on the any rigorous field work but in continuation of my earlier works on the same community.

The word Shia or Shiah like Islam, is an Arabic word which literally means 'a friend or followers' and in the present context the 'followers of Ali, first cousin of Muhammad and the husband of his daughter Fatimah' (TP Hughes 1885). The *Islamic Shi'ite Encyclopaedia* (1968) opines that this word is equally applicable to singular, plural, masculine and feminine without any variation. In general the term Shia is used for those who are devoted to Ali and his direct descendents called *Imams.* Thus, the term Shia has come to acquire a special connotation.

After the death of Prophet Muhammad the group closely affiliated to Ali, his cousin, associate and son-in-law, was called *Shia-tu-Ali* (the friends and devotees of Ali). The persons belonging to this group, while disassociating themselves from all others, formed a nucleous around Ali and believed in his *Imamate.* Thus, the term 'Shia' means all those who support the claim of Ali as the first and rightful successor of Muhammad. They consider Ali as the successor of Muhammad in temporal as well as spiritual matters. They hold unequivocal faith that Ali and the other eleven *Imams* were rightfully and divinely appointed to the *Imamate* of the Muslim community.

The Shia are in minority in the entire Muslim world, except Iran, where Shia Islam is the state religion. However, in Iraq, though they are believed to be the majority community, yet they do not exercise political power.

The present paper deals with the *Isna ashari* (twelve's or believers in twelve imams) Shias who constitute the overwhelming majority among the Shia community. The Shia being one of the two most important sects of Islam is further divided into three major sub-sects viz. *Isna ashari, Agha Khani Khoja* and the *Bohra.*

The *Isna ashari* Shias believe in twelve imams after Muhammad, the last as the hidden Imam believed to be alive and in hiding. Among the two remaining minor sub-sects, the *Agha Khani Khojas* maintain their faith upto the sixth Imam and branch out from this point following their own order leading to the present. Paris based Agha Khan, their Imam and spiritual head while the *Bohras* have faith upto the eight Imam beyond which they have their own line of spiritual heads the present being based at Bombay.

The major concentrations of the *Isna ashari* or for that matter the Shia of India are in Uttar Pradesh, Bihar, Jammu and Kashmir, Maharashtra (Bombay) and West Bengal (Calcutta). The Shias of Northern India and specially Uttar Pradesh (because of Nawabs of Awadh) hold the place of importance in the entire Shia universe of India and that is why they are the focus of the present study.

Religious System

The Shia Muslims share most of their religious beliefs and practices, the Great Traditions of Islam, with the rest of the Muslims. Hence emphasis is being laid, for the purpose of the narration and analysis, on those aspects which happen to be exclusive to the Shias with reference to the other Muslim sects. According to Shias, just as a tree has two parts i.e., roots and shoots (branches), the teaching of Islam fall under two categories :

- *(i)* *Usool-e-Deen* (Principles of religion) as roots of religion.
- *(ii)* *Furoo-e-Deen* (shoots of religion) as branches and leaves of the religion.

Usool-e-Deen implies the fundamental principles of religion. These are five in number and are *Tawheed* (oneness of God), *Adl* (justice of God), *Nubuwat* (prophethood), *Imamat* (guidance through the twelve Imams after the death of Muhammad) and *Qiyamat* (resurrection or the day of judgment). The first three are the fundamentals all the Muslims believe in while the Shias, in addition to these, also believe in the last two viz. 'Justice of God' and *Imamat* (belief in the twelve Imams after the Prophet), eliminating the institution of Caliphate.

The *Furoo-e-Deen* are (i) *Namaz* (prayers) offered five times a day but the Shias reduce it into three times – before sunrise, grouping the mid-day and pre sunset, and grouping the after sunset and midnight prayers. (ii) *Roza* (Fasting for one month) in a year in the month of *Ramzan*. (iii) *Haj* (pilgrimage to Mecca when one's means permits). (iv) *Zakat* (religious levy or poor rate). (v) *Khums* (also a religious levy for the welfare of the poor and needy equivalent to one fifth of the amount of an years' savings) and (vi) *Jehad* (holy war to defend Islam). According to the Shia belief *Jehad* is not possible in the absence of the twelfth *Imam* who is believed to be in hiding after his disappearance in 873 A.D. This, for all practical purposes, rules out any *jehad* on the part of the Shias though there is some difference of interpretation on this count. Of these six *furoo-e-Din* the Khums is exclusive to this Shias only.

Besides the above mentioned principles and doctrines the Shia faith also involves some more aspects of their religion exclusively held by them. Emphasis is being laid on these and hence being treated in a more detailed manner in this paper.

Ahl-e-Bait

The concept of *ahl-e-bait* is essential for a correct understanding of the Shia faith. Simply speaking it means the descendants of the Prophet Muhammad, through Fatima and Ali (including Fatima and Ali). Also pronounced as *ahlul bait* in Arabic diction it refers to "the people of the house"; a term used in the Quran (*Surah*, XXIV: 33) and in the *Hadis* (*Mishkat* XXIV: 21) for Muhammad's household" (TP Hughes 1885). Shia muslims are particularly devoted to the family of the Prophet – his cousin and son-in-law Ali, his daughter Fatima, and their sons, Hasan and Husayn – and the other Imams, succeeding leaders of the community and descendants of the prophet. "The Shi'i believe that these figures embody special holiness and spiritual power and knowledge through their relationships with the Prophet and his attachment to them" (John L. Esposito 1995). Relationships with the *ahl-e-bait* are intense and highly personal. Time and space are eliminated as the Shia believers think of them as their own brothers, sisters, mothers, fathers, sons and daughters. A popular Shia belief is that it is obligatory to love the *ahl-e-bait.* They believe that the two most precious things left behind by the Prophet is the holy book (Quran) and his *ahl-e-bait* and those who hold them steadfast will never be misguided. It obviously ignores and eliminates the popular Sunni belief in Caliphate.

Imamate

The *imamate* is one of the fundamentals of Islam but in Shia parlance it holds a different connotation. They believe that "just as it is necessary for Allah to send someone as a prophet, so it is also necessary for Him to appoint an Imam. It is necessary that at all times there should be an Imam to represent the prophet … showing them the way of goodness and prosperity in this world and the next" (Muhammad Rida-al-Muzaffar 1982). One of the greatest authorities on Shiaism, Allama Sayyid Muhammad Husayn Tabatabai, thus, says :

> "*Imam* or the leader is the title given to a person who takes the lead in a community in a particular social movement or political ideology or scientific or religious form of thought … the *imamate* and religious leadership in Islam may be studied from three different perspectives : from the perspective of Islamic government, of Islamic sciences and injunctions and of leadership and innovative guidance in the spiritual life. Shi'ism believes that since Islamic society is in dire need of guidance in each of these three aspects, the person who occupies the function of giving that guidance and is the leader of the community in these areas of religious concern must be appointed by God and the Prophet. Naturally, the Prophet himself was also appointed by Divine Command".
>
> (SMH Tabatabai 1981)

Therefore, Imam according to Shia faith, is the man who in direct succession to the Prophet, has the right to the absolute command of the Muslims in all religious and secular affairs. Thus the institution of *Imamate* begins with Ali and continues upto the twelfth Imam, Mehdi, who as per Shia faith is in hiding (*Imam-e-Ghaib*) and shall re-appear on the day of *Qayamat* to lead to the faithful to the paradise. In the physical absence of the last imam, guidance is taken from a recognized authority, *Mujtahid* (a high position of scholarship and learning). The very idea of an *Imam* in hiding is perhaps, a minority's inbuilt defence mechanism against religious persecution by the dominant majority. To a Shia believer, as I have gathered from my respondents, it gives him solace, confidence and security.

Ismah

The Shias believes that, like the Prophet, an Imam should excel the *Ummah* (believers) in all the virtues, such as knowledge, bravery, piety and charity, and should possess complete knowledge of the Divine Law. This qualification leads to *ismah* meaning infallibility. Shias believe that all the prophets are infallible and also that the *imams* too are infallible. *Ismah* means purity from all sins, both major and minor ones, and from mistakes and forgetfulness. Thus, the prophets and the Imams should be *masum* (free from error and sin). Only a *masum* coupled with his wisdom can perform the "esoteric function of interpreting the inner mysteries of the Holy Quran and the Shariah" (SMH Tabatabai, ibid). Hence only the *masum* (infallible) *imam* is worthy of *walayat* or the esoteric function of interpreting the Quran and the *Shariat*. Thus, the distinctive institution of Shiaism, the *Imamate* is inseparable from that of *Walayat* and *Ismah*. Most of the non-Shia Muslims do not follow this doctrine.

Taqqiyyah

This is the most misunderstood aspect of Shiaism. In the *Dictionary of Islam* (TP Hughes 1885), the author explains this concept in terms of "guarding onseself", a "pious fraud whereby the Shia'h Muslim believes he is justified in either smoothing down or in denying the peculiarities of his religious belief, in order to save himself from religious persecution. A Shia'h can, therefore, pass himself as a Sunni to escape persecution." Thus, *taqqiyyah* is dissimulation with the wider meaning of 'to avoid or shun any kind of danger.' Incidentally the same explanation is given by my Shia respondents.

In the entire history of Islam and Muslim societies, the Shia have been a threatened and persecuted minority including in India where they got protection wherever Hindu rulers ruled but often threatened and persecuted during Muslim rule, of course in varying degrees. Talking about the conditions under which a person could resort to *taqqiyyah,* Tabatabai writes :

> "The exact extent of danger which would make permissible the practice of *taqqiyah* has been debated among different *mujtahids* of Shiism. In our view, the practice of *taqqiyah* is permitted if there is definite danger facing one's own life or the life of one's family or the possibility of the loss of honour and virtue of one's wife or other female members of the family, or the danger of the loss of ones' material belongings to such an extent as to cause complete destitution and prevent a man from being able to continue to support himself and his family. In any case, prudence and the avoidance of definite or probable danger which cannot be averted is a general law of logic accepted by all people and supplied by men in all the different phases of their lives" (SMH Tabatabai 1981).

The critics opine that this practice goes against virtues of courage and bravery taught by the religion. But the qualities of bravery and courage could be perpetuated only if one survives, hence, as the respondents angrily retort, the demonstration of these so called virtues would be nothing but foolhardiness. This, definitely fits well in the worldview of a minority threatened by a vast majority.

Taqleed

An Arabic word, *taqleed* means to follow or to imitate (blindly). It refers to a practice of approaching a living *Mjthaid-e-Aalam* (the most learned guide of the world in religious affairs) for the interpretation of problems concerning religion with the intention of acting in accordance with his verdicts or pronouncements whenever the need arises. The verdict is known as *fatwa*. The *mujtahids* must pass comprehensive course of study in theology, law and other subjects. It is customary for Shias to select a *mujtahid,* to place himself under his *taqleed* and become his *muqqallid* (follower). Traditionally, the Indian Shias have been placing themselves under the authority of the Shia *mujtahid-e-Azam-e-Iraq* (the highest Shia *mujtahid* of Iraq). But lately, the religious authority of a *mujtahid* of Iran is also being adhered to by sections of Shias.

In this way, the Shia have always been divided on the basis of their preferences for one *mujtahid* or the other. Till the 19th century this *mujtahid* used to be so powerful that he used to interfere also in the non-religious affairs of his followers. But now the Shias took towards him for seeking guidance in the interpretation of religious issues only and he hardly commands any influence in secular matters. Significantly, *taqleed* of a dead *mujtahid* is also permitted (*Jaez*) on the basis of his *fatwas* left behind by him.

Religion and Society

"Religion is an important an even essential part of the social machinery as are morality and law, part of the complex system by which human beings are enabled to live together in an orderly arrangement of social relations" (Radcliffe-Brown 1952). Therefore, the social function of religion i.e. the contribution that it makes to the formation and maintenance of a social order may not be neglected or even underrated. Actually, every religion plays the same functionally significant role in maintenance of social order. Shiaism, too, influences the Shia society in a variety of ways. Apart from strengthening social and communal solidarity, it opens new avenues of ethics and morality as per its dictates and hence provides it's followers a particular code of social behaviour.

Among the Shia there are a number of occasions such as *majlis* (commemoration of Imam Husain's martyrdom at Kerbala) specially during the days of Moharram mourning and *mehfilor milaad* (commemoration of the birth of Prophet Muhammad and Imams) on which persons belonging to one *khandaan* or several *khandaans* (extended kin group) and friends assemble and spend some time together. Observance of *Azadari* (ritual mourning related with the tragedy of Kerbala) whose most important part is *majlis* during the two months of mourning is the best example of such congregations when the Shias assemble for the joint mourning. The size of gathering may stretch into thousands if the *majlis* is held in some popular *Imambara* and addressed by a popular *Zakir*. In such gatherings no segregation or distinction is observed between various socio-economic strata of the Shia. Some status differentiation may be observed sometimes if a majlis is held at an individual's place where sometimes some discriminatory treatment may be extended to the elite but in public *imambaras* there is total equality between all the mourners who come to pay their tributes to the 'martyrs of Kerbala'. Even the non-Shias or even non-Muslims are warmly welcomed[2] and the same amount of respect is paid to them by the host. The doors of *majlis* are open to everybody who wish to attend one. Actually, the *Azadari* plays an important and crucial role in a Shias' life. Imam Husain's self sacrifice imparts a number of outstanding lessons, such as to live with honour, self respect and dignity; to endure hardship and remain calm and peaceful in the face of trial and tribulation, to resist tyranny and aggression even at the cost of one's life; to realize that the grief for the loss of one's freedom must be deeper than the grief created by the loss of one's family, wealth and material possessions, and to appeal to the human sense of justice and sympathy by voluntarily undergoing sufferings for a just cause. Like the crucification of Christ, the *shahadat* (marytyrdom) of Husain has lent a halo to Shiaism.

The 'Tragedy of Kerbala' and the mourning related with it provides the Shias some sort of a 'psychological cushion' to absorb and withstand their own sufferings in day to day life. A *majlis* too follow as a part of post-death rituals in a Shia family and they try to derive consolation from the sufferings of Husain and his family. The usual 'punchline' in every *majlis* is the expression of the wish – 'we pray that the participants do not undergo or have to face any grief but the mourning of Husain. They draw parallels from the sufferings of Husain and his family and it provides them a healing touch or balm to their own sufferings. Thus, it is a popular saying in this part of the world that the 'heart of every Shia is a living tomb of Husain.'

The 'Tragedy of Kerbala' enacted thirteen hundred years ago offers such multicoloured scope for dramatic commemoration that kings and nobles and even well to do people over the centuries have utilized it for improving their own image in the eyes of the masses. Many Indian rulers, especially the Shia rulers of medieval Deccan – the Bahmanis, the Qutub Shahis, the more recent Nawabs of Oudh, the Nawabs of Rampur and even several Hindu rulers such as Scindias of Gwalior and the Raja of Benaras found in Muharram an excellent means of establishing a link, rapport and harmony between their Hindu and Muslim subjectgs.

Actually, in the mourning congregations called *majlis* not only the tragedy of Kerbala is narrated (which is the concluding part called *masaib* or tragedies) but the code of ethics and morality is also dealt with. Through these congregations one learns the lessons in virtues – equality, courage of conviction, honesty, truthfulness and righteousness etc. Thus, *majlis* serves as 'educational institution' in a Shia's life. Significantly most of the Shias derive knowledge about their religion, history, philosophy, ethics and morality not by going through books but by attending these *majlises*. With the growing materialism and status consciousness some of the Shias are also seen utilizing *azadari* and *majlis* for personal gains – image building, enhancement of social status, political gains or forging new relations and alliances with other groups. Distribution of expensive *tabarruk* (auguring articles like *prasada* distributed after some Hindu rituals like *Kathas*) is a means to display their wealth. Some persons, as the respondents report and also verified through empirical observation, may be seen using such occasions to propagate their political views or get political gains or to collect funds for any purposes. The *azadari* suffered a setback recently[4] as a result of increasing schisms and cleavage between Shia and Sunni population in Lucknow and adjoining districts, resulting in senseless violence.

Among the Shia, the ideals of individual virtue are many but honesty, truth and tolerance are the main three. These virtues are upheld in every religious text of the Shia. They believe that those who adhere to the path of honesty, truth, tolerance and industry will be rewarded by God on the day of judgement. Even the simple and initial religious texts they prefer for their children are full of praise for these virtues and ideals.

According to the Shia the major sins in the eyes of Allah are *shirk* which, in Arabic means to make anyone as a sharer in the authority and attributes of Allah (loosely translated as polytheism), murder, adultery, stealing, gambling, tyranny, consumption of intoxicants, back-bitting and false allegation (*bohtaan*). Miserliness is also considered an evil. Hoarding, black marketing and exploitation of labour are grave sins in the Shia perception of an ideal society. During the religious discourses and congregational prayers and priest delivers *Waaz* (sermon) in which these evils are condemned frequently and the followers are asked not to compromise on these issues. Regarding exploitation of labour some of the respondents quoted Muhammad as saying – "pay the labour before his sweat gets dried". Their most favourite, Ali the first Imam, earned his livelihood as a manual labourer who spent his whole life toiling in the orchards of the Jews to earn his livelihood and led an extremely simple life.

Another virtue that the Shia highlight is a definite attitude towards neighbours. According to them a maximum of forty households constitute a neighbourhood (*hamasaaya*). They believe that it is the duty of a Shia to be sympathetic to his neighbours and it is expected of them not to take meals until they ensure that none of their neighbours is hungry and starving. They quote the life of Ali and other Imams and their dictates as the sources of these 'commandments'.

In contrast to a small section, who has risen head and shoulder above their compatriots, the average Shia is not economically well off. And yet, like the proverbial poor Brahmin, he has to maintain his gentility and pride in his 'spiritual heritage'. Except in Iran, where Shiasim is the state religion, the Shias have been alway6s and everywhere, a minority; and like all the minorities they have been subject to the fear of persecution. But like most other such minority group0s these persecutions themselves have given an inner viability to them.

Like other minorities such as Brahmins and Jews, Shias have inherited a realization of the value of literacy. The overwhelming majority of Shias are found to be literate beyond the capacity to read and write. Their rate of literacy in India should definitely such higher than the National average and their share among the intelligentsia should be much more than their share in local population.

"The 'Iranian revolution' of 1979 and the emergence of Ayotollah Khomeini as a major force have brought about a perceptible change in the Shias' socio-religious behaviour" (Nadeem Hasnain 1988). They were exposed to a massive propaganda campaign through a vast amount of literature continuously pouring into India especially the cities with considerable Shia populations. As a result of the 'Khomeini Phenomenon' religiously has definitely increased among them. An increasing number of Shias are growing beards and going to mosques and size of Friday congregation has increased. Many Shia households display atleast one coloured portrait of Ayotallah Khomeini. The well versed Shias are vocally highlighting aspect of their religion. The long established lethargy and 'social inertia' of north Indian Shias, has to a substantial extent, given way to enthusiasm. They are trying hard to get more education and improve their economic lot. "Significantly, despite increased religiosity among them the yearning to achieve in secular affairs has also increased and the increased religiosity has not contributed to any alienation or disillusionment with India (Nadeem Hasnain, ibidA). The symbiotic relationship between Shias and India still seems to be as strong as ever because of historical reasons.

Acknowledgement

I am deeply indebted to my informants and respondents especially those who provided me deep insight into Shia religious beliefs and their impact on Shia society way back in 1972 in the wake of my fieldwork for my Masters dissertation on the Shias. Some of these respondents were again interviewed in 1986-87 as part of fieldwork for my research project on the Shias funded by the University Grants Commission. Again, some of the same respondents and a few more were interviewed for the present paper. Talking to some such persons over a period of 28 years has given me some idea about the attitudinal changes as a result of their new experiences, trials and tribulations.

NOTES

1. The persecution of Shias may be traced back to the times immediately after the death of Prophet Muhammad when the friends of Ali (*Shia*) sided with him and disassociated themselves from the Caliphs. When the contours of Shiaism were firmly established during the times of various Imams after Ali, the Shia have been a threatened minority everywhere. Ironically, they got shelter and patronage in India wherever Hindu rulers ruled. For details see *Imam in India and Pakistan* by Mrray Titus, 1959, Calcutta, YMCA Publishing House, *Tazkara –e-Majeed,* by SSH Hansvi, year not cited, Agra, *Mazar-e-Shaheed-e-Salis* and *Masaib-us-Shia* by Maulana Saadat Husain.
2. Moharram mourning is prevalent throughout India – a considerable section of Sunni Muslims and Hindus (especially of villages) also mourn the martyrdom of Husain. Among a number of Hindu peasant groups, Husain is another saint or *baba* who is shown reverence. The case of Mohiyal Brahmins, wherever they live, is a unique one. For details see *Shias and Shia Islam in India,* included in the list of references. A section of *Kashmiri Brahmins* are also known as *Husaini Brahmins*

REFERENCES

Al-Amin, Hassan (1968), *Islamic Shi'ite Encyclopaedia.* 2 (vols) Beirut : Publisher not given.

Al-Muzaffar, Mohd. Rida (1981), *The faith of Shia Islam.* Qum (Iran) : Ansariyan Publications.

Eposito, John L (ed.) (1995), *The Oxford Encyclopaedia of the Modern Islamic World* (4 vols) New York: Oxford University Press.

Hasnan, Nadeem & S.A. Husain (1992), *Shia and Shia Islam in India :* A Study in Society and Culture. New Delhi: Harnam Publications.

Hughes, T.P. (1992), *Dictionary of Islam.* Calcutta: Rupa & Co.

Tabatabai, Allama S.M. Husain (1981), Shia. Qum (Iran): Ansariyan Publications.

Radcliffe-Brown, A.R. (1952), *Structure and Function in Primitive Society.* London: Cohen & West Ltd.

NOMENCLATURE AND LEGITIMIZATION OF SAINT WORSHIP IN ISLAM

Hafeez-ur-Rehman Chaudhary

Introduction

It is not at all surprising that the traditions of saints (*zaddik*) and pilgrimages (*hillula*) were extremely powerful among the Jewish minority. Although Judaism goes back to the 14th or 13th century B.C., the genesis of the *zaddik* lies in the spiritual setting of the 15th and 16th century Kabbalists of Safad and other Palestinian towns. Among these Jewish mystics the tradition of prayer at the graves of rabbis and sages apparently began to take root (Deshen 1977). Grave sites became holy, powerful place-shrines and the legendary Talmudic sages and rabbis who were buried there took the form of the *zaddik*-pious, the righteous men, and ultimately, saints. Moreover, a tradition of making a pilgrimage to the grave of the saint on the anniversary of his death also developed. These periodic gatherings were known as *hillulot*, or memorial celebrations. Deshen describes the process in the following terms.

> The hillulot originally focused upon the death of especially pious men, a death that was seen to be a mystical union between the soul of the deceased and the God-head .... According to popular thought the belief developed that the zaddik (saint) in whose memory the celebration was held would intervene with God on behalf of his followers. Accordingly, persons who suffered from physical or mental illness might undertake a pilgrimage to the site of the zaddik in the hope and belief that their suffering would be lessened (Ibid: 110-111).

The rabbinic authorities typically condemned and sought to discourage these enthusiastic outpourings, but they confined to have widespread popular support, even spreading from Palestine to the other small Jewish communities located throughout the Middle East and North Africa. These traditions found a particularly sympathetic, not to say, luxuriant, environment in the *Maghrib*[1]. What Ben-Ami, the Israel folklorist, who has done the major documentary work on *zaddikim* in Morocco, calls "saint veneration" can be found throughout the North African Jewish communities (Ben-ami 1981). Indeed, his compendium of Moroccan Jewish *Zaddikim* lists more than 600 saints and their shrines, including dozen that were equally claimed and revered by both Muslims and Jews. Virtually each Jewish community had its "own" *zaddik*, and some places several local saints and shrines were worshipped. The *zaddik* were typically deceased Moroccan rabbis, although in other cases the shrine and the *zaddik* were named after Palestinian rabbis who had visited North Africa and died there. In still other instances, the shrined was named after a famed rabbi; the best known case is the Moroccan shrine of Rabbi Shimon bar Youchai, the Palestinian sage who was the reputed author of the *Zohar*, a book of mystico-religious cemetery, although in some instances "they were not in the cemetery proper, but in a special spot, for example, a cave , at some distance from it" (Goldberg 1983). A *zaddik's* grave was usually covered by a simple roof in order "to distinguish" it from among the tombs of famed marabouts. The fact that these shrines were located within the Jewish cemetery is itself important. Symbolically the Jews were is this way making a claim to exercise rights in the territory on an equal basis with that of the Muslims" (Ibid).

In common with the Muslim saints, the Jewish *zaddik* also possess *barkat*, or grace and holy power. The *zaddik* was believed to be able to act as an intermediary with God-prayer at the shrine and vows (*needs*) might result in the positive outcome desired by the supplicant. Beyond prayers, the true mark of a *zaddik* was his ability to perform miracles to heal the sick, bring about good fortune in love and bussines, cure barenness in women or provide male offspring, and, in addition, protect the wealthy exposed Jewish communities from their enemies. There also were important differences between *zaddik* and marabout, for example the miracles acts attributed to the latter were often "of amore spectacular kind".

With notable exceptions, moreover, there are no families or lineages of Jewish *zaddikim*; on the contrary, the saint was typically recognized after his death, and his descendants were not necessarily involved with his shrine. In comparison, the Muslim saints seem to have played much more active and critical political roles than did the *zoddikin* (Stillman 1982: 496).

In Buddhism the term *Arhat* is used for the saints, but his is not strictly correspond with the idea of the saints of history. These are rather the apostles of Buddha-sons, such as Anand the favourite disciple who did not win *'Arhat-ship'* till after Buddha's death[2]. The synonym term in Sanskrit is *muni* (means a hermit), which is used for an inspired saint, saint sage, holy man endowed with divine inspiration or one who has attained more or less divine nature by mortification and abstraction. In Sikhism the term *giani* (a learned men) is used for this purpose.

The orthodox saints amongst the Muslims form a heterogeneous group. Among the titles applied to them are *salik* (a traven in the world of Sufism), *faqir* (one who is wedded to poverty), *shaykh, mir, miyan* (chief master), *pir* (old *murshed), wal* (a friend, one who is very near), *abdal* (one ordained by God to handle administrative affairs of the world), *qutub* (pole, axis, pivot, the highest degree of sanctity among Muslim saints), *ghauth* (one to whom one may cry for help), and *Ghauth-al-Azam* (Shaykh 'Abd-al-Qadir Gilani), the head of them all'[4].

The word 'saint' is, therefore, the transation of many Arabic, Persian Urdu terms, *wali, murshid, shaykh, darvish, sufi, pir* or marabout (saint, shrine). According to Turner:

> "Arabic terms of marabout, *darvish, sufi, wali* cannot be translated into the Christian term of saint, because the history\, institutions and cultural frameworks of these religious are distinctive. The centralized complex and stringent process of canonization is crucial to the Christian understanding of saintship. Precisely because no such centralized, ecclesiastical machinery exists in Islam, there is no official or homogeneous terminology of maraboutism (saintship in Islam). When the Western anthropologists talk about Islamic saints, they use the term as a shorthand for a diversity of roles." (1975: 61).

In North Africa the term marabout is used for a Muslim saint or his descendants[5]. This term, which is derived from the 'Arabic *murabit* through the Portuguese marabuto (Spanish *marabito*), appeared under its present form in 1651 in the narrative of a traveler; for him the marabout is a "Muslim who devotes himself to the practice and the teaching of religion" (Block 1932). In the whole Maghrib, the classical marabit has given way to the dialectic form marabet (fem. *Marabtaq;* plur. *marabtin*[6]).

The institution of the *ribat* has gradually fallen into disuse in modern times; but the corresponding name *murabit* has survived, though changed a little in its original sense. This term is nowadays used only for Muslim saints, or, in certain cases, for their descendants.

Maraboutism was a major motif and generating power within Moroccan Islam (Geertz 1968; Westermark 1926). Eickelman's study (1976) of a Moroccan pilgrimage centre clearly summarized its main contours :

> "The most striking feature of North African Islam is the presence of marabouts .... They are persons, living or dead, to whom is attributed a special relation towards God which makes them particularly well-placed to serve as intermediaries with the supernatural and to communicate God's grace (*barkat*) to their clients. On the basis of this conception, marabouts in the past have played key religious, political and economic roles in North African society, particularly in Morocco ... A concrete indication of this is the proliferation of maraboutic shrines throughout the Maghreb .... In Morocco's rural areas, one rarely loses sight of the squat, whitewashed, and–in the case of the more popular ones –domed marabouting shrines. In towns more lavish shrines with green–tiled roofs are often found.

The themes underscored here–the marabout's *barkat,* his role as intermediary, the proiliferation of shrines–are basic elements in this pattern. The shrines served as pilgrimage points, and the more important among them grew into pilgrimage centres; the believers come there often to pray for the saint's intercession in various problems of daily living, and during the yearly festival dedicated to the saint entire group make the pilgrimage to the holy shrine, where they receive the blessings of the living saint. A few of these pilgrimage centres grew into small towns, replete with a market, numerous shrines, a religious lodge (*zawiya*) and various accommodations for pilgrims" (Austin 1983). To be sure the belief in saints was frequently attacked by the more orthodox Muslims theologians. Yet for many North African Muslims, maraboutism continuously to be a vital part of their religious belief system.

There is finally, another important dimension to maraboutism in the Moroccan Muslim tradition, *barkat* might be passed continuously along the generations, and saintly lineages played crucial political as well as ritual roles. In fact, the marabouts were frequently at the centre of local and regional political intrigue, and the long-lasting Moroccan pattern of periodic conflict between the central authorities, or *makhm* and the peripheral but powerful Berber tribes typically focused, upon the ambitions of the living saints (Eickelman 1976; Gelmer, 1969, 1981).

Traditionally speaking, the word *wali* is derived a room which in Semitic languages expresses the idea of adherence, attachment, more nearness. It means, firstly, one who is a close follower, friend or relative. In religious language the idea of nearness was extended also to the relation of man with God.[7] It generally means "someone who is close". In old Arabic usage the word was extended also the protector, helper and patron. Curiously enough, it also applied to divinely venerate beings of whom man believes that they help those who venerate the *Wali*, the devout, pious man, became *Wali* equipped with the attributed miracles (charisma, karamat), the intermediary (*shafi*) between God and man.

About term *shaykh*, Currie says:

> "The word *shaykh* has a variety of meanings–a venerable old man, the chief of a tribute or head of a village, a new convert to Islam[8]. But it is also used as a title which encompasses both the roles implied by *murshid*, and is, therefore, more useful as both functions tend to be performed by the same person. Thus, an Indo-Muslim, when referring to his *shaykh*, will often talk of his *pir-omurshid*.
>
> "It is misleading for the terms Sufi, *dervish, faqir* to be translated as 'saint'. They are wide-ranging in their meaning, and it is difficult, therefore, to be specific in their definition. For instance, a *shaykh, murshid*, or *pir* might define himself as a *faqir, dervish* or sufi but not all *faqirs, dervishes* and Sufis qualify as *shaykhs* or *murshids or pirs.*[9] A sufi is one who ends towards the mystic life as it has developed within the framework of Islam, whereas a *dervish* or *faqir* is one who is attached full-time to the religious life either as a dependent of a sufi establishment or as an independent wandering mendicant." (Currie 1989: 4)

The distinction between sufi and *darvish* (or *faqir*) is the difference between theory and practice. Whereas the sufi follows a mystical theory or doctrine, the *dearwish* practices the mystical way, the main difference being on the emphasis in practice. Some Sufis are predominantly intellectuals or of creative imagination, like Ibn-al-'Arabi, while others are *dervishes,* all feeling, emotion and action. In both instances Sufis and *dervishes* dispense with a guide and rely solely upon themselves (though frequently allowing for a spiritual guide), passively or actively, to achieve the annihilation of self and direct absorption into the divine Reality, one by intellectual exercises, the other by psycho-physical practices.

Also involved is the distinction between the sufi and the *malamati* (blameworthy ones), Abu 'Abda-Rahman as-Sulami (d. 1021) regarded the *malamatis* as the highest grade of God's slaves, above both the legalists (*fugaha*-class) and the theosophists, ahl-al-ma'rifa. He called the second category, the *khwas,* as Suffiya. The *malamati,* according to him, is one whose veins are saturated with the nourishment of pure virtue, who is really sincere, who does not want anyone to be acquainted with his ecstatic states and experiences. He is ready to be despised by men that he may lose himself in God. A *malamati* rejects all outward show, does not wear the special dress which characterized the sufi, and has no initiating *sheikh* though he is ready to seek guidance.

This distinction between a *malamati* and a *qalandari* is that the former hides his devotion and the latter externalizes it and even exploits it by going out of his way to incur blame. Confusion has been caused because of the derivation of the name *malama* (blame). Shahab-ud-din Sohrawardi writes:

> The term *qalandariah* is applied to people so possessed by the intoxication of 'tranquility of heart' that they respect no custom or usage and reject the regular observance of society and mutual relationship. Neither do they concern themselves with those earthly pleasures which are allowed by the indulgence of divine law.... The difference between the *qalandari* and the *malamati* is that the *malamati* strives to conceal his mode of life while the *qalandari* seeks to destroy accepted custom. *Qalandari* characteristics included the wearing of a distinctive garment, the shaving of head and facial hair with the exception of the moustache[10], the performation of hands and ears for insertion of iron rings as symbol of patience ... of which are forbidden (Trimingham: 267).

The terms *pir* and *murshid* are also controversial. These are used most confusingly by writers on the subject. The varying opinion on the meaning of the two words have been summarized by Mayer:

> Darling distinguishes between the *pir* as a healer (using this as a general term for the person who solves specific physical problems) and the murshid as guide (using this term to denote the giver of general moral and spiritual exhortation and teaching). Wilber distinguishes between the *murshid* as the spiritual preceptor and member of a sufi order and the *pir* as the centre of the cult of saint worship and Westphal-Hellbush marks, 'the *murshids* were and are holy-men, otherwise called *pir* or *faqir* but, in their capacity as spiritual leaders, they are called *murshid*. On the other hand, a number of writers use the two terms synonymously when speaking of the role of a spiritual guide. Titus, for example, states that "the spiritual guide is known as the *murshid, pir* or *shaykh*", and O'Brien speaks of the necessity of having a *pir* or *murshid*, spiritual adviser, a guide on the right path. (quoted in Currie 1989: 33-4).

Mayer (1967: 162-4) suggests that while both *pir* and *murshid* may refer to the role of a spiritual guide, *murshid* is not used to the role of a healer. He supports this conclusion with his observations. However, this distinction is more ideal than real. More people do not see any diference between the two words and refer them as interchangeable. An explanation of this twin usage is that was originally a Pesian word and the other Arabic. There is some truth in it because in common parlance the term *pir-o-murshid* is common everywhere.

So far as the qualities of a *pir* are concerned, an individual need to possess an ability to perform *karamat* (charisma, a sort of miracle) descent from the Prophet or his grandsons, connection with a prestigious sufi *silsilah*, a mastery of Islamic doctrines and sufi texts. A *pir* should have all these qualifications, or a combination of them.[12]

The possible combinations of these qualities could give rise to *pir* who approximates to the ideal portrayed in sufi hagiography – art of the greatest learning and spirituality, who guides his disciples along the mystical path and dispenses help and advice to all who come to his *khanqah*. He, therefore, his two functions to perform – he acts as a teacher and spiritual guide to his disciples. However, the number of individuals who were wholly dedicated to the spiritual life are few compared to those who come to the *pir* to 'exploit his spiritual powers to cure an ailment or fulfill a wish (Mujeeb 1967: 121). Since a *pir* is expected to heal both mental and bodily diseases by spiritual means, large crowds assmble in the *khanqah*[13]. People who seek the guidance of a *pir* in their perilous journey in the realm of the spirit (known as *saluki*) are quite few, as most of the visitors throng round him for the solution of their worldly problems, through amulets, blessings or recommendations.[14]

There are different types of *pir* in Pakistan : "some are quiet hermits, others active preachers; some take a useful part in the secular affairs of neighbourhood, some are mischievous stirrers of trouble, and some are charlatans pure and simple"[14]. Of these the *sajjada nashin pirs* are the most popular and powerful *pirs* and they exercise considerable influence on Pakistani politics. They are descendants of famous Muslim saints who either converted people to Islam or began reform movements. Unlike their saintly ancestors who lived as ascetics, these *pirs* benefited from royal patronage, often receiving landed estates or money to build beautiful mausolea and shrines in memory of the saints. The ruling classes forged an alliance with these *pirs* who commanded a vast body of hereditary followers, all of whom gave unswerving allegiance of religio-political parties like the Jamiat-e-'Ulama-e-Pakistan, the Jam'iat-e-Masha'ikh, the Pakistan People's Party and the Pakistan Muslim League. Some of them have formed their own parties from their followers (Gilmartin 1979: 485-417; Talbot 1982). The ideal *pir* is thought of as a physician of men's soul:

> The Pirs seldom allowed anybody to leave the *khanqah* unsatisfied ... With their deep insight into human character they assuaged the wounds of their visitors and gave them that unshakable faith in God and moral values which sustained them in the midst of the severest tribulations of life" (Nizam: 63).

To gain merit is a concept familiar to both Hindus and Muslims. It reinforces the universal appeal of the shrine. It is also central, in a somewhat different form, to Buddhism. However, there is accumulated merit for the Buddhist in religious giving, but not in everyday giving such as to build a school or contribute to the support of widow. Merit for Hindus to ensure a good rebirth is drawn from all actions. For Muslims, merit is seen in a different light. To Muslims, the concept has two important principles, neither of which is connected to ensuring good rebirth as they do not believe in the metempsychoses of soul. First, it is enshrined in principles of charity which represent social responsibility on the part of the individual towards collectivity[15]. Charitable acts are considered a true reflection of a *sharif*, or honourable, person. There are specific guide-lines in Islam as to their relative value. Some are compulsory (*fard*) while others are permissible or preferred (*mubark*). All forms possess religious merit (*thawab*) to a greater or lesser degree. The creation of a *waqf*[16], for example, and its scrupulous administration have a particular fitness for religious merit. Contrary to the Buddhism case, merit is applicable to more general acts of charity than any special purpose. Second, merit is seen as necessary to offset the bad accumulating effect of flouting Islamic instructions in the sphere of business. The constant opposition between religious values and styles of economic activity is thus regulated through gaining merit in the other more socially valuable areas. It is, therefore, a way of systematically ethicizing social behaviour.

The symbiotic relationship between a devotee and a shrine is maintained through regular rituals confirming their mutual dependence. Rituals are the practical, regular, reaffirmations of the relationship between devotee and shrine. These rituals may be performed daily, but are considered more efficacious if held on Thursday or Friday, and particularly in an annual *'urs* celebrations (called feasts by the Roman Catholics). It seems the power of the *pir* alone so long after his death was not enough to attract followers. A constant reaffirmation of the spiritual power he one held was also necessary, and this was achieved through ritual performance and material organization.

The devotees of shrines face a certain amount of opposition from their own religious community over the practice of visiting shrine particularly from some sections of *ulma*. The most prominent school representing opposing opinions in the debate are the Wahabi/Deobandish and Barelvi school of thought.

According to Shaykh Muhammad b, 'Abd-al-Wahab, the following practices may lead the believer to *shirk* (partnership with God):

1. To visit the toms of saints to gain God's favour.
2. To introduce the name of a prophet, or a saint, or of an into prayer.
3. Seeking intercession from any being but God.

Their insistence on the oneness of God can be gauged from the fact that on the cover of the Persian and Urdu editions of the *Al-Balagh-al-Mubin* is written the advice with Loqman[17] gave to his son:

> Do not consider anybody as a partner of God; undoubtedly associating partners with God is a great injustice (Quran xxxi.13).

The author of *Al-Balagh al-Mubin* described his view about saint reverence as follows:

> "When the devotees celebrate the death anniversary of a saint (*buzurg*), they come in crowds from far and near to his tomb; and reaching there on the day of the *'urs,* they perform more devotions than they do for obligatory rituals. To solve their worldly problems, they address their supplications to the tombs. They pray to the saint in his tomb to ask for children and food; they offer costly veils [*chadders*] for the tomb, sprinkle perfume on it, burn incense thinking it meritorious they adorn the tomb, light lamps, they think that with this superfluous expenditure, they will please the saint who resides in the tomb and will reach his proximity (*qurbat*). Hindu polytheists do for their idols (*asnam*)" (Persian Text: 77: Urdu Text: 159).

Such type of reverence of saints makes Muslim resemble the Hindu polytheists, with whom they have lived for centuries.

Aziz Ahmad (1964: 209)–relying mainly on the short and ambiguous preamble of *Al-Balagh al-Mubin*–states that *pir-parasti* "spread (in India) because of the social contacts (of the Muslims) with the Hindu polytheists" seems to believe that the main theme of the books is a borrowing from the Hindus. Nur Muhammad (n.d.) a modern reformer says more clearly that the practices of saint-reverence were borrowed from Hindus. The orthodox *'ulama,* therefore, also believe that the prevalence of such type of Muslim customs and beliefs might be due to the long association of Muslims with Hindus, and through the process of acculturation they might have adopted these socio-cultural and religious trait which in fact are contradictory to official Islam.

As discussed earlier one of the outspoken critics was Ibn Taymiyya (1263-1328)[18], who is even now often referred to as an authority on this subject. Reformist movements in the 18th century also condemned what they called the exploitative and parasitical shrine cult and the monopoly of landed property mostly stemming from the ideology of the "feudal" system. The reformists demanded a purification of Islam from local actions and rituals, and they postulated mystic reform.[19] this reformism, however, appealed mostly to restricted urban groups that adhered to the tradition of the Prophet Muhammad (*sunna*) in a scripturalist sense. Their reformism was designed mainly to legitimize their new social status as traders, bankers and representatives of "scribal groups", and to express an emancipatory world view[20]. The prevalent syncretism reflected in popular Islam and in "un-Islamic" practices could, however, not be crushed entirely, even if it was discussed critically in literary circles.[21]

Colonialism adopted this critique and developed it further in comprehensive attack on the "orient" with the objective to legitimize colonial power and pushing through its notion of modernization perceived by superstition. To Westerners, Islam had to be reformed and modernized: cults and "strange" patterns of belief were best abolished. This criticism seems to have had a decisive impact on those some groups which were directly exposed to the colonial system. The 19th century urban reform movement in India and elsewhere in the Muslim world was very much connected with this colonial expansion made encroachment on the minds of Muslims.[22]

The Wahabis were fundamentalists and did not believe in existence or tolerance in matters of religion. The moderate Muslim of the sub-continent did see some measure of common sense in what they said, but did not approve their rigidness and tough language which they used in expressing themselves. In Deoband, a town in Uttar Pradesh (India), a movement came into being to express the same views in a somewhat milder tone. In fact, it was a modern revivalist movement that datets back to the fundamentalist reformer Shah Wali Ullah of Delhi. Maulana Mohammed Qasim Nantvi (1832-80), influenced by ideology, opened (1867) an Islamic seminary at Deoband and started movement aimed at purifying Muslims from the customs and beliefs of saintship. Their main target has been the reverence of saints and shrine. This seminary produced many eminent Muslim leaders like Maulana Hussein Ahmed Madani, Maulana Mohammed Ali Jauhar, his brother Maulana Shaukat Ali, Maulana Shabbir Ahmed Uthmani, etc.

There was a reaction to this movement of fundamentalism in sub-continent. Ahmed Raza Khan (1856-1921), of Bareilly, another in Uttar Pradesh, started a crusade against the revivalist attack on institution of *pirs,* shrines and saint reverence, and gave coherent distinct groups, both intellectual and social (Metcalf 1982: 297).

The Barailavis formally recognize and promote the existence of shrines and the custom of *'urs,* while the Deobandis consider the processes of degeneration of Islamic values.. This is not to say Deobandis are opposed to Sufis or to *pirs* in principle, but they opposed to the entry of un-Islamic practices (*bid'at*) associated with rituals performed at shrines; hence their opposition in principle to *'urs* and shrine attendance. The view held by this body of opposition to Wahhabi/ Deobandism is that to p0ray for a saint's intercession with God for material benefit interferes with the individual's direct relationship with God, which places a human being (the *pir*) on an equal level with God[24]. Moreover all prayes to God are direct, not through an extraneous agency, e.g. very first chapter of Qur'an, *Al-Fatiha,* without which no prayer is complete.[25] Reverence of *pirs* and shrines is thus considered of questionable religious value or even blasphemy.

Patai (1987) points out some factors which make it difficult to explain folk/popular Islam. They are: firstly, Islam is the youngest monotheistic religion and it has retained many pagan features, and such pre-Islamic cultural elements have become part of official Islam; secondly, the officially sanctioned beliefs, doctrines and practices of Islam reached the masses by means of oral transmission and thus tended to be coloured by "folk" features: that is to say, the differences between the official and folk religion have been blurred; thirdly, the increasing number of Muslim sects, mystic and other religious orders have created a milieu for the mixing together of officially described elements of religion with folk features; fourthly, Islam absorbed much from the religions it displaced, especially in the places far from the heartland of Islam (e.g. in Asia and sub-Saharan Africa) many of these indigenous features survived within an Islamic framework without being differentiated from official Islam, or without being described as elements of folk religion, and finally, in Muslim countries it is difficult to establish a distinction between religion and other aspects of social life, because Islam is not a mere religion, but a complete way of life.

NOTES

1. *Maghrib* is the area West of Arabia upto the North-West Africa on the Atlantic Coast.
2. See *Encyclopedia of Religion of Ethics,* p. 49.
3. See *Dictionary of Urdu, Classical Hindi and English,* p. 1084.
4. As detailed nomenclature is given in the *Encyclopedia of Religion and Ethics,* p. 60. The full name of Shaykh Abdul Qadir Jilani (c. 1077-1166) is Mohyuddin Abu Mohammad bin Abi Saleh. It is said in books of *tasawwuf* that spiritually he is linked directly to Ali (c. 600-660) b. Abu Talib, the Fourth Caliph of Islam.
4. cf. the title al-marabitoun given to the Moor ruler of North Africa, Yusufbin Tashfain.
5. In the medieval Muslim society, particularly in the Maghrib, the *murabit* was a man who went into the state of *ribat,* a sort of conventual retreat coupled with ascetic practices and, occasionally, with military exercises which formed a training for the holy war.
6. Cf. *Al-Quran,* II. 254: Allah is the *Protecting Friend* of those who believe. He brings them out of darkness into light.
7. In 'Arabia the word *shaykh* is equivalent to the English title Mr. Anybody who is not a sayyid is called a *shaykh.* Sometimes sayyid is used for a Mr., in which case *Syed* is denoted by *Al-Sayyid.* In Punjab, however, a *shaykh* is one who is a converted Muslm from a Sikh.
8. One may illustrate the point by saying that every general is a solider, but every solider is not a general.
9. Cf. Iqbal: Come to the company of Iqbal and drink a peg or two; because although he does not have his moustache but he knows the art of *qalandar.*
10. On the other hand, Maulana Sher Mohammed, a Sufi of Sharaqpur in the Punjab, whose title is *Fanah-fir-Rasool,* regarded his life in complete conformation with Qur'an and Sunnah as his *karama.* The story goes that a man heard that Maula Sher Mohammed was a great *pir* came to Sharaqpur and lived in his mosque for about three months. When he did not see any *karama* he sought permission to leave. When Maulana Sher Mohammed asked him the reason for his sojourn, he replied that he had come to become his *murid,* but he had seen no *karama,* he wanted to return home. On this Maulana Sher Mohammed asked him whether he had seen any of his deeds against *Shariah* to which he answered in the negative. On it Maulana Sher Mohammed said that his conformity with *Shariah* was his *karama.*
12. In Morocco an *agurram* (saint) is, ideally, one who is descended from

the Prophet and is visibly a recipient of divine blessing, *baraka,* mediates between me and God and arbitrates between men and men, dispenses blessing, possess magical powers, is a good and pious man, observes Qur'anic precepts (oral held to be such), is uncalculatingly generous and hospitable (see Gellner 1969: 74).

13. The institution of *pirs* is so strong in Sindh that to question it is practically unthinkable. Regarded with a veneration bordering on worship, their worldly law, and they are considered almost as a separate species of human being. Ironically, the *pirs* 'power is equated with their spiritual prowess – although what is more visible is the materialism the institution perpetuates, why their relationship with devotees violates the basic Islamic concept of equality (Massoud Ansari, *The Daily News,* Special Report, February 16, 1996).
14. M.A. O'Brien as quoted in Hastings Donnan and Pnina Werbner (eds.) 1991. 224.
15. Cf. *Al-Quran,* II. 254: O ye who believe! Spend of that wherewith we have provide you eve a day come when there will be no trafficking, or friendship nor intercession.
16. To create a *waaf* is to transfer property to the name of the God, and income from such property should benefit not the individual but the collectivity.
17. According to *Qur'an* (XXXI, 12) Loqman was given wisdom, and was to told to give Thanks unto Allah.
18. See, e.g., Muhammad U. Memon : *Ibn Taimiya's Struggles Against Popular Religion,* with an annotated translation of his *Kitab ibtida as-Sirat al-mustaqim mukhalifat asbab al-jahim,* The Hague 1973.
19. However, it is still not clear to what extent reformers like Shah Wali Ullah really criticized shrine cult; see, e.g., M.A., Ansari: Shah Waliy Allah attempts to revise Wahdatul-Wujud, *Islam Quarterly,* 1984, pp 150-164. J.M.S. Baljon: Shah Waliullah and the Dargah in Troll (ed.) : *Muslim Shrines in India,* pp. 189-197; see also now *Muhammad Ashiq Puhliti* (ed.): *Al-qawl al-jali; Malfuz Hadrat Shah Wali Ullah Muhaddith Dehlawi,* translated and annoated by Taqi Anwar Alawi, Lakhnau 1988, which is a collection of rare *malfuzat* of the reformer particularly on this issue.
20. See, e.g., P. Gran : *Islamic Roots Capitalism : Egypt, 1760-1840.* Texas and London 1979: D. Washbrook: South Asia, The World System, and World Capitalism in *Journal of Asian Studies,* 49/3/1990, pp. 479-508.
21. See, e.g., Some of the verses of Sauda and Mir Taqi Mir in R. Russel/ K. Islam: *Three Mughal Poets,* Cambridge, Massachusets, 1968, and in Ahmed Ali : *Golden Tradition,* New Delhi/London 1973.

22. See, e.g., A. Hourani : *Arabic Thought in the Liberal Age,* 1798-1939, Oxford 1967.
23. Shah Wali Ullah (c. 1703-c.1762), whose real name was Azim-ud-din Shah, was the son of Maulana Shah Abdul Rahim. He received education of Hadith from Medinah. On his return to India in 1732 he started giving instruction in the hospice of his father known as Madrissah-Rahimiyyah.
24. A parallel can be drawn with the Roman Catholic priests, who do no allow the laity to invoke the Trinity directly.
25. Surah Fatiha reads as follows: Praise be to Allah, Lord of the Worlds, The Beneficent, the Merciful; Owner of the Day of Judgement, Thee (alone) we worship; Thee (alone) we ask for help. Show us the straight path, the path of those whom Thou hast favoured; Not (the path) of those who earn Thine anger, not of those who go astray.

REFERENCES

Ahmad, Aziz (1964), *Studies in Islamic Culture in the Indian Environment.* London: Oxford University Press.

Ali, Ahmad, (1973), *The Golden Tradition.* New York and London.

Ansari, M.A. (1984), 'Shah Waliy Allah Attempts to Revise Wahdatul Wujud'. *Islam Quarterly,* pp. 150-164.

Baljon, J.M.S., 'Shah Waliullah and the Dargah' in W.C. Troll (ed.) *Muslim Shrines in India.* pp. 189-197.

Ben-Ami, I. (1981), 'Folk Veneration of Saints among Moroccan Jews'. In S. Morag, I. Ben-Ami and N. Stillman (eds.), *Studies in Judaism and Islam.* Jerusalem: The Magnes Press.

Bloch, O. (1932), *Dict. Etymol de la langue Francaise.* Paris: S.V.

Currie, P.M. (1989), *The Shrine and Cult of Muin-al-din Chishti of Ajmer.* Delhi: Oxford University Press.

Darling, M.L. (1930), *'Rusticus loquitur', The old light and the new in the Punjabi village.* London.

Deshen, S. (1997), 'Tunisian hillulot'. In M. Shokeid and S. Deshen (eds.) *The Generation of Transition* (in Hebrew). Jerusalem: Ben Zn Institute.

Donnan, H. and Pnina Werbner (eds.) (1991), *Economy and Culture in Pakistan.* London : MacMillan.

Eickelman, D. (1976), *Moroccan Islam.* Austin : University of Texas Press.

———(1983), Religion and Trade in Western Morocco, *Research in Economic Anthropology,* 5, pp. 335-48.

Gilmartin, D. (1979), 'Religion leadership and the Pakistan Movement in the Punjab', *Modern Asian Studies,* 13, pp. 485-517.

Geertz, C. (1968), *Islam Observed*. New Haven Conn: Yale University Press.

Gellner, E. (1969), *Saints of the Atlas*. Chicago : University of Chicago Press.

———(1981), *Muslim Society*. Cambridge : Cambridge University Press.

Goldberg, H. (1983), 'The mimouna and the minority status of Moroccan Jews'. *Ethnology*, 17, No.1, pp. 75-88.

Goldzihar (1967-71), *Muslim Studies*. Trans S.M. Stern and C.R. Barber. London: Allen and Unwin.

Gran, P. (1979), *Islamic Roots of Capitalism : Egypt 1760-1840*. Texas and Lonxon.

Hourani, A. (1967), *Arabic Thoughts in the Liberal Age*. London : Oxford University Press.

Mayer, A.C. (1967), 'Pir and Murshid: An aspect of religious leadership in West Pakistan. *Middle Eastern Studies*, 3, pp. 161-2.

Metcalf, B. (ed.) (1982), *Moral Conduct and Authority. The Place of Adab in south Asian Islam*. Berkeley : University of California Press.

Muhammad, Nur n.d. 'Introduction' in the Urdu Translation of Qu'ran by Ashraf Ali Thanawi. Delhi: Kutub Khana Rashidiyaa.

Mujeeb, M. (1967), *The Indian Muslisms*. London : Allen and Unwin.

Nizami, K.A. 'Some aspects of Khanqah life in Medieval India', *Studia Islamica*, p. 6.

Pati, Rapheal (1987), *'The Folk Islam.'* In : Mirca eliade (ed.) *The Encyclopedia of Religion*, Vol. 5, New York : MacMillan.

Puhliti, Mohd. Ashiq (ed.) (1988), *Al-Qawal of al-jali, Malfux Hadrat Shat Wali Ullah Muhaddith Dehlawi*. Lakhnau.

Rose, H.A. *A glossary of the Castes and Tribes of the Punjab*, Vol. 1, Lahore, p. 522.

Russel, R. and K. Islam (1968), *Three Mughal Poets*. Cambridge, Mass.

Stillman, N. (1982), 'Saddiq and marabout in Morocco'. In I. Ben-Ami (ed.) *The Sephardi and Oriental Jewish Heritage*, Jerusalem : The Magnes Press pp. 489-50.

Talbot, A. (1982-1983), 'The growth of Muslim League in the Punjab 1937-46' and, 'Muslim Political Mobilization in Rural Punjab'. In P. Robb (ed.) *Rural India: Land Power and Society under British Rule*. London: Curzon Press.

Trimmming, Spencer, J. (1970), *The Sufi Orders in Islam*. Oxford: Clarendren Press.

Troll, W. Christian (1989), *Muslim Shrines in India*. Bombay: Oxford University Press.

Turner, B.S. (1975), *Weber and Islam*. London: Routledge and Kegan Paul.

Washbrook, D. (1990), 'South Asia, The World System and World Capitalism', *Journal of Asian Studies*, 49/3, pp. 479-508.

Westphal, Hellbusch S. and H. Westphal (1964), *The Jat of Pakistan*. Berlin: Duncker and Humbolt.

Watermarck, E. (1926) *Ritual and Belief in Morocco*. London: MacMillan and Co.

Wilber, D.N. (1964), *Pakistan : Its People, its society, its culture*. New Haven: Human Relation Area Files.

THE CORE AND THE ENVELOPE: THE DOMAIN OF THE GRAVE AMONG MUSLIMS IN THE MIDDLE EAST AND INDIA

Ifrah Zilberman

Introduction

The aim of this paper is to analyze the domain of the grave among the Muslims of North India, and to compare it to the same domain among the Palestinian Muslims. Exploration of the social and religious notions of death and burial is a journey into the core of the systems of belief of a society. At the same time, it is a journey into a zone of symbolic confrontation between different religions and societies. However, in the historical encounter between Islam and syncretism. Thus, the domain of the grave among the Muslims of North India also reflect syncretism and symbols which form a bridge between Muslims and non-Muslims in India[2].

Burial is used by the Muslims of India as a religious cultural signifier of their own uniqueness, and they symbolically contrast the Hindu practice of cremating their dead with their own custom of burial[3]. Thus, cremating the dead and burying them are two poles which represent the tensions and conflicts between Islam and Hinduism. There are tendencies among Muslim rulers in the past to make use of the sacred and political values of graves. Sacred graves and burial sites were transformed during the era of Islamic political domination in India into shrines and centres of pilgrimage, to denote the control of social and political arenas by Islam.

The concept of ritualistic pollution and purity shaped the ideology and the case system in Hindu society[4]. This concept however, is related to the practice of cremating the dead. For example, there is no cremation of a dead body in the case of pollution by disease such as the plague (Parry 1994: 68). This concept is also related to Hindu notions about the closed and eternal circle of cosmic unity, and about the reincarnation of the soul leading to retaining it in this world in a different form – as more or less pure. The practice of burial, however, reflects Islamic ideas about the transcendental destiny of the God-created world (Smith and Haddad, 1981: 31-63). Thus, graves became a source of ideological and symbolic contrast and conflict between Islam and Hindu society which cremated its dead. Nevertheless, in many cases, Muslim centres of pilgrimage in India – of which grave of a holy person is the symbolic centre - evoked among Hindus feelings of sanctity. The sacred graves of Muslim Sufi saints (Dargah) also attract Hindu pilgrims[5].

The main argument in this paper is that the core of rituals and beliefs in the domain of Muslim burial in India is similar to that of Muslim burial in Palestinian society, and indeed, among the Muslims of the Middle East. However, the envelope of rituals surrounding the acts of burial and the visiting graves among the Muslims of North India was influenced by Hinduism. The core embodies the original essence of Islam, and its envelope denotes adjustment to the deepest levels of culture among the Hindu people. Thus, the core signifies conflict with the values of the religion and the majority. The envelope is the symbolic locus signifying shared beliefs and values with this dominant culture. This paper contrasts the Hindu immanent-cosmological system of belief as articulated through the act of cremation, and the Muslim historical transcendental system of belief as articulated through the act of burial. This approach is broached in the work of Max Weber (1964)[6].

DEATH AND BURIAL IN IDEOLOGICAL PERSECTIVE

The core

Since the seminal work of Hertz (1960) which emphasized the relation between social order and the ritual of death and burial, the domain of the grave is recognized as reflecting also the symbolic order and the system of belief in society. According to Hertz (1960: 28) : "... death is the object of collective representation." Thus, the collective imprints the ritual surrounding the grave with its own unique reflection. The rituals of burial are also recognized as rites of passage (Van Gennep 1909), and represent the ideas of society about the cosmos and the other world.

Indeed, in Islam the rituals of burial are the signifiers for a successful passage to heaven or slipping down to hell (Granquist 1965). The grave creates a symbolic and cosmological orientation for the Muslims. The deepest core of Islamic cosmology, which is the same for Palestinian Muslim society for Muslims in India, shaped the way in which the body of the dead Muslim is prepared as the vessel carrying godly reward for the true believer. Thus, the head of the dead Muslim is pointed towards holy Mecca, the source of Islam and the place in which Islam was revealed to the Prophet. The face of the dead should according to orthodox Islam, be laid on its right cheek. The right side signifies a link to the domain of heavenly angels and godly justice. The left side, the unblessed one, denotes in the symbolic idiom of the dead believer's body the ideas of impurity and hell. The dead body is ritually washed and purified. Purity of the dead body in this context hopefully brings about purity of the soul, and hence a place in heaven. The orifices in the dead body are cleaned and sealed, in order to seal its boundaries against the penetration of polluting substances. The white shrouds with which the dead body is covered are another way to separate the pure from the impure. However, the body of the dead is the vehicle upon which the symbols of Islam are incised and imprinted.

For the believer who follows the Islamic sacred Law (Shari'a), death is only the corridor to the blessings of the afterlife, and the interlude to the Last Day of Judgment. Thus each member of the community of Islam has the potential to fulfill the historic transcendental density of the world : to begin and to end according to a predestined cosmic scheme. Hence the importance of the symbolic idiom of the core of rituals which dictates the way of Islamic burial in India and elsewhere. The key to the gates of Heaven is assumed to be Islamic piety during life, and Islamic practice such as the pilgrimage (Hajj) to Mecca. But the system of belief which shapes the way in which the Islamic tomb itself is constructed could be influenced by other symbolic needs of society. For example, royal Islamic tombs which are contained in impressive mausoleums in India articulated the needs of rulers for respect and deference. They embodied power and even conveyed the divine right of the sovereign to rule. These royal grave-structures break away from the need of Islam to symbolize through the domain of the grave and egalitarianism and a lack of embellishment. Egalitarianism in the case of the dead ruler is symbolized through the ritual of purification of the dead body, which is the same for everybody, and in the relatively simple appearance of the tomb itself. It is also articulated through the belief in godly justice to all on the Day of Judgment. In this context, egalitarianism means an equal approach to the godly rewards of the believers in the afterlife.

The cosmological outlook of Hinduism about the end of life combines the ideas of the indestructibility of the soul reincarnation, and the existence of the world as a cycle with no end. The practice of cremating the bodies of dead Hindus reflects these ideas . Furthermore, the rituals of cremation of the dead such as washing the dead-body before cremation with sacred water, preferably taken from the Ganges – reflect a religious need for purification. Cremation also means semi-deification, as the body releases the soul. Fire and water purify and lend on awe of sanctity and ritual cleanliness to the passage of the dead person to his next reincarnation. The effort to avoid ritual pollution from a dead body is related also to the wish to stop the circle of reincarnations, and to join the eternal cosmic unifying entity.

The Envelope

The Hindu notion of the cyclic nature of the cosmos is the opposite of the Islamic notion of its linear destiny. Therefore, there is a contrast between the Islamic and the Hindu symbolic idioms of the end of life. This contrast could be reconciled by an envelope of symbols, rituals and belief shared by the two communities. These shared symbols are in fact a part of syncretic trend in Indian Islam, blending Hindu with Islamic symbols. Through syncretism, the perceived Hindu/Muslim opposition could be partly dissolved, and the local tradition and the universal in Islam could be reconciled.

The Islamic mystic and ecstatic Sufi tradition and the Hindu Bhakti devotional tradition, for example, found common spiritual and ritualistic grounds in medieval India. The outcome was the North Indian medieval mysticism, which attracted members of

Hindu lower castes and low-status Muslims. An example of such a syncretic lend of religions was the school of Indian unifying mystic thought founded by Kabir – the son of a Muslim weaver born in the beginning of the 15th century (Ikram 164: 126-127). Kabir sang, as an example of his ideas: "O God, whether Allah or Rama, I live by Thy Name" (Sen 1961: 99).

This heterodox tradition of Kabir the saintly poet becaome in time a unique sect, the Kabir-panth, which still exists today. After Kabir's death his followers were involved in a conflict about whether to bury their saint or to cremate him. So, as a ritualistic way of taking care of their dead they neither buried nor cremated them, but weighed them down and immersed them in a river (preferably in Ganges) (Parry 1994: 70). In this way – rejection of both burial and cremation – they emphasized their unique position between Islam and Hinduism. This custom of immersion of the dead reflects a unique system of belief which creates symbolic bonds unifying this religious community into a collective entity with its own ritualistic and social boundaries.

The symbolic idiom of ritualistic cleanliness is central in different ways to Islam and Hinduism. While in Islam a part of this symbolic idiom is encapsulated in the domain of graves and burial shrines for saints, in Hinduism part of it is contained in the rituals of cremating the dead. Because the Islamic burial system reflects the belief in a universe created and then directed toward the Day of Judgment, the dead believer must attain ritual cleanliness before burial. Because Hindu cremation reflects the belief that life and death are only transformations in the eternal cosmos; the dead Hindu must achieve purity in order to improve his next reincarnation (Parry 1982).

In Islam ritual cleanliness (Wadu), as practiced before praying, is a precondition for the efficacy of prayer. Moreover, the state of ritual purity is binary. It means that though all male Muslims are equal in their inherent ability to achieve ritual cleanliness, they can be during a prayer either in a state of ritual purity or impurity. Yet, Indian Islam was influenced by the Hindu caste ideology. Therefore, some Indian Muslim groups were regarded as inherently less equal to others in their ability to achieve ritual purity before prayer, or in rituals relating to burial.[7]

Hierarchy in Hinduism is governed by the differences in ritual purity among different castes; and castes are linked to a complex division of labour according to their lever of ritual purity. Because Muslims were in many cases a minority in a Hindu caste-arranged society, they adapted themselves to it. They were influenced by the culture of the Hindu majority, as well as by the culture of Hindu converts to Islam. Therefore, Muslims as a distinct religious community became in some cases a caste-like group which filled unique economic roles in Hindu society. Indeed different Muslim groups were regarded in some cases as different sub-castes according to their assumed level of purity or pollution. Hindu ideas about the stratified hierarchy of castes in society influenced by Indian Islam and became the background to some important syncretic trait in it.

The village of Rampura on the plains of Mysore in South India, which was researched by Srinivas (1994), will serve as an example of the influence of the caste system on Muslims. In 1948, there were 179 Muslims out of 1523 inhabitants in Rampura – the third largest group in the village. These Muslims were usually artisans and traders. They gained a position in Hindu hierarchy of ritually pure diet and occupation as non-Hindu who did not eat pork nor drink any alcoholic drinks, and were not engaged in polluting occupations (except as catchers) and inclusion according to pollution and purity, were the norm for every group; and the Muslims were no exception. Therefore, they were regarded by the Hindu villagers as a caste like group. For example, the social standing of the Muslims in Rampura was better, and their caste-like position higher than the Harijans. The Muslims of Rampura were excluded, as were three other castes in the village, from making any contribution to the annual festival of Rama in Rampura. Nevertheless their cooperation was sought, and they participated in the deity's procession during the festival. Indeed, a Muslim had a traditional trade in it, of setting off the fireworks.

As any other small caste in Rampura, the Muslims took their disputes, even intimate ones, to the elders of the dominant Hindu peasant caste for settlement. For example, peasant elders mediated in a dispute about the conditions of religious services rendered by a Muslim clergy to the Muslims in the village. Though the Muslims had their own hierarchy of customary law courts outside Rampura, they regularly used the higher customary law court of the Indu dominant peasant caste in the area of Rampura as a court of appeals.

Hindus and Muslims in the village were involved in contractual relationships: Muslims invariably employed Hindus as servants, but agreed to be servants only to Hindu masters. Muslim families were linked into the networks of patronage in the village, and belonged to different political factions in it. These conditions cut across the caste structure of the village. For instance, the pesant Hindu headman of Rampura had a following of 58 families from different castes of village, including ten Muslim families as followers. These patrons mobilized their clients, including the Muslims, as "vote banks" during elections. The political role of the Muslims in the village also included their participation in its institutions, and in 1948 the local council of the village (panchayat) included Muslims.

The Indian Islamic practice of hypergamy was a part the dynamic which crated a social fabric resembling the Hindu hierarchical caste system. Among Indian Shi'a groups, ideas of purity and pollution relating to marriage were considered an integral part of relgion (Cole 1988: 117). For example, in Awadh during the 19th century notable (Sayyid) Shi'a families who could not afford to offer proper dowries to grooms of a high status refused to marry their daughters altogether (Cole 1988: 110), thus keeping the status and purity of their group.

In Hinduism ritual pollution is not binary, but relation to social status and graded along a continuum. Hindus are ranked in castes differing in the amount of their inherent pollution, and its meanings to society. Although each individual may wish to maximize his personal purity, he is limited by the boundaries and nature of his caste. Nevertheless, castes were known to improve their status by collective action.

The burial of the dead was an essential signifier of Muslim religious identity in India. That was so because the act of burial was ritually linked to Islamic ideas about the Last Judgment, the rewards of the true believer in heaven and the punishment of the wrong-doer in hell. Burial also stood in symbolic contrast to Hindu notions about the cosmic reincarnation of souls, and hence made the Islamic identity in India may distinct. For instance, the Meos of Rajasthan and Haryana who accepted Islam in the 15th century kept much of their Hindu Rajput identity and religious practices. However, they buried their dead (Ahmad 1976:99) – an act which established their Islam identity and a ritualistic boundary between them and they related Hindu social groups.

Among the Palestinian Muslims, burial is less important as a boundary between them and the Palestinian Christian because both religions practice burial. The religious boundaries between Islam and Christianity in this case are established to the different rituals surrounding the act of burial. For examples, Christians use coffins, while Muslims bury their dead without coffin, only clad in shrouds. The differences between Islamic and Jewish burial customs are even less than that. Both Christians and Islam hold almost the same notions about the Godly created and destiny of the world and about the character of the Judgment Day. Furthermore, Islam has accepted Jesus Christ as a true prophet emerging from the same "Tree of Prophecy" as itself, and regards his divine revelation as derived from the same source as the Islamic one.

The social organization of the rituals surrounding Hindu death reflects the way in which death was symbolically constructed. The religious values and meaning of death, however, influenced Hindu social structure. Thus, the castes of religious experts who deal professionally with death, invented rituals and reinterpreted their meanings in order to enhance their own position. However, their caste status was dependent on notions of ritualistic pollution. So there was a tension between a powerful hold over a domain of ritual, and an ambiguous social standing. The Brahmins, for example, who were involved with caring for dead bodies, were ritually polluted by their association with them (Parry 1994: 3).

In Hinduism, the concept of *karma* underlies spheres of dualistic activity including death. This concept means that all actions carried on during life influence the future of one's soul is an endless cycle of life, death and rebirth. The soul is locked into this cycle, but there is a wish to escape and be liberated from it. This liberation would be a final merging with what Hinduism conceives to be the cosmic unifying principle governing it.

In the act of cremation, the core of rituals representing *karma* is revealed, and the drama of cosmic creation is re-enacted. The dead body is consumed by fire, but at the same time the essence of the soul is regenerated. The material end and aim of the dead body is the renewal and regeneration of spirituality. Thus, Hindu death is an act of cosmic regeneration. Therefore, cremation is the enactment of Hindu cosmology, and a sacrifice which renews it (Parry 1994: 30-32).

The Symbolic Idiom of the Grave

In Indian Islam, the symbolic idiom of the grave is divided into two domains: that of its core of symbols, and that of the symbolic envelope surrounding it. As was mentioned before, the core embodies the unity of Islam and is a link between Middle Eastern Islam and Indian Islam. The envelope is composed of rituals common to both the followers of Hinduism and the believers in Islam. The syncretic symbolic idiom of the envelope is coded by smells, colours, and ritual offerings.

The efficacy of this envelope of symbols and rituals is sustained by the use of smells, incenses and fragrant essences which purify the area of the grave, mask the pollution of the dead body and create an invisible liminal threshold. This fragrant threshold also separates between the domain of the living and that of the dead, and also marks the liminal passage from the profane to the sacred. The relatives of the dead cross this threshold and visit their grave out of love, duty and custom. However, visiting graves of kin is different from pilgrimage to a saint's burial site. While visiting is a ritualistic obligation, pilgrimage is a devotional act.

Yet pilgrims to grave shrines are also endangered by the possibility of pollution emanating from the holy grave, and therefore the use of fragrant essences is widespread in such shrines. In the important Chishti dargah at Ajmer, for example (Currie 1989), incense sticks are used regularly. Such fragrant odors were used also to endow pilgrims who came to visit shrines with blessings. Thus, for example, in the most sacred dargah in Ahmadabad, a fragrant sandalwood paste was smeared on the tomb and then washed with water. The water is collected in a basin and given to the pilgrims as a carrying blessing substance (Desai 1989).

While there is some use of fragrant substances in Palestinian Muslim burials, it is limited to the purification of the dead body. Indeed, there is such use among Indian Muslims (for example: Sharar 1994). However, the use of fragrant substances among the Muslims in India is much wider than in the Middle East, and resembles similar practices among the Hindu population. The use of incense sticks and other substances spreading pleasant smells is general in relation to graves and such as the Chishti dargah at Ajmer (Moini 1989). They recognized the use of incense as part of their culture and as a purification agent, and this helped them to accept the pilgrimage as part of the overall Indian culture.

Colours in relation to death and burial rituals are indicators of liminality, and signifiers of different ritual categories. In the domain of the grave, colours usually indicate a wish for an aura of sanctity and purity. White, green and black are used in Muslim societies in the Middle East in the domain of death and burial. White indicates purity of soul and body and Godly justice at the Day of the Last Judgment. Green, is the colour symbolizing the House of the Prophet, signifies sanctity. Black means protest, collective anger and fierce grief. Among Muslims in Northern India other colours, such as yellow and red, are also used in the domain of the grave. This use reflects Hindu influence and the creation of a common symbolic idiom between Hindu and Muslim people.

In Palestinian society there are no offerings to the dead except for the of palm branches during Id al-Adha. This rejection was accepted by Islamic reform and revival movements. However, Muslim graves and burial shrines in Northern India are rich in the variety of offerings, which are used as part of death and burial rituals. People give offerings in order to show respect and deference to the dead; to gain merit, forgiveness and blessings; the endow the burial grounds with an aura of sanctity; to appease the souls of the dead, and to gain insight into their future fate. Such offerings are not found among Palestinian Muslims, but they are a common symbolic idiom between Islam and Hinduism.

Flowers are an example of such offerings. Flowers combine a pleasant smell and an attractive colour to create a powerful and sacred symbol. Flowers as an offering may be found in Indian Sufi shrines as well as in other types of graves. Important shrines of the Chisti Sufi order in North India such as dargah of Nizamuddin Aulya in Delhi (Siddiqui 1989) are an sample of the use of flowers in rituals. Flowers are brought to the grave of the saint as an offering. They are left on the grave and then taken back and given to pilgrims charged with mystic power of the saint. Flowers (and incense sticks) scent the atmosphere of the shrine. Their efficacy is also related to their smell; indeed, the area of the grave in Ajmer is washed with rose water (Currie 1989: 141-142). Flowers are chosen so their colours will be uniform, pleasant and conducive to the sacred feelings of the pilgrims. Flowers which were offered on a saint's grave assimilate some of its mystic power. For instance, in West Bengal women were given by an Islamic Moulvi an amulet (maduli) containing "dried flowers from a saint's grave" (Fruzzetti 1984).

Amongst Muslim societies in the Middle East, the sacrifice of a sheep is part of an offering to the grave of a saint. Among Bedouins, such a sacrifice is made during a pilgrimage to their local saint's grave-shrine. This notion of sacrifice at a pilgrimage was sanctified because of the importance of the holiday of Id al-Adha, in which a Muslim family is required to slaughter a sheep. This is done in order to commemorate the link of the Muslims to the origins of monotheism, as revealed in relations between Abraham/Ibrahim and his son Ismail. However, in India, Islam faced Hindu civilization, which regarded vegetarianism as status symbol and a religious value appropriate to the highest ranking castes. Moreover, the sacrifice of cows regarded in Hinduism as sacred – became a symbol of confrontation between Muslims and Hindus. Id al-Adha became known as Id al-Bakaram and slaughtering a cow could trigger a communal riots (Pandey 1993). Therefore, in order to enable Hindu pilgrimage to Muslim shrines in north India, and to keep open cultural bridges with the Hindu community, there is no regular sacrifice of animals in these shrines (except, perhaps sacrificing sheep during Id al-Adha). Instead, the symbolic idiom of the offerings which the pilgrims bring to the grave is taken from the rich repertoire of Hindu rituals.

At the dargah of Sayyid Salar Mas'ud Ghazi in Bahraich during the *Basant* fair (mela), many pilgrims – Muslims as well as Hindus – come and give offerings. Farmers dressed in yellow the colour of the fair, give to the shrine "green spikes of wheat fruit, vegetables and flowers, and they mainly pray for their crops". During the *Jeshth* Fair at this dargah, about 5,00,000 people come to the shrine and offer gifts to the main saint grave, and to grave of a woman saint – Zahra Bibi. These devotional offerings include, among other things, silver thrones, clothes embroidered with gold, silver and jewelry; and other things. Gold and silver wires are tied to an ancient sacred sandalwood tree located inside the compound of the shrine, in order to gain blessings and fulfillment of desires (Mahmood 1989: 34-37). Although the core of these rituals at the fairs – such as prayer inside the saint's grave – is similar to Muslim pilgrimages in the Middle East, the envelope of rituals in them is not. This envelope is shared by Muslims and Hindus, embodies a faith in the power of the saint to mediate between the local people and is supernatural, and is sustained by local syncretic traditions.

Graves as Indicators of Symbolic Struggle over Sacred Space and Political Power

Royal tombs and burial sites are known to reflect the politics and ideology of the State, and to reflect its wish to shape a collective identity for society. Royal burial sites also reflect the political aspirations of the ruling stratum in society. For sample, the Merina of Madagascar used their kings' tombs to embody their collective entity and to create a symbolic centre for their kin-groups (Bloch and Parry 1982).

In some cases, cohesive kin-groups used graves as the embodiment of their collective entity. For instance, the Palestinian Hebronite Muslim migrants to East Jerusalem practiced burial in common tombs. Each kin-group buried its members in its common tomb, and the bones of all members intermingled, creating a powerful symbol of leveling differences in status before God. The burial in common graves also enforced the social borders of the kin-group and symbolized these migrants' new hold over the urban sacred space of Jerusalem. The presence of the Hebronite migrants in Jerusalem clashes with the social position and the symbolic hegemony of the established urban Muslims of East Jerusalem. The Muslim graveyards of Jerusalem reflect this clash between the old, established and notable (sharif) kin-groups of Jerusalem and the rural migrants : the common graves of the migrants have taken over most of the sacred space of these graveyeards (Zilberman 1988: 246-253).

In areas of India ruled by Islam there was in some cases a use of symbol denoting control of territory and dominance over sacred space. Religious symbols were also created and used to achieve political hegemony[8]. Muslim royal grave sites, graveyards and Sufi shrines utilized in this struggle, and they denoted control of the sacred geography of the land.

During the history of relations between Islam and Hinduism, the act of a Muslim burial became a challenge to the symbolic domination of Hinduism over the sacred geography of India. Burial could be regarded by Hindus as an unsatisfactory way to dispose of bodies because it could produce spirits of malevolent dead to haunt everybody, regardless of religious identity[9].

Burial could be used in different ways by different political and social parties to challenge each other. It was used, for example, as an articulation of secularism and atheism and as a negation of traditional Hinduism. E.V. Ramaswamy Naikkar called as Periyar, a Tamil Hindu secular leader in Madras led an important secular Tamil party. He ordered his body to be buried and not to be cremated, and intended this act to enshrine his atheist beliefs and to protest against the Hindu caste system. His body was buried beside the headquarters of the party he established, symbolizing protest against the ideas of purity and pollution embodied in Hinduism (Naipaul 1991: 216-218).

Burial was used by Muslims to symbolize their defense of their sacred sites. For instance, Ayodhya a town located in the plains of North India – is a centre of Hindu pilgrimage as it is known to be the birthplace of lord Rama. In Ayodhya lives also a Muslim population. Both Hindus and Muslims there believed that the central Mosque in the town – the Babri Masjid – was built intentionally during the 16th century over the temple marking the birthplace of Lord Rama. The site of the mosque temple became an arena of strife between Islam and Hinduism. Seventy-five Muslims were killed in an armed struggle between Muslims and Hindus in 1855 over the possession of the Babri Masjid, and were buried in a common grave under the stairs of the mosque by the entrance. This common grave symbolized for Muslims the sacrifice of their people and their hold over the mosque. It also signifies the essence of the sacred notions of the Muslim martyr (Shahid).

For the Hindus this grave became a source of ritual pollution, because they believed it was located over the site of their destroyed temple which, in their view, should have remained ritually pure. Therefore, during 1949, when the subcontinent of India was still in turmoil after its division to Pakistan and India, Hindus groups tried to take over the Babri Masjid . Their first act was to dig up the Muslim common grave in the mosque and remove the remains of the dead. They then ritually purified the grounds of the mosque in order to convert it into a temple for Rama (Srivastava 1991: 14). This common grave was obviously regarded by the Muslims as a symbolic defense of their sacred site. At the same time, it was regarded by the Hindus as a ritualistic barrier to the holiness required for their temple[10].

Islam in India was shaped by Sufi traditions, which originated in the Middle East but were influenced by Hindu beliefs. The Sufi order, with the Muslim Saint as its charismatic centre, was one of the main means of converting non-Muslims to Islam. The grave of the Sufi saint was usually the centre of a pilgrimage complex. It was the linchpin linking earth and heaven. The other monuments and buildings in the saint's burial complex only serve the purpose of illuminating the sacred grave which cuts across different components of society in Islam in India. The sanctity of the saint in his life, and the belief in the efficacy of his blessing as well as the blessings emanating from his sacred grave, convinced people to convert to Islam. For example, the dargah of Shaikh Bakhtuyar Kaki (d. 1235) in Delhi, who belonged to the Chishti line, became since the 14th century a centre for adoration and pilgrimage. Non-Muslim villagers who came to the dargah to seek blessing were impressed by what they regarded as its spiritual power, and in some cases adopted Islam (Siddiqui 1989: 10-12).

Many Sufi burial shrines are surrounded by tombs. There is a considerable number of such tombs in the dargah at Ajmer (Currie 1989: 103). Important and affluent Muslims wished to be buried as close as possible to the grave of the saint. These notables and ulama believed that the saint's grave was endowed with blessing radiating out of it to the benefit of those who were buried beside it. They also believed in the ability of the saint to mediate before God on their behalf on the Day of the Last Judgment.

Nevertheless, the Sufi rituals through which Islam was practiced in these complexes of sacred graves and centres of pilgrimage were rejected by some Muslim scholars (Friedman 1971), who believed these rituals were influenced by the Hindu majority culture. They suspected that the conversion to Islam brought about by the Sufi orders in these dargah were a two-edge phenomenon-recruiting new Muslims, but also introducing into Islam non-Muslim rituals and beliefs. Therefore while some Muslim rulers – such as Akbar (d. 1605) – did not oppose the rituals of the Sufi leaders, others – like Aurangzeb (d.1707) – tried to purge Indian Islam from what they considered to be unorthodox rituals.

The case of the important dargah and pilgrimage centre located in Bahraich, about 130 km. from Lucknow, revealed the tensions in the assimilation of new converts to Islam, and the rejection of their tendency towards syncretism. Sayyid Salar Mas'ud Ghazi, the Muslim saint believed to be buried in Bahraich, died in the year 1033 AD; and since that time his grave has been a centre of pilgrimage. Aurangzeb, who wished to purify Islam from syncretic Hindu influences, prohibited devotional processions of pilgrims to the dargah of Sayyid Salar and even stopped the Sufi rituals there (Mahmood 1989: 25).

Muharram Processions and Symbolic Burial in Indian Islam

Among the followers of the Shi'a in the Middle East, the first ten days of the 'Ashura' during the month of Muharram are a time of emotional drama rooted in the collective means of the Shi'a. These ten days, especially the last of them the Ashura, commemorates the tragic massacre of the descendant of the Prophet, and signify a demarcation line between the Shi'a and the Suna in Islam. Nevertheless, the Ashura is a voluntary fast day for the Suni Muslims.

This sacred time is composed mainly of ritual liked to death, burial, burial shrines, and to sainthood, and in this sense it indicates deep layers of belief. During this time Shi'a Muslims meet at home in a mosque or in a special meeting hall. They pray, listen to devotional songs about the tragic events at Karbala (the sacred site in Iraq), and join religious processions[11].

In India, this time of mourning and festivity during Muharram became a symbolic tapestry related to death and burial, shard by Suni and Shi'i alike, and even by poor and low-caste Hindus. While the Suna in India mixed gaiety with mourning during the Muharram, the Shi'a there observed only mourning (Fruzzetti 1984: 91). The Muharram festival according to Saiyed (1984:114) became a flexible system which created inter-community cohesion. What denotes in the Middle East a separate sectarian identity was transformed by the symbolic representation of death and burial in India into an integrative Suni-Shi'a ritual. Yet, in some cases, the Muharram events resolved deep dividing lines between the Suna and the Shi'a, and in some cases violence erupted during Muharram processions (Schuble, 1993:79). Sacrifice – the evil power of rulers and the denial of cosmic justice – become an explosive power which can change social structure during Muharram into anti-structure (Turner 1977).

Through the Muharram rituals and processions the symbolic elements of burial, grave shrine and martyrdom uphold the Islamic

Indian collective identity, and create a syncretic ritualistic bridges to Hindus. In Northern India, for example, there was widespread participation of Hindus in the Muharram processions. Hindus influenced these processions by introducing into them offerings and rituals taken from the symbolic idiom of Hinduism. Thus, Islamic and Hindu elements were woven into a unified syncretic tapestry of rituals. For example, Hindus interred a cenotaph (an Islamic symbol of burial representing the Shi'a martyrs) but they offered to these symbolic graves, "rice, corn, flowers and cups of water" – offerings taken from Hindu rituals (Cole 1988: 116-117). Furthermore, these Muharram celebrations resembled in some ritualistic details of Hindu festival for Durga, the Goddess of Death.

For the Shi'a, this participatory role of Sunni Muslims and Hindus in the days of the Ashura is a proof of their just cause and piety, and of the universal importance of the murdered Imam. They believe that the events at Karbala, in particular the death of the Imam were on a cosmic scale and these events evoke in human beings – Muslims and non-Muslims – powerful emotions (Schubel 1993 : 95).

The Muharram festival in Bishnupur in West Bengal is an example of the dynamics of the social and religious interaction in town in which there are only Suni Muslims (they are some 5% of population there), living in 13 different Muslim neighbourhoods (Fruzzetti 1984). During the 1930's, Hindus also participated in the Muharram procession. This procession in Bishnupur started in a shrine of local saint and ended in the Muslim burial site in the town, which is symbolically considered to be Karbala. The Tazziya – a replica of the murdered Imam Hassan's mausoleum – was buried in the past in this graveyard but today only the flowers which decorated it are buried there.

This is a symbolic burial for the Imam, a burial that was denied to him by his enemies at Karbala; and thus this symbolic burial is an act of cosmic justice (Schubel 1993: 1111). The notion of symbolic sacred burial is exhibited in Bisnupur also by the Asthana, a symbolic sacred grave located in each Muslim neighbourhood, which contains soil from the grave of an important saint endowed with godly blessing (*barakat*), or even soil from the Imam's sacred burial site in Karbala. The procession carrying *Taziyas* passed through each Asthana before finally reaching the Muslim graveyard. In some other Muslim communities (Sayyid 1984:

114-133), a custom exists of digging symbolic graves which are filled with earth by the end of the Muharram, and the burial in them of the *Taziyas*.

In Kanpur, to give another example, the Muharram processions also exhibited Islamic symbols and cohesiveness Muslim groups ('castes') with strong corporate identities paraded *Taziyas*, and controlled the public spaces for a short time. However, in Bombay during the early 20th century, the Muslim neighbourhoods (muhallas) were composed of different Muslim sects, and ethnic and linguistic groups. These groups' muted antagonism was articulated throughout the Muharram procession. During the Muharram each muhalla paraded a Tabut (a symbolic model of a coffin) which represented the tomb of the martyr Imam, and in some cases the muhalla clashed with other muhallas. These processions also included many poor and the low caste Hindus. The Tabut was the symbolic essence of Ashura, yet it also symbolized the different identities of the various Muslim groups of Bombay at that time. The Muharram ritual in Bombay came to an end on the final, tenth day. The Tabuts were then brought to the seashore and symbolically immersed in the sea, a ritual linked to Hindu traditions (Freitag 1988: 116-123, 129).

The Muharram in India became an indicator of collective Islamic identity. In order to show Islamic uniqueness, symbolic burial – which stood in contrast as ritual and ideology to Hinduism – was selected and enacted collectively. The Muharram procession became a universal dram presenting life and death, sacredness and evil, cosmic justice and human treachery. It is a liminal event which could articulate integration and solidarity between Muslim and even non-Muslim groups. However, the Muharram procession could become a contested political and symbolic arena between Shi'a and Suni groups. It also has the potential to bring about violence.

NOTES

1. This article is the outcome of field research during two brief visits to North India during 1994-5. I have retained the spelling of Indian and Indian Muslim names, terms and places as I found them in the sources used. On Palestinian Muslim graves in Jerusalem, see Zilberman (1988).
2. On Islamic folk-beliefs, syncretic components, and regional cultural traits in India, see Ahmad (1984: 7-16) and Roy (1983). On syncretism in Indonesia, see Kahana (1993) and Brakel (1995).

3. Though cremation is the main method of handling the dead among Hindus in India, there are also other ways. Laying the dead on stone platforms on tops of hills is a custom among some small groups, and it resembles the Parsi Zoroastrian way of handling dead bodies (The Trustees of the Parsi Punchayet 1984). Floating dead bodies down a river is another way (Parry, 1994). The broad spectrum of belief, ritual and religious organization embraced by the term Hinduism creates diversity in custom and rituals. I thank Prof. G. Kressel and Dr. P.R. Kumarswami for their help and comments.
4. On ritual purity and pollution, see Dumont (1970), and Srinivas (1994).
5. See, for example, Jackson (1992); Tahir (1989); Moini (1989); and Currie (1989: 112-113).
6. See the way in which Aho (1981) uses this contrast.
7. On castes in Islam in India. see Ahmad (1978).
8. See, for example, the case of 'Rallying round the Cow' in the Benares area (Pandey, 1983).
9. On this idea, see in Parry (1994: 70).
10. The Muslim-Hindu struggle over the site of the Babri Masjid-Temple came to a climax in 1992, when Hindu crowds stormed the mosque and destroyed it. On the history of the conflict, see Srivastava (1991).
11. On the rituals of Muharram in Lucknow, see Sharar (1994: 215-217) and Hjortsoj (1987). On these rituals in Lebanon, for example, see Peters (1963: 159-200).

REFERENCES

Ahmad, I. (1976), "Exclusion and assimilation in Indian Islam" in *Socio-Cultural Impact of Islam on India* edited by Attar Singh, Chandigarh : Publication Bureau Punjabi University.

Ahmad, I., (Editor) (1978), *Caste and Social Stratification Among Muslims in India.* Columbia, Mo.: South Asia Books.

———(1984), *Ritual and Religion Among the Muslims in India.* New Delhi : Manohar.

Aho, J.A. (1981), *Religious Mythology and then Art of War.* London: Aldwyh.

Bloch, M. and J. Parry (1982), "Introduction : Death and the regeneration of life" in *Death and the Regeneration of Life* edited by M. Bloch and J. Parry. Cambridge : Cambridge University Press.

Brakel, C. (1995), *Islamic Syncretism in Indonesia.* Jerusalem : The Truman Institute, Peace Papers No. 3.

Cole, J.R.I. (1988), *Roots of North India Shi'ism in Iran and Iraq, Religion and*

State in Awadh 1722-1859. Berkeley and Los Angeles : University of California Press.

Currie, P.M. (1989), *The Shrine and Cult of Mu'in al-Din Chishti of Ajmer,* Delhi : Oxford University Press.

Desai, Z.A. (1989), "The Major daragahs of Ahmadabad" in *Muslim Shrines in India* edited by C.W. Troll Delhi : Oxford University Press.

Dumont, L. (1970), *Homo Hierarchicus : The Caste System and its Implications.* London: Weindenfeld and Nicolson.

Freitag, S.B. (1988), "The roots of Muslim separatism in South Asia : Pesonal practice and public structures in Kanpur and Bombay" in *Islam, Politics and Social Movements* edited by E. Burke and I.M. Lapidus. London : Tauris.

Friedman, L.M. (1984), "Muslim rituals : Household rites us public festivals in rural India" in *Ritual and Religion Among Muslims in India* edited by Imtiaz Ahmad N. Delhi : Manohar.

Granquist, H. (1965), *Muslim Death and Burial.* Helsingfors. Private Edition.

Hertz, R. (1960), "A contribution to the study of the collective representation of death" in *Death and the Right Hand* (Translated by R & C Needham) London : Cohen and West.

Hjortsoj, K. (1987), "Shi'a identity and the significance of the Muharram in Lucknow" in *Shi'ism, Resistance and Revolution* edited by M. Kramer, Boulder Colorado : Westariew Press.

Ikram, S.M. (1964), *Muslim Civilization in India.* New York: Columbia University Press.

Jackosn, P.S.J. (1989), "Perceptions of the daragahs of Patna" in *Muslim Shrines in India* edited by C.W. Prott. Delhi Oxford University Press.

Kahane, R. (1993), "Modern interpretation of animistic metaphors : An example from Indonesia". *Social Issues in Southeast Asia* 8 (1): 11-34.

Mahmood, T. (1989), "the dargah of Sayyid Salar Mas'ud Ghazi in Bahraich : Legend, tradition and reality" in *Muslim Shrines in India* edited by C.W. Troll. Delhi : Oxford University Press.

Moini, S.L.H. (1989), "Rituals and customary practices at the dargah of Amjer". *Muslim Shrines in India* edited by C.W. Troll. Delhi : Oxford University Press.

Munir, D. (1987), 'The Shias of Pakistan" in *Shi'ism Resistance and Revolution* edited by M. Kramer. Boulder, Colorade Westview Press.

Naipaul, V.S. (1991), *India, a Million Mutinies New.* London : Mandarin Paperbacks, Minerva.

Pandey, G. (1993), "Rallying round the cow : Sectarian strife in the Bhojpuri Region c. 1988-1917 in *Subaltern Studies II. Writings on Southern Asian History and Society* edited by G. Ranjit, Delhi : Oxford University Press.

Parry, U. (1982), Sacrificial death and the necrophagous ascetic" in *Death and the Regeneration of Life* edited by M. Bloch and J. Parry. Cambridge: Cambridge University Press.

Peters, E.C. (1963), "Aspects of rank and status among Muslims in Lebanese village" in *Mediterranean Countrymen* edited by J. Pitt-Rivers. The Hague : Mouton.

Roy, A. N.D. *The Islamic Syncretistic Traditon in Bengal.* Princeton : Princeton University Press.

Sayyid, A.R. (1984), "Moharram : A behavioural interpretation" in *Ritual and Religion Amoing the Muslims in India* edited by I. Ahmad, New Delhi : Manohar,.

Schubel, V.C. N.D. *Religious Performance in Contemporary Islam: Shi'a Devotional Rituals in South Asia.* Columbia: University of South Carolina Press.

Sen, K.M. (1982), *Hinduism.* Harmondsworth : Penguin Books.

Sharar, A.H., (1984), *Lucknow : The Last Phase of an Oriental Culture* (translated and edited by E.H. Harcourt and H. Fakhir). Delhi : Oxford University Prèss.

Siddiqui, I.H. (1989), "The early Chishti daragahs" in *Muslim Shrines in India* edited by C.W. Troll. Delhi : Oxford University Press.

Smith, J.I. and Y.Y. Haddad (1981), *The Islamic Understanding of Death and Resurrection.* Albany : State University of New York Press.

Srinivas, M.N. (1994), *The Dominant Caste.* Delhi : Oxford University Press.

Srivastava, S. (1991), *The Disputed Mosque.* New Delhi: Vistaar Publications.

The Trustees of the Parsi Panchayet (1984) *Towers of Silence and Doongerwadi* in Bombay. Bombay : The Trustees.

Turner, V. (1977), *The Ritual Process : Structure and Anti-Structure.* Ithaca: Cornell University Press.

Van Gennep, A. (1909), *Les Rites des Passage.* Paris : emile Nourry.

Weber, M. (1964), *The Sociology of Religion.* Beacon Press.

Zilberman, I. (1988), Change and Continuity Among Muslim Migrants in A Suburb of Jerusalem. Ph.D. Thesis, Department of Social Antlrapology, Cambridge University.

ABU BAKR TUSI HAIDARI QALANDARI (BABA MATKA PIR, MATKEY SHAH) IN HISTORY, MYTH AND LEGEND

Kumkum Srivastava

Introduction

Mysticism has no genealogy. It is the eternal quest of man to directly experience the Ultimate Reality. Hamilton Gibb (1957, 1970) remarks that the history of popular religion in Islam runs parallel to that of the mystical movement. It was through the mystic channel that dynamic and progressive forces entered the structure of Islam and facilitated its adjustment with new situations and circumstances. Within Muslim societies, there is a permanent, if sometimes latent, tension and opposition between the two styles of religious life (Gellner 1981:159). On the one hand, there is a puritanical, unitarian, individualist, and scripturalist ideal of a single deity, which has disclosed its final message in a definitive Revelation available to all literate people. This version spurns mediation; thus has no clergy and no church organization. As Tocqueville explains: "Islam is the religion which has most completely confounded and intermixed the two powers...so that all the acts of civil and political life are regulated more or less by religious law" (quoted in Gellner 1981:1). In contrast to this view, there is the other ideal, which allows mediation, propitiation ritual and devotional excess and religious hierarchy. The pure, disinterested love of God, without hope of reward or fear of punishment is the leitmotif of Sufism throughout the centuries. 'Ecstatic' Sufism persisted alongside legalistic Islam, challenging the conventional religiosity of the 'Ulema' establishment. Incidentally, the Ulema constitute a literate class of scribes who act as guardians and exegetes of the revelation (Ruthven, 1997: 65).

The Sufi masters were renowned for their spirituality. They were known as the 'friends of God', i.e. Wali, a term translated as 'saint', though there is no church and no canonization process in Islam. The intercessionary powers attributed to God's friends endow them with the religious authority that leads to the creation of the Sufi orders (*tariqa*, path) (Trimingham 1973). Just as every *hadith* is supplied with a line of transmitters (*isnad*), tracing it back to the Prophet, so the different Sufi disciplines are provided with a chain (*silsila*) of authorities, extending back to the Prophet, his earliest companions and the eponymous founders of the various orders. From the mid twelfth until modern times, Sufi brotherhoods flourished all over the Islamic world, from rural outbacks to the dense human fabric of cities. (Gellner 1981; Hasan and Roy, eds, 2005).

A majority of the Sufis insisted that the inner reality of Islam (*haqiqa*) could only be approached through the observance of Sharia (*bashara*), the outward or exoteric law. Under the umbrella of their different *tariqas*, they developed organizations bound by personal ties of allegiance to their leaders. The *tariqas* soon became important sources of social and hence political power – hence considered a threat. The other kind of Sufis were the 'withdrawn' from the world (*beshara*), indulging in ritual practices regarded with hostility by the ulema. They did not show the orthodoxy of the *bashara*. Traditionally, the *tavez, tona, jharphunk* (boons, curses, blessings, magical amulets, 'blessed water') are connected with the *beshara* order. The *faqir* (mendicant) roaming in towns and villages is likely to belong to this order. The Malamatis, Qalandariyya, Siyahposh, Suhagiya, Rasul Shahi, Madari are some of them (see Kumkum Srivastava 1998, 2003).

In the beginning, the *beshara* ideology started as a philosophy of freedom. In practice, however, it degenerated into licentiousness among some sects. In the sixteenth century, there were a number of 'mad men' (*majdhub*) and 'naked men', who were respected because of the supernatural powers they were believed to possess (Mujeeb, 1967:296). They did not have any permanent institutions such as a *zawiya, khanqah, dargah*, which were associated with a Sheikh (the leader of an order). The *khanqahs* survived as long as their founder's *baraka* (grace) continued and pilgrims and offerings flowed in over time. It developed characteristics which did not harmonize with the principles and ideals of the services for which it was founded.

The *khanqah* served as a mediating institution between the saintly qualities of the Pir on one hand and the believers on the other. From there, he could reach out to a vast multitude of the faithful. Aid could be disbursed to the needy in terms of money, food and other worldly goods. After the Pir's *wisal* (union with God), his Khalifa observed the rituals, cherishing his memory, guiding the pilgrims on how to receive the *baraka* of the saint interred there. The *khanqah* also became the place of pilgrimage (*ziyarat*) for the members of that order. The dead saint now becomes the center of a cult and his *khanqah*, a shrine (*dargah*).

Morphology of the Shrine of Abu Bakr Tusi

Driving towards Purana Qila, Delhi, just ahead of Pragati Maidan, one notices branches of *kikar* trees sticking out from within the compound of what seems to be a place of worship. On the branches of these trees hang inverted clay plots (*matka*). The shrine of Abu Bakr Tusi Haidari Qalandari (Rehmat Ullah) urf Baba Matka Pir Matkey Shah would have gone unnoticed, had it not been for these innumerable earthen pitchers lining the compound walls, hung on bamboo sticks dug in the ground and serving as lamps atop the poles on either side of the arched gateway proclaiming the name of the saint. Earthen pitchers of all shapes and sizes, plain and decorated, painted and glazed, adorned with mirrors and *gota patti, kinari,* old and new, in different hues, can be seen inside and outside also. On a Thursday, one can witness the actual placing of the empty *matka*s on the branches and walls.

A flight of marble steps leads to the main tomb of the revered saint, twenty-eight feet above the ground on a *tila* (*mound*). Down below, on the left are two shops, their signboards proclaiming clearly in Devanagari and Urdu that these are Abdul Hamid Phoolwale and Qadimi Dukan (old shop). The items sold here – *elaichidana* (sweet cardamom), roasted Bengal gram (*bhuna chana*) –constitute what will become transvalued (or blessed) food (*tabarruk*) after being offered at the grave. In addition, rose petals, garlands, *chadar* (sheet, usually green bordered with silver or golden *gota,* laced and embroidered), earthen pitchers of all shapes and sizes, other ritual ingredients, incense sticks, *loban,* low priced books, cassettes and posters of religious import are also sold here.

Once you have stepped in the sacred geography of this *dargah,* on the right is the Nur-al-Islam mosque. On the flight of stairs, on every landing, one will find beggars and urchins equipped with tin bowls, waiting for the occasional visitor to drop a coin or two. At the end of the first flight of stairs is the residential complex of the *sajjadanashin* (keeper of the prayer carpet) Mohammad Naseem Sultani (who is also a government employee) and his children. Above that, after sixteen steps, is another covered courtyard (*sahn*). Saint Abu Bakr and his Khalifa, Sheikh Rahimuddin, lie buried here. The tomb of Abu Bakr is not very large. It is a flat-roofed structure with the grave covered by a green velvet sheet in the center. The *qibla* (western wall) has three recessed arches that serve as shelves while the other three sides have latticed doorways.

The tiled floor is also covered with a green carpet. The roof, the cenotaph and the *matka* motifs are painted red and green. A plaque on the *qibla* wall has a Quranic injunction and an inscription in Urdu, stating that 'this is the *rauza*' of Sheikh Abu Bakr Tusi Haidari Qalandari who died on 20 Ramzan 655 A.H. A partially dislodged wooden board outside the enclosed grave also bears the same information.

> Shaikh Abu Bakr Tusi Qalandari qadas sarah mashrib-i-Qalandariyya dasht. Sheikh Jamaluddin be-ghayat muwarzat-bud-o-Sultan alam Sheikh neztar Khanqah hazir shude. Majlis wasle 22 Rajab 700 azeen jahan pardonamud.
>
> [Sheikh Abu Bakr Tusi was affiliated to the order of the Qalandars. There existed great affection between Sheikh Jamaluddin and him. And, Sultans and Sheikhs used to sit in his Khanqah and participate in the assembly. He left this mortal world on 22 Rajab 700 A.H.]

The *khadim* (ritual officiant) is the only employee, whereas the two *qawwals* present mostly on Thursday (when a crowd is expected) fend for themselves, collecting whatever the visitors offer them.

Not only the visitors but also the administrators term it a *dargah* (Dargah Sharif), but in my opinion it is just a *mazar* and not a *dargah.* The institutions and appurtenances that are associated with *dargah* such as hospices, school (*madarasa*), dispensary, etc, are absent here. Let me clarify certain terms associated with a Muslim shrine. The term used for grave is *qabr*, but one that is venerated (*ziyarat*) is called *mazar*. It is always covered with a velvet cloth (*gilaf*). Thus, a *dargah* includes the *mazar*. There are examples of *mazars* that do not have a *dargah*, or it may be established later, as the popularity of the saint grows. A *mazar* may be defined as a raised, rectangular, cemented platform underneath which rest the mortal remains of the venerated saint. It may or may not be roofed, nor housed within four walls (*maqbara*). When a *mazar* is on its way to becoming a *dargah*, the first step is the construction of a *maqbara*, of marble, preferably, which is absent here. The distinction between *mazar* and *dargah* is also important socially – women may be permitted entry into the precincts of the *dargah* but not the actual grave (*mazar*). When the saint is buried at the same place where he had lived, it is called *rauza*, a word that literally means 'garden' (de Tassy 1997:40). Since Abu Bakr's *khanqah* and his *mazar* are at the same place, the term *rauza* is used for it. As noted earlier, the plaque in the mausoleum also refers to it as a *rauza*.

Sources for Life-history

How do we begin the story (or legend, or life-history account) of a Sufi master? We begin by looking into the literature, which was produced when he was alive. This literature consists of writings of the Sufi, memoirs of the *murids*, the letters written by the saint, the descriptions of the travelers who visited the Sufi and stayed at his *khanqah*, and perhaps, in more recent times, historiographic accounts.

Notwithstanding this orientation of the Sufis to writing, there was always an impulse to record the sayings of the saint, his biographical details and travels, the austerities he performed, the first-hand account of his discourses, his participation in assemblies (for instance, *mehfil-i-sama*), his opinion of other Sufis, if he ever expressed it, etc. Unfortunately, under the canopy of such writings have flourished apocryphal and fictional accounts (Rizvi 1978:5). The researcher should, first of all, know which of these writings are authentic and which spurious.

Lawrence (1982:31-3) identifies certain kinds of literary evidence that have proved notable in the institutional phase of Sufism. The first is the genealogical tree (Shijra), which functioned to confirm the consanguineous relation of the Sufi to the earliest generations of Muslims, and perhaps even to the Prophet

Muhammad himself or his family members. The other genealogy, which has precedence over the consanguineous links, is of spiritual relationship; we may call it 'spiritual genealogy'. It describes the relations of initiation (*bait*) – who initiated whom?

The other literary evidence consists of anecdotes. Lawrence (1982:31) writes: 'Sufis delighted in anecdotes on every topic – whether moral, having to do with sensual restraint and subtle codes of conduct, or miraculous, pertaining to food, procreation, conversion, and the like'. These conversations of the Sufis were committed to writing by their disciples. The letters (*maktubat*) and didactic essays (*isharat*) of the Sufis had the same content. They were all meant to illuminate a point of spiritual, social, legal, and even behavioral import (see Digby 1991).

Abu Bakr Tusi in History

No biological or spiritual genealogical tree of Abu Bakr Tusi has been discovered. Nor do we have his *malfuzat*, *maktubat*, or *isharat*. We do not know if he ever lectured, preached, or corresponded with other saints or his disciples. No eulogy of this saint is known to us. We know that he was fond of *sama* gatherings, but no information is available on his participation in them. We find scanty references to him in Abdu'l-Ha'i's *Nuzhatu'l-Khawatir*, Hamid bin-Fazlu'llah's (also known as Dervish Jamali Kamboo Delhavi) *Siyaru'l-Arifin*, Shaikh Abdu'l-Haqq's *Akhbaru'l-Akhyar*, Mir (also Amir) Khurd's *Siyaru'l-Auliya*, Ghulam Muinuddin Abdullah Khweshgi's *Ma'ariju'l-Wilayat* and Zia-uddi'n Barani's *Tarikh-i-Firuz Shahi*. A point needs to be reiterated here. Visitors to Matka Pir are least interested in the genealogy of the saint. They believe that their wishes would be fulfilled once they present themselves before the saint and ask him for his intercession. Devotion and faith supersede the academic quest.

There is a problem of chronology with respect to Abu Bakr Tusi. We noted earlier that the inscription on the plaque (installed after 1971) inside the mausoleum reads that he left his mortal remains in 655 A.H. (1235 A.D.), but *Nuzhatu'l-Khawatir* (p.123; c.f. Hussain 1960: 7) records that between 664 A.H. (1244 A.D.) and 684 A.H. (1264 A.D.), he came to Delhi. Hussain's booklet (1960: 54) notes that Abu Bakr died (*wisal paya*) on 22 Rajab 700 A.H.

Abu Bakr was a resident of Tus in Khorasan. When he migrated to Delhi, Sultan Ghiyasuddin Balban was the reigning monarch.

Abu Bakr set up his *khanqah* on the banks of the river Yamuna (according to *Akhbar-ul-Akhyar*, p.3-74; Rizvi 1978: 307) after demolishing a temple standing there. Abu Bakr's year of birth is uncertain. Hussain (1960) estimates that he lived to be seventy or eighty years old. We have little information of his life before coming to Delhi, about his birth or his *ilm-o-fazl* (learning and accomplishments). His contemporaries were Sheikh Nizamuddin Panipati, Sheikh Ali Zanbali, Sheikh Nuruddin Yar Parran, Maulana Husamuddin, Shaikh Nizamuddin Auliya, Sheikh Jamaluddin Hasan Hansvi, and other Chishtiyya saints (Hussain 1960:14). They used to visit his *khanqah* and were aware of his external (*zahiri*) and internal (*batini*) achievements. He was well known for his attempts to transcend his baser self (*nafs*) and was educated in the precepts of Islam (*tabligh-i-din*). Abdu'l-Ha'i (p.123) writes that Abu Bakr was committed to prayer and closely followed the religious instructions; so he was both *abid* and *zahid*. He was a 'high level' (*buland*) dervish.

We also learn about Abu Bakr in references in the *malfuzat* and *maktubat* of his contemporary sufis. Rizvi (1978: 308) writes that Abu Bakr's relations with his contemporaries were not cordial. One of the first disagreements was with Nuruddin Malik Yar Parran, attached to the *silsila* of Shaikh Abu Kaziruni. Nuruddin, a resident of Lar in Fars, came to Delhi around the same time as Tusi. Abu Bakr was well established by then and was held in high esteem. Nuruddin also planned to build his *khanqah* in the proximity of Abu Bakr's. Considering it to be an encroachment on his spiritual territory (*wilaya*), Abu Bakr asked him to bring an order (*farman*) from the Sultan as well as permission from his Pir. *Siyaru'l-Arifin* relates that the Sultan was away from Delhi; even then Nuruddin was able to procure the required documents from the Sultan and also, his mentor in no time. Impressed with his 'flight', Abu Bakr bestowed on him the title 'Yar Parran' meaning 'flier' (Hussain 1960:7-8; Rizvi 1978:308). Nuruddin's *mazar* is in the Bagh-e-Bedil, opposite Tusi's *dargah*.

Another interaction he had was with a famous Chishtiyya Saint, Jamaluddin Khatib Hansvi, Baba Farid's first Khalifa. The former visited Abu Bakr frequently and respected him for his spiritual accomplishments. Sheikh Jamaluddin himself was a profound and reputed scholar. Abu Bakr Tusi always organized a *mehfil-i-sama* in his honor. The Sheikh gave the title Baz-i-Safed (the white falcon) to Matka Pir for his 'rare mystical achievements' (Rizvi 1978:307). Hussain (1960:22) assumes that it was due to his fair complexion. Abu Bakr Tusi must have been handsome as well (*khushindam*). The falcon symbolizes the 'spiritual flight' too. 'Once we meditate on Allah, our materialistic lust is ever transcended, and the human body becomes light and can 'fly' anywhere' (Ibid). If white stands for 'complexion' and 'purity', falcon is a symbol of 'lightness' and 'supernatural flight'.

Shaikh Abdu'l-Haqq's *Akhbaru'l-Akhyar* refers to another incident that shows the cordiality and closeness of their relationship. Maulana Husamuddin (the Head Khatib and Qazi-ul Qazah of Delhi) was a disciple of Sheikh Jamaluddin. Once when he went to meet Abu Bakr, the latter told him that he was planning to go on Hajj. When he returned to Hansi and met Jamaluddin, the latter's first query was regarding the welfare of the 'white falcon' (Hussain 1960: 8; *Akhbar-ul Akhyar*, p. 163). Hearing the Maulana's reply, the Sheikh asked him to proceed to Delhi saying, 'You leave, I am going to follow you soon.' He wrote a *rubai* (quatrain) in honour of Abu Bakr Tusi and handed it to the Maulana to be delivered to his friend.

> *Bar paye tera saram nashara wali terast*
> *Yak sar che bud balke hazara wali tar*
> *Dar gar-i-walan saz chun bu bakr az an kah*
> *bu bakr muhammadi be gara wali tar*
> (If my head is sacrified at your feet, it will be a good thing to happen,
> What to speak of one head, if even a thousand heads are sacrificed, it would be better still,
> Like Abu Bakr converted this cave into a home,
> So like the lover of the Prophet, Abu Bakr, for us the cave should be better than anything else.)

Hazrat Nizamuddin Auliya's visit to the *khanqah* of Abu Bakr Tusi to attend *sama* session is also documented (Hussain, 1960:29), justifying that it was of a 'high religious order' and met with the 'stringent expectations' of the Chishtiyya saints who vehemently opposed those auditions which were for mundane, secular enjoyment. Amir Khurd's *Siyaru'l-Auliya* gives a detailed account (p.201) of one such *mehfil*. Khwaja Jahan Ahmad Ayaz in Nizami Bansari (1945: 214-5) also details this incident.

Hazrat Nizamuddin, Khwaja Sayyed Mohammad (Imam) and his brother, Khwaja Jahan Ahmed as well as fifty others attended the *sama*. Finding the *mehfil* lack lustre and dull, the saint enumerated the requisites of a good *mehfil-i-sama*. His narration of the life histories of saints generated waves of ecstasy (*wajd*). Singing resumed and the saint entered into *wajd* and started dancing along with Sheikh Zanbali. It is not clear whether Abu Bakr Tusi participated in the above proceedings, but this is evident that the Chishtiyya saints visited the *khanqah* of Qalandari saints and were themselves visited by Jawaliqs, Qalandars, and Haidaris (*beshara* sects). Abu Bakr Tusi, though a Haidari Qalandari, was not a peregrinating or wandering dervish. In many aspects of his lifestyle, he bore similarity with the Chishtiyya *silsila* (permanent residence, *majlis*, *mehfil-I-sama*). Ziauddin Barani, a contemporary historian, in his *Tarikh-i-Firuz Shahi* (p.173) remarks on the political involvement of a dervish of his caliber in the scandals of the court. This is the first reference to Abu Bakr Tusi by a contemporary historian, therefore worthy of mention.

The Attack On Sidi Muwallih: Sufis in Court Politics

Abu Bakr Tusi was also involved in a controversy. One of his disciples mortally wounded the founder of the Muwallih Sufi *tariqa*, Sidi Muwallih, in the reign of Jalalu'd-Din Khalji. The story as narrated in Barani's *Tarikh-i-Firuz Shahi* (c.f. Lal 1967: 23-7; Rizvi 1978:308-9; Digby, 1984: 67-8, 91, 106) is as follows.

On his way to Delhi from Persia, Sidi Muwallih met Baba Farid (at Ajodhan) some years before 1265 A.D. Baba found him exceptionally ambitious and advised him to keep himself away from the company of political elites (Sultans, Shehzade, Amirs, Maliks), for such associations were calamitous for dervishes (Rizvi 1978: 308). But, Sidi did not heed Baba's advice, and during the reign of Balban, he bought his way into the inner circle and established contacts with prominent people. In the reign of Mu'izzu'd-Din Kaiqubad, he was more successful and gathered around him an adulatory entourage. His popularity further rose during the reign of Sultan Jalalu'd-Din Khalji. The Sultan's eldest son, the Khan-i-Khanan, became Sidi's ardent devotee. Sidi fondly called him 'son'. Besides him, many other outstanding nobles and religious functionaries such as Qazi used to visit his *khanqah*.

However, mystery surrounds the source of Sidi's immense wealth, since he accepted neither land grants nor any other largesse from anyone. Although he himself was austere, his guests were treated royally and bestowed with expensive gifts. The story goes like this that whenever he had to pay somebody, he would ask the person to reach a specific spot. There the person would find freshly minted coins (*tanka*). This was considered quite intriguing. In his personal habits, he performed strenuous ascetic exercises but never attended the Friday prayer. He was an enigma to all, and the rumor spread that he was a 'magician' and 'alchemist', having the knowledge of *kimya-o-simya* (as he was able to create wealth).

A plot to assassinate Sultan Jalaluddin Khalji was exposed. Sidi Muwallih was alleged to have conspired with the rebels. He was arrested along with some nobles and Maliks. Barring Sidi, the others were transferred from the capital. However, a debate ensued regarding an appropriate punishment for the arch-conspirator, Muwallih Sidi. The Sultan had called a large number of nobles and religious personnel for consultation. This group included Abu Bakr Tusi and his disciples. Sidi was brought before the court in fetters. The punishment prescribed was that the offender be trampled to death under an elephant's feet.

The presence of Sidi threw Jalaluddin into a rage, and he asked Sheikh Abu Bakr Tusi 'to avenge him of Sidi Maulah' (Lal 1967:26; *Akhbar-ul Akhyar*, p. 162-4). At that very moment, Bahri Haidari, a follower of Abu Bakr, attacked Sidi with his razor and *juwal-doz*. Sidi was wounded and fell down. The other son of Jalaluddin, named Arkali Khan, signaled to a mahout to bring his elephant forward to trample Sidi to death. The orthodox criticized this method of execution. Unfortunately, a number of natural calamities (dust storms, failure of the monsoon, drought and famine, and devastating floods the following year) followed Sidi's (unlawful) and the Sultan was unequivocally blamed for this. To the Chishtis, the moral was clear: the Sufi should distance himself from politics and power struggle. And, to Barani, the lesson was clearer – 'A king could ill afford to kill a dervish' (Rizvi 1978: 309).

Isami's *Futuhu's-Salatin* (ed. Usha, Madras 1948) argued that the Sufi impostors (*khirqa-poshan-i kham*) falsely accused Sidi. The actual conspirator was the Khan-i-Khanan, who was a contender with Arkali Khan for the throne. Sidi's finances came from the merchants and the Sultan's son, the Khan-i-Khanan. The wide spread belief that Sidi was obtaining wealth from magical practices was a myth. In this power struggle, Arkali Khan enlisted the support of many Sufis, Sheikh Abu Bakr being one of them. Rizvi (1978: 309) concludes from this that Sheikh Abu Bakr was also 'ambitious', but we do not know what his ambitions were.

Abu Bakr Tusi in Myth and Legend

One day, a thirsty traveler approached Abu Bakr. The Hazrat offered him water from an earthen pitcher. The man told the Sheikh that he was suffering from an incurable disease. The Sheikh offered to pray for him. A few days later, the traveler returned, now completely cured. He thanked the saint and spread the word to his fellow men. Soon, more people started visiting him with their problems. His prayers and intercession, they believed, would rid them of their misery.

It is said that Sheikh Abu Bakr was very fond of *sherbet*. The visitors and his followers used to bring it for him in earthen pitchers (*matkey*), water pots of clay (*lutia*), oval long necked containers (*kunde*), and the well to do in silver kettles. One does not know much about their disposal; metal ones must have been kept safe but what about the clay ones? The tradition of keeping the pots at the shrine, or suspending them from the branches of the tree in its compound dates back to September 1947 (Hussain 1960: 29). During the months of loot, plunder and rioting, thousands of Muslims took refuge near the shrine and at Purana Qila. The earthen pots were perhaps used as cooking utensils, or for storing water and grain. To keep them safe and prevent breakage the pots were suspended from trees, or placed upside down on the parapet and walls. At that time, Hussain writes: the entire area appeared like a 'city of pots'. Soon this practice of suspending *matkey* became a tradition and lent an exotic flavor to the shrine. The standard item brought as an offering to the shine was a *matka*, sometimes kettles of brass, copper and silver were also offered, which were displayed during the Urs ceremony by the administrators of the *dargah*.

Due to the Sheikh's preference for sherbet, its ingredients (milk, sugar or jaggery (*gur*) are included in the list of ritual offerings at the fulfillment of a vow (*mannat*). Besides the *matka*, which they invariably buy from the shop at the foot of the shrine (Qadimi Dukan), *elaichidana*, vials of perfume, *agarbatti* (incense sticks), *chadar*, flowers (rose petals) are the other ritual ingredients. The quality of the *chadar*, the visitors bring varies according to their financial position. The administrators of the shrine advise visitors to bring the sherbet ingredients as oblations, rather than the prepared drink. Often, on a Thursday, pilgrims bring readymade sherbet and offer it as *tabarruk* to other visitors and waiting beggars.

Once a disrespectful (*bad aquida*) person, intending to test the spiritual prowess of the saint, offered *lohe ke chane* (iron balls resembling gram) on a platter to him. Cynical of the saint's power, he wanted to expose him (*qalandari kirkiri ho jayegi*). The saint took a fistful of *chanas*, rubbed them between his palms, blew off the husk and ate them. Ashamed of his action, the man apologized profusely, and begged to be taken in as a servitor (*khadim*). Since then a well-known saying about the Sheikh is oft recited (Hussain 1960: 28).

> *Abu Bakr Tusi, khaye chane, udaye bhusi*
> [Abu Bakr Tusi, (he) eats horse-grams, blows off husk.]
> *Abu Bakr Tusi, mare phunk, udebhusi*
> [Abu Bakr Tusi, when he blows on it, the husk flies off.]

The popularity of Abu Bakr, it is said, prompted Ghiasuddin Balban, the ruler of Delhi, to test the saint. He sent him a platter full of iron balls and a lump of mud for lunch. Unfazed, the Baba prayed to God and when he uncovered the plate, the iron had changed to roasted gram and the lump of mud into *gur* (jaggery). The Baba mixed a part of *gur* with the gram and part with water, which changed into sweet milk. Since then, it has become a custom to offer gram, *gur* and milk in earthen pitchers once someone's wish is fulfilled. Another story, quite similar to the above, tells of a man who sent horse droppings in an earthen pitcher to the Sheikh with the intention of witnessing his *karamat* (miraculous power). When the cloth covering the pot was lifted, the fecal material had transformed to *gur*. These stories abundantly establish the sheikh as being a *karamati* (ability to perform miracles).

Ironically it was the Baha's miraculous powers that ultimately led to his death. He was known to convert lumps of mud into gold to help the poor. This set his disciples thinking that he had a large treasure hidden somewhere. They murdered him to get to the booty but found nothing. The *dargah* is located on the site where he was murdered.

The Saint is Alive

In this section are discussed the reasons why graves become the object of veneration. The Deoband School of Islamic Thought has strongly opposed the worship at graves. Shah Waliullah's criticism of such practices is well known (Gaborieau 1983, 1989; Baljon 1989). However, when we examine the composition of people who visit the *mazars* with an explicit aim to venerate them, or as pious Muslim would say, 'to read' (*padne ke liye*, meaning 'reading certain verses from the Quran'), we find that the orthodox Muslims are as much present there as are the more liberal ones. Mahmood (1989: 40) recalls the names of many Deobandi ulema who used to visit the *dargah* of Sayyad Salar Mas'ud Ghazi.

I remember one of my first visits to the shrine of Abu Bakr Tusi, with a family friend of ours, a devout Muslim, who is critical of the way in which the 'keeping of graves' has become an occupation, an instrument of making money. Although orthodox in many ways, he, like many other Muslims I had met during the course of this work, visited the *mazars* of prominent saints, as and when he 'felt' like visiting them. His rituals included no offerings (of flowers, scented-sticks, sweets, etc), but 'recitations' from the Quran.

After he had 'read' at the *mazar* of Abu Bakr, he told me that he had the feeling that the saint was present. I asked him to describe this experience, but he said it was ineffable: 'You have a strong feeling in your heart (*qalb*) that the Saint is present there.' He said that he had not fixed a particular day to visit a *dargah*. Whenever he had a strong 'feeling', he knew that the saint (*buzurg*) wanted him to visit him. I learnt the same from many other visitors to the shrine of Abu Bakr. Many claimed to have 'seen' the saint: they all believed that the saint was 'alive' and 'alert' (*zinda javed*).

Stories of the miracle of omnipresence of saints are common in other religious traditions (see Babb 1986; Laidlaw 1995; V.K. Srivastava 1997; Whitehouse and Laidlaw, eds, 2004, for examples from other cultures). A servitor at the shrine called Chand described one of his experiences falling in this category. He was handling the case of a woman who had been possessed by an evil spirit. She was in Dehradun, and it was not possible for her kin to bring her to Delhi for 'supernatural treatment'. Chand had to go there to perform the rites of exorcism (*utara*). When he started reciting the verses from the Quran, he realized that the 'dangerous' (*khatarnak*) and 'sullied' (*gandi*) entity was extremely powerful. Then, he had a strong feeling that the saint, Abu Bakr, was present there: he was 'sitting on a cot', and continued to be around till the *utara* rituals were in progress. The woman started recovering gradually after the ritual performance. Chand attributed the success of rituals to the presence of the saint.

I asked the *sajjadanashin* of the shrine, Muhammad Naseem Sultani, what he understood by the term Qalandar. He said the Qalandars have a special attraction (*kashish*) that cannot be ignored. In this context, he described one of his experiences, which is given below. This also illuminates the concept of Qalandar.

One day, Naseem Sultani was sitting at the *mazar* as a 'ritual officiant' when three women (from Reghar Pura, Delhi) came for *ziyarat*. They had brought with them a clay pot which was empty. Naseem Sultani told them that the earthen pitcher was never offered empty, and advised them to fill it with a fistful of roasted horse-grams or sweet balls of cardamom. They women knew of this, but had brought an empty earthen pitcher on the advice of a holy man (*baba*) who had appeared in the dream of one of them. The moment the women finished saying this, Naseem Sultani saw an old Muslim gentleman (in shirt and trousers) standing behind them. Presumably, he had come for *du'a* (prayers of supplication), he thought.

The man had a strong magnetic power. Even when Naseem Sultani was reading the *fatiha*, while offering the women's oblations at the shrine, he seemed to be transfixed. The man sat on the parapet. Naseem Sultani was extremely keen to talk to him. Just a few seconds before he finished the ritual (of distributing the *prasad*), he saw that the man was stepping down the staircase. Immediately, he ran after him, went even up to the main gate to the shrine and the road beyond it, but that man was to be seen nowhere: 'he became invisible'. Naseem Sultani narrated this incident to his father, who remarked that the man was a *buzurg*. That night, in a dream, Naseem Sultani received a confirmation of his father's conclusion about the identity of that man (Abu Bakr Tusi).

He saw three old men sitting on a wooden cot (*takht*). The one in the middle sat cross-legged.Naseem Sultani paid homage to them. The *buzurg* seated in the middle had a receding hairline, but long wavy hair; he sported a thin moustache and beard, wore *kurta* (shirt) and *tehmad* (lungi), on his chest were iron chains (quite like what the prisoners are made to wear), and in one of the chains around his neck was suspended a big locket. Unmistakably, he was a Qalandar.

The three men stood up and asked Naseem Sultani to follow them. The entire pathway was brightly lit. Suspended to the branches of small trees were lamps. Naseem Sultani wanted to touch them, but the elders advised him against it, warning him that if he did so, the whole place would be engulfed by fire. They asked him not to follow any further and return. Suddenly, he woke up and realized that it was a dream.

The following morning he did not feel like going to work. He had made a commitment to three of his office colleagues. They had decided to teach a lesson to their officer who troubled them no end. Since Naseem Sultani absented himself from office, the other three went ahead with their plan of waylaying the office and thrashing him. The injured officer lodged a complaint with the authorities. The three disgruntled fellows had a hard time saving their jobs. Nadeem Sultani reached the office the following day and was told about the deeds of his colleagues. The interpretation of all those who listened to Nadeem Sultani's proclamation of supernatural experiences was that it was the divine intervention of Sheikh Abu Bakr – the *buzurg* standing behind the women in one episode and the one sitting in the middle, in the other – which saved him from disgrace.

Interviewing people about their reasons for visiting the shrine, many of them told us the incredible experiences they have had of 'feeling' the presence of the saint. Many claim to have benefited from the guidance the saint provided them in their 'dreams'. The belief of people is that the saint is alive; he is *zinda* and *javed*. Findings of researchers who have studied other shrines corroborate my observation; for instance, Pinto (1989: 118) writes:

> Continued interviews with those who visit the dargah regularly...revealed their unmistakable faith that Hazrat Nizamuddin is alive. They often said, 'He is not dead. He has only put a veil between himself and us, ordinary mortals. That is why was cannot see him.' But sometimes he is believed to appear to some people. These appearances are taken as a mark of special favour and love.

After leaving the body (*jism*), the soul (*ruh*) of ordinary mortals rests at one of the two places (*muqam*), respectively known as Illin and Sijjin, which lie beyond the 'seventh heaven' (*satwan asman*). Their destination will be known on the day of judgment (*roz-i-mahshar*). But, the *arwah* (plural of *ruh*, soul) of saints do not ascend to the places meant for ordinary people. They go to the Ka'ba, from where they travel, on their own volition, to places they like most, and one of them is their graves. The bodies of ordinary mortals putrefy, 'they are eaten away by worms', but those of the saints remain as they are; 'they are beyond the process of decay.' One of my respondents, quoting from the Holy Book, said: 'The Quran pronounces that those who sacrifice themselves in the path of Allah are not dead. They are alive, but you do not know it.' On Thursdays, when shadows lengthen, the *arwah* of all dead descend to their graves, wherever they may be located. They expect their dear ones to visit them and light candles. That is why, Thursday is regarded as extremely important for a pilgrimage to the *mazars* of saints, because they are likely to be there, and may grant boons to their visitors.

REFERENCES

Abdu'l-Ha'i (1965), *Nuzhatu'l-Khawatir*. Lahore.

Babb, Lawrence A., (1986), *Redemptive Encounters, Three Modern Styles in the Hindu Tradition*. California: University of Chicago Press.

Baljon, J.M.S. (1989), Shah Waliullah and the Dargah. In Christian W. Troll (ed), *Muslim Shrines in India, Their Character, History and Significance*. Delhi: Oxford University Press (pp. 189-97).

Digby, Simon (1984), Qalandars and Related Groups. In Yohanan Friedman (ed), *Islam in India*. Jerusalem: Magnas Press.

———(1991), Anecdotes of a Provincial Sufi of the Delhi Sultanate. Paper presented at the International Seminar on Sufism, ICCR, New Delhi, 11-13 November.

Gaborieau, Marc (1983), The Cult of Saints among Muslims in Nepal and North India. In Stephen Wilson (ed), *Saints and their Cults*. Cambridge: Cambridge University Press.

———(1989) A Nineteenth-Century India 'Wahhabi' Tract Against the Cult of Muslim Saints: Al-Balagh al-Mubin. . In Christian W. Troll (ed), *Muslim Shrines in India, Their Character, History and Significance*. Delhi: Oxford University Press (pp. 198-239).

Gellner, Ernest (1981), *Muslim Society*. Cambridge: Cambridge University Press.

Ghulam Muinuddin Abdullah Khweshgi, (1855), *Ma'ariju'l-Wilayat*. Delhi.

Gibb, H.A.R. (1957), *An Interpretation of Islamic History*. Lahore.

———(1970), *The Arab Conquest in Central Asia*. New York.

Hamid bin-Fazlu'llah (also known as Dervish Jamali Kamboo Delhavi). (1893) *Siyaru'l-Arifin*. Delhi.

Hasan, Mushirul and Roy, Asim (eds). (2005) *Living Together Separately, Cultural India in History and Politics*. New Delhi: Oxford University Press.

Hussain, Akhlaq (1960), *Hayat-e-Tayyaba: Hazrat Sheikh Abu Bakr Tusi*. Delhi: Dargah Committtee (in Urdu).

Isami (1948), *Futuhu's-Salatin*. Madras.

Laidlaw, James A. (1995), *Riches and Renunciation, Religion, Economy and Society among the Jains*. Oxford: Clarendon Press.

Lal, K.S. (1967), *History of the Khaljis (1290-1320)*. Bombay: Asia Publishing House.

Lawrence, Bruce B. (1982), Islam in India. In Richard C. Martin (ed), *Islam in Local Contexts*. London: E.J. Brill.

Mahmood, Tahir (1989) The Dargah of Sayyid Salar Mas'ud Ghazi in Bahraich: Legend, Tradition and Reality. In Christian W. Troll (ed), *Muslim Shrines in India, Their Character, History and Significance*. Delhi: Oxford University Press (pp. 24-43).

Mir (also Amir) Khurd (1885), *Siyaru'l-Auliya*. Delhi.

Mujeeb, M., (1967), *The Indian Muslims*. London: George Allen and Unwin.

Mustafa Sheik Abdul Haqq Muhaddis Dehlvi, 1309 A.H. *Akhbar-ul Akhyar*. Karachi: Medina Publishing Company. (Translated by Maulna Sabhan Mahmud & Maulna Mohd. Fazil Darul Uloom.)

Pinto, Desiderio S.J. (1989), The Mystery of the Nizamuddin Dargah: The Accounts of Pilgrims. In Christian W. Troll (ed), *Muslim Shrines in India, Their Character, History and Significance*. Delhi: Oxford University Press (pp. 112-24).

Rizvi, S.A.A. (1978 & 1983), *A History of Sufism in India*. Volume 1 and 2. Delhi: Munshiram Manoharlal.

Ruthven, Malise (1997), *Islam, A Very Short Introduction*. Oxford: Oxford University Press.

Shaikh Abdu'l-Haqq (1914), *Akhbaru'l-Akhyar*. Delhi.

Srivastava, Kumkum (1998), On Sufism and the Qalandars: The Case of the Shrine of Sheikh Abu Bakr Tusi. Unpublished M.Phil. Dissertation. University of Delhi: Department of Anthropology.

———(2003), The Qalandars and the Qalandariyya Path (*tariqa*). In Anup Taneja (ed), *Sufi Cults and the Evolution of Medieval Indian Culture*. New Delhi: Indian Council of Historical Research and Northern Book Centre (pp. 247-86).

Srivastava, Vinay Kumar (1997), *Religious Renunciation of a Pastoral People*. Delhi: Oxford University Press.

Tassey, Garcin de (1997), *Muslim Festivals in India and Other Essays*. Delhi: Oxford University Press.

Trimingham, J.S. (1973), *The Sufi Orders in Islam*. London.

Whitehouse, Harvey and Laidlaw, James (eds). (2004), *Ritual and Memory, Toward a Comparative Anthropology of Religion*. AltaMira Press.

Zia-uddi'n Barani (1860-2), *Tarikh-i-Firuz Shahi*. Calcutta.

BAY'AT: SPIRITUAL RELATIONSHIP BETWEEN PIR AND MURID IN PAKISTAN

Hafeez-ur-Rehman Chaudhary

Introduction

Shrines are complex social institutions with a number of characteristics distinctive to their role in the life and culture of Pakistan. They have an internal organization, are usually led by a resident *pir*-manager and include a number of functionaries essential for carrying out the diverse activities of the shrine. How these individual recruited to their respective roles, trained for their specialties, and how they carry out their tasks contributes to success and reputation of each shrine. The shrines also develop networks of affiliation with other shrines. Not only are there important historical connections between them, but cooperative economic and visiting arrangements often exist. These networks include the followers or *murids* attached to individual shrines. Such networks extend to many areas of Pakistan, including those which are geographically remote, and include people representing virtually all social and economic classes of the Pakistani society. Thus, shrine function as linking institutions, bringing together people in a common interest despite the diversity of their individual backgrounds. In this way, the shrines have the capability of making positive contributions to the integration and unity of the Pakistani society. According to Schimmel (1975).

> The visitor to India and Pakistan is always amazed when he discovers the innumerable shrines, saints tombs and places of pilgrimage, and some authors have rightly remarked that there seems to exist a certain mystical relationship between the people and the saints.

Some of the important shrines in Pakistan are those of Syed Ali Hajwari in Lahore, popularly known as Data Gunj Bukhsh, Khawaja Farid Shakar Gunj at Pak Pattan, Shah Abdul Latif at Bhit, Shah Baz Qalandar at Sehwan, sachal Sermast in Sind and Ghazi Shah Baba in Karachi. This is only a cross-section as the list is very long. As Ewing says,

> The Saints of Pakistan ... are identified with the areas in which their shrines are situated. In rural areas many tribes are associated traditionally with a particular saint, who is thought to have originally converted that tribe to Islam.

These shrines are known for their ubiquity all over the country and are primarily identified for their spiritual attributes. Nevertheless their latent functions go well beyond the realm of the sacred and cover, for the major part, the social, cultural, economic and political life of the communities around them.

It is estimated that in the rural areas of Pakistan the majority of the people believe in a system popularity known as *Pir-Muridi*. If some one does not believe in *Pir-Muridi* he is labeled as *Bey Pira*[1] or *Bey Murshada*[2], i.e. without an elder and religious guide. According to system of *Piri-Muridi*, the *Murid* (follower) is supposed to have *Baiyat* (to follow) at hands of *Pir* which in common parlance means that the *Murid* has accepted the *Pir* as his spiritual master. Once the *Baiyat* is made the *Murid* refers all the problems he cannot easily handle to his *Pir* and requests him to have them solved by Allah through his *dua* (prayer) supplication. People believe that the *Pir* is possessed with spiritual powers. He can boost their business and cure their family members, and even their animals, from sickness and disease. They also think the *Pir* is the protector of their crops. Above all, they believe that the *Pir* can bring them salvation on the Day of Judgement (*qayamat*).

The aim of the present paper is however, to focus on the *Bay'at* at system of the shrine of Pir Mehr Ali Shah which is located at Golra Sharif.

The Village of Golra

Golra is a medium-size village in Rawalpindi District of the Punjab, Pakistan. As stated earlier it is situated nearly eleven miles north east of Rawalpindi. The distance of Golra from the Federal Capital

Islambad is approximately five miles. It is connected with Islamabad and Rawalpinid both by *katcha* and metalled roads. If one travels from Islamabad to Golra by *Katcha* road the distance is further reduced by almost half to two and a half miles. In fact, in the map of Islamabad Master Plan for metropolitan area, the village of Golra is shown as a part of Sector E-II of Islamabad. A link road connects Golra with Rawalpindi. The traveling time between Golra-Rawalpindi by bus is approximately one hour.

The village rests at the foot of the Margalla Hills. It is situated just where the slopes of Margalla meet the relatively flat area of Rawalpindi Sub-District. As such, part of the village land is undulated along the slope of Margalla Hills. The remaining portion is in the plains which extend upto the Grand Trunk Road running between Lahore and Peshawar. A *kass* (stream) flowing almost in the middleof the village divides the slopes from the plain. The total area of the village is approximately 654 acres.

The Line of Pirs

Village Golra has many shrines. However, the most well known shrine of Golra is that of Pir Mehr Ali Shah (1859-1937). He is accepted by his followers as having been an outstanding religious leader and a great spiritualist. It is believed that during his lifetime he performed miracles. Several stores of his spiritual power are narrated by the followers and those who visit the shrine during the annual *urs* festival. The present Pir Sahib is the grandson of Pir Mehr Ali Shah and serves as the executive head of the entire establishment.

The Baiyat

The spiritual system of the shrine at Golra Sharif owes it origin to, and is drawn from Sufi Imam. According to Sufi system the universe is divided into two spheres, *majaz* and *haqiqat*. Both spheres are believed to be the creation of the same Supreme Being. As such, both operate under His absolute power and control. Nothing moves in both worlds without His command and will. *Majaz* is the world of reality which one can see, observe and feel through one's sensory perceptions. However, the ultimate objective of a man is not to immerse himself completely into *Majaz* for it is purely temporary in its existence. The main reality is to be searched for in the realm of *Haqiqat* which is sublime, pure and everlasting.

It is ultimate Truth and perfect Beauty. While the two spheres are separate, Sufism, unlike orthodox views of Islam, does not believe that there is no connection between the two. On the contrary, it is believed that *Majaz* is only the first step leading towards the ultimate goal of *Haqiqat*. *Majaz*, may, in fact, be taken as a reflection of *Haqiqat*. One can achieve true experience of *Haqiqat* only when one has gone through the stage of *Majaz*. Thus *Majaz* and *Haqiqat* are a part of a single continuum, interconnected as well as complementary to each other. For instance, beauty is to be seen and observed in *Majaz* and eventually it is to be experienced in *Haqiqat*. Similarly if one seeks nearness to the Supreme Being – the ultimate form of *Haqiqat*, one should cultivate love for all of his creation (*Majaz*) which are observable around one in this world.

It is further believed that a person seek for *Haqiqat* should take a guide to led him to the 'right path'. This guide is the *Pir* or *Murshad* who has himself found the path through penance, self mortification, meditation, and through complete submission to the will of God. Having gone through all these states leading to *Haqiqat* a person is capable of holding the hand of a seeker of Truth and leading him to his destination.

This system of accepting an intermediary for the attaining of spiritual guidance is known as *Baiyat* which means 'taking an oath' or marking a firm promise to follow. When a man makes a *Baiyat* to another person by placing his hand in the hand of the other, he accepts the other as his spiritual guide and makes a firm commitment to him to follow his dictates without questioning. The holding of the hand is a symbolic way of accepting the spiritual power of the *Pir* or *Murshad*. A man thus promises that he will obey the directions of the *Pir* and order his life according to the dictates of Islam. It also means that the *Pir* has accepted him as his *Murid* and will henceforth provide him with every possible assistance in resolving his worldly problems so that he can attain his objective, viz. the experience of *Haqiqat*.

Once the *Baiyat* is done the *Murid* enters into the fraternity of which all the following of the *Pir* are members. Other *Murids* treat him like their own brother. The *Murids* of the same *Pir* are known as *Pir Bhai*, a fictive kinship term indicating a sibling relationship.

In an interview with the Pir Sahib, he explained to me that when a person makes a *Baiyat* he is required to self evaluate himself with regard to his life in the past, and recollect all the sins that he had committed previously. This process, according to Pir Sahib, leads him to a realization that he should henceforth change his mode of life and spend the rest of his time in complete submission to the will of God, and follow the path of truth and righteousness. The *Pir* supports the *Murid* in his determination and assures him that if he corrects himself in his conduct all his previous sins will be written off and he will have the chance to start all over again. The *Pir*, through the application of his spiritual powers, would see that he is protected from the influences of evil forces, and that the usual worldly problems do not distract him from his determination to achieve his new goal. Thus, according to the Pir Sahib the system of *Baiyat* infuses new hope and provides strong faith to the *Murid*. It awakens the inner conscience of a man and provides a mechanism for self restraint, self discipline and motivation in his endeavour to lead a pious life.

Method of taking Baiyat

The method of accepting *Baiyat* is highly ritualistic. Whenever a person seeks *Baiyat* at the hands of Pir Sahib he is asked first to perform ablution (*Wazoo*) and then approach the Pir Sahib in his chamber. The Pir Sahib takes the hand of the seeker in his own and recites verses from the Holy Quran for a new minutes. Following this the Pir Sahib directs the man to rub the hand on his face and pray five times with the congregation in the mosque. After each prayer he should recite *Darood Sharif* ten times, and also read on the beads ten times. During this period he should concentrate on the benevolences of God the merciful and make a firm commitment to himself that he will follow the path of Islam. Toward the end of these rituals the Pir Sahib raises his hands for *Dua* (blessings) and the *Murid* is asked to follow him in his prayers. This being over the person is declared as a *Murid*.

When the seeker for *Baiyat* is a female the same procedure is followed with the exception that the Pir Sahib does not take the hand of the woman in his own, for holding the hand of a female other than of one's own wife and daughter is considered sacrilligious in Islam. Instead of holding her hand, the Pir Sahib asks the woman to hold a piece of cloth at one end. The other end is held by him and the whole ritual is followed in the same fashion as in the case of a male.

During the period of the ritual for *Baiyat* both male and female are asked to keep their heads covered with a cap, a piece of cloth or some kind of head dress. This is done to intensify the purity of the ritual.

It is interesting that no record of names and addresses of *Murids* is kept either by the Pir Sahib or in the shrine secretariat. It is also not recorded how many persons have been accepted as *Murids* on a single day. On certain occasions the rush of seekers is so high that the Pir Sahib holds the hands of two or three persons at a time and accepts them in the fold of his *Murids*. Similarly, many women were noted to have held the other end of the piece of cloth at the same time on special occasion for accepting *Baiyat*.

Eligibility for *Baiyat*

There is no minimum qualification laid down for attaining the status of *Murid*. Anyone can take *Baiyat* provided he is in a proper frame of mind. Young and old are treated equally. The only condition which seems significant is that the seeker should not be a child or a non-Muslim. If a non-Muslim wants to be accepted as a *Murid* he should first convert himself to the faith of Islam.

The status of *Murid* can be terminated at the will of the Pir Sahib. This is done when a person has committed blasphemy or violated the rules of the shrine. For instance, a person who has accepted the Pir Sahib as his spiritual guide and has become his *Murid* is not allowed to take *Baiyat* as the hands of any other *Pir*. If he does so his membership of the fraternity is terminated automaticalloy.

Piri-Muridi

The system of *Piri-Muridi*, as stated above, is deeply enshrined in village communities all over the Punjab, and also in other parts of Pakistan. If a person has no *Pir/Murshad* he is nicknamed as *Bey Pira* or *Bey Murshada*. Both terms are derogatory and earn for such person a lower status in the society, for it is believed that he does not have a source of spiritual guidance and his sins cannot be written off on the Day of Judgement. He may also be treated as an imperfect individual in his worldly life. Persons without a *Pir* for spiritual guidance have few contacts in the community. It is noted that sometimes the relations between real brothers get strained if either of them has no *Pir* of his own. Hence, normal social community relationship such as inter-marriage or gift exchange (*vartan*) is not entered upon the *Bey Pira/Bey Murshada* persons. This is explained by arguing that a religious bond is stronger than an actual blood relationship. Therefore, a person who does not have such a religious bond cannot be accepted in other types of social relationships. Numerous cases have been noted when persons have been ostracized from their *Biradari* (local kindred group) if they do not have a *Pir* or *Murshad* to follow. One of the most common practices is for parents who are *Murids* of a particular *Pir* to ask their children to become *Murids* of a *Pir* too, preferably their own. If they do not listen to this advice they are threatened first by such admonitions as, "God will never forgive them for their sins" and if they still persist with their own course they are asked to leave the house. The parents feel guilty that their children have not listened to their advise and think there is something mentally wrong with them.

As stated earlier, generally a person has only one *Pir* at a time to follow. If there are reasons for him to believe that his Pir is not effective or that his personal character is not above board he can change his *Pir* and replace him with another. However, such cases are rare because traditionally the *Murid* is supposed to justify the actions of the *Pir* under one pretext or the other. In case he decides to change his *Pir* and accepts some other persons as his spiritual guide his membership with his previous fraternity terminates automatically. However, if the *Pir* with whom he has taken *Baiyat* dies, he need not choose another *Pir* because the spiritual relationship once established continues even after the death of the *Pir*. Among the visitors of Golra Sharif a large number of persons interviewed were the *Murids* of Babooji, the father of the present Pir Sahib. They did not take *Baiyat* at the hands of the present Pir Sahib. They attend the shrine as in the past and ask for the *Dua* (blessings) of the present Pir Sahib just as they did from Babooji. This is done in terms of a bnelief that the son of a *Pir* is also a *Pir*. Thus the spirituality of the *Pir* is believed to be a hereditary trait transferred lineally from father to son and grandson etc.

NOTES

1. *Pir* is derived from the Persian word *pir* which literally means a person of old age. Since the person of old age are looked upon with respect,

the heads of the shrine are given this title for the respect they command from their followers.

2. *Murshada* is given derived from the Persian world *murshad* which means a person from whom spiritual guidance is drawn by his followers.

REFERNCES

Schimmel, A. (1975), *Mystical Dimensions of Islam*. The University of North Carolina Press.

THE SPREAD OF COMMUNAL RIOTS TO SOUTH INDIA

Theodore P. Wright Jr.

Introduction

The ideology of Muslim nationalism in British India in the 1940s held the Muslims were an homogenous nation, distinct in every respect from other Indians and especially from Hindus (Ikram 1964: 294). The fieldwork of anthropologists published in the 1970s and represented by the series of volumes edited by Imtiaz Ahmed of Jawaharlal Nehru University (Ahmad 1973, 1976, 1981, 1983) contended to the contrary that South Asian Muslims are regionally, linguistically, ritually, by sect and behaviourally diverse. Our purpose here is to reexamine these alternative paradigms. However, true diversity may have been present a quarter century ago. Have both external and domestic pressures produced a trend toward homogenization of South Asian Muslims at the end of this century ? This paper is about the spread of communal (i.e. Hindu-Muslim) riots, the most damaging common experience of North Indian Muslims (Wilkinson 1995). This violence had culminated earlier, in 1947 in the near genocide of the Muslim population of the Eastern Punjab and has recurred since the 1970s in the rest of the "Hindi belt", plus Maharashtra, Gujarat and Hyderabad City (Das 1990). It was my contention in 1965 however (Wright 1965: 580) that the Dravidian South of India (Tamil Nadu, Kerala, Karnataka and Andhra Pradesh save for Hyderabad) afforded a sharply different picture with an almost total absence of communal strife, a model of inter-religious harmony for the North. Evidence is accumulating that this key distinction between what one might call "Hindustan by conquest" and "Dravidistan by peaceful immigration", between North and interior India and south and coastal India, in fast eroding in 1990s and a negative homogenization is bringing Muslims all into one subordinate and oppressed community. It is, furthermore, my tentative explanation that the agents of this homogenization are an incongruous combination of internal and external enemies, the *Sangh Parivar* and Inter Services Intelligence (ISI) of Pakistan.

The communalization of the South began, as Fanselow details, with the sudden conversion to Islam of several villages of Scheduled Caste people in Tamil Nadu in 1981 ((Mujahid 1989). Young men educated with the help of Scheduled Caste admission quotas came home to see in a new light the age-old discrimination from which their parents suffered. They determined to escape this subjection by converting out of Hinduism to another religion. Instead of Christianity, the logical choice of the colonial era, or Buddhism, the path of Dr. Ambedkar in 1956, they with great risk chose Islam, the religious faith of Pakistan, the national enemy of India. Perhaps the Gulf oil boom of the 1970s with its promise of lucrative jobs and powerful Arab friends implicitly or explicitly influence their choice although they denied it (Wright 1982: 239-245). The phenomenon, not unprecedented in South India was blow up out of proportion by the media and led to the revival of the dormant *Virat Hindu Samaj* by Dr. Karan Singh the *Yuvraj* of far off Kashmir (Mathew 1982). Other 'untouchables" used the threat of conversion to extract concessions from the Hindu castes above them. Some were reconverted to Hinduism by *shuddhi* or ritual cleansing. All of this gave the Hindu militants represented by the R.S.S. (*Rashtriya Swayamsevak Sangh*) and the *Bajrang Dal* and their political wing, the B.J.P. (*Bharatiya Janata Party*), the opportunity to break out of the confines of the Hindu belt and Central India. Without penetrating the Dravidian South, the party had no hope of becoming a truly all-India majority party. Frank Fanselow concludes his retrospective analysis of the Meenakhsipuram conversion by asserting that "the conversions and the reaction they triggered changed the political culture of Tamil Nadu. They contributed to the emergence of a communalist social psychology and led to the foundation of an organization infrastructure for inter-religious communalism ... and a new pattern of inter-religious violence in the state." (Fanselow 1999). A new local organization, the *Hindu Munnani*, struck root

(Krishnaswamy 1995: 380). Part of the reason for the benign character of inter-religious relations in Tamil Nadu therefore had been that the main political confrontation was between the anti-Brahmin Tamil nationalist movement (Hardgrave 1965) and the Brahmin social, religious and political elite. As in Lucknow in the North, where the fact that the main feud was between Sunni and Shia Muslims, left little attention to be paid to communal enmity (Varshney 1997: 7). The B.J.P. has still failed to penetrate Tamil Nadu (if not Karnataka) significantly, but in 1998 it won the alliance of the Tamil fraction of Jayalalitha, the A.D.M.K., which gave it a winning margin in New Delhi for a year (Dasgupta and Bhaumik 1998); and of the D.M.K. in 1999.

Kerala is the state where the minority strategy (Khalidi 1995:200) of having an exclusively Muslim political party, the Muslim League, bargaining to ally itself successfully with Congress Party-centered and Communist Party-centered coalitions has had the greatest payoff (Abdul Azeez 1992). The relatively large minority percentages in the state's population (Christian 24%; Muslim 19%) and the evenly balanced coalitions, kept the R.S.S. out until disputes over job reservations for "backward castes" (all Muslims are defined as backward in Kerala despite their Gulf remittance wealth in the 1970s, *Times of India*, Oct 28, 1994) aroused the powerful Nair caste. After that Muslims became the target of a devastating riot in the state capital, Trivandrum, at the end of 1982 (O.J. 1983; "A Jurist", November 1973).

The *Sangh Parivar* also used the agitation to demolish the *Babri Masjid* in Ayodhya and replace it with a Ram temple at Ram's birthplace (Wright 1991) to extend its influence in the South. *Yatras* or processions, chariot and all, brought donated bricks all the way from Cape Comorin to Ayodhya. The severest post demolition riots in December 1992 were orchestrated by the B.J.P.'s Bombay ally, the *Shiv Sena* in the hitherto cosmopolitan and relatively peaceful city (Padgaonkar 1993).

Muslim militants then turned in anger and frustration to terrorism and "fundamentalism." With the aid of Muslim gangsters (Wright 1979) and possibly with the collusion of Pakistan, they set off several huge explosions in the metropolis in March 1993 (Burns 1994 and *Illustrated Weekly of India* 1993). Some of the alienated Muslim youth in the Dravidian South were recruited into new terrorist groups like *Al Umma* of S.A. Basha

(Murari 1997), the *Islamic Seva Sangh* of Abdul Naseer Madani and the *All India Jehad Committee of Palani Babu* (Subramaniam 1998). It may be conjectured that the decline of jobs in the Arab Gulf states in the 1990s created a reservoir of unemployed Muslim youth in Kerala for whom the Muslim League could do little. Indeed, the Muslim League itself had split into two.

In any event, speakers of the Hindu Munnani bated Muslims by defaming the Prophet in the industrial city of Coimbatore in Tamil Nadu (Subramaniam 1998). Bomb blasts damaged the R.S.S. and Hindu Munani offices in Chenai (Madras) in 1993-94 (*India Today,* August 31, 1993: 16). In revenge Palani Babu was assassinated (Bhaskar 1998). In the right electoral competition between the Tamil parties, Karunanidhi of the D.M.K. (Dravida Munnetra Kazhagam) was seen to favour Muslim voters, so his rival, Jayalalitha of the A.D.M.K., leaned to the Hindu militants (*Deccan Herald,* Dec. 18, 1998). A major communal riot broke out in Coimbatore at the end of 1997 (*Frontline,* March 20, 1998: 119). In retaliation, when the B.J.P. leader, L.K. Advani, was scheduled to come to Coimbatore during the February 1998 election, major bomb explosions and police firing killed 46 persons and injured over 200 others (*The Hindu,* Feb. 21, 1998:1). Basha and other Muslim militant leaders were arrested and their parties banned. South India had come to lok like North India in its polarization of communal relations.

Asgher Ali Engineer points out parallel developments in Karnataka (Engineer 1995: 30) where the B.J.P. succeeded in boosting its vote from 2.5% in 1989 to 28.8% in 1991. Provocations in this state were protests over the Urdu broadcasts on Doordarshan (All India radio) (*Loc.sit.*) and the hoisting of the national flag over the Muslim Idgah in Hubli (Karnad 1994) and more recently disputes over celebrating the bicentennial of the Muslim ruler of Mysore, Tipu Sultan (*Times of India,* May 12, 1999).

As to the accusation that Pakistan's Inter-Services Intelligence (ISI) facilitates Muslim terrorism in South as in North India and as it certainly does in Jammu and Kashmir in aid of the rebellion of much of the Muslim majority in that state (Swami 1999), the white paper of the Tamil Nadu intelligence agencies about the Coimbatore blasts admitted that they had "no specific information" regarding ISI involvement (*Times of India,* April 7, 1998). The ISI seems to have replaced the C.I.A., as the Indian press's favourite whipping boy in the 1990s But Kerala police reported that an arrested youth recruited by Madani was sent to Pakistan for training in terrorism (Surendran 1998). It stands to reason that Pakistan, the smaller and weaker state of the two in the bitter struggle over Kashmir, would resort to infiltration and subversion of India just as the latter no doubt does in Pakistan (Joshi & Chakravarty 1998; Baweja 1998). The point for this paper is that Indian Muslims, North and South, have been homogenized in the 1990s with respect to insecurity and communal violence against them. The results can only be disastrous for this huge, harassed and disaffected minority.

Acknowledgement

This paper was prepared for the panel on "South Asian Muslims at the end of the Twentieth Century: Homogenization or Differentiation?" (Sponsored by the South Asian Muslim Studies Association) at the annual meeting of the American Council for the Study of Islamic Societies, Villanova, Pa. April 30 – May 1999.

REFERENCES

Ahmad, I. (ed.) (1973), *Caste and Social Stratification among the Muslims.* New Delhi: Manohar.

———(1976) (ed.). *Family, Marriage and Kinship among Muslims in India.* New Delhi: Manohar.

———(1981), (ed.). *Ritual and Religion among Muslims in India.* New Delhi: Manohar.

———(1983), (ed.) *Modernization and Social Change among Muslims in India.* New Delhi: Manohar.

Azeez, Abdul (1992), *Rise of Muslims in Kerala Politics.* Trivandrum: CBH Publications.

Baweja, H. (1998), "Terrorism Spreads its Net", *India Today,* December 7.

Bhaskar, B.R.P. (1998), "Telling Video Evidence", *Frontline,* March 20.

Burns, J.E. (1994), "Riot Scars are Gone, but Bombay is Still Healing", *New York Times,* April 17.

Das, V. (ed.) (1990), *Mirrors of Violence.* Delhi: Oxford University Press.

Dasgupta, S. & Bhaumik, S., "Atal Bihari Vajpayee: Crown of Throns", *India Today,* March 16, 8-14.

Anon (1998), "Karunanidhi has Alienated Muslims: Jaya", *Deccan Herald,* December 18.

Engineer, A.A. (1995), "Asghar Ali Engineer on Bangalore Disturbances", *Muslim India*, No. 145, January 30.

Fanselow, F. (1999), "The Genesis of Communalism in Tamil Nadu: the Minakshipuram Mass Conversion of Harijans to Islam", Presented at Association for Asian Studies, Boston, March 13.

Anon (1998), "An Anti-Muslim Pogrom", *Frontline*, March 20: 115-119.

Hardgrave, R. (1965), *The Dravidian Movement*. Bombay : Popular Prakashan.

Anon (1998), "48 Killed as Blasts Rock Coimbatore", *The Hindu* February 21, 1.

Ikram, S.M. (1994), *Muslim Civilizations in India*. New York: Columbia University.

Anon (19930, "Wanted: The Dawood Network", *Illustrated Weekly of India*. March 27 – April 2, CXIII, 13.

Anon (1993), "Deadly Blast Rocks RS Den", *India Today*, August 31, 16.

Joshi, J. & S. Chakravarty (1998), "Trail to Pakistan", *India Today*, March 30.

"Jurist" (1973), "RSS and Tellichery Riots", *Secular Democracy*, November 19-20.

Karnard, G. (1994), "Girish Karnad on Hubli Incident", *Muslim India* No. 142, October, 468-469.

Khalid, O. (1995) *Indian Muslims Since Independence*. New Delhi: Vikas.

Krishnaswamy, V. (1995), "Hindu Munnani Tamilnadu", *Muslim India*, No. 152, August 380.

Mathew, G. (1982), "Politicisation of Religion: Conversions to Islam in Tamil Nadu", *Economic and Political Weekly*, XVII, 25, June 19, 26, 1027-1034, 1068-1072.

Mujahid, A.M. (1989), *Conversion to Islam: Untouchables' Strategy for Protest in India*. Chambersburg, PA.: Anima.

Murari, S. (1997), "Communal Cauldron Boils Over", *Deccan Chronicle*, February 10.

"O.J." (1983), "Kerala: Political Backdrop to Trivandum Riots", *Economic and Political Weekly*, February 12, 209-211.

Padgaonkar, D. (1993), (ed.). *When Bombay Burned*, New Delhi: UBSPD Publishers.

Subramaniam, T.S. (1998), "A Time of Troubles", Frontline, March 20: 16, 17-20.

Surendra, P.K. (1998), "Madani's Arrest Reveals ISI Role in Kerala", *Times of India*, April 7.

Swami, P. (1999), "Extending Terror", *Frontline*, March 26: 16-20.

Anon (1994) "All Kerala Muslims get OBC status", *Times of India*, October 28.

Anon (1998), "TN had No Information on ISI Presence ..." April 24.

Varshney, A. (1997), "Postmodernism, Civic Engagement, and Ethnic Conflict", *Comparative Politics*, 30, 1 (October), 7.

Wilkinson, S.I. (1995), "What Large Datasets can Tell us About the General Explanations for Communal Riots", *Towards Secular Democracy*, I, 4 October.

Wright T.P. (1965), "The Muslim League in South India since Independence : A Study in Minority Group Political Strategies", *American Political Science Review*, LX, 3, September, 580.

———(1979), "Muslim Mobility in India through Peripheral Occupations", In M.Gaborieau and A. Thorner (eds.) *Asie du Sud, Traditions and Changements*, Paris: Editions du Centre National de la Recherche Scientifique, Collection des Colloques Internationaux.

———(1982), "The Movement to Convert Harijans to Islam in South India", Muslim World, LXXIII, 3-4, July-October, 239-245.

———(1991), "The Babri Masjid vs. Ramajanmabhoomi Controversy in Ayodhya, India". In Andre Wink (ed.), *Islam, Politics and Society in South Asia*. New Delhi: Manohar.

RISE OF COMMUNALISM IN TAMIL NADU

Frank S. Fanselow

Introduction

Until recently Tamil Nadu was known for its harmonious inter religious relations. The political unifying force of Tamil nationalism had been a stronger force than the potential divisiveness of religion. Among the Hindu majority Tamil nationalism had developed out of the anti-religious and anti-Brahman movement which was hostile to Hindu and Brahman-dominated religious organizations and political parties. As elsewhere in India, the minorities too supported secular forces and the overwhelming majority of both Muslims and Christians identified with Tamil nationalism. As a result Tamil Nadu was one of the few areas in which no Hindu-Muslim communal violence occurred at the time of partition and inter-religious relations remained largely peaceful in the subsequent decades. Communal violence in the state was not of a religious nature, but took the form of local antagonisms between particular castes, such as that between Maravars and Harijans, Maravars and Nadars, and Nadars and Paravars.

But since the early eighties there has been a marked deterioration of inter-religious relations in the state and a growth of communalism on all sides. This process manifests itself in a turn to religion among many Tamil nationalist politicians and thus the gradual abandoning of secularism and anti-Brahmanism, the growing influence of North Indian political and religious organizations on all sides, and most tragically in periodic eruptions of communal violence on a scale not previously witnessed in the state. With the decline of Tamil nationalism as a unifying force with which al religious communities could identify, patterns of antagonistic inter-communal relations hitherto more characteristic of North India began extending themselves into the South.

In this paper I seek to show how the conversions of Harijans to Islam which occurred in the village of Minakshipuram in Tirunelveli District in 1981 became important catalyst in the growth of the communalism[1]. In the first section I will describe the circumstances that led to the conversions and show how they can be explained in terms of a particular constellation of local factors. The second section shows how the conversions were exploited by outside communal forces to mobilize political support in the state and beyond. The third section shows how the publicity surrounding the conversions created by communal forces was then exploited by Harijan leaders all over the state and beyond by using threats of further conversions as a political weapon to pressure state and central governments. The final section examines the effects, which the Minakshipuram affair had on the political situation in Tamil Nadu and its role in the deterioration of communal relations in the state.

The Conversions

Minakshipuram is a village in Tenkasi Taluk in the western part of Tirunelveli District in southern Tamil Nadu. In 1980 it consisted of 300 households of whom 280 were Harijans of the Pallar caste and the rest belonged to the dominant Maravar caste. The land around Minakshipuram belongs to a Hindu monastery and is cultivated mainly by Maravar and Harijan tenants from Minakshipuram and surrounding villages. In 1969 the tenants formed a co-operative society under Maravar control but it split in 1980 when the Harijans formed their own association. The Maravars regarded this as a challenge to their traditional dominance and relations between the two castes deteriorated sharply.

These relations had already been strained earlier when in 1997 a young Harijan from Minakshipuram eloped with a Maravar girl. Both converted to Islam in neighbouring Kerala and married under Muslim law. After their return to the village the man worked on a nearby estate and in December 1980, he was accused of involvement in the murder of two Maravar guards on the estate. Police inspector in charge of the investigation was a Maravar, who owned land under his wife's name in Minakshipuram and allegedly colluded with local Maravars against the Harijans.

In the face of what they saw as severe police repression, a group of Harijans from Niakshipuram decided in early February 1981 to convert to Islam. They had considered this option on earlier occasions; but older, more conservative Harijans had opposed it. The older generation of Harijan leders had gradually been replaced by a younger and more educated generation resentful of caste discrimination. The conversions were conducted on 19th February 1981 by the Isha-Athul Islam Sabha (IIS) a Muslim organization based in the District headquarters Tirunelveli that provides support to converts. Originally, 220 out of the 280 Harijan families had agreed to convert, but only 200 applied for conversion and of those who applied only 180 actually converted. A second group of 27 families converted on 23rd May 1981 (Khan 1983). The converts decided to change the name of their village from Minakshipuram to Rahmatnagar[2].

The Causes

Crucial in understanding the Minakshipuram conversions are two factors : firstly, the long history of conflict between the Maravar caste, and its equivalents elsewhere in Tamil Nadu (such as the Kallar and Vanniyar) and the low ranking Nadars and Harijans; and secondly, the upward socio-economic mobility of Nadars and Harijans during and after the colonial period.

In many villages of northern Tirunelveli District, most of Ramnad, and parts of Madurai District, the Maravars are the dominant caste. In the pre-colonial period they were the mainstay of the traditional village guard system (*kaval*) and provided the military manpower to the Poligar warlords who fought the Muslims and the British during much of the 18th century. With the defeat of the Poligars in 1801 by the British and the subsequent abolition of the *kaval* system, they became an important element in the newly established police force and remained a dominant agricultural caste in many areas.

The Harijans, on the other hand, experienced considerable upward social mobility in the southern districts of Tamil Nadu, where low ranking castes had benefited from educational opportunities provided by Christian missionary institutions during the colonial period, and from the reservations policy in education and government employment during the post-independence period. As a result, there has been a significant rise in literacy rates, educational achievements and socio-economic expectations among younger generations of Harijans in the area. Tirunelveli District has with 26 percent the highest literacy rate among Harijans in the whole of Tamil Nadu with the exception of Madras City (Census 1971). Better education and upward social mobility increased the resentment of the younger generation of Harijans who experienced continued caste discrimination. The Maravars, on the other hand, finding themselves in relatively stagnant socio-economic position resented the upward mobility of many Harijans.

This constellation of factors in the post-Independence period has resulted in a pattern of communal antagonism between Maravars and Harijans in Tirunelvli and Ramnad districts which regularly occurred. Shortly after these clashes, there was a wave of Harijans converting to Islam. In April 1981 there were similar riots between Marvars and Harijans in the same area following an alleged incident of 'eve-teasing' of a Maravar girl by Harijans. Soon after the police arrested large number of Harijans, mass conversions to Islam occurred in the area (India Today 16-31, 1981: 73). Similarly, Madurai District conversions occurred among the Harijans in the face of harassment by Maravars and Kallars (Wingate 1981). Indeed the IIS, which conducted the conversions, was established after an earlier wave of mass conversions in southern Tamil Nadu in 1944. That wave followed the return of Harijans who had been drafted into the army during the Second World War, and who after serving abroad, resented their treatment at the hands of caste Hindus. The first, conversions occurred in Seelayampatti in Madurai District and later the same year 235 Harijan families converted into Tirunelveli District (Mathew 1982). Between 1969 and 1978 there were conversions to Islam almost every year in parts of Madurai District (ibid). There was thus in southern Tamil Nadu an established pattern of Maravar-Harijan antagonism leading to conversions to Islam.

Subsequent independent inquiries[3] into the Minakshipuram conversions agreed that a combination of harassment by caste Hindus and police repression were responsible for the mass conversions. Although the Anna Dravida Munnetra Kadhgam (ADMK) government of Tamil Nadu denied allegations that police behaviour had caused the conversions and accused the Congress-led central government of trying to make political capital of the issue, the Maravar police inspect in charge of the murder investigation was transferred and later charged with corruption. In an opinion survey conducted by a sociological, Mumtaz Ali Khan, shortly after the conversions in and around Minakshpuram, 280 out of 350 respondents agreed with the statement that "Harijans get converted because of unbearable ill-treatment from the caste Hindus". Predictably, all converted (N : 100) and non-converted Harihans (N : 50) agreed with the statement, whereas none of the 39 Maravar respondents did. But interestingly, 50 out of 60 Brahmans also agreed with the statement indicating that this was more of a Maravar-Harijan, rather than caste Hindu-Harijan conflict (Khan, 1983).

In addition to the factors that led the Harijans in Minakshipuram to reject Hinduism, we must consider the factors, which directed them to convert to Islam rather than to Christianity. Minakshipuram is located near the border between Tamil Nadu and Kerala. Most Muslims in this area belong to the Ravuttar (horseman) community, who are descendants of converts who served in the army of the Nawab of Arcot defending the area against neighbouring Travancore in the early 18th century[4]. For these reasons Tenkasi Taluk has one of the highest concentrations of Muslims in Tamil Nadu and is a Muslim political stronghold. At the time of the conversions, the member of the Tamil Nadu Legislative Assembly for nearby Kadayanallur constituency (A. Shahul Hamid) was the only representative of the Indian Union Muslim League (IUML) in the Assembly, and his brother A. Rifai was a former IUML Member of the Central Parliament. Both were leaders of the IIS, which conducted the conversions.

There are interesting parallels in the history of both Maravars and Muslims: both communities have a military tradition, the former in the service of the Poligar warlords and the latter in the army of the Nawab of Arcot, and there is some evidence that the Muslims are partly descendents of Maravars who converted to Islam in the 18th century. But whereas today the Maravars in the area are predominantly an agricultural community, most Muslims are traders. There are no Muslim landowners with Harijan tenants or wage labourers in Minakshipuram. On the contrary, Muslim smallholders, like Harijans, work their land themselves. Conditions were thus favourable for a Muslim-Harijan alliance: There were no potential conflicts over political and economic interests between the two potential conflicts over political and economic interests between the two communities. Instead their interests coincided: Muslims were good alliance partners because they had the necessary (political) muscle power to counterbalance the Maravars, and Harijans could provide electoral support for Muslim candidates, since together the two communities controlled one third of the votes in the parliamentary constituency.

The relations between Muslims and Harijans in this western part of Tirunelveli District are very different from their relations in the southern parts of the district, where the *poligar* system was not deeply rooted and Maravar power was much weaker. In some places Mulsims and Nadars actually held the *kaval* rights which were elsewhere the prerogative of Maravars (Pate 1917). In the southern parts of the district, particularly in Nanguneri and Tiruchendur Taluks, the main Muslim community are not the Ravuttar, but Marakkayars (boatmen) who have a long history of maritime trade in the Indian Ocean, which has made them considerably wealthier than the Ravuttars. Rich Marakkayar have invested in agricultural land and become major landowners. Muslims in these areas never participate in agricultural labour but employ Nadars and Harijans as tenants and wage labourers. In the coastal town of Kayalpattnam, Kulasekarapatnam and the interior towns of Eruvadi, Panakkudi and Kalakkadu, Muslims constitute a powerful element in the population and are sometimes the dominant community. Communal conflicts between Muslim landlords and Harijan tenants and labourers are not uncommon. In Eruvadi, for example, a long standing conflict between the town's almost exclusively Muslim population and local Harijans led in May 1982 to serious communal riots following a minor dispute between a Muslim shopkeeper and Harijan. In these areas Muslims therefore occupy a position in the stratification system analogous to that of the Maravars around Minakshipuram. The factors, which account for conversion to Islam in Maravar-dominant areas, are absent in further south. Instead, conditions favour conversions to Christianity. The southern parts of Tamil Nadu, including southern Tirunelveli and neighbouring Kanyakumari District, therefore have been the highest proportion of Christians in the state, particularly of the low-caste Nadar and Harijan converts[5] and in these areas communal relations are characterized by a Hindu-Christian antagonism, which periodically erupts into violent confrontations.

The Minakshipuram conversion were therefore neither new nor unique. They fall within an established historical pattern in this area. They are less of a protest against the existing social order, than an opportunistic move by an underprivileged community seeking to improve its position within the existing order by allying itself with powerful groups, formally outside the caste structure. They are, therefore, not unlike the conversions to Islam and Christianity which occurred during the periods of Muslim and British rule. Rather than being the vanguard of a strategic Muslim resurgence aimed at subverting Hindu society, they were at the tailend of a long established pattern of tactical conversion.

The Hindu Reaction

It is therefore more remarkable that the Minakshipuram conversions attracted unprecedented national and international publicity that seems completely out of proportion to the significance of the actual events. Indeed the very first conversions on 19th February 1981 attracted no outside attention, even though the organizers had sought publicity. Only after the conversion of another 27 families on 23rd May 1981 were conducted by Abdul Hasan Nadvi, a well-known Muslim scholar from Lucknow, were they reported in the Hyderabad Urdu daily *Rahnuma-e-Deccan* on 4th April. Eight days later the Madras edition of the *Indian Express* covered the Minakshipuram conversions on its front page (Khan 1983). Within days the conversions became front-page and cover-story material for most Indian newspapers and magazines. Minakshipuram and its fallout received daily coverage in the regional and national press sometimes with upto a dozen articles a day dealing directly or indirectly with the conversions and their aftermath. Eventually, news of the conversions even made it into the international press[6].

It is the purpose of this paper to understand how rather insignificant event in a remote village in southern Tamil Nadu, could produce such a massive Hindu reaction and become a catalyst in the Hindu revivalist movement. Minakshipuram became a crucial rallying point in the Hindu revival. Long established Hindu organizations were reinvigorated and new organizations were established to mobilize Hindus against any further conversions and to bring about reconversions. Among the existing organisations that became involved were the Arya Samaj, the Viswa Hindu Parishad (VHP), Rashtriya Swanmsevak Sangh (RSS) and the Bharatiya Janata Party (BJP). The RSS General Secretary declared the Minakshpuram conversions as the main concern of his organisation and indeed of the entire Hindu society (*Indian ExpressI* Jan. 3, 1982). Due to the mistrust of Brahman-dominated and predominantly North Indian organisations in Tamil Nadu, the initiative in opposing the conversions fell to the Hindu Unity Front (Hindu Munnani), allegedly a front organisation of the RSS. At the national level, the main new organisation to emerge was the Virat Hindu Samaj (VHS). Its founder and leader was the former Education Minister and Vedic scholar Karan Singh, a descendant of the former Hindu dynasty of the predominantly Muslim state of Kashmir. In response to the conversions he convened in late September the Hindu Unity Conference in New Delhi with participation of over sixty Hindu organisations, which decided to come together under the umbrella of the VHS with the aim of preventing conversions. A large number of organisations with the same aims suddenly emerged all over the south. Already by August 1981, in response to the Minakshipuram conversions over a dozen new organisations sprouted almost overnight throughout the country to look after the Harijans and eradicate untouchability.[7] These anti-conversion organisations were supported by prestigious Hindu religious institutions and leaders, particularly the Sankaracharya of Kanchipuram, the Swamiji of Pejawar Mutt in Udipi and the head of Maduari Adhinam as well as by various political parties, particularly the BJP. Their common aim was opposition to conversions to Islam through the formation of a united front of Hindu religious, political and social organisations to promote the idea of Hindu solidarity and fighting 'casteism'. They employed two strategies in their reaction to the Minakshipuram conversions : appeals for solidarity of Hindu society and accusations of subversion against Muslims.

Call for Hindu Solidarity

Modern Hindu reformism has a long history going back to the 19th century intellectual confrontation with the West. The Minakshipuram conversions provided a forum for reiterating many of its arguments and claims, but this time in the context of a confrontation with Islam and Arab influence rather than with Christianity and the West.

The eradication of 'casteism' was seen as a necessary condition for the prevention of further Minakshipurams. The most radical demands called for a revision of Hindu scriptures. A Harijan MP, for example, demanded that all reference of Untouchability and the caste system should be removed from the Laws of Man[8]. Others called for a reinterpretation rather than revision of the scriptures. Karan Singh, for example, argued that the traditional interpretation of Hinduism was obsolete and ought to be replaced by one which is more appropriate to modern conditions. The most common argument, however, was that Hinduism needed neither to be revised nor reinterpreted, but to be realised. The argument depends on a distinction between Hindu religious and Hindu society. Untouchability and the caste system are not part of Hindu religion but a contemporary distortion of which Hindu society should be purified. The MP for Tenkasi, in whose constituency Minakshpuram falls, declared that Harijans should not run away from a great religion because of some passing disabilities. Karan Singh claimed that the Vedantaz contained conept of brotherhood and unity, which have not yet been realised in Hindu society and that untouchability contradicts the spirit of the unity of creation (*advaita*). Untouchability and the caste system were not the ideals of Hindu religion, but its very negation: untouchablity has no place in any religion, let alone Hindu religion. A speaker at the Hindu Solidarity Conference held in Minakshpuram claimed that none of the Shastras and Vedas preached Untouchablity, which was a manifestation of the ego (*ahambavam*). The presidents of four major opposition parties, the Lok Dal, Congress-U, BJP and Janata, jointly declared the caste system to be :

> "Contrary to the highest religious ideals of this land. It has not only nothing in common with the noble ideals of Hindu religion and philosophy, but is antithetical to the fundamental principles on which the edifice of this religion rests" (*The Hindu* Aug. 6, 81).

Having thus defined casteism as a social rather than religious evil, political and religious leaders then blamed each other for the persistence of casteism in Hindu society. The snior Janata leader, Krishna Kant demanded in an open letter to the Sankaracharyas that they call for the abolition of the caste system, declare anybody who practises untouchability a traitor to Hindu religion and that they call for the abolition of the caste system, declare anybody who practises untouchability a traitor to Hindu religion and that they themselves should lead ceremonial entries of Harijans into temples and interdine with them (*Onlooker* Oct. 16, 1981). Hindu religious leaders, on the other hand, blamed the perpetuation of the caste system on the government's reservation policy. The head of Maduari Adhinam, for example, claimed that the Hindu ideal of human equality could not be realised as long as the government continued to segregate Harijans and the Sankaracharya of Kanchipuram predicted that if the government were to case asking for caste membership in applications for education and employment, the caste sysetm would disappear within ten years.

The reformist rheotoric was accompanied by symbolic and ritual demonstrations of Hindu solidarity in the form of mass rallies (*sammelan*), footmarches (*padayatra*), mass interdining (*bhojanam*), temple entry, reconversions, and charity. The first mass rallies were the ones organised by the Hindu solidarity conferences in July 1981 at the two major centres of conversion at Minakshipuram and Ramnad organised by the VHP and attended by leaders of a wide variety of Hindu religious, cultural and political organisations and institutions, such as the RSS, BJP, Arya Samaj, and the head of the Pejawar Mutt, who addressed local audiences of upto 2000 people. The biggest such rally was the Virat Hindu Sammelan held in New Delhi in October 1981 under the auspices of the VHS. The organisers claimed an attendance of one million, though police estimated it at four hundred thousand. There were representatives of over sixty Hindu religious organisations as well as Jains, Sikhs and Buddhists. Although the conference was officially non-political, a wide range of political leaders from all over India representing both the ruling and opposition parties also attended. A large number of similar rallies were held all over Tamil Nadu as well as in other parts of India.

Most of the public rallies held in the wake of the Minakshpuram conversions included foot marches by religious and political leaders entering Harijan villages and mass meals in which they interdined with Harijans. On independence Day -15 th August 1981 – the Tamil Nadu Department of Hindu Religious and Charitable Endowments instructed temples to hold communal lunches with Harijans and the next day the Arya Samaj organised community lunches in Tenkasi and neighbouring Shenkottai taluks for 9000 people, half of them Harijans, in which temple trustees and government officials participated. At a temple in Panpoli near Minakshipuram alone, 3000 people took part, 450 of whom were Harijans and in Minakshipuram "top politicians and religious leaders rubbed shoulders and shared meals" with Harijans (*India Today* Sept 15, 1981 : 31).

The symbolic breaking of caste barriers also extended to the issue of temple entry and common worship of Harijans with what came to be called "non-Harijan Hindus". In Minakshipuram the Arya Samaj conducted prayers and performed a sacrifice with the participation of Harijans. The Swamiji of Pejawar Mutt inaugurated *tiruvillaku puja* at the Kaliyamman temple in the village with participation of 300 women and a sanctum for Lord Venkateswara of Tirputi was set up at which villagers queued up for worship. In Kuriyar village in Ramnad District the BSS organised the local Murugan festival at the request of unconverted Harijans. In AP Chatram near Madras, Harijans "beamed with joy when enthusiastic caste-Hindus took out, for the first time, the Mriamman idol in procession to the Harijan's colony during Sunday's temple festival" and in Perambalur in Tiruchirapalli District caste Hindus were reported to worship with Harijan in the local Shiva temple and the 'Hindu Equality and Brotherhood Organisation' called on them to visit and worship in Harijan temples. The head of Madurai Adhinam performed *sumangai puja* for the welfare of the people in honour of five women scavengers employed by Madurai city, instead of the usual Brahman women, because he considered them as "equals". The International Aryan League began a campaign to teach Harijans the *Gayatri mantram*, traditionaly privileged knowledge of Brahmans. The *jeer* of Sriperumbudur temple assured the Hindu Solidarity Conference in Minakshipuram that his temple has employed Harijans as temple servants and the Kanchipuram Sankaracharya announced the establishment of a school to train Harijans as temple priests. In June 1982 he inaugurated the *gnana ratham* of the VHP, a mobile idol of the Palani Murugan-one of the most famous temples in South India-mounted on a van in order to bring Brahman religion into Harijan settlements all over the state. Apart from ritual paraphernalia, it also carried a public address system, cinema equipment, as well as leaflets and books for distribution. From the start of its tour of the state, its visits repeatedly led to violent communal clashes, which will be discussed below.

A logical implication of the assumption that casetism was an affliction of Indian society rather than of Hindu religion, is the argument that it equally affects other religious communities in Indian society and that consequently conversion to Islam was no way to escape Untouchability. Soon after the first news of the Minakshipuram conversions reports appeared about the converts' disappointment with Islam and their desire to reconvert. A reconvert in Ramnad was reported complaining that they would remain isolated from mainsteam Muslim society and not be able to intermarry with the Muslims. The General Secretary of the BJP predicted that "those getting converted would be 'disenchanted' in Islam as that religion was also beset with practices which widened the gap between groups of people" and claimed that many converted women wanted to reconvert to Hinduism.

In addition to facing the same Casteism as among Hindus, converts were said to face additional oppression due to gender discrimination in Islam. Converted women were reported to find the restrictions on leaving their houses unbearable, particularly as they prevented them from performing agricultural labour. The MP for Tenkasi, for example, claimed that Hindu women had the utmost freedom and honour, while Muslim women were oppressed. Others claimed that such women had never really wanted to convert in the first place and had been forced by their male relatives. Together with calls for a reform of Hindu society went therefore the allegation that Muslim society was even more oppressive. Instead of the brotherhood and equality which Harijans sought by converting to Islam, they had to labour under the double oppression of casteism and sexism, one of which Hindus were trying hard to eradicate and the other they had never known.

Demands for reconversion were reported to be widespread and many of the mass rallies featured reconversion ceremonies. Already fifty reconversions were claimed to have taken place by the time the Hindu Solidarity Conference was held at Minakshipuram five months after the first conversion. At the Second Hindu Solidarity Conference in Ramnad the organisers had secured agreement of a number of converts to reconvert, but these failed to turn up at the planned ceremony and in their place five

Christians were reconverted to Hinduism. The main Hindu organisation active in organising reconversions was the Arya Samaj. During a visit of its leader to Minakshipuram on Independence Day 1981 eleven Harijans reconverted and during another visit by Arya Samaj leaders reports spoke of the reconversion of several more families. After a visit to the village the Janata Party leader announced that 25 families of converts had expresed their intention to reconvert and in November another five people reconverted in Minakshipuram in a ceremony arranged by the Arya Samaj. Within a year of the first conversions, the Sankaracharya of Kanchipuram claimed at a conference held in Maduari that there had been a large scale return to Hinduism.

Since the causes of the conversions were defined as socio-economic rather than the religious, charitable donations and development measures were a logical strategy in the prevention and reversal of conversions. These generally took the form of distributing *saris* and *dhotis* to non-converts and reconverts, for example, when Arya Samaj leaders vitied Minakshipuram. The Swamiji of Pejawar Mutt announced that during his viit to Minakshipuram and Ramnad he would not only give spiritual advice against conversions, but also entertain request for financial assistance from Poor Harijans. A delegation of BSS camped in Minashipuram and inaugurated a well project at the temple. The Tamil Nadu Sarvodaya Mandal promised that it would start village industries, a spinning unit, and other projects for creating employment, such as a cooperative farm. It also announced that seventeen of its members had adopted twenty Harijann children from Minakshipuram and surrounding villages for whose education and boarding they would pay and the General Secretary of the Janata Party declared after a visit to Minakshipuram that his party had decided to adopt all Harijan villages in the District for economic development.

As a result of intense political pressure the government itself began to take economic measures to prevent further conversions. Following a visit inn July the Union Home Minister blamed the government of Tamil Nadu for the conversions because of its failure to implement socio-economic reforms and protect Harijans. Although the state government rejected this criticism and accused the minister of trying to make political capital out of the issue, already the following day the Tamil Nadu Minister for Hindu

Religious and Charitable Endowments visited Minakshipuram. He criticised local officials for not implementing socio-economic development plans and instructed them to regularly visit the village and implement welfare measures within two months as well as to take measures against those who practised untouchability. Two weeks later the District Collector held a 'mass contact programme' at Minakshipuram during which inhabitants were invited to submit petitions. Of the 425 petitions received nearly half were grantned on the spot.

The Hindu reaction to the Minakshpuram conversions seems completely out of proportion to the significance of the actual events. In the first section we sas that the conversions involved a relatively small number of persons in a remote village that fit a historical pattern in the area and can be explained with reference to a specific local context. In this section we have seen how these events triggered a massive reaction at the national level and were used as a rallying point by the Hindu revivalist movement. The reaons for such an incongruous reaction cannot be found in the events themselves. Instead we have to look at how the Minakshipuram conversions were reinterpreted within the dynamics of Hindu-Muslim relations at the national and international level.

Accusation of Muslim Conspiracy

The reverse of the calls for a reform of Hindu society and the appeals for solidarity were accusations which blamed sinister Muslim organisations for the conversions. These accusations took two forms : allegations of internal Muslim subversion of Hindu society and of an external threat against India. The Minakshipuram conversions were represented as part of an international consipracy between external enemies and internal traitors aimed ultimately at destorying India and turning it into another Pakistan.

Given that charitable donations and development measures were widely used by Hindu organisations to prevent conversions and bring about reconversions, it is perhas ironic that the main accusation against Muslim organisations ws that they were using economic incentives to allure Harijans to Islam. Minakshipuram is located nor far from the Courtallam waterfalls, a popular resort during the hot season for many people from both Tamil Nadu and neighbouring Kerala. Many Muslims, particularly wealthy

Muslims from Kerala employed in the Middle East, undertook excursions to Minakshipuram and brought preents for the converts. The total number of visitors to Minakshpuram in the wake of the conversions was said to amount at fifty thousand. When the Parliamentary Committee visited Minakshipuram it heard allegations that busloads of Muslims from Kerala had come and given large donations and that a Saudi preacher, who had laid the foundation stone for a mosque had promised Rs. 20,000 towards its construction. The joint Secretary of the RSS claimed that he had information that truckloads of clothes and money had been brought to Minakshipuram to induce conversions and both he and the General Secretary of the VHP claimed that their research had shown that each of the 765 converts had been paid a flat rate of Rs. 500 plus new clothes.

Minakshipuram was alleged to be part of a Muslim conspiracy encompassing the entire nation. The General Secretary of the VHP claimed that five hundred villages in southern Tamil Nadu with a total population of a 100,000 were considering to follow Minakshipuram. The General Secretary of the VHP Tamil Nadu branch claimed that even though few mass conversions were reported, they continued unabated and more systematically that before avoiding publicity and sensitive areas. Reports from all over India provided further evidence for these allegations. Although the Minakshipuram conversions in the south ahd received most publicity in contrast to other areas, "the fact remains that the insidious and quiet conversions (which) are taking place in areas like Assam and Kashmir pose a much greater threat to Hinduism than what is taking place down South (*The Hindu* Sept 15, 1981). In August 1981 Kanpur4 and Lucknow were swept for rumours that a group of Arabs in alliance with the Dalit Panthers were organising secret conversion of Harijans (*Sunday*, Aug. 30, 1981). Reports from Kashmir recalled that the Iraqi Miniser of Waqf and visited the state in May 1980 and distribtued 40 lakh to Islamic institutions and that during his stay "long queues of Moulavis used to meet him to get aid for uplift of the poor Muslims in Kashmir." This was met by a swift response from rival Muslims when in June 1981 Iranian officials visited Kashmir and distributed funds "to counter the Iraqi influence in Kashmir (*Indian Express* Oct. 12, 1981)."

The alleged moving force behind these conversions were Muslim organisations within India collaborating with organisations aborad all financed from the Middle East. The immediate target of attack was the IIS allegedly a front organisation of the IUML. It was accused of not merely conducting the conversion formalities but to be actively organising mass conversions. Another organisation allegedly behind the conversion conspiracy was the Tablighi Jama'at, sometimes described as the Muslim equivalent of the Arya Samaj. It was accused of not simply pursuing its declared aim of deepen knowledge of Islam among Muslims, but to spread Islam by conversion. In April 1981 a world meeting of the Tablighi Jama'at was held in Tiruchirappali in central Tami Nadu attended by 500 delegates from Arab, Asian and European countries. At this convention a master plan was allegedly hatched to begin a massive conversion campaign of Harijans throughout India. For this purpose Inda was said to have been divided into twelve separate Jama'ats, each with the task to explore the possibilities of converting Harijans in its area.

The largest Muslim organistaion in India, the Jamaat-e-Islami Hind, sometimes described as the Muslim counterpart of the RSS, too was allegedly behind the conversion campaign. In March 1981 it had held its All-India Conference at Hyderabad, attended by delegates from various Muslim countries, including Saudi Arabia, and Britain. At the meeting, converted Harijans were reported to have been presented to the participants and the possibility of further mass conversions was debated.

These Indian organisations were allegedly financed by Muslim organisations abroad, particularly in Pakistan, the Middle East and Britain. The Karachi-based Motamar-al-Alam-al-Islami, set up to bolster Pakistan's image in the Middle East as an active Muslim nation engaged in spreading Islam, was said to be planning moves to convert 50,000 Harijans in 1981 and four times that number the following year. Suspicious were further fuelled by the attention which the conversions received in a number of Middle Eastern newspapers. A Kuwati newspaper, for example, was reported to have quoted a press release from the Islamic Cultural Centre in London according to which fifty Harijans families who had benefited from a $50,000 irrigation project had converted to Islam and which pointed to potential future conversions (*India Today* July 16-30, 1981). Later a representative of the Centre was reported to have visited Ramnad and met converts under the auspices of the Jamat-e-Islami. The Jamat-e-Islami was reported to have donated

Rs. 300,000 to 33 mosques in Tamil Nadu, which it allegedly received from the Supreme World Council of Mosques in Mecca. In October, press reports maintained that "according to unconfirmed reports three Gulf countries have sanctioned about Rs. 26 crore to sustain new converts and also to induce fresh conversions (in Tamil Nadu). The petrodollars were allegedly pumped into the country by such organisations as the World Islamic Jama'at, the World Supreme Council of Mosques and the Islamic Cultural Centre in London, which wee planning to convert 80 million Indian Harijans to Islam.

The conversion thus appeared to be part of a conspiracy aimed not only at the Hindus as such but at the Indian nation as a whole. There was "a growing fear that sinister forces overseas are at work to create communal and religious discord in the country (*Indian Express* June 26, 1981). The RSS Joint General Secretary alleged that the Minakshpuram conversions indicated the existence of :

> "international conspiracy to Islamise the country in ten years" as "Muslim religious and political organisations appears to have launched a plan to convert eight crore Harijans on the strength of Gulf money so as to increase the Muslim population to 20 crores in the next ten years".

The RSS claimed that:

> "such conversions do not merely imply a simple change in the way of worship but destruction of national culture and sentiments, growth of separatist and secessionist tendencies and extra-territorial loyalties and communal animosities and flare-ups as well, which directly strike at the roots of our national integrity and security ... such conversions should be a matter of serious concern to all patriotic and nationalist people .. (and appealed to) our Hindu Harijan brethren to stand united, as in the past, with the main body of Hindu society, keeping in view the interests of our nation and refuse to play into the hands of such antinational forces" (*Indian Express*, June 15, 1981).

The Congress-I General Secretary declared that the conversions threatened the secular character of the constitution. The Janata Party Secretary after a visit to Minakshipuram described the conversions as "a potential time bomb" and on a visit Minakshipuram the BJP leader, A.B. Vajpayee, described them as "part of a sinister conspiracy by elements both within the country and outside to undermine the demographic and secular complexion of the country and turn it into a theocratic state like Pakistan and Iran" (*Indian Express* Aug 15, 1981). At a VHP convention in Calcutta alarm was expressed about "the constant decline in Hindu population" (*The Hindu* Oct. 19, 1981). Support for these demographic predictions came from sections of the academic community. A political scientist from Karnataka University argued on the basis of statistical predictions that by the year 2041 non-Hindus would outnumber Hindus in India if all Harijans converted to Islam and warned that therefore any further conversions like those of Minakshipuram threaten national unity and disturb the present demographic "balance" (*Organiser* Sept. 13, 1981). A leaflet of the Hindu Unity Forum warned:

> "Minakshipuram-the moment one hears this word, there is concern in him. Meenakshipuram is the advance warning of an international conspiracy to separate 12 crore neglected Hindus from their religion and convert them to Islam. Thereby they want to make India Islamic. But now this conspiracy is exposed. Hindus are going to thwart ths international ambition" (*Indian Express* Nov. 24, 1981).

The conversions ultimately assumed historical and even mythical proportions. Some writers divided Indian history into the pre and post-Minakshipuram periods. In a speech in Minakshipuram a BS leader "reviewed history of India to show how many nations in the past came and tried unsuccessfully to destroy the Hindu culture. He claimed that Minakshipuram would go down in history as the place where Indian Muslims' true intention was exposed and became the focal point of Hindu resistance" (*Indian Express* Nov 6, 1981).

Speakers at the Virat Hindu Sammelan in Delhi claimed that not since the legendary battle of Kurukshetra in the Mahabarata had so many Hindus assembled in the name of religion (*India Today* Nov. 15-30, 1981: 142).

Harijan Threats of Conversion

The allegations that Muslim purchased converts with petrodollars, implied that Harijans were sufficiently immoral or ignorant to accept such offers. Thus the RSS state Committee alleged that the gullible people in the lower strata of society who never understood our religion were lured away by coercion, money and untenable promises. Tabilighi Jamat was accused of "exploiting the gullibility, if not the frustration, of the Harijans", whereas caste Hindus were called on to start:

> "organizing themselves and appealing to their Harijan breathren not to fall a prey to the lure of the Muslims. In some of the areas, non-Harijan Hindus are visiting Harijan colonies to enlighten them on the 'far reaching ramifications' of mass conversions" (*The Hindu* Aug. 14, 1981).

Harijans were variously described as "misguided" by the RSS Organizing Secretary in Tamil Nadu or "illiterate" by T.S. Rao of Benares Hindu University. The VHP claimed that "in all the conversion game, the HindunPallar caste were the victims."

But the representation of Harijan as gullible and innocent victims proved counterproductive because Harijan leaders resented the patronizing assumptions implicit in these allegations. The veteran Harijan leader Jagjivan Ram rejected all such allegations (*Current* July 22, 1981; *Indian Express* Sep. 24, 1981) because they implied that Harijans were a purchasable commodity at a rate of Rs. 500 plus a *dhoti* or *sari*. In a joint letter to *The Hindu* (Aug. 25, 1981) a number of social scientists from the Indian Social Institute and the Institute of Religious Studies in Delhi complained that this was merely a case of letting caste-Hindu prejudice against untouchables in through the backdoor.

In fact it soon became clear that far from being gullible pawns in the conversion game, educated Harijans were quick to exploit the Hindu-Muslim antagonism for their own political advantage. The transformation of a local Harijan-Maravar conflict into a national Muslim-Hindu issue put a powerful political weapon into their hands that could be used to pressurize the local and state administration. If anything it were therefore the Harijans who used Hindu organisations and government agencies to their advantage.

Soon after the Minakshpuram conversions had become the focus of attention in the mass media, seventy Harijan families from Devarayapuram in Salem District submitted a petition to the District Collector on 25th June 1981 demanding that they be allowed to enter the village temple, draw water from the public well and that the government continue the free distribution of house plots to them, which they alleged was stopped due to pressure from caste Hindus. If these demands were not fulfilled, they threatened to convert to Islam on 1st August. During the next few days the District Collector, police and revenue officials visited the village in turn, and within a week a handpump was installed and public land cleared for distribution as house sites. The Harijans were reported to have reacted by saying that:

> "if the government gives us water and land *pattas* and houses why should we take to Islam?" (*Indian Express* July 3 and 10, 1981).

On 6th July 1981 senior police officials from Pondicherry rushed to a nearby village after receiving reports that three hundred Harijan families were planning to convert to Islam. This followed a long standing dispute they had with caste Hindus in surrounding villages which had two months earlier led to a mob of two hundred caste Hindus threatening the village. The Harijans threatened to convert to Islam unless assurance were given that water supplies to land they cultivated were released, that there would be no interference in the allotment of house sites, that women labourers should receive fair wages and all ill-treatment by caste Hindus should cease. Senior government official negotiated an agreement whereby each family would lease land and be provided with water by the landlord; the demand for fair wages was referred to the Law Department. In return the Harijans agreed to withdraw their threat to convert (*Indian Express* July 7, 9 and 11, 1981). There were many other similar conversion threats from villages all over Tamil Nadu.

The conversion threats soon spread to the cities. At the Kalpakkam nuclear power station near Madras, 700 Harijan workers threatened to convert with their families on Independence Day after several of them had been insulted and assaulted by high caste employees who had remained unpunished. Their grievances were resolved before the deadline and their conversion plan was abandoned. At a lorry factory at Avadi 200 Harijans threatened to convert to Islam in July. This threat followed a dispute about special concessions between Harijans and Forward Caste members during which a Harijan leader had assaulted a Forward Caste member and had been dismissed. The Harijans demanded the reinstatement of the General Secretary of their union. The management refused to revoke the dismissal but only seventeen Harijans converted in November.

In September the leaders of the Urikara Nayakar caste threatened with the conversion of their entire caste claiming a quarter of a million members in the state, unless they were designated a Scheduled Tribe, given guarantees of protection from harassment by caste Hindus, received interest free loans for business, and house plots were distributed to them by the government.

Soon a wave of conversion threats swept through Tamil Nadu From Ambasamudram in Tirunelveli District, the General Secretary of the Janata Party claimed that during his visit 22,000 Harijans had agreed to postpone their intended conversion until 15th September 19081 to give him to ensure an end to harassment by police and caste Hindus, and from Tirupattur it was reported that residents of R.S. Puram Colony in Gudiyatam taluk have withdrawn their decision to embrace Islam following their demand of removing a bathroom and lavatory constructed by the Textiles Labourers Cooperative Society (*Indian Express* Oct. 9, 1981).

Conversion fever soon spread to other states. In Bangalore, 500 youth leaders of the Karnataka Harijan Welfare Association announced that 15,000 Harijans from different parts of the city would convert to Islam on 15th August 1981. This date is of symbolic significance and frequently recurs in the conversion threats because it is Independence Day. No conversions took place in Bangalore on the day, instead after a meeting with the Swamiji of Pejawar Mutt, who assured them that he would strive to rid Hinduism of its evils, "The Harijans of Gowathamnaager who had threatened to embrace Islam en masse, gave up the idea and affirmed their faith in Hinduism". At Kanpur the Dalit Panthers announced that on the same day a total of 25,000 Harijans would convert to Islam, Buddhism and Christianity in protest again caste oppression. In this case heavy police repression was alleged to have prevented the mass conversion and only one Harijan converted to Islam during a Congress-I Party meeting. Even the Hindu holy city of Benaras was not spared of conversion threats of Harijans at a function of the Harijan-Muslim Ekta Sammelan were reported to have threatened with converting to Islam, but let it be known to Congress-I sources that if they were satisfied with various facilities provided by the government, if they would see no need to convert. From Delhi it was reported that the Harijan poet Yad Karan Yad and his family had converted to Islam and soon afterwards rumours spread in the capital that Jagjivan Ram would convert to Islam and assume the name Jehangir Khan.

Posters appeared in Delhi announcing his conversion to Islam as well as that of his son Suresh Ram and other Harijan leaders on 21st August at the Jama Masjid. Four days before this date Ram denied any such intention in Parliament and claimed that these allegations were a ploy of his political enemies to discredit him.

With the mere mention of the word "conversion" guaranteed to cause panic, other communities soon got into the game. Back in the Ottapidaram Taluk of Tirunelveli District members of the dominant Nayakkar caste, who in alliance with the Maravar had been the mainstay of the Poligar system, threatened to convert to Islam following a land dispute with Harijans. The Nayakkar claimed that in the face of unbearable provocation and harassment by the Harijans they had "no other escape than to trust in Allah and embrace Islam" (*Indian Express* Aug. 29, 1981; *The Hindu* Aug. 30, 1981). Following conversion threats by a group of Harijans at Villupuram, a group of caste Hindus led by the freedom fighter P.T. Thulasingam Pillai threatened that if the Harijans converted to Islam, they would convert themselves into Harijans. Around the same time a company manufacturing electric fans began advertising its product under the slogan "Mass conversions to Minar Fans".

With the dialectic conspiracy theories and conversion threats escalating into the realm of absurdity both gradually exhausted their credibility when it became clear that the first could not be substantiated and the second were rarely carried out. In Parliament the Minister of State for Home Affairs repeatedly denied that there was any evidence of foreign money received by religious and cultural organizations being used for conversions and investigations by the Intelligence Bureau also proved negative (*The Hindu* Aug. 28, 1981; *Indian Express* Sep. 18, 1981; Oct. 12, 1981). Newspapers began to report disappointedly from all over the country that "there are no reports of Arab Sheikhs doling out funds in Hariyana and the state of Himachal Pradesh has also not attracted Arab Sheikhs" (*Indian Express* Oct. 12, 1981). On the other hand, the alarmist tone with which conversion threats had been met by press and politicians was gradually replaced by cynical headlines such as "Mass Conversion Hoax in Bangalore", "Kunnaloor conversion just a threat" and "Avadi a far cry from Minakshpuram". Reporters who investigated the announcement by the Karnataka Harijan Welfare Association that on

Independence Day 15,000 Harijans would convert at Sriramapuram, found the Harijans in the town surprised at the suggestion. Elsewhere, closer investigation revealed that the alleged converts could not even remember their Muslim names the next day. The political magazine *India Today* (Sept. 1-15, 1981: 34) aptly put a bottom time to the affair with the headline "Converted into an Issue".

The Aftermath: National in the Local

But while the publicity surrounding them died down, the conversions and the reaction they triggered changed the political culture of Tamil Nadu. They contributed to the emergence of a communalist social psychology and led to the foundation of an organizational infrastructure for inter-religious communalism. In December 1981, the IUML Tirunelveli District Unit decided to support Harijan candidates in upcoming panchayat elections, and shortly afterwards the Society for Equality and Brotherhood (*Samathuva Sahodarathuva Sangam* or SSS) was funded in the town of Kadayanallur near Minakshpuram through the initiative of A. Shahul Hamid, the local member of the State Assembly for the IUML, and his brother, an ex-MP for the IUML, both previously mentioned as leaders of the ILS. The leadership and membership of the SSS were made up equally of Harijans and Muslims and its stated aim was to unite the two communities not through mass conversions but through a political alliance. Muslims and Harijans together held the single largest block of votes in Kadayanallur constituency due to the fragmentation of the rest of the vote along caste and party lines. Within a short time of its foundation the organisation had 61 branches in the District.

On 8th June 1982 the SSS held a rally at Kadayanallur on the occasion of the birthday of the Harijan leader Ambedkar, which was addressed by A. Shahul Hamid and the IUML president. On the same day the propaganda vehicle (*gnana ratham*) of the VHP was scheduled to tour the town of Puliaangudi located half-way between Minakshipuram and Kadyanallur but following protests from local Harijans police prohibited its entry into the Harijan quarters. While passing through town of Chokkampatti on their way to Kadayanallur by lorry, Harijans from Puliangudi shouted insulting slogans about Maravar women. The Maravars responded by stoning the lorries and wounding one Harijan. The injured was then paraded at the SSS rally with a headbandage; outraged by this crowd attacked a bus on which they had identified a Maravar and beat him up. Further violence occurred on the way back through Chokkampatti in which 15 Harijans and Muslims were injured. Later the same day a shop in Pulianguid owned by a Maravar from Chokkampatti was looted and one worker wounded.

In the days following the town of Puliangudi, Chokkampatti and Kadaynallur were swept by widespread communal violence, which started when SSS members attacked arches erected for the visit of the *gnana ratham* the previous day, followed by the looting arson and attacks on public buses in which three youths and a Police Inspector coming to their help were injured by SSS members. Later Puliangudi police station was attacked by a crowd of a thousand SSS members, which was driven away with lathi charges and warning shots. On Thursday a quarrel between a Muslim and a caste Hindu woman over drawing water from a public tap erupted into widespread violence in the town in which at least 156 houses and many shops and a Vinayakar temple were destroyed by country bombs. A police party making a lathi charge to disperse the rioters was attacked by the crowd with stones and sticks and eleven policeman were injured and so were many rioters one of whom later died. Enraged by this a mob of Harijans again attacked Puliangudi police station, forcing police to open fire in which another Harijan was killed. Police charged 2000 people with attacks on buses and the looting of shops. On the same day violence spread further north to Vasudevanallur where one Muslim was killed during attacks on Muslim shops. The following morning a long standing dispute between Harijans and Maravars over the use of water wells in a village about 10 kilometers from Puliangudi turned into violence when a mob of about 1500 Maravar attacked the village in which a local branch of the SSS had been established. The attackers massacred seven Harijans with knives and axes, wounded another 21 and set fire to about fifty houses. Another Harijan village in the area was attacked by a 200 strong mob armed with knives which set fire to 18 houses and ransacked another 14 houses. The following day a Harijan colony a few kilometers from Puliangudi was attacked by a mob which set fire to 30 houses and injured an elderly woman who was unable to escape in time. Just after midnight the nedxt day a provisional thatched mosque in

Minakshipuram built after the conversions burnt down. The converts registered a case of arson with the police, but following an investigation the police claimed that the fire was caused by an accident. Later in the day violence spread to neighbouring Ramnad following an incident in Rajapalayam in which a Harijan youth knocked down a Maravar girl in a bicycle accident. The girl's father gathered a group of Maravar to beat up the youth, who in turn collected a group of Harijans to take revenge. Maravars then attacked a lorry carrying Harijan workers, who they claimed wre armed with deadly weapons, though these seemed to have been agricultural implements which sometimes are used as weapons. A total of 11 civilians were injured in the attack, including seven Harijans, two Maravars and two policemen before police could bring the situation under control. On 14th June rumours of an impending clash between Maravar and Harijans swept the town of Sankaranainarkoil, 16 km north of Puliangudi and streets remained empty and shops closed. Nothing happened that day, but on 17th June a long-standing dispute over cattle grazing between Harijans and Maravars in two nearby villages erupted into violence. A fight broke out when a group of Maravars approached the Harijan colony in which one Maravar was killed. Police arrested 13 Harijans. Apart from direct confrontation, large numbers of banyan and coconut trees as well as haystacks, pumpsets and sugarcane fields belonging to the Maravars, Harijans and Muslims were destroyed by fire in villages throughout the area.

The situation was gradually brought under control by police through the formation of peace committees in the area comprising representatives of all religions, castes and political parties, and by the arrival of heavy police reinforcements from other districts, six companies of the Tamil Nadu Special Police as well as two contingents of the Armed Reserve and the Central Reserve Police from Bangalore. On 18th June the chairman of the Hindu Temples Protection Committee was arrested under the National Security Act for inciting communalism and A. Shahul Hamid was arrested under the Criminal Procedure Code. His brother A.K. Rifayee was arrested two days later under the same section but subsequently released after charges against him were dropped. In all 185 people were arrested in connection with the violence in Tirunelveli District and another 66 in Rajapalayam.

The Tenkasi riots in the wake ot the Minakshpuram conversions are only one example of a new pattern of inter-religious communal violence in the state. The following year similar riots occurred in Tiruchirappali District when the *gnana ratham* of the VHS visited Puthanatham in January 1983 and again on the first anniversary of the visit in January 1984 when a large procession by the Hindu Munnani threatened to attack a mosque. The growth of inter-religious violence has also characterized relations between Hindus and Christians in the state. Already in December 1981 and again during March and April 1982 the neighbouring District of Kanyakumari saw some of the worst communal clashes ever in Tamil Nadu. Here too a local, traditional inter-caste antagonism between the Paravars and Nadars turned into a communal confrontation between Christians and Hindus which left six people dead and 21 seriously injured. On a subsequent visit to the District, M. Karunanidhi, the president of the anti-Brahman and anti-religious DMK opposition party attributed he riots to the growing influence of radical Hindu organizations in Tamil Nadu. He threatened that unless the RSS and Hindu Munnani ceased to hold self-defence drills (*Shakhas*), his party would respond by training its young men in the martial arts. The IUML Tirunellveli District Unit too decided to provide such training to its members. A growing radicalization of intercommunal politics has therefore occurred among all the major political actors in the state; the Hindus, the Muslims, the Christians and the secular Tamil nationalists and this has set the scene for an escalation of communal violence in the eighties and nineties.

Conclusion

This chronicle of the Minakshipuram conversions, their causes and their consequences, is based primarily on reports in the mass media. But these reports are treated here not as documentary sources for the reconstruction of a particular historical event and there is no attempt of source criticism to sort out fact from fiction. On the contrary, many of the 'events' I refer to are clearly misrepresentations, distortions, exaggerations and outright inventions. Apart from the first section, the paper is therefore not meant as a historical account of the Minakshipuram conversions. Instead it tries to show how the conversions were publicly interpreted and re-interpreted within a communalist discourse which thereby attributed national and even global significance to what were essential local events. What to the outside observer appears as an absurd cycle of suspicions, claims and counter-claims, accusations and threats, appears from the inside as evidence of a dangerous, all encompassing conspiracy. Instead of reason, communal discourse uses an arabesque repetitiveness as a means of establishing its truthfulness and thereby mobilizing political support.

What made the erosive cycle of suspicion generated by the Minakshipuram conversions spin out of control, was that it could serve the communal political interests of all the sides involved. It was used by Muslim propagandists to draw a picture of Islam on the march forward and of Hinduism on the defensive. It served the interests of Hindu propagandists to mobilise a massive Hindu reaction against Muslims. It put into the hands of Harijan leaders a powerful political weapon for pressuring the national, state and local administrations to achieve their political and economic goals. Since an exaggeration of the conversions was in everybody's interests a vicious circle developed: the more massive the conversions appeared to be, the more dangerous they were represented. The more dangerous they appeared to be, the more effective political weapon, the more conversion threats they invited, and the more threats there were, the more the conversions appeared as massive and dangerous.

NOTES

1. Looking into the future M.N. Srinivas in a lecture entitled "Caste and Its Future" given at the Institute of Economic Growth of Delhi University predicted an impending increase in communal violence due to increasing Hindu militancy arising out of mass conversions to Islam (*Indian Express,* 1.4.84). Looking backwards, the press summarised the significance of the conversions : "The current Hindu mood started with a slow burn in 1981, after the mass religious conversions at Meenakshipuram" (*India Today,* 31st May 1986). "The new wave of *senas* have their origin in save-the-religion battle cries raised by the Vishwa Hindu Parishad (VHP)- the intellectual arm of the RSS – in 1980 (sic) following the mass conversion of Harijans of Meenakshipuram to Islam." (*India Today,* 15th October 1986).
2. 'Minakshi' is the name of a Hindu goddess famous in Tamil Nadu' 'Puram' refers to a temple town, 'Rahmat' means 'grace' in Arabic

and is one of the name of 'Allah'; 'Nagar' refers to a town whose function is more commercial than religious.

3. These inquiries were conducted by the Union Minister of State for Home Affairs, who visited the village in July 1981, by the Parliamentary Committee on the Welfare of Scheduled Castes and Scheduled Tribes, which sent a delegation to Minakshpuram in August 1981, and by the Commissioner for Scheduled Caste and Scheduled Tribes.
4. For a detailed historical analysis of the origins of the different Muslim communities in Tamil Nadu see Fanselow (1989).
5. The paravars converted as early as the 1530s collectively to Roman Catholicism when they allied themselves with Portuguese against the local Hindu rulers, who were in alliance with Muslim merchants in the coastal towns. Conversions by Nadars, Iluvans and Harijans were the result of mainly protestant missionary activities since the late 18th century. The low ranking and poverty-striken Nadar caste, in particular, was regarded as an ideal target of protestant missionary efforts, which provided them with opportunities for considerable educational and economic upward mobility (Hardgrave 1969).
6. My own first encounter with the Minakshipuram conversions interestingly occurred through an Arab newspaper *Egyptian Gazette*, June 29, 1981.
7. *India Today*, September 1-14, 1981: 31. These included the movement to protect religion started by the International Aryan League (*The Hindu* Aug. 11, 1981); the 'Indian Hindu Forum' in Karnataka (*Indian Express* Aug 18, 81); the 'Hindu Equality and Fraternity Organisation' formed in Perambalur in Tirchuriapalli District and the 'Hindu Front' established in Kulittalai (*The Hindu* Aug. 14, 81).
8. *India Today* (Nov. 15-30, 1981). An article in *The Hindu* (Sep. 23, 1981) argued that the Laws of Manu and reference to *Chaturvarna* are infact not legally applicable to the present age of Kaliyug, during which only the Prasara Smriti read with Yajnavalikya Smriti were valid and these emphasise collective strength (*Sangha Shakti*) and strife (*Sangrama Yojna).*
9. Of the 124 petitons for family ration cars, 115 were immediately issued. A fair price shop was sanctioned and opened on the same day. The Divisional Engineer sanctioned the construction of a branch road to link Minakshipuram to the main road and ordered work to begin immediately so that a bus service could start the following month. A large sum was also sanctioned for the construction of a water supply system and the District Welfare Officer granted requests for a child welfare centre (*The Hindu,* July 21, 1981).

10. *Indian Express* Oct. 7, 1981. The international Hare Krishna Movement attributed the conversions to lack of proper knowledge and an Italian member of its delegation to Minakshpuram declared the main cause of conversion to be the "lack of information on spiritual aspect of Hinduism" which leads a "drift towards materialism" due to which Harijans "were more susceptible of allurements as they were not in the mainstream of Hindu society and did not have a religious tradition like the caste Hindus (*Indian Express*, No. 17; Sep. 29, Nov. 6, 1981).
11. On 26th July Harijan leaders at Villupuruam and surrounding villages established the "Harijans Protection Society" with the aim of initiating conversions to Islam, but they also held talks with Hindu religious and political leaders from whom they demanded the extension of the reservation system from education and employment to the awarding of government contracts, the allotment of agricultural land to Harijans and adequate representation of the constituencies in local elections. The government immediately instructed local officials to prepare a "minimum programme" of welfare measures, which would forestall the conversions. The Hiarjans said that before committing themselves to convert, they wanted to discuss their grievances with the Prime Minister and the Sankaracharya of Kanchipuram. Two weeks later their delegations met the Sankaracharya who assured them that he would do his best to redress their grievances in consultation with the government and in return the delegation promised him that they would dissuade the Harijans of Villupurum from their intention to conver (*Hindu Bindu* Aug. 11, 1981). On 5th August 1981 Harijans from Unnalur in Tanjavur District sent a petition to the Prime Minister and to the Chief Minister of Tamil Nadu threatening to convert to Islam unless their eviction from land belonging to a local temple was stopped. The District Collector immediately started a two day mass contact tour of the area promising the Harijans a fair solution and announced that a comprehensive drinking water supply scheme had been drawn up for the area. In the end only about a dozen families were reported to have converted to Islam (*Indian Express* Aug 22 and 6, 1981; *The Hindu*, Sep. 6, 1981).

REFERENCES

Census of India (1971), District Census Handbooks : Tirunelveli.

Fanselow, F.S. (1989), "Muslim Society in Tamil Nadu: An Historical Perspective", *Journal of the Institue of Muslim Minority Affairs* 10 (1), 264-289.

Hardgrave, R. (1969), *The Nadars of Tamil Nadu*. Barkeley : University of California Press.

Khan, M.A. (1983), *Mass Conversions of Minakshipuram: A Sociological enquiry*. Madras : Christian Literature Society.

Mathew, G. (1982), "Politician of Religion L: Conversions to Islam in Tamil Nadu", *Economic and Political Weekly*, 19th June 1982, 1028-1033.

Pate, H.R. (1917), *Madras District Gazetteers : Tinnevelly*. Vol. I Madras: Government Press.

Wingate, A. (1981), "A Study of Conversion from Christianity to Islam in two Tamil Villages," *Religion and Society* 28 (4), 3-36.

LIFE-SPACE OF INDIAN MUSLIMS

Qamar Hasan

Introduction

The word 'life-space' is a keyconcept in the field theory proposed by Lewin (1951) under the influence of field concepts of Physics Lewin made use of a picture of circle enclosed by but not touching an ellipse to represent life space. The circle represents the person and the ellipse psychological environment as distinct from the non-psychological environment existing outside the ellipse. Lewin (1936) insisted that behaviour of a given individual is to be derived from the psychological facts that exist in the life space at a given movement. One of the principles of Lewin's field theory which is of great relevance for us is the principle of contemporaneity which states that only present facts can produce present behaviour However, the facts can remain in existence throughout the intervening years (Lewin 1936: 1836).

Considering life-space of Indian Muslim we are acknowledging the fact that the behaviour of the members of the community cannot be considered independent of psychological environment in which they find themselves and also the fact that historical events, so far as they are 'facts' remaining in existence, can influence the contemporary dynamics of their behaviour in interaction of Muslims with their compatriots.

Muslims are in India for more than a millennium. They first came in contact with coastal inhabitants of Malabar in 7th century A.D. and within a short space of time could have a permanent settlement in the area by ingratiating with the ruler of Malabar and obtaining generous grants from him. However, as a member of the community which could bask in the reflected glory of conquerors and rulers, their advent in India began with th expeditions of Mohammed Ibn Qasim in Sindh around A.D. 705-715, Mahmud of Ghazni (A.D. 1000-1026) and Ghori who conquered Multan in AD.716.

The permanent foundation of 'Muslim rule' in north India was laid by Ghori's slave Qutubuddin Aibak. During the slave dynasty the Hanafi School of Jurisprudence came to dominate. Many scholars migrated from Iran, Bukhara and Samarkand, including the famous historian Al-Biruni, the author of *Kitabul Hind*. Most of the rulers of Delhi were ardent devotees of Sufism. Two great Sufis who migrated to India in the 11th century were Saiyed Salar Masood Ghazi and Shaikh Ismail. Sufis with their message of love converted thousands to Islam.

The Mughal period (A.D. 1527-1858) began with Babar's victory over Lodis in Panipat (A.D. 1526). This period is known for Akbar's consolidation of India under the Mughal empire, his inductions of native Hindus in administrative services and nobility (Husain 1991) has creation of revenue system. Shahjahan's construction of Taj Mahal, Dara Shikoh's indulgence in the study of Hindu scriptures and later on dominance of ideas of Shaikh Ahmad Srihind who came to be known as 'Twelth Renovator'. The Shaikh rejected the Ibn Arabi's philosophy of 'unity of existence' as he argued that religion becomes meaningless without the distinction between God and his creation.

The Mughal empire disintegrated between A.D. 1707-1857 but a significant feature of the closing years of the Mughal empire was flourishing of Urdu language with the contribution of poets like Meer Taqi Meer, Asad Ullah Khan Ghalib and Ibrahim Zauq. Reference is also to be made to the impact of revivalist movements led by Shah Walliullah (A.D. 1703-1762), Shah Abdul Aziz (A.D. 1746-1824), and Sayyid Ahmad (A.D. 1786-1833) of Rai Barelli.

Three different views are expressed about the impact of 'Muslim rule' on the Hindu-Muslim relations. The first is that to a very large extent Hindu-Muslim relations were good and there was much synthesis between Hindu and Islamic elements (Husain 1961: 203-204). The other view is quite opposite to the above observations about Hindu-Muslim relations. According to this view Hindus were suppressed, put to sword, forced to convert to Islam, and Hindus places of worship were demolished. A third view is that the two religious groups existed like two banks of a river bounding the stream but far away from each other.

The only comment which can be offered about Hindu-Muslim relations during the 'Muslim rule' is that the past can be reconstructed to justify one's ideological orientations, one can delve out historical episodes that are congruent with one's beliefs and elaborate them to justify the basic tenets of the ideological orientation and the kind of society which one wants to be established.

With the beginning of 19th century Muslims experienced a hard blow to their self-identity and esteem as this century brought with it the dominance of British in India, Dutch in Indonesia, French in Africa, and Russian in Central Asia. This onslaught made Muslims anxious with the awareness that, "something is awry between religion which God has appointed and historical development of the world which it controls" (Smith 1957: 41). Muslim's intellectual response to this awareness of disjunction led to a number of movements which are identified by Smith (Ibid) as below :

1. *Revivalism*: Discard of accretion and attempt to retrieve the 'golden age'.
2. *Liberalism*: Willingness to reinterpret the creed according to the demands of contemporary life and allowing the exercise of learned discretion and judgement.
3. *Dynamism*: Getting rid of passivity, self-negation, emphasis on change, toughness and active participation in the construction of Islamic society.
4. *Apologetics*: The defense of Islam against criticism, asserting that Islam cannot be against modern humanistic ideas because it was propounder of such ideas. This mechanism helped in soothing the consciousness of westernized Muslims who were somewhat guilt-ridden at their deviation from Islamic norms.s

Muslims in Post-partition era

Let us now have a brief account of Muslim's situation in India in post-partition India which truncated the community into two parts. This era brought Muslims face to face with the feelings of remorse, helplessness, insecurity and anxiety of being accepted without loss of the identity. The following account of Muslim's situation in India is based on reports, articles and letters published in newspapers in different decades.

1947-1959

This period was marked by migration of people from across the border both way. Refugees from Pakistan were pouring in different towns of northern and western India carrying with them the tales of treatment meted to them. The main concern of Indian Muslims was the fear of their property being declared evacuee property and being harassed by the 'custodian'.

The Indian constitution with its provision making no discrimination in government service, according rights to have freedom of conscience and faith, to establish and manage educational institutions and welfare associations, etc., assured Muslims that they could lead a peaceful and honourable life as citizens of India. Despite the reference to desirability of having uniform civil code for all citizens of India, Muslims were happy that at least their legal status was not different from Hindus, who form the majority. However, in 1950 there was protest against some comments about Prophet Mohammad in the Bharati Bhawan Publication *Religious Leaders*. There were also press reports of Muslims expressing pro-Pakistan sentiments by not paying respect to the national flag, not singing national anthem, shouting pro-Pakistan slogans and similar other instances. The displacement of Urdu which they regard as the vehicle of composite culture and treasure of and the source of religious knowledge was a matter of great concern of Muslims.

1960-1969

The main event of this period was the 1965 Indo-Pak war which gave Muslims an opportunity to show their patriotism. The war was also an occasion for Muslims to be sure that they would not be treated as fifth columnists and harassed. However, this period witnessed more frequent and more destructive communal violence. Jabalpur riot of 1961 occurred following molestation of a Hindu girl by a Muslim youth. The destruction that followed was perceived by the Urdu press as a conspiracy to hurt Muslims economically. The police and local administration was criticized for its inefficiency and laxity. Riot at Rourkela in 1954 was studied by a group of social scientists, B.B. Chatterji, P.N. Singh and G.R.S. Rao (1967). The group reported that besides economic anxiety, a rumour that refugees from East Pakistan were served poisoned food when their when their train halted at a station inflamed communal passion.

The rioting in Ahmedabad in 1969 is an example of a combination of different events leading to communal violence. In December 1968 a congregation of Rashtriya Swayamsevak Sangh (R.S.S.) volunteers was addressed by Guru Golwalker. He is reported to have observed that Hindus would continue to suffer until Bharat is declared 'Hindu Rashtra'. Shah (1984: 180), who did a content analysis of letters to editor, found that Hindus in Gujrat supported the theory of Hindu Rashtra as they believed that Muslims destroyed Hindu culture and were continuing to receive favour from the government.

The treatment meted out to the Indian delegation at Islamic conference at Rabat was extensively discussed in the press. Balraj Madhok made a statement (*Times of India* Sep. 28, 1989) that :

> "Today India is a communal state which works for the interest of Muslims and treat Hindus as second class citizens. So there was need to declare India a Hindu state."

This statement can be regarded as an early formulation of the concept of "pseudo-secularism."

1970-1979

The most momentous event of this period was the independence of Bangladesh which exploded the myth that religion is a key element in defining nationalism. Nevertheless there were bloody riots in Bhiwandi (1970), Firozabad (1972), Varanasi (1978) and in Aligarh during 1978-82. In Aligarh riots occurred again and again till 1982 with normalcy returning for short intervals; there was counting of 'scene' on both the sides and the shortfall was immediately met by killing of innocent visitors to the town not familiar with lanes, streets and lalities. The district administration and police were not effective in controlling riots that occurred at different places. Regarding the role of police and administration, Naidu (1980: 120) observed that they:

> "carry a burden of emotion with regard to intercommunity problems which seems to tilt the balance of their judgement. The burden of emotion is also most often a pre-conscious experience so that there is often not a clear awareness that a particular act is prejudiced or discriminatory of minority."

During this period the media discussed job reservation for Muslims, modernization of Muslims, the status of Muslim University as a minority institution and management of Muslim trust (*Awqafs*) and their regulation by the government. The Muslims who came to limelight in this period and had a role in the events to occur in the coming years were Shahi Imam Abdullah Bukhari and Syed Shahabuddin.

The shifting of population from the mixed localities to new settlements and colonies where majority of neighbourhood were of the same community was also observed in different cities. In Aligarh a thinly populated area-Dodhpur-close to Aligarh Muslim University, witnessed construction activity at large scale. There were two reasons for the construction activity: recurring communal riots in the city which created feelings of insecurity, and earning from lucrative jobs in the middle east. Muslims' economic prosperity became visible in the form of construction of houses and religious places and also in extravagance in celebrations.

1980-1988

The happenings of this period were of such a great significance for the Muslim minority and Hindu majority that it would be better to put aside for a while the division of time dimension in decade-long intervals. What happened in the second half of this decade cannot be delinked with the events in the early years of 90s. Riots in Moradabad (1980), intermittent riots in Aligarh since 1977, and riots in Meerut in 1987 were devastating. Muslims accused police, particularly Provincial Armed Constabulary of partiality and killing innocent Muslims in cold blood in Milani and Hashimpura areas of Meerut while Hindu organizations like RSS were attributing Muslims' aggressiveness to foreign money and its role in making Muslims more fanatic and indifferent to the sentiments of the Hindu majority. Certain new and alarming signals were identified by Kumar and Khan (1987) in Meerut riots:

(a) The involvement of neighbours in attacking neighbours of the other community living in the same *mohalla*. In earlier days the participation in riots was limited to hired riff-raff, delinquent youths, a small number of artisans, petty shopkeepers, unskilled workers and hawkers.

(b) The participation of people from the lower middle and middle strata, an indication of degeneration of human values and brutalization of human psyche symptomatic of the pervasive and increasing appeal of communal feelings and antagonism.

(c) Patronized anti-social elements coming to the forefront to represent the community to which they belonged in the peace-keeping and dispute-settling committees.

Many important events including conversion of some Harijan families to Islam in Meenakshipuram in Tamil Nadu (1981), which cast a shadow on the next decade and led to the discussions on the differences between semitic religions and the Indian religions, conspiracy to convert India into a Muslim-majority land, appeasement of Muslims under the cover of the notion of secularism which had been obstructions in the realisation of Hindu cultural and national aspirations, made the later half of the decade a tumultuous period. The defeat of Congress Party in several assembly elections in 1985-86 after the Supreme Court judgment in Shah Bano case compelled the Congress leadership to falter by placating Hindu and Muslim voters turn by turn. The Supreme Court ruling that a divorced Muslim woman is entitled to maintenance in a situation of destitution and also the reference to Article 44 of the Indian Constitution which provides "that the state shall endeavour to secure for citizens a uniform civil code", was regarded by many Muslims as an infringement of the "covenant" of composite nationalism and secularism. The threat to meddle with personal law, which is regarded as a guarantee of the preservation of collective identity of the community, as to be removed by a legislation which could make some arrangement for token maintenance of divorced Muslim women and also to remove the religious anxiety of the minority community. The Muslim women (Protection of Right on Divorce Act, 1986) and the ban imposed on the Salman Rushdees' book *The Satanic versus* in 1988 were construed by the RSS, BJP and other organizations as appeasement of Muslims for electoral advantages. The Congress government also decided to open the locks of the disputed Babri Masjid in February 1986 to counter the accusation of appeasing the minority and to restore the balance.

A few examples of intergroup attitude of Hindus and Muslims prevailing in this period were reported by Tiwari (1983) who had interviewed some members of both communities living in different cities and reproduced their responses. A Muslim is quoted to state:

> My generation accepted the humiliation heaped on us but the youngsters are getting aggressive and why not *hamara bhi haq hae es mulk per*".

Rajiv Tiwari (ibid) reported the following opinion expressed by a political activist:

> "Muslims are getting more and more aggression and they need to be put back in place ... vast sums of money is coming from Muslim nations to fuel the rise of Islam in India and that, by and large, Muslims are lazy and idle or of criminal bent of mind besides being dirty and breeding like rabbits. Also every Muslim *mohalla* is an armed fortress bristling with weapons."

To remove the misgiving of the majority community and relax the mounting the mounting tensions Maulana Wahiduddin published two articles in the *Times of India* on July 15, 1988 advising Muslims to disengage themselves from confrontation and make themselves as inconspicuous as possible, desist from making grievances and follow the example of Asian Americans who ignored their disadvantages and made the best possible use of the advantage they have.

1990-1999

The simmerings and accumulations of illwill in the previous decade, particularly 80s, made the environment very hot for the Muslims. There was from their point of view, the deterioration of secular environment and diminution of support for secular values. Over and above the condemnation of Congress-brand secularism as 'pseudo' there was an attempt to give new meaning to the term by talking of a secular nature of *Hindutva*. With the events occurring in this period there was regression of Muslims to the situation that prevailed just after partition. Though there were some saner voices on both the sides of communal divide, almost the whole Muslim community and the Hindu majority community were in confrontation on the mosque–temple issue. A common Hindu was made to believe that the issue was as simple as this : Hindus constitute 80% of Indian population, the site of Janambhumi which was destroyed to build the mosque be restored to them by Muslims in partial repentance of their ancestors so as to soothe the hurt feelings of Hindus and to enable them to live with a sense of pride in their homeland. For Muslims the issue was more complex as it was the question of myth-versus historical record, victimization and humiliation of the present generation for perceived misdeeds of Muslim rulers, submission or firmness in the face of unreasonable demand and high-handedness, and the test of secular bonafides of the state in protecting the minorities. Muslims were having their self confidence and feeling of affiliation with the homeland shattered by an environment polluted by the communal virus. The disputed structure was demolished on December 6, 1992 in the presence of security forces and the occasion was celebrated. Then followed riots in different parts of the country; the most devastating in Mumbai.

Many articles and editorials appearing in newspapers and magazines calmed ruffled feelings of Muslims with the assurance that all members of the majority community did not approve the vandalism. Muslims were also advised to come to terms with the reality. About a week after the demolition of Babri Masjid, Girilal Jain in an article published in the *Times of India* on December 12, 1992 exhorted Muslim leadership to realize that : It was not possible for Muslims to get the Ramlala's idol removed from the site and the dispute would continue to poison Hindu-Muslim relations; the issue could not be put in cold storage and no compromise solution was possible; with the demolition Muslims had lost bargaining power; they should realize that Indian nationalism is rooted in Hindu ethos, and they should not ignore the dramatic changes that have taken place in recent years. Moreover, riots must have convinced them that they need the goodwill of Hindus as no administration can guarantee their safety and well-being. Another article by Dileep Padgaonkar entitled "India in 1993- No Respite from Chaos" lamented that : (a) the principle of many paths of truth found no favourable echo in the Muslims particularly when the prospect of living no permanently under the rule of majority community is imminent; (b) the ideology of *Sangh Parivar* is almost couched in negative terms; abolish privileges of minorities, destroy symbols of Muslim tyranny, compel minorities to adhere to the symbols and substance of Hindu faith and so on. Padgaonkar warned the *parivar* of consequence of this scheme of things, : "it appears to have learnt no lessons from the tragic development in Punjab and Kashmir ..."

The illegal migration of Bangladesh Muslims, the use of TADA, the restriction of the construction of *madarasas* (schools) and mosques have been matters of concern and discussed in the press. The treatment meted out to the Christian missionaries is also making Muslims anxious because of the apprehension of diversion of vandalism from a minority group which is not only appreciated for sharing the Hindu believe that all humans can share the same vision of truth, but was also more mingled and less conspicuous.

In a seminar on 'Muslim situation in India' held in Aligarh, an appeal was made to Hindu elites.

> "not to read Indian history and contemporary Islamic world in a manner that imaginary Islamic legions may appear to be on a march, the Indian Muslims serving as fifth column."

Participating in the seminar sociologist Imtiaz Ahmad warned against the contention that due to decline of secular pretensions Muslims' social advancement is being blocked and reversed through administrative and popular action. He advised Muslims to find out as to why the wider society harbour hostility towards them and entertain the fear that it might be run-down by them (1989: 46). Ahmad further observed that:

> "...by and large the Indian Muslims have not paid adequate attention to the question of working out an efficacious strategy for struggle for distributive advantages and social advancement. Their orientation has been focused on a strategy of asking for certain group rights, seeking to convert their cultural identity into a political pressure group at the zero-sum game in which gains to the Indian Muslim can taken place only where there is corresponding loss to the wider society" (Ahmed 1989: 46).

Important as they may be, the opinion and views expressed by those who have access to the columns of newspapers, are not the views of an ordinary member of one or the other community; though there is no denial of the fact that public opinion is shaped by opinion leaders and also that the image of a community is created by what is discussed about it in the press. However, social scientists are more comfortable with the empirical studies in which unbiased data are collected using objective instruments and representative samples. As far as studies on Muslims are concerned, the sample used in the study are confined to a city or a few towns of a state but the findings are generalized to all Muslims living in any nook or corner of this vast country who have more resemblance to the ethnic community of their neighbourhood than to other members of the religious community living thousands of kilometers away. Besides the problem of representativeness of the sample there is the problem of confounding the focused variable by the operation of uncontrollable extraneous variable. One may come across a finding where the difference observed in the independent variable(s) because the relationship between the two kinds of variables may be mediated by their covariance with the third variable. One can give the example of the difference in attitude of Hindus and Muslims towards family planning. This difference may be attributed to the relationship of attitude towards family planning with variations in socio-economic status. One should also be conscious of different sources of response distortions which come in the way of generating data and also of the fact that opinions and attitudes are not stable and what is found at one time may not be true at another time. The findings of the empirical studies discussed below are to be considered in the light of the above mentioned methodological limitations. The resume, of the empirical work presented under different categories, in the interest of exposition, is not claimed to be comprehensive.

Intergroup Orientations and Intentions

This section includes the studies on social distances, prejudices, discrimination and intergroup perception. The boys of Patna said that Rankings of different kinds of interaction with Muslims showed no distance in informal relations but social distance was found to increase with change from informal to formal and from formal to kinship relations. Kuppuswamy (1961: 223-24) in a study on Madras University student reported :

> "We find each group rank itself as the first in order to preference... on the whole we find that the Parsis, the Muslims, and the Sikhs are placed at the lower end of the scale.

Do Muslims discriminate and are discriminated against in letting out house? Kuppuswamy (1956) conducted a study to answer this question. Using Brahmins and other upper castes, Harijans, Muslims, Christians as respondents, he found that:

> "43.6 percent of Brahmins (n =188), 54.5 percent of non-Brahmins (n=290), 61.1 percent of Muslims (n=36), 48.1 percent of Christians (n=77) asserted that they would let out house to any one. As against this 36.3 percent of Brahmins, 34.1 percent of non-Brahmins, 16.7 percent of Muslims and 6.8 percent of Christians asserted that they would let house only to the members of the same community".

Studies on intergroup prejudice made an attempt to answer the question who are more prejudiced, Hindus or Muslims? And what are the psychological, demographic and situational factors that are related to intergroup prejudices. Mohsin (1976) explained the relationship between prejudices and such psychological variables as self-concept security-insecurity, parental attitudes and ethnocentrism. Intergroup prejudices were measured by giving a list of socially desirable and socially undesirable characteristics to the subjects and asking them to tick and qualities found in a specified group. The difference between the number of desirable and undesirable qualities ticked by the subjects indicated the degree of prejudice. More ethnocentrics were found to be more prejudiced. There was also some tendency on the part of insecure, low self-regarding, and those who have positive attitude towards parents to give more positive evaluation of the in-group but none of these variables were found to be related to negative evaluation of the in-group. The variables which were found to be significantly correlated to negative evaluation of the outgroup are: security-insecurity, positive evaluation of in-group, and ethnocentrism. The theoretical proposition that self-acceptance is related to acceptance of others was not supported by the finding that self-concept has zero correlation with negative evaluation of the outgroup.

Studies have been conducted on the relationship of intergroup attitudes with personality variables – like security-insecurity, locus of control (whether a person believes that outcome of his behaviour is contingent upon his own effort or on the doings of external agencies), contingent upon his own effort or on the doings of external agencies, alienation, feeling of deprivation, residence in Muslim/Hindu mohallas, and living in towns where occurrence of communal riots are frequent/less frequent (Jahan 1988; Sharma 1991; Hasnain 1998; Hasnan et al. 1998; Ghufran 1998). The main findings are : those who are more insecure are more prejudiced; those who are more willing to do self-disclosure are less prejudiced;

caste Hindus are less prejudiced than scheduled caste Hindus; those living in tension prone areas are more prejudiced; and less educated are more prejudiced. Residence in tension prone area in interaction with low education further added to increment in prejudice, and those who are deprived are more prejudiced. There are contradictory findings about the question as to who are more prejudiced, Hindus or Muslims?

Most of the studies referred to above mentioned prejudice scores by finding difference between the counts of attribution of positive and negative characteristics to the members of outgroup. This kind of quantification is more suitable for statistical treatment of the data but such an approach obscures the content of mental images and opinions about the members of the outgroup. Realizing this fact Hasan (1987) made use of a semi-preojective method in which the subjects were asked to estimate the prevalence (percentage of the population) of certain themes of opinion among Hindus and Muslims. Three different formats were used – 'Hindus think', 'Muslims think', and matter of fact format in which the holder of opinion was not specified. Subjects were also requested to indicate, on a 5-point scale, how far what is stated in an item was 'true' or 'false'. The themes were the general allegations which Muslims make against Hindus and Hindus make against Muslims such as : Muslims are more loyal to Muslim countries, are bent upon population explosion, quarrelsome, blow up their grievances and problems to extract appeasement, are aggressive due to religious belief and upbrining, are not getting equal opportunities of education and employment. Hindus are: not willing to give Muslims the status of equal citizens, regard Muslims as unpatriotic and traitors. Besides the general allegations made by Muslims against Hindus, there were two statements of extremist position:

> "to prevent frequent occurrence of communal riots Muslims have to show that they are capable of retaliation by inflicting more losses on the life and property of Hindus"; "Muslims should not depend on the goodwill of Hindus and have to make their own arrangement for education, employment and security."

The findings of the study are discussed in detail elsewhere (Hasan 1987; 198-229). A brief summary of the findings is as follows : Most of the allegations are placed by both Hindus and Muslims in between 2 and 3 on a 5-point scale, that is slightly lower than the natural point on the True side. The statement about Muslim aggressiveness and Muslims' view that retaliation is necessary to prevent communal disturbance have been rated above 3 (on false side) by Hindus; but Muslims place the statement about their aggressiveness on 'True' side below the neutral point.

When Muslim and Hindu respondents were asked to give estimation of percentage of Muslims holding certain beliefs, two findings deserve attention : Muslim respondents estimated that 49%, members of their community are of the view that they are not regarded 'equal citizens' by Hindus, while according to Hindus' estimation this percentage is 56.79. Similar disparity is observed in Muslim and Hindu respondents, estimation of prevalence of belief among Muslims that they are not getting equal opportunities of employment and education.

The most striking finding of the study was that there was no discrepancy in Muslims' estimation of prevalence of negative characteristics when the themes were presented to them in matter-of-fact format and "Hindus Think" format. But in the case of Hindus' estimation much difference was observed. This disparity in Hindus' estimation implies that while lesser percentage of Muslims are to be blamed their coreligonists (Hindus) are attributing negative qualities to a higher percentage of Muslims.

Social and Political Attitude of Muslims

A number of studies are available on Muslims' social and political attitudes. The findings of a survey carried out in 1971 in 35 districts of India are reported by Gopakrishna (1986). The respondents were asked questions to probe their sentiments about secular and democratic values. Krishna concluded :

> "Indeed the distribution of responses in the Muslim cross-sectional sample was more congruent with non-Muslim equivalent. The data would suggest, however, elites' disagreement on the representativeness of parliament, and both the cross-section and the elite view that the courts of law are not above discrimination, suggest disenchantment with political and legal process" (p. 181).

Two thirds of Muslims were also found to be satisfied with territorial (non-communal) representation while a bare majority of cross-section of Muslims (50.29%) and a large majority of Muslim elite (61%) were of the view that Muslims should work through other (not their own) political parties. More sense of alienation among Muslim elite than in Muslim masses was reported by Krishna. Nandy (1975a; b) conducted studies on acceptability of democratic norms and different kinds of political marginalities among Indian people. He could not find any difference in respect of support for the democratic norms in the two communities; about 50% respondents from both the communities were found to be supporters of democratic norms, and the remaining were opponents. Categorizing Hindu and Muslim respondents in eight kinds of marginalities formed by the three dimensions of alienation – political powerlessness, normlessness, and isolation, Nandy (1975 a; b) noted that Muslims have a low proportion of 'active insiders' (active and efficacious supporters of the system) and active dissenters (active and competent nonbelievers) in the norms.

Table 1
Kinds of Marginalities Prevailing in the Two Communities

	Muslims (%)	*Hindus* (%)
Insiders	6.00	20.00
Passive supporters	4.67	2.67
Inefficacious conformist	4.67	7.40
Ineffective supporters	6.67	6.67
Mechanical participants	2.67	5.40
Passive dissenters	9.33	2.67
Active dissenters	2.00	5.40
Outsiders	14.00	2.67

More than a decade after Nandy's study, Khatoon (1987) used Nandy's 3-dimensional measure to compare the kinds of marginalities prevailing in the two communities. The distribution of respondents in different categories of marginalities as in Table 1 indicates that the percentage of Insiders is higher among Hindus and percentage of outsiders is higher among Muslims. Muslims have a higher percentage of passive dissenters and Hindus have a slightly higher percentage of active dissenters.

Hasan (1987) had put open-ended questions to Hindu and Muslim respondents: Who is responsible for riots, and what you will do to prevent the government from making a law which you consider undesirable and harmful? The content analysis and frequency count of responses showed that : (1) police is more frequently blamed by Muslims (16.04%) and 'internal vested interest' by Hindus (8.86%). As many as 15.31% responses of Muslims also fell in the category of 'internal vested interest'. It is to be noted that in 7.88% of responses of Hindus police is blamed for communal riots. Analysis of responses was also done to know what purpose is served by communal riots as designs against Muslims such as not allowing Muslims to prosper economically, keeping Muslims under domination, preventing Muslims to follow their religion. Situational factors related to 'person' and related to 'property', which led to communal riots are also mentioned by both the groups. The means of Hindu and Muslim respondents on the measures of political efficiency, isolation, and civic tolerance were not significantly different and were indicative of the fact that both groups are doubtful about their political efficacy, are not certain about their participation-isolation from political activities and are indefinite about their sense of civic tolerance.

Haqqi (1989) carried out a study of attitudes of Muslims in which 100 subjects from a town in eastern U.P. and 100 subjects from a town in western U.P. were asked questions about their perception of social status, children's future, changing economic conditions along time, possibility of getting job, getting a rented house, and getting relief from official machinery. The two towns were given code names of Ramnagar and their children's future 'bad' and in their perception of economic deterioration 30% Muslims from Ramnagar reported 'great deterioration' and 38% 'deterioration'; the corresponding percentages of respondents from Alipur were 16%, and 25%. On the basis of responses to questions about rented house, employment, and relief from official machinery, Haqqi observes:

> "They (Muslims) believe, by and large, that the Muslim has practically no chance of getting a house whether it belonged to a Hindu landlord or government agency, and similarly no chance of being recruited or promoted against a similarly qualified Hindu. In regard to relief and rehabilitation assistance provided by the government agency, a majority of Muslim respondents believed that there is "bias and discrimination" (Haqqi 1989: 55).

Using self-anchoring ladder scale Hindus and Muslims were asked by Hasan (1987) to locate their past, present, and future on the ladder of happiness. The two groups were not found to differ with respect to their ratings of past and future life but Muslim were slightly but significantly less happy with the present. While in respect of past and present both groups located themselves in the middle of worst-happiest ladder steps, both groups expected greater movement on the ladder of happiness in future. The study of the concepts of best and worst possible life indicate that both the groups were more concerned with achievement of personal goals, possession of good personal qualities (honesty, intelligence, etc.), status and prestige of oneself, and psychological and physical well-being. Taking into consideration those conditions of happy life which have implication for intercommunity relations, it was found that the two groups differed significantly in percentage of responses falling in the categories of social harmony (Muslim 7.45%, Hindus 9.37%) removal of social irritants (Muslims 5.21%, Hindus 7.9%), and conformity to norms (Muslims 2.8% and Hindus 1.44%).

In a study of intergeneration gap of modernity among Muslims Enayatullah (1998) compared modernity scores of father and son with different levels of education. The measure of modernity was the scale developed by Singh (1984) which includes items representing the dimensions of personality, socio-cultural and political outlook, and beliefs about illness and health. Enayatullah concluded that education is an important modernizing factor among Muslims too; more educated sons have more modernity scores than their poorly educated fathers. The new generation of Muslims has developed a scientific outlook on the etiology and therapy of physical and mental illness, diet, nutrition, family planning, child care; it has more favourable attitudes towards democracy and secularism, is more consciousness of civic rights, and has it has a rational approach to social and cultural issues.

Muslims' Educational-economic Backwardness, Quality of Life and Sense of Deprivation

There is no controversy about the fact that Muslims of India are a backward community whatever criteria one may employ to identify the overall backwardness of the community. There is, however, a controversy regarding the reasons of this backwardness; the blame is attributed by Muslims to the state and the system, and by others to Muslims' mentality of defeatism and motivational deficit.

Gopal Krishna had conducted a study of Muslims' attitude and their place in Indian society during 1973-74. As the study was sponsored by the Ministry of Home Affairs, its findings are not available but Saxena (1983) revealed that Gopal Krishna found that educational level of Muslims is lower and dropout rate is higher in all parts of India and in every economic category. This state of backwardness of Muslims has been found to prevail even in Muslim managed schools and colleges where there is no possibility of discrimination against them. A survey of Muslim managed schools and colleges showed that there was dropout from 83.8% enrolment percentage at school level to 40.4% at the college level. As many as 14 reasons of this state of affair are listed by Shah (1983) who conducted the study.

The most common refrain of Muslim parents' lack of encouragement to Muslim children to go for education was reported by Nian in the Indian Express, Oct. 10, '83:

> "What he will do after finishing education? At the most he would be employed as a clerk and earn a salary of Rs. 500/= per month; at this place the child would do the job and earn between 20 to 50 per day."

Muslims are not only educationally backward in the north, they are also backward in all parts of India. In Tamil Nadu as many as ten associations are working for the cause of Muslim education and yet Muslims are classified as a backward class eligible for educational concessions (Ali 1989). The picture is dismal in the case of Calcutta too where Muslims constitute 15% of the population out of which three-fourths live in slums. The total enrolment of Muslims in schools is 2.2% and at higher level the percentage of 0.50% (Siddiqui 1989).

Associated with the economic conditions of Muslims is their representation in government and quasi-government jobs. Abdussalam (1989) developed a quantitative index of equality (CE) based on the ratio of percentage of presentation of a community to percentage share of that community in the total population. The ratio multiplied by 100 provides the coefficient of equality (CE). The departure of the CE from 100 on the lower side is an indication of backwardness of a community. The CE found for different levels of jobs in public and private sector provides a picture of miserable condition of Muslims' employment even in class four posts in public and private sector undertakings and state government jobs. Most of Muslims are earning by working as electricians, mechanics, craftmen and artisans. However, one finds certain islands of prosperity in some towns of Uttar Pradesh (Moradabad, Aligarh, Mau, Varanasi) and Maharastra (Bhiwandi) where Muslims entrepreneurs can be found among manufacturers and wholesale traders in textiles, carpets, locks and brass utensils.

One recent study (Barkat 1999) on organizational development has revealed that entrepreneurs' quality of work, life and effort to bring organizational change have been the important factors and organizational development for both Hindu and Muslim entrepreneurs. As a result of entrepreneurs' higher motivation, the yearly turnover rates of their establishment have witnessed an increasing trend in the case of Hindu entrepreneurs even when they are in a minority in Bhiwandi town of Thane district, Maharastra. They have an average annual turnover of Rs. 57.2 lakhs whereas, Muslim entrepreneurs have a slightly lower average annual organizational turnover of Rs. 53.3 lakhs. This difference in yearly turnover rate has been found because of the difference in opting technological change as Hindu entrepreneurs are more prone to modernize their textile industries by replacing the old looms by automatic looms.

Muslims live in dirty localities, a fact which cannot be denied despite their protest on being called *malech*. One can find heaps of garbage and filthy drains in Muslim areas. The residents lament about indifferent attitudes and discrimination on the part of municipal administration but they do not take any step to get the locality cleaned regularly.

Realizing the interactive nature of economic deprivation and degraded environmental quality under which slum developers find themselves, Siddiqui (1997) carried out a study to find out the type of coping strategies which Muslim slum dwellers adopt in dealing with the economic and environmental degradation stressors which they confront daily. The sample comprised of 140 slum dwellers from Allahabad and 140 slum dwellers from Delhi. From both the cities equal numbers of males and females were interviewed. The findings of the study show lack of any significant correlation between perceived economic condition and environmental stressors of air, water, noise, garbage, traffic, and crowding males reported greater social support. The regression analysis showed economic stressors were better predicators of psychological health than that of physical health but environmental stressors were found to be better predictors of physical health than that of psychological health.

The possibility of prevalence of feelings of relative deprivation among Muslims has been empirically explored. The term 'Relative Deprivation' was proposed by Runicman (1966) and Gurr (1970) in recognition of the role social comparison in giving rise to the feelings of deprivation. Egoistic Relative Deprivation (Crossby 1972), Just Deserts Frustration (Miller and Jukam 1981) and Subjective Rank Disequilibrium (Galtung 1964) are the other concepts which take into consideration individuals' assessment of what he is getting.

The salience of deprivation in social, economic and political areas among Muslims and the effect of salience of deprivation in different areas on integroup attitudes of Muslims was studied by Tripathi and Srivastava (1979). Data collected from a sample of 112 Muslim students of Allahabad University showed that deprivation was highest in economic area and lowest in social area. Moreover, Muslims suffering from greater feelings of deprivation were found to attribute higher negative qualities to the outgroup but the difference of level of deprivation was not found to be associated with the difference in attribution of positive qualities to the outgroup.

Khatoon (1989) conducted a study in which 180 Muslim and 1290 Hindu students of Aligarh Muslim University (age range 21-27 years) were administered different scales including measures of Just Desert Frustration (JDF), Subjective Rank Disequilibrium (SRD) and questions about situation of life – housing conditions, medical care, influence in community, educational opportunities, and life in general. The respondents were required to indicate how did they feel about each condition and to give 'Yes' or 'No' response to indicate that their condition was as good as they deserved. Yes was scored 1 and No 0. The measure of SRD was made of three questions dealing with one's comparison with that of one's education, income, occupational prestige and status, and extent 'say' in various matters. The respondents were asked that considering their level of education do they feel that their income level, occupational status, etc. would be as good as they deserved. The response was to be 'Yes' or 'No'. If the response was 'No' the respondents was to indicate disparity on a three point scale, somewhat worse, much worse, very much worse. The three categories were assigned scores of 1,2 and 3 respectively. The measure of Treatment Evaluation named police, railway staff, electricity department, and municipal authorities and asked the respondent to indicate how they feel toward these agencies in different situation of life. The respondent's feelings toward the agencies were assessed with a set of four statements asking the respondents to indicate whether they themselves or other members of their community were given a hard time and their problems were not looked into. The scoring varies from – 2 to 2 (no hard time given – very hard time given). The statistical analysis of the data showed that the two groups differed with respect to JDF and SRD but not with respect to Treatment Evaluation.

Studies on Traits, Minority Complex, Assimilation and Identity

It is often reported that minorities have peculiar personality traits and psyche which can be collectively designated as oppression/ minority complex (Miller 1924; Dewy and Humber 1951). Hyper-sensitivity, self-hatred, helplessness, defensive pluralism, and siege mentality are the components of minority complex. Assertion of rights granted by the constitution and invoking U.N. Charter on human rights, is also a salient feature of minority reaction to its situation.

Though much work has been done on the attitudes and traits of minorities in the U.S.A., U.K. and other countries, we shall discuss only those studies which have been conducted in India. In his study of 'Adolescent Fantasy', Kureshi (1975) used a set of pictures to arouse fantasy manifestation of different motives. The stories told by 62 Hindus and 57 Muslim boys matched with respect to age and socio-economic status were thematically analyzed according to the scheme of scoring for different motives, developed by McClelland and his association (1958). Muslim and Hindu subjects were found to differ with respect to the strength of affiliation and power motives; they were equal in respect of intensity of achievement, aggression and security motives. The rank order of motives' and aggression. The rank order of intensity of motives among Hindus was security, aggression, achievement, power and affiliation. The implications of the finding as brought out by Kureshi are : Muslims have more affiliative tendency for forging solidarity for preservation; the need for power is an indication of lack of damage to their self-image of dominance which persists despite their post-partition situation; the lack of difference in need aggression is a refutation of the refrain and population stereotype of Muslims as an aggressive community. The security motive can be broken into the components of 'hope' for attaining friendly and congenial atmosphere, and 'fear' but overall scores conceal this fact. Achievement motive can also be broken into hope for success and fear of failure and Muslims and Hindus differing in respect of fear of failure.

A study (Fatima and Hasnain 1998) to find the difference between the level of adjustment and defeatism among Hindus and Muslims showed that the groups do not differ significantly in respect of either of the two variables. However, in a study carried out by Khan and Hasan (1997) Muslims were found to have les faith in their personal capacity to bring about the desired outcome in 20 different situations some of which were of the nature where outcome is more contingent on effort and some in which the outcome is more contingent on chance.

There are studies showing that Muslims have gradually and spontaneously accepted certain Hindu influence and yet they assert their distinct identity. Umar (1973) reported adoption of a large number of Hindu rituals related to marriage ceremony among Muslims. The persistence of the impact of Hindu culture on Muslim living in Bihar was studied by Madani (1993) who collected data using participant and non-participant observations, interview, census, case studies, office records, and photography. He listed rituals after birth, marriage customs, dress and food, ornaments which are common to both the communities. Impact on social relations (and stratification) and observations of festivals were also recorded. Farooque (1984) has also reported as many as six different ways of Indianization of Islam.

It is not difficult to understand the existence of the opposite tendencies of accepting Hindu influence and assertion of distinct identity by Indian Muslims. The acceptance of Hindu influence was gradual and outcome of spontaneous interaction; it was not under threat or as a price of condition of acceptability. Moreover, it was a manifestation of expansion rather than a case of loss of identity. Even now, as Madani (1993) found, Muslims are observing Hindu rituals without the awareness that what they do is an accepted influence; for them the rituals are their own.

Those who demand Muslim to make a choice between either Indian identity or Muslim identity are not aware of the fact that a person has many identities some of which remain submerged and in different contexts different identities are aroused. Weinreich (1991), who defined identity as a totality of one's self-construal and ethnic identity as a part of totality of one's total construal, reported that Black youth in South Africa, when they are situated with Africans, cue into identity states which are quite different from that they are with English speaking Whites.

Subscribing to the theoretical view that one of the multiple identities of a person is aroused by the situational cues and coming across the instances where peace loving and tolerant persons become prejudiced and violent under certain situations. Hasan and Khatoon (1996) conducted a study in which 38 Muslim students of Aligarh Muslim University were required to indicate on a 5-point scale as to what extent 20 listed situations arouse religious identity among them. Analysis of the data showed that the following situations were identified to be highly identity-arousing among Muslim youth: when objectionable statements are made against the community; when people of the community indulge in prohibited acts; when members of one's community are selected to represent the country; and when members of one's community win national/international awards. The following situations were found to be lest identity-arousing : when one has to restrain oneself from participating in a discussion due to fear of being singled out; when one is bound to conceal religious identity because of fear; when one visits a religious shrine of another community and stands aloof with a sense of non-participation; when there is some critical situation, natural calamity or difficult situations.

Studies have been conducted to find the development of religious and ethnic identities in different groups. Singh (1985) on the basis of such studies, mostly done in the Ranchi University observed that religious and ethnic identities among Hindus, Muslims, Sikhs, and Christians emerge at the age of 4-5 years and are fully blown by early adolescence. Singh also noted that children of 14-15 years of age have correct information about their own religion but not even 25% of them have correct information about other religions. Minority group status was found to hasten and strengthen identity and to influence social distance with other religious groups.

To conclude, Muslims of India though forming a religious community with sharing of basic Islamic precepts, do not form a homogeneous community in a sociological respect. The empirical studies provide central tendencies or minimal common elements of Muslims' reactions. Muslims have different kinds of identities (Srinivasan 1981). There are many among them who are willing to dissolve their identity or to pass as Mohammadan Hindu, there are those who believe that their problems of life are due to their not being true Muslims, there are those who want to lead a simple life of an ordinary citizen who is fairly treated and is not oversensitive to his minority status and realizes that in our society nepotism is a fact of life. Also, Muslims show same kinds of reactions as are manifested by other minority groups wherever they are found.

REERENCES

Abdussalam, C.A. (1989), "Muslim Backwardness: A Quantitative Analysis". In I.A. Ansari (ed.). *The Muslim Situation in India,* New Delhi: Sterling Publishers.

Ahmad, I. (1989), "The Problems of Indian Muslims: Methodology for Analysis." In I.A. Ansari (ed.). *The Muslim Situation in India.* New Delhi: Sterling Publishers.

Ali, N.A.A. (1989), "Educational Landscape of Tamil Nadu·Muslim Contribution." In I.A. Ansari (ed.). *The Muslim Situation in India.* New Delhi: Sterling Publishers.

Barkat, S.A.(1999), "A Study of Organizational Development as a Function of OC and QL – A Comparative Study of the Hindu Muslim Entrepreneurs." Unpublished Ph.D. Thesis, Department of Psychology, Aligarh Muslim University, Aligarh.

Chatterji, B.B., P.N. Singh and G.R.S. Rao (1967), *Riots in Rourkela: A Psychological Study.* New Delhi : Popular Book Service.

Crossby, E.A. (1976), "Egoistic Relative Deprivation," *Psychological Review,* 83, 5-19.

Dewey, R. and H.J. Humber (1998), *The Development of Human Behaviour.* New York: MacMillan Co.

Enayatttulah (1998), "Modernity in Muslims: A Study of Generation Gap." In N. Hasnain (ed.) *Social-Psychological Dimensions of Muslims.* New Delhi: Institute of Objective Studies.

Farooque, J. (1984), "Cultural Contacts between Hindu and Muslims". Proceedings on Seminar on "Intra-Societal Tension and National Integration" held at Aligarh Muslim University, Aligarh.

Fatima, T. and N. Hasnain (1998), "Adjustment Alienation and Defeatism in Muslim and Hindu Adolescence." In N. Hasnain (ed.). *Social-Psychological Dimensions of Muslims.* New Delhi: Institute of Objective Studies.

Ghufran, M. (1998), "Prejudice in Relation to Education and Alienation Among Muslims of High and Low Tension Areas." In N. Hasnain (ed.) *Social-Psychological Dimensions of Muslims.* New Delhi: Institute of Objective Studies.

Gaur, T.R. (1972), *Why People Rebel.* New Jersey : Princeton University Press.

Haqqi, S.A.H. (1989), "Muslim in India: Behavioural Introduction." In I.A. Ansari (ed.). *The Muslim Situation in India.* New Delhi: Sterling Publishers.

Hasan, Q. (1987), *Muslims in India: Attitudes, Adjustment and Reactions.* New Delhi: Northern Book Centre.

Hasnain, N. (1998), "Prejudice Across Communities." In N. Hasnain (ed.) *Social-Psychological Dimensions of Muslims.* New Delhi: Institute of Objective Studies.

Hasnain, N., S. Riaz and T. Fatima (1998), "Ethnocentrism Among Hindu and Muslim Adolescents and Muslim Dominated Areas". In N. Hasnain (ed.) *Social-Psychological Dimensions of Muslims.* New Delhi: Institute of Objective Studies.

Hasnain, N. (1961), *The National Culture of India.* Bombay: Asia Publishing House.

———(1991), *Nobility Under Akbar and Jahangir.* New Delhi: Manohar.

Jahan, Q. (1988), "A Study of Communal Prejudice as Related to Self Disclosure and Adjustment". Unpublished Ph.D. Thesis. Department of Psychology, Aligarh Muslim University, Aligarh.

Khan, H.R. (1978), "Development of Religion Identity and Prejudice in Children. Unpublished Ph.D. Thesis, Magadh University, Bodh Gaya.

Khan, S.R. and Q. Hasan (1977), "Locus of Control Among Hindus and Muslims", *Indian Psychological Review,* 1, 19-24.

Khatoon, N. (1987), A Comparative Study of Political Alienation of Hindu and Muslim Youth. Unpublished M.Phil. Dissertation, Department of Psychology, Aligarh Muslim University, Aligarh.

———(1989), A Comparative Study of Patterns of Political Alienation and their Socio-psychological Correlates Among Hindu and Muslim Youth". Unpublished Ph.D. Thesis. Department of Psychology, Aligarh Muslim University, Aligarh.

Krishna, G. (1986), "Problems of Integration in the Indian Community: Muslims and Political Process." In D.K. Bose and S. Richards (eds.) *Social and Economic Development in India,* New Delhi: Sage Publications.

Kumar, P. and D. Khan (1987), "Meerut Riots – Some Alarming Signals, " Patriot, July 18.

Kuppuswamy, B. (1961), *An Introduction to Social Psychology*. Bombay: Asia Publishing House (reprint 1980).

Kureshi, A. (1975), *Adolescent Fantasy*. Calcutta: Minerva Associates.

Lewin K. (1936), *Principles of Topological Psychology*. New York: McGraw Hill.

———(1951), "Field Theory in Social Sciences": In D. Cartwright (ed.) *Selected Theoretical Papers*. New York : Harper & Row.

Madani, M.S. (1993) *Impact of Hindu Culture on Muslims*. New Delhi: M.D. Publications.

McClelland, D.C. (1958), "Methods of Measuring Human Motivation". In J.W. Atkinson (ed.) *Motives in Fantasy, Action and Society*. Princeton: D.Van Nostrand.

Miller, E.N. and T.O. Jukam (1981), "Discontent and Aggressive Political Participation," *British Journal of Political Science* 13, 159-179.

Miller, A.H. (1924), *Races, Nations and Classes*. Phildelphia: J.B. Lippincott.

Mitra, S.K. (1977), "Social Prejudice and Personality in Adolescents." In B.De and Durganand Sinha (eds.) *A Perspective on Psychology in India*.

Mohsin, S.M. (1976), "Reinterpretation of Dynamics of Attitude Formation and Change." Indian Journal of Psychology, 51, 1-60.

Naidu, R. (1980), *Communal Edge to Pluralistic Societies*. New Delhi: Vikas Pubishing House.

Nandy, A. (1975a), "Insides and Outsiders: Aspects of Political Alientation." D.L. Sheth (ed.) *Citizens and Parties-Aspects of Competitive Politics in India*. New Delhi: Allied Publshers.

———(1975b), "The Acceptance and Rejection of Democratic Norms in India." *Indian Journal of Psychology*, 50, 265-278.

Runicman, W.G. (1966), *Relative Deprivation and Social Inequality in Twentieth Century England*. Berkley : University of California Press.

Saxena, M.S. (1983), "Why Muslims don't fare well", *Times of India*. May 31.

Shah, G. (1984), "The 1969 Communal Riots in Ahmadabad." A.A. Engineer (ed.) *Communal Riots in Post Independent India*. Hydrabad : Sangam Books.

Sharma, R. (1991), "A Study of Communal Prejudice in Relation to Locus of Control Security – Insecurity and Prolonged Deprivation among Students." Unpublished Ph.D. Thesis, Department of Psychology, Aligarh Muslim University. Aligarh.

Siddiqui, M.A.K. (1989), "Muslim Education in Calcutta." In I.A. Ansari (ed.) *The Muslim Situation in India*. New Delhi : Sterling Publishers.

Siddiqui, R. (1997), "Effect of Economic and Environmental Stressers on Health." Unpublished Ph.D. Thesis, Department of Psychology, University of Allahabad.

Singh A.K. (1984), "Health Modernity: Concepts and Correlates." *Social Change*, 14, 3-36.

———(1985), "Developing Secularism and National Integration in India." Presidential Address, Section of Psychology and Educational Psychology, 77th Session of Indian Science Congress.

Smith, W.C. (1957), *Islam in Modern History*. Princetone: Princeton University Press.

Srinivasan, N. (1981), *Identity Crisis of Muslims*. New Delhi: Concept Publishing House.

Tiwari, Rajiv (1983) In the *Times of India*, Oct. 30.

Tripathi, R.C. and R. Srivastava (1979), "Relative Deprivation and Protest Behaviour". Proceedings of 66th Indian Science Congress.

Umar, M. (1978), *Hindustani Tahzib ka Mussalmano Par Asar*. New Delhi: Government of India.

Weinrich, P. (1991), "Ethnic Identities and Indigenous Psychologies in Pluralistic Societies, *Psychology and Developing Societies* 3, 73-99.

MUSLIM SOCIETY AND CULTURE IN BENGAL: TRADITION AND CHANGE

Sekh Rahim Mondal

Introduction

Muslims constitute the largest religious minority of India. The social and cultural life of the Muslims, living in various parts of the country, display distinctive features, as they are influenced by both the Islamic as well as regional and local traditions. Muslims are the members of Islamic community (*Umma*) out of common belief and faith. But it is not concern of everyday practical life, where they interact with the local cultures. Therefore, curiosity arises in many quarters to know the nature and character of this community with special reference to their society and culture.

Bengal has a significant Muslim population. Bengali Muslims adhere to basic principles of Islam and at the same time share the local traditions of Bengal. There is no conflict between the two spheres, although both the boundaries are sharply defined by their respective ideology and practice. Bengali Muslims share little traditions of Bengal, i.e. the Bengali culture, which is common to both Hindus and Muslims of this region. But unfortunately due to lack of research studies we do not know much about the social matrix and cultural dynamics of the Bengali Muslims.

The present paper is an attempt to highlight the dynamics of Muslim society of India in general and Bengal in particular. To deal with this, the traditional social organization of Muslims shall be discussed in brief and the trends of change therein shall also be highlighted. This paper presents an analysis of social structure and social organization of the Muslim on the basis of groupings, interrelations and interactions among various units of this society,. In this paper the interaction between the great tradition of Islam and little traditions of the place in the framework of Muslim society and culture shall also be pointed out.

The paper is based on data gathered from primary and secondary sources. It is the product of empirical research on the subject with which the author has been engaged for more than two decades.

Islam and Muslims in India

The word 'Islam' derived from the Arabic root "SLM", means peace, submission and obedience. In religious sense the word Islam means submission to the will of God (*Allah*) and the obedience to His laws. The great tradition of Islam is found on a world view which is apparently non-hierarchical, egalitarian and historical in ethos. Islam has oriented towards holistic principle in its conception of social and cultural order. Thus, Islam is not only a religion but a complete way of life. The followers of Islam are known as Muslims.

During early part of seventh century the new monotheistic religion of Islam emerged in Arabia. Prophet Muhammad was the founder of this religion. The message of God as revealed to Prophet is noted in the Holy book called *Quran*. The entire life, words and deeds of the Prophet recorded by his followers in another book(s) called *Hadith*. Islam emerged as a reaction against exploitation in the land of Arabia and played a vital role in reform and revolution of the Arab society and culture of that time. Though Islamic tradition is based upon non-hierarchical world view with monotheistic ideology and its followers abiding the common code of conduct application to the peoples of all colou8rs and creed, yet pluralism gained impetus, as it never remained confined to a region for long. Islam spread from Arabia to other countries in various phases of history and thereby adjusted with the local situations.

The spread of Islam in India is very interesting one. India has an age old contact with the Arab world. The Arabian preachers, central Asian traders and the Muslim rulers played a very significant role to spread Islam in Indian subcontinent. The commercial relations between Central Asia and India, the religious mendicants (saints), the various Muslim invasions followed by continuous Muslim rule in the country, the immigration of people from various parts of Arabia, central Asia and neighbouring places and finally the conversion of the local people into the fold of Islam facilitated the spread of this religion in India. Various social, religious and political causes are considered for the growth and spread of Islam in various parts of this country., Islam spread and propagated in India mostly between eighth to seventeenth centuries.

Bengal's contact with Islam and the foreign Muslims, specially in the field of trade and missionary activities, began much earlier than its conquest in the thirteenth century. Many Muslim scholars and saints or *Sufis* are believed to have come even before the conquerors. To spread Islam in Bengal the activities of the former were no less significant than those of the latter. In Bengal Islam expanded mostly in rural areas, while in other parts of the country Islam mostly spread in urban areas (Wolf 1951, Levy 1957, Sarkar 1972, De 1974, Imam 1975, Islahi 1978).

Muslim Population in India

Muslims from about 25 percent of the world's total population and India has the second largest Muslim population of the globe. Out of 1000 millions of world Mulsim population 100 millions live in India. According to 1991 census, total Muslim population in India was 101,546,057 (12.12%) of which 52,631,365 were males and 48,964,692 are females. The sex ratio of Muslims was 930 females per 1000 males.

The Muslim population is spread over the length and breadth of the country in all the States and Union Territories in various frequencies. Maximum concentration of Muslim population is found in the state of Jammu and Kashmir (64.19%) and the Union Territory of Lakshadweep and its neighbouring Islands (94.31%). The lowest percentage of Muslims are found in the states of Mizoram (0.66%) and Sikkim (0.85%). About 74 per cent of the Muslims of this country reside in three states namely Assam (28.42%), Kerala (23.33%) and West Bengal (23.61%). Over 55 percent of Muslim population of India reside in the States of West Bengal (23.61%), Uttar Pradesh (17.33%) and Bihar (14.81%). The States and Union Territories where Muslims form 5 percent or more but less than national average of 12 percent are Andhra Pradesh (8.91%), Gujarat (8.73%), Karnataka (11.64%), Maharashtra (9.67%),

Manipur (7.27%), Rajasthan (8.01%), Delhi (8.91%), Andaman and Nicobar Island (7.61%) and Pondicherry (6.54$) as per 1991 census. In Arunachal Pradesh, Himachal Pradesh, Nagaland, Orissa, Punjab, Sikkim, Chandigarh, Dadra and Nagar Haveli their population is between 1 to 3 percent of the total population. And the rest of the states have above 3 but less than 5 percent of the total population. The widespread distribution of the Muslim population through out the length and breadth of the country is clearly indicative of the fact that it has grown mainly out of indigenous population (Siddiqui 1998, Mondal 2000).

Bengal Muslims – Aspects of Their Social Organization

The idea of homogeneity and equality among the Muslims was practiced during the initial state of the rise of Islam in Arabia. But in successive stages the homogeneity and equality of Islamic society has to face a serious challenge due to its contact with the plural societies and the complex cultures, like in India. When Islam reached India the concept of equality, homogeneity and brotherhood only remained an ideal one as the Muslim society in this country is characterized by various social groups which exhibit a clear trend of diversity in social customs.

In this section I shall briefly discuss the system of social organization and patterns of social groupings among the Muslims. In course of discussion I shall highlight the features among Muslims of India in general with Bengal in particular. Through empirical studies it is noted that the Muslim population is significantly divided into certain social groups of varied backgrounds. The groups among the Muslims may be considered as macro as well as micro units of the society. The macro units of the Muslim society are based on the theological schools, sects and sub-sects, *khanqahs* and *sisilas*, history of descent, ethnicity and social status of the people which are operating at the wide level. Besides macro groupings of the Muslims, they are also segmented into several smaller units like kinship, neighbourhood and local community. These smaller groups among the Muslims are the micro units of the society as these are localized and their features are typical to the people living in specific region. The nature and character of these groupings are described below.

The empirical study among the Bengal Muslims reveal that, despite the equalitarian ideology of "Islamic brotherhood" the

Muslims of this provide are segmented into various orders at macro and micro levels. At macro level, first, the Muslims are segmented on the basis of various schools theological jurisprudence (*majahabs*). There exists two major Muslim groups on the basis of *Majahabs*. These are *Hanafis* and *Shafeis*. There is a sharp difference between these two groups, particularly6 in regard of *ijma* (consensus). The *Hanafis* reject the concept of *ijma*, while the *Shafeis* accept it as valid. Each group maintains its social boundary through limiting social contacts with members of the other group. These two groups are endogamous and they built up their respective mosques to pray *namaj*. However, inspite of their jurisprudential differences, the *Hanafis* and *Shafeis* are interacting with each other in their day76 to day life various social needs.

Secondly, the Muslims are divided among themselves into certain sects and sub-sects. Three major sects have been identified among the Bengali Muslims. These are *Sunni, Shia* and *Ahle-e-Hadish*. The Sunnis are numerically dominant in this provice and they are further subdivided into two main sub-sects. These are *Barelvis* and *Deobandis*. The *Sunni Barelvis* show the highest degree of assimilation of little traditions and they are also least critical in containing the traditional (pre-Islamic) customs and rituals. They are well integrated with the local society of Bengal. While the *Sunni Deobandis* are willing to differentiate them from the *Barelvis* by virtue of their involvement in missionary works and activities of puritan nature. Actually their main goal is to strengthen the process of Islamization among the Muslim masses. Though there are differences of opinion between *Barelvis* and *Deobandis* in matters of social customs and religio-ritual practices, yet they interact with each other in all matters of day to day social life. The sectarian affiliation of Muslims also cuts across various social boundaries among them, like ethnic (*jat*), and class divisions.

Thirdly, the Muslims are segmented on the basis of their affiliation and association with the various spiritual (*Tariqat*) orders, based on *Khanqahs* and *Silsilas* i.e. saints and their schools of thoughts. Around *Khanqah*, there exists two fold divisions of the people viz., *Pir* (saint) and *Mureed* (disciple). The *Mureeds* of a common *Pir* are known as *pir-bhai*, who have some duties and obligations to each other. Various social problems among *Mureeds* are generally solved by their respective *pirs*. The *pir-bhais* are related to one another through their clientship to a common *silsila,* and this helps them to interact with each other in various social contexts. Interaction among the *Mureeds* of different *Khanqah* is also not uncommon among the Muslims. The belief in *pirism* among Muslims is identical with the *guruism* among Hindus. The Pir-bhais among the Muslims and Gurubhai among the Hindus are also identical in character. Belief in spiritualism (*tariquat*) among Muslims cut across various social boundaries among them. A notion of social inequality exists among the Muslims around affiliation to different spiritual orders and *pirs*. Muslims of higher social status usually associate themselves with some famous *Khanqah* of distant places. Whereas the commoners who enjoy lower social status affiliated to the *Pirs* and *Khanqahs* of their locality which are not very renowned one. A notion of superiority complex among the *Mureeds* over the non-*Mureeds* has also been very often noticed among the Muslims.

Fourthly, the Muslims are also segmented into various groups on the basis of their ethnic identity and social status and which are arranged in stratified order. The traditional informal system of social stratification among the Muslims of Bengal is the division of people into several *jats* and social categories on the basis of social honour through place of origin, ethnicity, descent and degree of distance from original converts., Besides *jat* categories, there are many occupational groups among the Muslims. Inequality in social position on the basis of traditional occupations is also noticed among Bengal Muslims. Maintenance of group identity on the basis of social boundary through endogamy, and limited social interaction in various spheres of social life among the Muslim groups is very conspicuous one. All these facts reveal the "caste like" characteristics among the Muslims. The difference that emerged among Muslims in this context is between the descendants of the so-called "foreign ancestors" and the "indigenous converts". The former segment is called as *Khas* or *Asraf,* while the latter is known as *Aam* or *Ajlaf* or *Atraf.* Those who called themselves as *Khas* are the gentry section and considered them as aristocrat of *Aaimadar*. They are the land owners, civic or religious leaders and comparatively wealthier. The *Khas* or *Asraf* constituted the elite category of the Muslims. They are further subdivided on the basis of their ethnicity and place of origin. Among them there are four major groups viz.,

Sayyad, Shaik, Mughal and *Pathan.* The *Sayyad* and *Shaik* are believed to have descended from Arab ancestors. While *Mughal* and *Pathan* are claimed to have descended from *Mughal* (Mongol) and *Afgan* conquerors. But the people of *Ajlaf* or *Aam* category are the toiling massesw and peasants, therefore, could not lay6 any such claim of noble ancestry. There are several occupational groups among the Muslims of *Ajlaf* category. Social gradation amongst the Muslim occupational groups is also noticed. Actually the social gradation among the *Ajalaf* occupational groups is determined by their past caste characteristics. At the bottom of social ladder there are those Muslims who do scavenging, sweeping, and such other unclean jobs. They are commonly referred as *Arzals* or *Raizals.* It is estimated that more than two-third of Muslim population belong to *Ajlaf* and *Arzal* categories and they are considered to be marginalized in their social position. Owing to impact of the notion of nobility among the *Asraf* and caste back-ground among the *Ajlaf* and *Arzal,* the segments of Muslim society are generally arranged in a stratified order. Although Islam does not recognize any caste differentiation among its adherents, but several categories of Muslims belonging to *Ajlaf* and *Arzal* sections have traditionally been treated as 'low castes' i.e. *nichu-jats* in their occupations and in matters of social relations. It is also to be noted here that, the traditional social gradation among the Muslims on the basis of place of origin, ethnic identity and traditional occupation has been changing in recent times and which has been replaced by "status group" and "class-like" divisions among them. The most popular emerging "status groups" among the Muslims in Bengal are *Miya* (well todo), *Garosthi/Chhasa* (poor) and *Kamina/Itar* (degraded/ fallen). The emerging status groups among the Muslims are also ranked in stratified order in terms of their social position. There is limited social interaction among the Muslims of various status categories as each of them occupies a definite position in the social ladder. Many of the marginalized Muslim groups belonging to traditional *Ajlaf* and *Arzal* categories or emerging *Garosthi* and *Kamina* status categories are now awakening and organizing movements for social equality. They called themsevels as OBC Muslims. In 1980 the Mandal Commission considered 90 percent of Muslim population in India as backward and declared 82 Muslim groups as OBCs. In West Bengal there are Muslim groups who are known as OBCs Muslims of the state.

The pattern of social stratification among the Muslims clearly reveals that the traditional *jats* distinction is more an ascribed and closed system, while the emerging status group or class inequality is achieved, flexible and open in character. The structure of traditional *jat* stratification developed in the background of feudal conditions whereas the emerging pattern of status group distinction is an outcome of changing situation. However, inspite of separate social boundaries, various Muslim groups interact with one another in economic, social, political and cultural contexts, in their day to day life as well as on ceremonial occasions. This enables them to cut across ethnic, social and class boundaries.

Beside above groupings among the Muslims, they are also segmented into Muslim kinship is constituted by a sect of kin categories. Broadly, there are two sets of kins, i.e., *Khandan* and *Kutumb* or *Meheman*. So far the groupings and relationships are concerned, the members of *Khandan* and *Kutumb* are further sub-divided into several clusters. The members of *Khandan* or lineage (consanguinal kins) are divided into *Parivar* or *Ghar* (family), *Bhaiad* or *De-deiji* (minimal lineage) and *Gusti* or *Bangso* (maximal lineage). And similarly the *Kutumbs* (affinal kins) are categorized as *Baper-kutumb* (father's side), *Maer-kutumb* (mother's side) and *Nejer Kutumb* (one's own side). The inter-relations and interactions among the members of *Khandan* are basically face to face, intimate and informal. They closely interact in their day to day life as well as on ceremonial occasions. Whereas the pattern of relationship and interaction among the *kutumbs* is mostly formal and occasional.

The neighbourhood (*parsi*) occupies the most important position in structure and organization of the Muslim society. It is an another dimension of social interaction among the Muslim people other than their kinties. The neighbourhood is considered as the smallest element of *umma* (brotherhood) among the Muslims. The neighbourhood relations are developed on the basis of physical proximity, sense of belongingness, fellow feeling, solidarity, and mutuality. The interactional pattern among the members of neighbourhood is both informal as well as formal, which is mutual and co-operative in character. There exist a define organization to look after the various socio-religious issues of the residents of a neighbourhood. The informal council of neighbourhood is termed as *para-majlis* on *Malat-majlis* or *mohollsh-majlis*.

The local community or *solo-ana* is constituted by the residents of the neighbouring villages is also a very important unit of interaction among the members of Muslim community at the base level. It is the amalgamation of many neighbourhoods (*parti*) of a locality. The members of local community not only co-operative in economic, political, social and ceremonial contexts, but also re-enforce the relations among them as members of the same community at the local level. Thus the individuals of the local community behave as a micro- unit of Muslim *Umma* by developing a close relation of fraternity, co-operation and interdependence for various social and religious needs. The interactional pattern among the members of local community is basically formal in character. The local community is organized through its own council termed as *Saloana-majlis*, or *Grami-majlis* or *Gram Salisi Majlis*.

There are structural and functional overlapping i.e. fusion among various components of social segments in Muslim society at the micro level. For example, in case of necessity, the *parivar* (family) merges with *Bhaiad* (minimal lineage) and which in turn also unites with *Khandan* (maximal lineage). Likewise, *Khandan* (lineage) merges with the *Parsi* (neighbourhood) and which again relates to *Solo-ana* (local community) for various purposes. The extent of this horizontal fusion of social segments is the fundamental feature of social organization of the Muslim society at the base level (Ansari 1960, Ahmed 1973, Siddiqui 1974, Ahmed 1981, Mondal 1994).

Social Mobilization Among the Bengali Muslims

Islam spread in Bengal due to contact, conquest and conversion through middle eastern traders, rulers and *Sufis* or *Pirs*. In course of conquest and conversion, the great tradition of Islam underwent a significant modification due to adjustment with the local cultures and forces of change that emerged from time to time in this region. There were diffusion and acculturation of culture traits between Islam and the local society. In the process of culture contact there were always mutual cultural adjustments. As a matter of fact, Islamic tradition in Bengal existed side by side with the local Hindu traditions without losing its basic identity.

In matter of way of life, initially the *Asrafs* used to maintain the traditional orthodox customs of the place of their origin for maintaining exclusive identity through certain social mechanisms. Likewise, the *Ajlafs* who were converted from local society, continued to retain many of their earlier pre-Islamic customs and traditions. However, due to close association with the Bengal society, the *Asrafs* gradually acquired the local customs from the *Ajlafs*. Under such a condition there were certain significant modifications in the great tradition of Islam in Bengal. On the whole, the great Islamic tradition, which was borrowed from outside, did not face any serious trouble to propagate in Bengal. This was because of the fact that Islam did not want to alter the basic socio-economic structure Bengal society. The cultural synthesis between Hindus and Muslims which emerged in the medieval era had attracted the attention of orthodox religious leaders of the Muslim community who stood against it for socio-political reasons. The emergence of orthodox culture pattern in Muslim society commenced in the later phase of eighteenth and early phase of nineteenth centuries. The religious leaders of such an orthodox ideology called for Ismalization of the Muslim masses for removing their so-called un-Islamic and extra-Islamic practices. This was beginning of first religio-revival movements among the Muslims in Bengal.

The Muslims of upper stratum i.e. the *Asrafs* enjoyed privileged and politically dominant position in Bengal from thirteenth to seventeenth century. They controlled army and administration. While the *Ajlafs* were the peasants engaged in agriculture, craft making and some other occupations to serve the local needs. On the other hand the land, trade and commerce were under the control of Hindu higher castes. As the Muslims enjoyed enough facilities in administration and politics, the dominant position of the Hindus in business sector did not disturb the communal peace. But with the gradual and rapid expansion of British power the entire situation drastically changed. As the British altered the administrative as well as economic structures the Muslims lost their pre-eminent position under the British rule. This led to the development of a new type of personality among the Muslims, which resulted in seclusion and isolation of the community from the changes that emerged at that time. The life of the Bengali Muslims was almost stagnant due to their association with the decaying feudal structure and their obedience to orthodox religious elites (*Ulemas and Mullahs*) who were under the spell of tradition.

During British rule the Muslims as a whole faced serious socio-economic problems due to their negligence of the situational reality. They did not accept English education and western value system of capitalism and materialism for fear of losing their so-called cultural identity. The notion of such a character was propagated among them by the orthodox religio-political leaders of that time. On the other hand, the Hindus found no difficulty in finding satisfactory adjustment under the British power. They easily took up English education in place of Persian and employed in mercantile houses and administration. They also participated in modern trade, industry and banking. The Hindus had also shown considerable social mobility during this phase due to works of social reformers who initiated renaissance in Bengal. But due to absence of rational outlook of Muslim leadership the community was deprived of renaissance and which forced them to develop a unique personality in matters of adjustment with the changing situation. The gap between Hindus and Muslims in matters of resource competition gradually emerged due to this uneven development. As a consequence, during this period, the Muslim community lost more and more of its earlier liberal tendencies and in its place orthodoxy and revivalism became their preoccupations.

For breaking the stagnation of Bengali Muslims during the British rule two solutions emerged. The reactionaries advocated seclusion and isolation of Muslims from the thrust of westernization. Thus, they called for Islamization of the Muslim masses. While the liberalists and progressivists advocated for modernization among Muslims for situational adjustment of the community under the British empire.

In order the emancipate Muslims from degeneration, the traditional *Ulemas* launched various religious reform movements (Farazi, Wahabi, Ahl-e-Hadish, Tayyani, etc.) of orthodox nature. Consequently, during the eighteenth and nineteenth centuries vast areas of Bengal were affected by these movements. The movements were basically religious in character but acquired the socio-economic programmes.

In religious sphere the movements strengthen the process of Islamization among Muslim masses. And in the politico-economic spheres the movements stood for defending the economic and political interests of the local *Zamindars* Britishers. The revivalists not only asked for reform of religious and social customs, but also generated a political consciousness among the Muslims. Thus the movements were not only the religious revivalism but the peasant movements too. In nineteenth century Bengal various pulls of religious reform movements of the Muslims began to polarize into two major camps i.e. orthodoxy and militarism on the one hand and peaceful liberal reform on the other. In this context it is necessary to mention the religio-political movements of Titumir (1931) and religio-social movements of Karamat Ali which had a very serious impact on religious, social, political and economic life of the Bengali Muslims. The British suppression of various socio-religio-political movements made the Muslims more secluded and isolated in all matters.

Traditionally, *Maktabs* and *Madrashas* were the main institutions through which the process of Islamization was cultivated among the Muslims. These institutions followed the traditional path of learning through Arabic and Persian languages and placed much more emphasis on Muhammadan Laws and jurisprudence. The basic goal of *Madrasha* was to impart the Islamic education and also to establish contact between religious leaders and the common Muslims for organizing the people to maintain their religious and cultural identity. The organizers of *Madrasha* education did not realize the importance of English language nor they gave any importance to learn scientific subjects. However, the situation started to change in successive stages.

Due to slow acceptance of western (English) education the middle class in Bengali Muslim society could not be formed until the middle of nineteenth century. Being influenced by Sir Sayed's reform movement at Aligarh, during later half of nineteenth century a small section of English educated Muslims began to realize what a mistake was committed by their community. In Bengal Moulavi Abdul Latif, Kazi Abdul Bari, etc. were the persons who played a major role in awakening their co-religionists. They keenly felt that the Muslims must participate and adjust with the economic-socio-political situation which emerged under British rule. To cultivate the process they founded an association named Calcutta Mohammedan Literary Society (CMLS) in 1863. The organizers of the association worked for the spread of English education among the Muslims along with the traditional Islamic education in *Madrasha*. Their aim was more in social and cultural and less in political matters. Their activities were mainly confined among the members of upper class of Muslims living in Calcutta and other towns of Bengal. Thus for obvious reasons only a small section of urbanized *Asraf* Muslims were benefited through it and a vast majority of *Ajlaf* Muslims of rural Bengal were far from the benefit of its activities.

After CMLS, another group of Calcutta Muslims formed a separate association named Central National Mohammedan Association (CNMA) in 1878. The leading spirit behind this association was Sayed Amir Ali. The organizers of this association were professional men, government officials and men of middle class. The association worked as a democratic body, it established contacts with the Muslims of different districts of Bengal and also or urban and rural areas of the province. The association had branch offices in the name of *Anjumans*. The association mainly devoted its activities towards social and educational aspects of the Bengali Muslims. It also maintained a friendly relationship with the Hindus. Its basic goal was to organize the Muslim masses in a way that they were receptive to modernization. But unfortunately, for various reasons, by 1890's the early activities of the association had lost its tempo.

The gradual loss of vitality of CMLS and CNMA motivated a few other Muslims to work for their society. In 1886 the Muhammadan Reform Association (MRA) was formed by the men of legal profession who published *Muslim Chronicle* and highlighted the Muslim issues and problems. This association was basically devoted to the advancement and the welfare of the Muslim community by all legitimate means. The social situation of Bengali Muslims in colonial era, particularly the status of women, drew the attention of a scholarly woman named Begum Rokeya Shakhawat Hussain. She organized a movement for women's education and social reform during first half of twentieth century. She was the spokeswoman of Muslim women's education of her time.

Due to effort of all the above associations the traditional Bengali Muslism society gradually started to change towards modernity. A new middle class emerged in Bengali Muslim society by the last quarter of nineteenth century. From this incipient middle class a neo-political elite also emerged. But due to poor spread of English education among the Muslim masses the growth of middle class and neo-political elite sustained a setback and remained confined among the rich and well to do Muslims of *Asraf* category.

Since the factor of English education was the most important in determining the position of middle class and neo-political elite, the Hindu community had undergone such an orientation much earlier than the Muslims. From beginning of the nineteenth century the progressive section of Bengali Hindu community passed through a series of social reform movement under the leadership of Raja Rammohan Roy, Vidyasagar, Kesabchandra Sen and many others. But contrast, the movements of such a progressive nature was not started by Muslim intelligentsia for several socio-political reasons. The difference between the Hindu and Muslim intellectual elites of the nineteenth century Bengal was also noticed in their approach to Bengali language and culture. Since the Hindu intelligentsia of Bengal emerged from the local soil, they used to cultivate Bengali along with the English. While the major portion of Muslim intelligentsia belonging to the *Asraf* category preferred Urdu in lieu of Bengali as a mark of their social honour within the community.

Due to failure in competition with the Hindus in matters of economy and politics and also for other reasons the elite section among the Muslims started to maintain their exclusive identity. This affected the growing process of integration between these two communities. By that time the emergence of revivalists in both the communities further aggravated the inter-community relations.

During the late nineteenth and early twentieth centuries when the concept of nationalism was in motion a sizeable section of Muslim population in Bengal participated in the freedom movement along with the Hindus. But during this phase, the attitude of the extremist group of Congress Party towards Muslims on leadership question was very critical one, which further aggravated the political minds of the Muslims. Under such a circumstance a section of Muslim political elite developed a political organization of their own in the name of Muslim League in 1906. During the phase of India's freedom movement the Bengali Muslims were divided into two major political trends like secular nationalism with anti-partition strategy under the leadership of Indian National Congress and Muslim Nationalism with pro-partition tendency set by Muslim League.

The birth of Muslim League introduce a new era in socio-political life of the Bengali Muslims. Consequently, the growing process of interaction and integration between Hindus and

Muslims received a serious setback. Finally, the partition of Bengal greatly affected the growth of educated middle class in Muslim society, when a good number of them migrated to East Pakistan (now Bangladesh). This created a great vacuum in the rising middle class and its leadership in Muslim society of Bengal.

The above situation started to change after independence of India., Like other parts of the country, the Bengali Muslims irrespective of their ethnic, social and class position gradually participated in developmental process of the nation. But for various reasons the impact of the change among them is not very significant one. The historically emerged incipient Muslim middle class is still suffering for its healthy growth. Owing to the lack of expansion of middle class and also due to insignificant and egocentric role of the emerging neo-political elite the modernization of Muslim society as a whole has been suffering. Even in contemporary times the elite structure in Muslim community and also the authoritarian role of traditional religious leaders have not significantly changed. This has created a social atmosphere which enhances the growth and activities of the traditional elites (*Ulemas* and *Mullahs*). They are still controlling the masses by virtue of their hold on them. Thus the contemporary Bengali Muslim society is passing through a transitional phase. On the one hand, there is a small section within the community which is in the path of modernization, while on the other hand there is a large section which is still motivated by the tradition. The self imposed isolation which was the characteristic of Muslim society during the colonial era is still continuing to a certain extent due to fear psychosis, minority syndrome, and overall socio-economic backwardness of the Muslims. The spread of communal politics followed by frequent communal riots in the country further aggravated the situation from which Muslims are unable to come out for obvious reasons. However, the situation of Bengal is somewhat different and unique one. The progressive outlook and leftist liberal political atmosphere of Bengal somehow maintained communal peace and harmony in the state. This enabled Muslims of all social strata to change their traditional socio-cultural condition to a certain extent. But still there are several constraints to change towards modernity and development of the Muslims (Singh 1973, De 1974, 1982; Hasan 1975, Nazrul Karim 1980, Engineer 1985, Mondal 1988, Mondal and Begum 1999).

Conclusion

The fact presented in the foregoing pages clearly reveal that Islam as a religion and a way of life has a definite and well defined concept of society and culture. The ideal society which is set by Islam is egalitarian, democratic, holistic and dynamic in character. But in course of history Islam has acquired an adaptive spirits as it never remained confined to a particular region. Thus, pluralism has gained impetus in Islam when it spread from Arabia to various parts of the globe owing to adjustment with the local situations.

The relationship between Islam and India is a very old one. There are various economic, political and socio-cultural reasons behind the spread of Islam in India. When Islam reached India it had adjust with the multiple little traditions of the country and thereby acquired a unique character. Islam made a significant contribution to Indian society and culture, but the reverse is also very true. The followers of Islam in India i.e. the Muslims constituted 12 percent of country's total population. They are living in all parts of the country in varied numbers and represent diverse customs and traditions inspite of their common characteristics as a member of a particular religion.

Nearly one fourth of Indian Muslims live in Bengal. The Muslims of Bengal adhere to basic principles of Islam and also follow the local traditions of the region. The Bengali Muslims are mostly inhabiting the rural areas. Their widespread distribution in rural hinterlands is indicative of the fact that it has grown out of indigenous population. Like other parts of the country, a large concentration of Muslim population in Bengal fall in the category of low income group, live below the poverty line and lag behind in education. As a matter of fact they are considered as very tradition bound.

The social organization of the Muslim community in Bengal is characterized by concrete social divisions of varying types with complexities of relations and interactions with one another. Therefore, in spite of egalitarian teachings of Islam, various segments have emerged in Muslim society both at macro and micro levels. At the macro level the units of the Muslim society are sects and sub-sects, *Pirs* and *Mureeds*, ethnic groups (*Jats*) and status groups etc. And at micro level the Muslim social units are kinship, neighbourhood and local community. All these facts suggest that the social organization of the Muslim community is characterized by concrete social groupings of varying types. Therefore, it is observed that, in spite of egalitarian teachings and social homogeneity of Islam, various segments have emerged in the Muslim community both at macro and also at micro levels. At macro level various social units have been formed within the Muslim society owing to varied interpretation of theological/jural (*Shariat*) and spiritual (*tariqat*) aspects of Islamic great tradition. Further, the units have also emerged out of basic social groupings of the people on the basis of ethnic, descent, status and other social backgrounds. Similarly, at the micro level the units are formed due to degree of distance among the kinsmen and also among the neighbours. Various units of the Muslim society are not the isolable components. Moreover, there are structural and functional overlaps amongst those segments both at the macro and the micro levels. The functions of this social framework are adaptive in its external and integrative in internal aspects. Further, the social stratification and social inequality which is observed among the Muslims, is a situational development both for adaptive purpose and also for financial necessities to operate within the larger framework of the larger Indian society. This feature is inconsistent with the egalitarian norms of Islamic social order. Therefore, it is seen that, there is a gulf of difference between the text (Islamic ideology) and the context (the practices of the Muslims). Thus the social organization of the Muslims is determined by some traditional values and customs.

The analysis of social mobilization of the Bengal Muslims clearly shows that Islamization was favoured and extensively followed by the masses. As a result, the process of modernization received a setback. The various forms of social movements have extended the path of Islamization for integrating the members of the Muslim community on one hand and to protect them from the forces of westernization/modernization on the other. The process of Islamization is an age old phenomenon among Muslims not only in Bengal, but also in India and world at large. Ismalization in the form of solidaristic movement has reinforced communal, cultural and political consciousness among the Muslims. In economico-political arena it has provided a good bargaining medium, while in socio-cultural sphere it has generated an integrative symbolism leading towards ideal monolithic Islamic community. All these generated a social and cultural exclusiveness among the Muslims. The process of Ismalization contributed to a greater conservatism among them and increased the holds of religious elites amongst the Muslim masses.

The conventional process of Islamization by less educated religious leaeders extended the path of traditional and orthodox religious revival movements. As a result, the cultivation and propagation of liberal Islam as well as Islamic modernization by way of *jtehad* (reinterpretation of Islamic prescriptions under new situation) is very far from their consideration. Though in Islamic ideology there is no place of blind imitation, yet Islamization has never been able to break away from conservative attitude of the Muslims. Under such a situation, the Muslim society is unable to organize a strong social reform movement or renaissance on secular and modern lines. But what is very important to note that, due to several forces of change the Muslim today are also struggling for a new identity by participating in developmental process of the country. To sustain this process the government and non-government organization (NGOs) should come forward to help and cooperate with the Muslims for strengthening their endeavour.

REFERENCES

Ahmed, Imtiaz (ed) (1973), *Caste and Social Stratification Among Muslims in India.* New Delhi : Manohar Publications.

Ahmed, Rafiuddin (1981), The Bengal Muslims 1871-1906: *A Quest for Identity.* Delhi : Oxford University Press.

Ansari, Ghaus (1960), *Muslim Caste in Uttar Pradesh: A Study in Culture Contact.* Lucknow: Ethnographic and Folk Culture Society.

De, Amalendu (1974), *Roots of Separatism in Nineteenth Century Bengal.* Calcutta : Ratna Prakashan.

———(1982), *Islam in Modern India.* Calcutta P: Maya Prakashan.

Engineer, A.A. (1985), *Indian Muslims–A Study of Minority Problems in India.* New Delhi: Ajanta Publications.

Hasan, Mushirul (1975), *Some Aspects of the Problems of Muslim Social Reforms,* in Zafar Imam (ed.) *Muslims in India,* Calcutta: Orient Longman.

Imam, Zafar (ed.) (1975) *Muslims in India,* Calcutta : Orient Longman.

Islahi, Sadruddin (1978), *Islam at a Glance.* Delhi : Markazi Maktaba.

Levy, R. (1957), *The Social Structure of Islam* Cambridge: Cambridge University Press.

Mondal, S. Rahim (1987), *Elite and Middle Class in Bengali Muslim Society: A Study in Modernization Problem of a Minority Community*. Occasional Paper No. 1, Deptt of Sociology & Social Anthropology, University of North Bengal.

———(1988) Tradition versus Modernity in Muslim Society : An Analysis of Social Movements Among Muslims in India, *Islam and the Modern Age*, Vol. 9, No. 3, pp. 179-200.

———(1994) *Dynamics of Muslim Society*, New Delhi: Inter India Publications.

———(1997), *Educational Status of Muslims*. New Delhi: Inter India Publications.

A SOCIO-HISTORICAL STUDY OF WASIQA AND WASIQA HOLDERS OF AWADH

Haider Mehdi

Historical Background

The history of Awadh starts with the founder of Avadh Dynasty, Mohammad Amin, a resident Nishapur in Iran. He left Iran in 1708 to try his luck in India.

A brief sojourn in Gujarat, he came to Delhi where with the help of Rai Ratan Chend, Divan of Qutbul Mulk Nawab Abdullah Khan, he was able to have access to the court of emperor Farukhsiyar. After getting a stronghold in the court he was rewarded by Mohammad Shah with the governorship of Agra and title of "Sadat Khan Bahadur". However, as he failed to contain the Jats, he was transferred to Avadh as Subedar in 1772. From this date commenced the history of Avadh as a Shia Muslim principality. In 1722 he married off his daughter to his nephew, Mirza Maqin and appointed him as his deputy.

In 1739, Nadir Shah invaded Delhi and it is stated that Saadat Khan went over to the side of the invader to humiliate Ahmad Shah, but committed suicide shortly afterwards. On the intervention of Nadir Shah, Safdarjang, the son-in-law of Burhan-ul-Mulk was appointed subedar of Avadh by the emperor of Delhi. On Mohammad Shah's death, Safdarjung was appointed Wazir by his successor Ahmed Shah but he could not last long. On account of internal conflict, he had to return, with his reversion as Subedar, to Avadh in 1753, and died shortly in October 1754 at Paparghat near Sultanpur.

Jalaluddin Haider Shuja Ud Daulah succeeded as subedar of Avadh. In recognition to his services, he was appointed Wazir by the empeor Shah Alam on the recommendation of Ahmad Shah Durrani. After defeating Marathas, with the help of the British, at Ram Ghat in 1773 and occupying Rohilkhand the same year, he appointed one of his sons, Saadat Ali Khan as Governor of Rohilkhand but he himself could not enjoy fruits of his victories and died on 26th January 1775 when he was merely forty two.

The period of Asuf-ud-Daula (1775-1797), son and successor of Shuja-ud-Daulha, saw rise of British influence over Avadh. His life was very sad because of the over bearing attitude of the British resident and his frequent interference in his administration. He died broken hearted in 1797. to excess his devotion to Imam Husain, Asaf-ud-Daulah built Bara-Imambara or Imambara Asafi in 1784.

Saadat Ali Khan, brother of Asaf-ud-Daulah, who was living at Banaras (now Varanasi) in the state of neglect, was now the British choice as the ruler of Avadh but the story behind his selection as ruler was dangerous because they wanted to take advantage from him. The amount of tribute payable to the Company was not only raised from 52 lacs to 76 lacs of rupees but Lord Wellesely forced on him an army for maintenance of which he was made to part with half of his territory as well. In this way, he was unable to bear the humiliating attitude of the British and died shortly afterwards in July 1814.

Saadat Ali Khan was followed by Ghaziuddin Haider who ruled Avadh from 1814 to 1827. He gave a loan of Rs. 1,08,50,000/- and then 1,00,00,000/- amounting to Rs. 2,08,50,000/- to East India Company in 1819 and 1825. Ghaziuddin Haider crowned himself as King of Avadh at the instigation and with the approval of the Governor General and thus he broke the normal tie of subordination to the Mughal emperor. It was the sum of Rs. 2,08,50,000/- given as loan, to the Britisher which laid foundation of *Wasiqa*. Besides Ghaziuddin Haider, other Nawabs and Bahu Begum (wife of Shuja-ud-Daulah) contributed a huge amount for the same purpose. An agreement was entered into that interest of the lent amount would be distributed as a *Wasiqa*, which helped to sustain Shia nobility and maintain Shia institutions even after the fall of Avadh, among the members of the royal family and those listed in agreement.

Thus, *Wasika* or *Wasiqa* is an Arabic word which means a document which has been strengthened (by writing) or written agreement, a bond or obligation. As all stipends are paid on the authority of the agreement made between the donors and the East India Company they are called *Wasikas/Wasiqas*.

In 1808 the Begum executed a will, making the British Government heir to the residue of her property, after maintaining certain *jagirs* and pensions, and paying certain sums for the construction of a mausoleum, etc. The Government, however, declared its intention of yielding the legacy to the Wazir and making over the residue of the property to him. The will was subsequently revoked, and a Deed of Deposit (No. XLII) was executed under the provisions of which the British Government guaranteed to execute so far as dependend on them. The proposed arrangements were, with the Begum's consent, disclosed to the Wazir, who was assured that he would be acknowledged by Government as the Begum's heir on his agreeing to the whole of the purposes of the will. To this management Ghaziuddin Haider intimated his assent in a letter to the resident, received on the 4th August 1814.

The Begum died on 15th December 1815, leaving property to the value of Rs. 99,48,916/-. After her death it was proposed to embody the obligations of the British Government and the Wazir in regard to her property in a treaty. But as the Nawab expressed an unwillingness to execute any further documents, which were unnecessary6 after his engagement in 1814, the treaty was not pressed on him.

All the personal property of the Begum was made over to the Wazir on his paying into the British treasury Rs. 56,84,082/-, the interest on which was to yield certain persons which by the Deed of Deposit were to be defrayed from the funds left by the Begum. These pensons are now known as the *Amanat Waskias* or trust pensions. But besides these there were certain *jagirs* and pensions payable from the Oudh treasury, in case of the diminution or resumption of which by the Wazir the British Government was to make a provision of corresponding amount for the holders from the residue of Begum's property. To this class belonged the pensions of Mirza Ali, Salar Jung and his three sons, and several members of the Khas Mahal. The pensions of Mirza Ali, Salar Jang and his three sons were subsequently provided for in the arrangements made with the Wazir for the payment of first Oudh loan. Of the Khas Mahal pensions, there, namely, those of Lutf-un-Nissa, Mirza Mohammed Taki Khan and Mirza Nasir and their children, aggregating Rupees 6,000/- a month, were secured by the guarantee of the British Government. These are now known as the *Zamant Wasika* or security pension.

Now it is clear that Bahu Begum deposited her all cash and personal property into the coffers of the British at fixed rate of 6% interest annually to save the future of her close-relatives and dependents so that they all might live with 'royal grace' and at the generosity of others.

Thus, *wasiqa* is a fixed interest, on the entrusted money to the company, was to be distributed among the persons listed in the accompanying list prepared according to her own wish at the time of Dee of Deposit executed in 1813. A close and careful study of Deed of Deposit and accompanying list reveal that interest on two types of deposits were to be drawn. The first category was of cash and gold deposit called *Amanat* (Trust) and the second category deposited related with property and articles was termed as *Zamanat* (Security). Because of this two types of pensions viz. (1) *Amanat-wasiqa* (trust pension) and (2) *Zamanat wasiqa* (security pension) came into being.

Act No. XXI of 1886 passed by the Governor-General of India in Council, defined *wasiqa* as under :

> Whereas, on the death of Her Highness the Bahu Begum. His Highness the Nawab Vazir of Oudh delivered to the British Government a sum of money with intent that the interest occurring thereon should, in compliance with the wishes of her Highness the Bahu Begum as expressed in a Deed of Deposit executed by her in the year 1813, be applied by the British Government to the payment of certain pensions, which pensions are known as *Amanat Wasikas*.
>
> And whereas, in the year 1831 the said Government guaranteed the payment of certain pensins to persons connected with the Khas Mahal of her Highness the Bahu Begum, which are known as the *Zamant Wasikas*. Accordingly Oudh Wasikas Act 1886 came into existence.

Therefore, *Wasiqa* may also be called as a political pension paid to the descendants of Avadh rulers and others under the arrangement entered into between the East India Company and the members of the Avadh Royal family. Thus, the *Wasiqdars* (endowment holders) came from the following classes :

1. Descendants of the Royal family
2. Relatives
3. Servants and other dependents

In other words, interest on the sum given to the Britishers by different Nawabs as loan, distributed to the members of the Royal family and those listed in the agreement between the East India Company and the Nawabs, is called *wasiqa*. This arrangement was made by them as a help to their family members, and those shown in the list of agreement. In this place, it would be appropriate to indicate the names of those kings, who made these arrangements showing sympathy to their family members and others.

1. Bahu Begum, wife of Shuja-ud-Daula.
2. King Ghaziuddin Haider
3. King Nasiruddin Haider
4. King King Mohammad Ali Shah
5. King Amjad Ali Shah

II

Today, *wasiqa* is a status symbol for those related either to the Royal family or of the others listed in the agreement between the East India Company and the Nawabs. It was always not only focused on their dignity and stateliness but also showed their or proximity with the Royal family. They, with this honourable rank, passed their life cheerfully and maintained their superiority and excellence during the Nawabi period. But, it may be recalled that those who have been getting *wasiqa* till today are basically feudalistic because their descendants have been of noble descent at a certain stage of feudalism and *wasiqa* is the creation of that time and age.

Wasiqa helped them, during the prevailing feudalistic conditions and they passed their life gorgeously and sustained their nobility but the situation has changed for them. The *Wasiqa* which was given to *Wasiqa* holders was adequate, the period of early Nawabs, to survive and maintain their status accordingly but after the feudalistic stage stood terminated, the conditions of endowment holders took a miserable turn and those who were accustomed to pass a luxurious life became the victim of the circumstances of the lost feudalism which had gone against their grain. It is now clear that the amount to be paid to *wasiqa* holder is so meager that it is unable to sustain their status maintained as before and the result is that they could not adjust themselves in the society.

At this stage let us see how this changed condition affected them socio-culturally, economically and psychologically, what feelings were created among the *wasiqa* holders due to the 'shocking circumstances' which brought down their status from grandeur to penury.

The respondents in the present work are the *wasiqa* holders who are on the pay roll of *Wasiqa* officed and Husainabad Trust, Lucknow. There are various categories of *Wasiqa* holders depending upon the original deposits and sources, income from which is derived and distributed among the *wasiqa* holders. A broad spectrum of *wasiqa* holders can be viewed at a glace from the following chart :

Description of *Wasiqa* and Beneficiaries as in year 2002 at a Glance

Sl. No. Sources of Wasiqa	*Wasiqa more than Rs.10/-*				*Wasiqa less than Rs.10/-*				*Total No. of beneficiaries*				
	Male		*Female*		*Male*		*Female*		*Male*		*Fèmale*		*Grand Total*
	No.	*%*	*No.*	*%*	*No.*	*%*	*No.*	*%*	*No.*	*%*	*No.*	*%*	
1. Amanat	85	23	104	28	97	20	89	23	182	49	193	51	375
2. Zamanat	52	29	53	29	38	21	38	21	90	50	91	50	181
3. Mahal of Mirza Ali Khan	13	30	15	35	5	12	10	23	18	42	25	58	43
4. Mahal of Salar Jung	11	31	7	20	7	20	10	29	18	51	17	49	35
5. Mahal of Qasim Ali Khan	8	16	20	41	6	12	15	31	14	29	35	71	49
6. First Awadh loan	32	30	30	29	28	27	15	14	60	57	45	43	105
7. ThirdAwadh loan	75	33	91	41	20	90	39	17	95	42	130	58	225
8. Sixth Awadh loan	30	27	29	26	25	23	56	24	55	50	55	50	110
Total	306		349		226		242		1123				

(beneficiaries gettingWasiqafrom different heads altogether)

The sample units are spread over almost whole of the old Lucknow city. Source list is made of about more than 1123 units. Hence the size of sample has to be brought to the practical position. Accordingly, 300 persons were randomly selected in such a manner as to represent from each categories of *Wasiqa* holders viz., *Amanat, Zamanat* and Awadh loans etc. and conclusion drawn after the processing and analysis of data remain unbiased and meaningful.

In the present study, the respondents are members of urban conglomerations, claiming themselves from the elites of the Royal family of Avadh. To elicit information from such culturally 'snoberred, typical Lucknow *Nafis* and *Nazuk* (sophisticated) persons was really a tough task. Hence, I used interview schedule for collection of data.

Present Social Condition of *Wasiqa* Holders

In the present study, data were collected from *wasiqa* holders drawing *wasiqa* from various heads/sources called *Amanat, Zamanat,* Awadh loans and others such as *Three Mahals.* It is clear from the Table 1 that maximum number of *wasiqa* holders that is, about 39% are drawing *wasiqa* from the deposit of the Bahu Begum. It is also clear from the Table that about 56% of *wasiqa* holders are drawing less than Rs. 50/- per month as *wasiqa* and the amount is inadequate even to their conveyance charges to collect it every month. This also indicates the defect of very purpose of *wasiqa* which was made for maintenance of dignified life of the *wasiqa* holders. *Wasiqa* holders drawing above Rs. 100/- is limited only to 7% of *wasiqa* holders. This also includes the highest amount of *wasiqa* being Rs. 569.99 drawn by only one person named Nawab Haider Ali Khan. Obviously, the present amount of *wasiqa* is the result of division of the amount in subsequent generations.

Distribution of *wasiqa* holders age-genderwise is an important factor in the study of *wasiqa* holders. Table 2 indicates that female *wasiqa* holders outnumber the male *wasiqa* holders and their percentage is 57. Not only this 30 per cent women fall under the age group 50 to 90 years as against only 18% of men in that age group. This also indicates about high life expectancy of women *wasiqa* holders and their deep interest in their registration at the *wasiqa* office to claim their legacy and draw economic benefit.

As regards younger generation of *wasiqa* holders falling in the age group of 20 to 40 years, we find again the women outnumbering men. About 17% women *wasiqa* holders and 14% *wasiqa* holders fall in that age group. This again proves the greater awareness of women *wasiqa* holders about their linkage with royal family and desire for economic benefit and betterment.

Table 1
Source, Type and amount of *Wasiqa* and Distribution Thereof

S. No.	*Head*	*Number of Wasiqa holders with Wasiqa per month andPercentage thereo*								*Total no. of wasiqa*	*Per cent*
		Below (Rs.10)	*%*	*Above (Rs.10)*	*%*	*Below (Rs.50)*	*%*	*Above (Rs.100)*	*%*		
1.	Amanat	48 (41%)	44	52 (45%)	47	12 (10%)	21	5 (4%)	23	117	39
2.	Zamanat	19 (37%)	17	14 (28%)	13	15 (29%)	26	3 (6%)	14	51	17
3.	Loan	12 (19%)	11	17 (27%)	15	22 (35%)	37	12 (19%)	9	69	21
4.	Other	30 (43%)	28	28 (41%)	25	9 (13%)	16	2 (3%)	9	69	23
	Total	109		111		28		22		300	100

Values within the parenthesis indicates the percent of the respondents number.

Table 2
Agewise-Genderwise Distribution of *Wasiqa* Holders

S. No.	*Age group (in years)*	*Gender of wasiqa holders*				*Total No. of wasiqa holders*	*Total percent*
		Male		*Female*			
		Number	*%*	*Number*	*%*		
1.	20-30	18(40)	14	27(60)	16	45	15
2.	30-40	24(50)	19	27(50)	14	48	16
3.	40-50	33(50)	26	33(50)	19	66	22
4.	50-60	30(42)	23	42(58)	25	72	24
5.	60-70	18(37)	13	30(63)	18	48	16
6.	70-80	6(33)	5	12(67)	7	18	6
7.	80-90	-	-	3(100)	1	3	1
	Total	129		171		300	100

Values within the parenthesis indicates the percent of the respondents number.

Further, the total percentage of non-graduates is more than 80% and many of them come under the income group of Rs. 5000/- to Rs. 10,000/- per month and above. Obviously, this income does not come from the *wasiqa* alone but from the other economic activities. Economically, about 36%, that is to say about more than one-third population of the *wasiqa* holders, is poor and they draw *wasiqa* as status symbol.

Table 3
Religion/Sectwise and Marital status-wise Distribution of Wasiqa Holders

Sl. No.	*Religion/ Sect*	*Marital status of wasiqa holders*								*Total No. of wasiqa holders*	*Total per cent age*
		Married		*Unmarried*		*Single*		*Widow*			
		No	*%*	*No.*	*%*	*No.*	*%*	*No.*	*%*		
1.	Shia Muslims	190 (68)	91	3 (1)	100	6 (2)	75	80 (29)	99	279	93
2.	Sunni Muslims	6 (100)	3	–	–	–	–	–	–	6	3
3.	Hindus	12 (80)	6	–	–	2 (13)	25	1 (7)	1	15	5
	Total	208		3		8		81		300	100

Values within the parenthesis indicates the percent of the respondents number.

It is evident from the Table 3 that about 93% of the *wasiqa* holders hail from the Shia sect, 2% from the Sunni sect and 5% are Hindus. This is quite natural because Nawaba of Awadh were of Shia faith and descendants and most of the dependants were Shia Muslims, *wasiqa* being a sort of economic provision for their progeny. What is more important here is the presence of the Sunnis and Hindus. This indicates not only the secular approach of Nawabs of Awadh as also co-existence of various communities in high power echelon of the ruling elite. This also gives a certain mirror view of basic foundation of Lucknowi-culture and communal peace prevailing at Lucknow not only in the past but also at present.

III

The socio-cultural impact of *wasiqa* on *wasiqa* holders is quite significant. Its impact can be seen in all the aspects of life like birth ceremony, initiation into schooling, celebration of entrance into puberty/adolescence, pre-marriage celebrations after settlement of marriage, post marriage celebrations, religious occasions and festivals. Here it should be borne in mind that about 93% of *wasiqa* holders are Shia Muslims and therefore the socio-cultural impact of *wasiqa* is most visible among them in the form of various customs and traditions which do not have any relevance to Islam. These customs and traditions seems to have been borrowed and adopted from the Iranian-culture and Mughal Darbar of Delhi. Some of them also appear to be adaptation from Indian soil that is 'Hindu culture'. Thus assimilation of various traditions has actually contributed to the evolution of "Ganga-Jamni Tahzeeb" (syncretic culture) of Lucknow. Even today various customs and traditions are being observed by the *wasiqa* holders with different intensity6 and adherence depending upon their social and economic status. Though great pomp and show is no more present in their social ceremonies yet remnants are clearly visible. At the time of a birth of child in a family there is a gathering of close relatives and friends who congratulate the parents and in turn the father of the child distributes some gifts and presents among the family members, *sadaqa*, (ritual offering) on behalf of the child and money is also donated to the poor and beggars. Not only this, some times eunuchs are invited for song and dance and given appropriate gifts. After the attainment of age of five years, the child before being introduced to school or *madarsa*, a ceremony called *Bismillah*, initiation to writing, celebrated. In this ceremony relatives and friends gather at home and a religious teacher (*maulana*) or an elderly member of the family intiates child into writing with the name of *Allah* on a paper or with a silver pen on a silver slate. There is get together and a 'party' in the family on this occasion. This may also be grand party in case of a rich family. Likewise there is again a grand party when the child learns and completes the reading of *Quran*. This ceremony is called *'Aamin'*. This means a joint prayer by the family of the child to bestow upon him (child) *Ilm* (knowledge) in the coming years. There are several other ceremonies demonstrating their kinship with the erstwhile ruling class.

Significantly, *wasiqa* acts as an impediment in occupational mobility among *wasiqa* holders. Because of higher social status attached to *wasiqa* holders, they find it difficult to adopt profession like that of general masses. *Wasiqa* holders are very choosy and selective on this score. Thus areas of economic activities have shrunk for the *wasiqa* holders. It can be inferred that *wasiqa* is also acting as an impediment in the economic progress of *wasiqa* holders. This economic retrogression has direct bearing on the socio-cultural life of the *wasiqa* holders.

However, social change is also sweeping the *wasiqa* holders. For instance many families are not observing the '*Bismillah* ceremony' (initiation ceremony for education) of their child due to schooling of their children in the English medium schools and also due to unnecessary economic burden on the family. Likewise *Sanddaling* ceremony of moustache (putting paste of sandalwood on the moustache of young boy as an initiation on ceremony for adulthood) and *Goud-Bharai* ceremony for young prospective mother, before the marriage ceremony etc., are being observed only by a few families particularly rich families. It is also important to note that the second or third marriage with living spouses is altogether absent. Furthermore, '*Mutah marriage*' (temporary marriage) which used to be not rare among the ancestors of the *wasiqa* holders is totally absent now-a-days. However various religious traditions and customs are being followed with great adherence particularly the rituals to be observed at the time of '*Moharrum*' . Participation of *wasiqa* holders in the *Nawroz* festival' (first ay of the year as per Iranian calendar) in which water and colour are on each other is also decreasing perhaps because of its disorganized system of celebration, economic reasons as also to the religious objections raised by other Muslim sects.

Future Imperfect of Wasiqan Hoders

Observance of *Pardah* (veiling) among *wasiqa*-holder families has declined radically. About 50 years ago *wasiqa* holder families are said to have used strict *Pardah* and ladies were also prohibited to step out of house even for shopping purpose. Cloth-sellers, tailors, jewelers and bangle-sellers used to visit houses of the *wasiqa* holders. Even for the treatment of ladies, *hakim* and doctors were called in *Zanankhana* (ladies quarters) with *Pardah*. Now-a-days such a life style is now history. This may also be due to the fact of poor economic conditions which compel the females to undertake certain social and economic activities for survival and also because of forces of modernization.

They are under tremendous pressure to adopt economic activities which have not been compatible with their erstwhile high social status and dignity. A large number of *wasiqa* hoders are serving as peon, guard and guide in various *Waqf* properties of

Lucknow. Besides this some of them have opened shops of grocery, crockery and material of embroidery. A large number of *wasiqa* holders are dialy wage earners and working as handicraft workers in the workshops (*Karkhana*) of embroidery called *'Aari-Zardozi'* and *'Chikan'*. Not only this in order to earn two meals, even their females are actively involved in such economic activities as earning wages through *Kamdani* (embroidery with metallic wire), *Chikan* work and embroidery, etc. Thus, a new kind of economic independence has come to the females and they have now more confidence and stronger role in family education have adopted services in the government departments, teaching, engineering medical, law profession and business.

Thus, we find that the institution of *Wasiqa* and the stake holders, *wasiqadaar*, have no parallel in the Indian society. The story of *wasiqa* holder in that of riches to rags. However, those who made quick adjustment with the changed socio-economic and political situation are able to retain their elite status in the society but the majority of them present a sad scenario. This may be good area of research for any interest future researchers.

SELECT BIBLIOGRAPHY

Akbarpuri, Anwar Husain (1991), *Awadh ke Tarikh Nigar (urdu).*

Bird, Major R.W. (1966), *Awadh Ki Loot* (Hindi), Lucknow: Hindi Samiti, Soochna Vibhag.

Haider, Kamaluddin (1907), *Sawaneh hayaat-Saltatin-e-Awadh* (urdu), Vol. 1, Lucknow: Munshi Nawal Kishore Press.

Hasan, Amir (1992), "Wasiqa-The Inherited Curse", *Pioneer,* Sept. 19.

Llewellyn-Jones, Rosie (1985), *A Fatal Friendship: The Nawabs, the British and the City of Lucknow,* New Delhi: Oxford University Press.

Mohan, Surendra (1997), *Awadh under the Nawab: Politics, Culture and Communal Relations*–1722-1855, New Delhi: Manohar Publishers.

Rajkiya Press (1991), *Wasiqa Manual,* February 15, (Hindi).

Sleeman, Sir W.H. (1989), *Kingdom of Oudh* in 1849-1850, Vol. I & II, Lucknow: Helicon Publications.

INFLUENCE OF GULF MIGRATION ON IDENTITY ASSERTION PATTERNS: DENOMINATIONAL CONTESTATIONS AND THE EMERGING PUBLIC-SPHERE AMONG MUSLIMS OF KERALA

Shareena Banu C.P.

Introduction

The identity of a community is not only a conscious construct of the group members but is perpetually influenced and redefined through the mediation of various historical and socio-political circumstances. Contemporary social-identity studies have broadened the scope of the concept of identity from individual role-conflict to a larger socio-political issue. Thus, identity is seen as constantly in the process of construction rather than a static entity. Communities are today understood as constantly redefining their boundaries along with the dynamics of socio-political forces. To be regarded as an ethnic community of distinct identity, the members should have a sense of being distinct from the rest of the society and institutionalized boundary marking mechanisms through which they maintain social and cultural differences. Any community with a shared cultural history and traditions tends to create a 'we feeling' among its members. Though the cultural traits of ethnic groups change over time, the sense of distinctness, of belonging to an ethnic group persists through the maintenance of cultural and symbolic boundaries. Frederic Barth (1969) emphasized the importance of boundary marking mechanism in the process of identity formation and maintenance. He makes a very crucial observation that the cultural content enclosed by boundaries can vary from setting to setting and across time.

For the Muslims in India, religious beliefs and practices are an important part of their ethnicity. These beliefs and practices are in turn shaped by history and socio-economic events as well as the regional culture. It is generally acknowledged by scholars on Muslims in India that, the religious culture undergoes change responding to the challenges of modern society. However, these religious/cultural changes are, generally speaking, not a consequence of any particular enthusiasm towards emulation of the western value system (see Metcalf 2002). Various socio-religious reforms taken place within the community are generally not rotted in any comprehensive attempt towards incorporation of modern/western lifestyles and values – the basic religious principles followed by the group define the contours of religious and cultural reform, if any. The motivation for reform is derived from a reaction to the western modernization agenda. The orientation towards religious/cultural reforms remains more or less ethnocentric, except a few attempts like the Aligarh movement, for the Muslims in India.[2]

This has particularly been so in the case of Muslims in contemporary Kerala, also who are categorized among the backward communities. The community is experiencing tremendous strain in order to come to grips with the rapid social change. There are various endogenous and exogenous factors contributing towards this tension. Some of the anxiety or challenges in front of the community are the Islamic values and discrepancy with modern education, fast changing society and changing value systems, globalization or homogenization of western culture, international politics, clash of civilization discourse, terrorism etc. Alongside these endemic concerns of all Muslim, the Muslims in Kerala are also wedged up in the debate on the legitimacy and authenticity of the local cultural influence on the religious practices of the community. In recent times, they have engaged in serious religious polemic concerning the community's response towards many social challenges. These pressures, in fact, have expedited the process of initiating innovating strategies to comprehend these complexities. There exist different voices within the community in response to the challenges of local and global social situations. Deciphering the unsettled discourse and counter-discourse on religious practices and customs is an interesting exercises for the local scholars and intellectuals. Kerala has been able to provide an amiable secular atmosphere conducive to such dialogue. This has not been possible for the members of Muslim community in other parts of India on account of the psychic insecurity and perception of discrimination.[3]

To put it differently, the community is witnessing internal differences, as various groups and denominations following alternative religious ideologies and worldviews are increasingly critical of the socio-religious traditions followed by members of other denominations. Each group offers a different interpretation of various religious issues, such as theological matters, religious legitimacy of many of the local customs and practices such as the *nerccha* festivals, marriage rituals, dress pattern, issues regarding modernization of education and education of women along with other ethical issues. These contestations had been there in the past also to some extent, especially during the British rule, as a reaction to colonial rule and cultural domination (see Pannikar, 2001). Another instance was during the period of active involvement of some of the socio-religious reformers and leaders of the community. These reformers had attempted to encourage the common mass to actively participate in the debate on issues regarding the community, especially modernization and social-cultural reform. Though these efforts had a historical impact on the socio-cultural life of the community, they were confined to the social sphere. What distinguishes the previous engagement and the present is the dynamic participation and mobilization of the community members in these dialogues, leading to fractures in the community on the basis of contesting religious ideas. The manifestations of these contestations are present equally in public and private life of the members.

This article maintains that the rising activism towards cultural and religious dialogue is part of the change in socio-economic structure of the Muslim community in Kerala in the recent decade brought about by the Gulf migration. A large section of the Muslim population has been continuously migrating to the Gulf countries since the 1960s. The resultant economic prosperity and the emergence of 'neo-rich' within the community had a deep impact on their socio-economic culture, affecting the class composition and religious orientation of the community.[4] The article argues that, Gulf migration is an important factor shaping the reformulation of religious identity and engagement of the community members. Similarly, in relation to the capacity to initiate dialogue on the existing religious observance and practices, Gulf migration is one of the crucial factors behind it.

International migration in no way is confined to the economic influence as its effect is all-encompassing; it has latent potential for inducing new meanings to socio-cultural practices. Among other things, this article argues against the hitherto practiced uni-dimensional analyses confined to the consequences of Gulf remittance on the material culture of Muslims or the sweeping generalizations related to the pan-Arabic influence. This article brings forth the need to look into these dimensions with a fresh perspective. It advocates for a multilevel exploration essential for delineating the gamut of contemporary social change among Kerala Muslims. The 'Gulf connection' and the emerging intra-community dialogue/conflict contribute towards redefinition of the social identity of the Muslim in Kerala. It is argued in the paper that this contestation is latently favourable, contributing towards the formation of new social space. It is initiating a process towards formation of a fragmented 'public sphere' with accommodative ethos enabling a re-orientation of socio-cultural aspects of life. It is expected to infuse Muslim religious identity with new enthusiasm while providing room for accommodating multiple or alternative worldviews. Thus this intra-community contestation/conflict is a process of adjustment and preparation of a 'community in transition'.

This paper is an attempt to delineate some of the recent trends emerging among the Muslims in Kerala. It explores the process of construction and reconstruction of identity of the community in the changing socio-political scenario. It raises the question of community identity – what is to be a Muslim in Kerala in contemporary times – and how their consciousness of being a member of Muslim community is asserted. It also looks at the role played by some of endogenous and exogenous factors, which influence the nature and character of Muslim social life. The Muslim 'community' in Kerala today faces manifests and latent challenges from various socio-political aspects in relation to the modernization process while it is attempting to maintain and negotiate cultural and symbolic boundaries.[5]

Rather than looking at identity as a static entity, the study proposes to look into the dynamic nature of identity construction. The religious and cultural identity is negotiated and asserted through an engagement of various socio-historical forces. The study takes into consideration how in the changing scenario, new meanings are attributed to a range of symbolic religious activities associated to community life. In this process the agents are initiating innovative strategies to make a requisite array of meaningful association with the changing social world, where new identities are being forged and existing orders either challenged or in some way reasserted.

Revisiting Collective Memory: A Brief Survey of Social History

Historical events and conjectures provide a basis for a community's disposition towards social life. A sense of historical roots is essential for the formation of a collective consciousness and cultural continuity. The community constantly relates with its cultural past to legitimize its socio-religious practices and traditions. Collective history is embedded in the narratives of folklore, myths and memories of collective living. To a large extent, local cultural symbols, language and local metaphors and folklore, along with the socio-political events of Kerala shape the cultural and religious experiences of the Muslim community. Religious culture is symbolized through local experiences of the community. Nevertheless, the customs and traditions have an Islamic quality.[6] The Muslims in Kerala share a common socio-political history with other communities; they have always been able to maintain their distinct religious and cultural identity (see Miller 1992).

The origin or spread of Islam in Kerala[7] is generally traced to the peaceful and extensive economic and social relationships between the early Arab traders and the native Keralites. Alongwith economic relations the Arab traders established conjugal ties with the native women, which led to the spread of Islam in Kerala. Arnold (1896) in his study, *Preaching of Islam*, provides an elaborate picture of the missionary preaching in Kerala. He gives a detailed historical account of the spread of Islam in the Malabar Coast. Instead of coercive force, peaceful preaching of Islam by Muslim missionaries and *Sufis* was responsible for large-scale conversion. Many *Sufi* saints and theologians have contributed towards establishing a strong religious base in Kerala. Though there is scanty information on the early missionary tradition, the local folk tradition narrate the account of various *Sheikhs* and saints for whom people still have high esteem. The folklore and Muslim songs, extensively sung, and the *nercca* festivals, extol the activities and miracles of these saints (see Kunju 1989).

The tradition of Malik-ibn-Dinar and his disciples has played a major role in spreading the religion. The tradition suggests that Chereman Perumal, the last Perumal ruler of Kerala embraced Islam. On his return journey from Arabia, he was accompanied by the family and friends of Malik-ibn-Dinar. When the king died at Zufar on the Arabian coast, he instructed his friends to proceed to Kerala and spread the new faith. They landed at kodunnallur, visited different parts of Kerala and established several cathedral mosques in different parts of the state.[8] In one of the earliest travel accounts about Muslims in India, Ibn-Batuta, describes the extent of religious activity on the Kerala coastal region. He visited Kerala around AD 1342. He mentions that many distinguished theologians and saints from the Middle East, for instance from Baghdad visited the place. The theologians were honoured by the local rulers and people from different parts, including the Chinese, sent offerings to them. He visited some of the famous hermitages in Khozhikode (Calicut). The Arabi-Malayalam linguistic form, which is Malayalam written in the Arabic script had developed. Innumerable Mappila folk songs, written in this linguistic form, are a rich resource on the saint tradition among the Muslims.

There are different explanations about the spread of Muslims in the interiors of Kerala coast. Extensive trade and economic links existed between Kerala and the Middle East in the first century AD. The Arabs controlled the trade in the Arabian Sea. Arab merchants had managed to establish a monopoly of the import and export trade of the Zamourins. The long-distance voyage in the Arabian Sea and the changing climate, made it necessary for the Arabs to stay in the western coastal areas for longer durations, sometimes even for months. Trade relations provided opportunity for Arabs to get married to the native lower-caste women with the permission of the Zamourin. The alliance of lower-caste women with the Arab traders led to the improved status of the castes, as the Arab traders were attributed an equal status to that of the upper caste Nayars. Changed social status enabled these women to enjoy freedom hitherto not possible in the restrictive caste structure. This might have attracted many low castes to encourage this type of alliance. Thus, the Muslims of Kerala are the descendents of the offspring of the Arab traders and the lower-caste women. However, in later days, many lower caste Hindus also converted and embraced Islam.

The Muslims in Kerala also witnessed many socio-religious reforms and modernization movements during the colonial period and after independence. Response to reforms was not in consonance with the expectation of the leaders as the community was deeply rooted in traditional local practices and dogmatic beliefs. Logan (1951) recorded that the only education received was religious in content. Curriculum included the Holy *Quran, Hadith,* Arabic and jurisprudence. Education was confined mostly to the *Madrasa* attached to the mosques. The study of Malayalam, especially by females is opposed on the grounds that it was an *Aryan* language.[9] Similarly, the reason for indifference towards English education was antagonism towards the British with whom the Mappilas had historic hatred.

Modernisation among the Muslims in Kerala started during the late nineteenth century under the able leadership of socio-religious reformers such as Makthi Tangal (1847-1912) and Vakkam Maulavi (1873-1932). The early movement they initiated is known as the *Islahi* movement, which was later on known as the Aykya Sangam Movement. The *Islahi* movement advocated modern educational and social reforms among Muslims in different parts of Kerala (see Seethi, 2000). It also attempted to disseminate Islamic knowledge through printing and publications and opening up of numerous educational institutions. Most popular among the later leaders were Vakkam Maulavi, both a nationalist and a socio-religious reformer, who started Newspapers, like *Deepika* and *Swadeshabimani*. Maulavi spread a rational outlook towards the world, criticized religious fanaticism, superstition, and all kinds of un-Islamic practices. To propagate modern education and overcome backwardness of the community they started numerous educational institutions and banks. The Aligarh movement initiated by Sir Sayed Ahmad Khan and the ensuing educational reform had its influence on the early Islamic socio-religious reformers like Maulavi in Kerala. Maulavi and others emphasized the need for modernization of religious education and incorporation of modern secular education in the curriculum. He organized the Muslim youth under various cultural committees, the 'Muhamaddeya Sabha', is one among the several cultural groups which initiated educational activity among Muslims. Efforts were made to translate Arabic religious texts into Malayalam. The old syllabus and curriculum was criticized as it hardly left any scope for the youth to gain the relevance of contents is Islamic texts or to inculcate critical literary ability. The new syllabus gave emphasis upon both the religious and non-religious education (see Samad, 1998 and Seeti, 2000).

The reformists were later on called by the more conservative Sunni section as Mujahids. The Mujahid group generally criticized superstitious practices and engaged in puritanical reforms. They were critical of the native Muslim practices like *Nerccha, Mulid, Malappattu,* which were conducted anticipating the intercession by the dead saints and prophets. The Sunnis were in favour of practices like *Nercca, urus, Chanandankkudam, Maulid, Malas,* and *Ratib,* which are prayers done in the name of saints as an act of piety and valid in Islam. The Mujahids consider all kinds of worship other than of *Allah* as un-Islamic and equivalent to idol worship. This counter-argument about religious practices and local tradition is contested among the community members on religious grounds. Gulf migration has augmented this trend, discussed in detail in the following sections.

Gulf Migration and Kerala Muslims

Geographic relocation through international migration forces the imagination and articulation of personal and group identity, especially in cultural terms (Appadurai, 1996). As mentioned earlier, the relation of Muslims of Kerala with the Persian Gulf has a history of centuries, when the native Keralaites from the coast had peaceful and extensive economic and social relationships with the early Arab traders and settlers. After a long gap, the old relationship to the Persian Gulf is renewed in the mid-twentieth century, i.e., around the 1930s. There were migrants from Kerala in the Persian Gulf region as early as the 1930s when the oil industry in the region began to develop. But large-scale migration began only during the oil boom of the early 1970s. In the last few decades there has been large-scale migration, particularly of Muslims from Kerala to the Middle East.[10] This migration to the Gulf countries for around three decades has deeply influenced the economic behaviour, religious culture and tradition of native Muslims in Kerala. It has resulted in the emergence of neo-rich in the community. This group is playing a principal role in the social transformation of the community members, in terms of setting standards and influencing social behaviour, attitude and aspirations. Before analyzing this dimension an exploration of the nature of migration is attempted here.

Till today, Kerala, a small state in India has been a major labour exporter to the Middle East countries. Although the state's population of around 30 million comprises only 3.43 per cent of the population of the country, around 35 to 50 per cent of the migrants from India have been from this state. The influence of gulf migration is much larger among the Muslims in north Kerala as compared to other parts, in spite of the fact they account for only one-fifth of the total population of the state. Statistically, they constitute as much as 78 per cent of the migrant population. Hindus and Christians account for only about 12 and 10 per cent of the outflow. Reports show that at least one male member of every Muslim household is working in the Middle East at this point of time. A survey conducted in 1998 estimated that there were 33 international migrants for every 100 households. Entire village populations sometimes migrate affecting the very social structure and composition of the village. Researches show that economically and culturally, there are distinct characteristics of these villages which distinguish them from the non-migrant village.[11]

Social scientists, especially economists, have been interested in the emerging trends and characteristics of this international migration, especially nature of the migrant labour. Various studies in this area substantiate the fact that more or less, all the migrants are unmarried males[12] in the age group of 20-30, with low levels of education. It is neither the traditional rich nor the extremely poor who migrate. Most of the migrant labour in the Gulf belongs to lower middle-class consisting of unskilled and semi-skilled workers, relatively less qualified population in the region.[13] They also come from poor, rural families engaged in low productivity, traditional activities such as fishing, agricultural labour, cottage industry, and service sector jobs, such as helpers in tea shops and salesman in grocery stores. Only a few migrants come from well-to-do families of plantation owners or professionals such as engineers, doctors and college teachers and middle-level industrialists and businessmen. Mostly, the migrant labourers are engaged as construction workers, employees in private firms, employees in government and public sector institutions, traders and businessmen and domestic servants.[14] Professional or technical education initially was not an important prerequisite for migration. In the majority of cases, vocational training played a more important role than higher technical education.[15]

The migrants' return to the country is inevitable due to emigration policy of the Gulf countries, which put variety of restrictions regarding Asian expatriate labour, the length of their stay and the admittance of dependants. As the labour importing gulf countries allow only a few years of stay till the contract period ends, the migrants live frugally so that they can remit a large portion of their incomes to their families. Consequently, due to the fear of repatriation migrants are perpetually oriented toward their home communities, visiting them frequently. Thus, the domicile continues to influence all aspect of the migrant's social life in the Gulf countries.[16]

The economic condition of the home state influences the magnitude of migration to the Gulf countries, and correspondingly the return migration also. Economic opportunities in the state determine the factors contributing towards large-scale migration and the nature of remittance investment of the return migrants.[17] In contemporary Kerla, tardy growth of employment opportunities in the agricultural or industrial sector continues despite mass internal and international migration from the state. Thus, financial crisis is attributed to the inhospitable investment climate and also to the non-productive investment habits of the Malayali people. Future migration is greatly dependent on the generation of employment and investment opportunities within the state and also migration policies of the Arab countries. In recent times, the Middle East countries have promoted *Arabisation* policies and the legal control on labour import has tightened. Alongside this, the migrants face competition from others with better technical skills in the competitive market. Zachariah(2002) and others underline the need for immediate steps to be taken by the state government to improve the technical skill of migrant workers. They warn that Kerala workders are going to lose out in the international competition for jobs in the Gulf market. The new immigration policy of the Gulf countries deter unskilled Asian workers and the future demand will be for skilled workers, technicians, and computer operators, professional categories such as doctors, nurses, engineers, and teachers. The Keralite workers are increasingly finding themselves incapable to compete with other South Asian countries. The solution lies in equipping the workers with better education and technical skill. The future emigrants should be equipped to meet the changes and development of labour market in the Gulf countries. As a major section of migrants are from the Muslim community and lacking proper higher education and technical skills, they will be seriously affected. This issue needs to be addressed immediately and measures should be taken to improve the labour standards of the migrant workers.[18]

In spite of this dismal picture, Gulf migration has been able to enhance the economic condition of the individual migrant family by increasing the overall income level of the family, especially in the last two decades. The impact of migration can be observed in terms of the socio-economic status, attitudes and behaviour, values and religious practices of migrants and their family structure and gender roles,[19] the very nature of investment, and cultural influence.[20]

In comparison to other communities, Muslims in Kerala have witnessed rapid enrichment of the lower classes by Gulf remittances. A change in life-style, increased demand for consumer goods such as vehicles, ornaments, jewellery, gadgets like TV, refrigerators and other electrical appliances, increased spending in marriage and other ceremonial functions, land purchase and construction are most visible signs of the accumulating wealth. In fact, a large proportion of Gulf remittance is being used by the newly rich Muslims in showing off affluence by buying real estate, palatial houses, school and hospital construction, *salkkaaram* (feasting relatives and neighbours on special occasion), and religious philanthropy. Wealth has become a claim for higher social status. Besides enhanced status brings about privileged positions in the local power structures.

However, it need not be emphasized that this zeal about material wealth and ostentatious spending is in no way an indication of change in the core values and attitude.[21] In fact, in many quarters, profligate exhibition of wealth is observed as a sign of the acceptance of western values and a manifest challenge on the way to the sacred life. However, quite contrarily, there is also an augmentation of religiosity among the return migrants and their family. This is partly explained in terms of cultural contact of the migrants with the Islamic state and society in their workplace. In a Mappila Muslim village, a great deal of importance is attached to distribution of wealth in a large circle of people within the community and support of religious activities. Migrant's families flaunt their wealth for religious rituals, donation for construction of religious institutions like mosques, *Madrasas* and religious-cultural organizations and charitable activities. In this sense, economic prosperity and outside exposure has not led to a decline in religious faith and practice; religious attitude and feeling remain unchanged in the community (see Nair 1986).

However, what is interesting is the way Gulf money is used for redefining religious identity. The middle classes are in a process of status assertion to gain better social position and recognition in the community. The Gulf tradition provides a new legitimacy to their religious existence. Their attempt to gain space within the community is reflected in their increasing criticism of the religion followed by native Muslims. There is an attempt of re-conceptualization of meaning and significance of their identity, concretely manifested through modifications in ritual practices to attribute Islamic quality and religious sanction to many of the practices. One important trend is the increasing attention towards proper etiquette in both private and public life.[22]

Increased status in society is appropriated through renewed interest in religious etiquette.[23] Religious etiquette here can be understood as the set of moral values and standard for guiding Muslims in all aspects of life such as eating, drinking, dressing, sleeping, talking, family life, marriage etc., the mastery of etiquette helps to discipline and train and endows Muslims the qualities to follow an exemplary life. The theory of etiquette ensures that all Muslims become capable of spiritual discipline and self-realization. Believers whether saint, teacher, craftsmen, family head, women all have equal potential to be blessed. The behaviour of every Muslim should be shaped in accordance with the moral values exemplified by the Prophet Mohammed through his life. His life and commandments are compiled in the form of *Hadith*. This was compiled after the death of Prophet by his associates and eye witnesses. There are various narrations and interpretation among which the compilation of Malik, Bukhari, Tirmidhi, and Ibn Majah are considered to be the most authentic.

Etiquette governs the interpersonal conduct between relatives, family members, and strangers in public forums.[24] Etiquette determines status in society and position in the social hierarchy. The neo-rich enhance their prestige through imitating the normative patterns of the traditional elite. The traditional elite attempt to de-legitimise these efforts by attributing innovative symbolic meanings to etiquette and ritual practice. The traditional elite assert their identity through the historical legitimacy of the family to maintain their superior status in the local hierarchies.

The influence of migration on etiquette in the case of Kerala Muslims, has started redefining well-mannered behaviour for Muslim women. The increase in number of women wearing *Parda* compared to earlier periods is an illustration of this phenomenon.[25] Etiquette has evolved as a form of the value of social capital through which, the dedication towards religious life is demonstrated. Manners are symbols of ones higher status, manifested through modifications in ritual practices which have religious connotations.

Muslim Community in Transition: Denominational Contestations and Emerging Public Sphere

Though in Kerala there is already a relatively well-established public sphere, there are many discourses, which have not found their appropriate place. Among the different communities such as Nayars, Dalits and Christians there has been much dialogue and engagement with regard to problems and prospects within their community. The Muslim community is generally considered as passive in its reaction to and response to various socio-political changes it faces. The discourse of conflictual interpretation has not gained much attention in the public sphere, with some exception being during the British period. With the emergence of a newly rich class trying to assert its status and the increasing assertion of multiple identities within the community, a large section of the community is today stimulated to participate in religious contestations in the social sphere. The diverse voices within the community along with emergent new faces among the leadership augments this process.

At this moment, there is a strong tendency towards branding oneself as the authentic representative of Islamic values and consequent marginalization of oppositional groups. The various revivalist and reform movements have lead to more and more intra-community division on the issue of tehological matters, jurisprudence and modernization. It is not possible to talk about a monolithic Muslim community in Kerala in its real sense as differential identities are emerging from conflicting ideologies. In recent times there exists an intensified and open expression of differences. Here we try to understand the intra-community relation, looking into some of the socio-religious movements and ambiguities involved in the diverse religious ideologies and worldviews discussed within the community.

The differences between various sections became more and more visible and open. Miller calls the period 1976-1991 as a history of struggle (Miller 1992). Muslims in Kerala developed many approaches on theology, law etc. During this period the Sunni majority experienced a division into two groups: A.P. Sunnis and the E.K. Sunnis, major cause being the Gulf money. The A.P. or the Kandapuram group is lead by A.P. Abu Bakr Musaliar, known for his strong Gulf connection which enabled him to accumulate large amounts of donation through charity boxes in Gulf and in Kerala to establish his group in Kerala. They established, as cultural complexes, a large number of educational institutions for the propagation of Islamic values. This group opposes political involvement of Muslims, which is a departure from the Sunni leadership, which maintain faith in the political involvement with the Muslim league for the transformation of Muslim life. The group is popular among the youth having their own organization called the Sunni Students Federation (SSF).

The E.K. group is the other section of Sunni group with the leadership of E.K. Abu Bekr Musaliar. They support the theological tradition and the legitimacy of Muslim saints saying the saints do posses special powers and grace. Praying at the shrine is both permissible and helpful. They provide support to the political party, Muslim League, and actively engage in political issues. They are critical of the Mujahid argument, and favour *Ijtihad* or the private interpretation of *Quran*. Their youth organization is called the Samasta Kerala Sunni students Federation. Both A.P. and E.K. groups differ in political and financial matters but otherwise share the same theological positions. Their main fight is with the Mujahs and Jamaat-Islam group spread Islamic principles with the goal of creating an Islamic society. They also give much emphasis to character building like other groups, the major difference being that they do not allow the members to engage in government service or government grants, or any kind of political involvement. They have their own student wing called the Students Islamic Organisation (SIO). They also started a newspaper named '*Madhyamum*'.

There are also other less significant sections such as the Tabiligh Jammat group, Islamists, the Ahamadiyas, and the Chekannur Maulavi group working with differential perspectives on religion trying to spread religious values among the community members. The differences between various groups become evident, as the hardcore followers strictly follow the commandment of their *Ulama*. Different sections have also started their own educational institutions such as Kerala Nadvattul Mujahindin, Jammat-I-Islami of Kerala, Samastha Kerala Jamiyyathul Ulama to propagate their own theology (see Samad 1998).

Here, Habermas's concept of 'public sphere' is important to apprehend the recent transformation of the Muslim community in Kerala. The denominational rivalry among Kerala Muslims over the issue of the authentic religious behaviour provides an interesting case of multiple validity claims to legitimize their understanding of Islam as authentic. Though there were differences during the colonial and post-colonial periods, what characterizes the recent period, especially after 1991, is the expansion of the public sphere. Increased awareness due to the earlier religious and political discourse and the newly achieved self-confidence of the neo-rich provides opportunities for engagement in serious polemic in everyday interaction within the community.

It is widely accepted that the traditional intellectuals (*Ulama, Musaliar, Quazis*) had a crucial role in the Kerala Muslims' social life. The leadership had strong linkages with the community and is involved in various aspects of socio-political life. They provide socio-political, religious leadership and guidance to the community. In shaping the outlook of the rural Mappillas, they played a dominant role. Their influence was not limited to ecclesiastical matters, but also extended to everyday life issues

(Pannikar, 2001). Though there are many religious and political leaders who still have authority over the community, their influence is being contested now. In recent years the domination of the traditional religious authority is weakening, as new leadership has come up, which is a challenge to the traditional leadership. The factionalism within the Sunni community is an illustration of this fact. This challenging and questioning may lead to a collapse of the earlier hierarchical notions of religious authority. The religious interpretation of social life today is not a monopoly of any particular leadership. Earlier, the situation was of a general acceptance of the prescriptions of political-religious leaders, without much debate. Now, there exist differential 'validity claims' by various denominations projecting their ideologies as authentic and their interpretation of religious life and community activity as proper.

These developments form the core of contestation in everyday life. Within one family it is possible today to find different members following different interpretation of theological matters. The meaning of religion is being contested in the public and private life. Legitimacy of the local is in contestation with the so-called universal aspects of Islam. Local Islam is challenged in the process of the inclusion and exclusion of social life. The universal tenets of Islam are being underlined as the basic principles in which any kind of local innovation is to be put into the array of serious polemic and contestations. Any native innovation is facing a threat from the puritans. This is not only a specific feature of Kerala Muslims but a similar phenomenon is being observed in other South Asian countries, for instance in Sri Lanka.

Migration may also lead to change in socio-religious identity and status to the migrants in society and even spiritual relationship with God may be reformulated in the process. As Gardner and Osella (2003) point out in several cases the "..... migrant move away from Islam based on the local shrines, saints and hierarchies, and engage in a new global form of Islamic purism and brotherhood". Here the "tradition" assumes a central role in the struggle not only over status and power, but also in the peoples' attempts to reformulate their relationship with god' (p.xxiii). The historically evolved cultural life is redefined to suite to the changing orientation towards religious life. The contestation is not confined to the linguistic polemics only as they are engaged in serious observance and practice of their religious ideology. The youth is also actively involved in this contestation as members of the youth wings of various groups and denominations. Active participation thus, necessitates the sharpening of views and critical outlook and a boost to mass education.

Ordinary people now have unprecedented access to information about religion and other aspects of their society. Mass Media is playing an important role, especially print and audio-visual media. Sensitisation and acceptance of the possibility of multiple interpretations of Islam and Islamic values may be one of the outcomes of the expansion of media's reach and importance (Eickelman, 1999). Forums like newspapers, journals, pamphlets, new television channels and marketing of religious and political sermons through audio-cassettes, are important sites of dialogue and debate. The marketing of religious sermon through audiotapes especially during religious occasions has an important role in the process. It is pertinent to look at Hirsch Kind's study (2000) which provides an anthropological analysis of role of audio tape-recorded sermons in the Egyptian revivalist movement. Tapes are considered as an extension of religious sermon in the mosque. These sermons are used to reinforce moral values and self-discipline, especially among women. The Friday prayer (*kuttuba*) and cassette sermons have an important role not only for promotion of religious values but also for educating people of various interpretations of social issues. These kinds of denominational polemics through mass media lead to 'spiritualization' of every day life. Thus, conflict is an expression of creating legitimate space for itself in public domain.

Concluding Comments

The community, in the process of social life, is experiencing a tremendous exertion to comprehend and interpret the rapid form of social change in all spheres of life. These socio-psychological pressures, in fact, augment the process of initiating innovative strategies and imagination to handle the complexities. In recent times, the community is engaged in serious religious polemic and self-introspection on the community's response towards various social and cultural challenges. Deciphering this state of interpretive ambivalence is indeed a challenge for scholars and intellectuals.

Difference of opinion can be seen as an indication of the intellectual and religious vibrancy of the community. With the community actively engaged in dialogue, it is expected that this 'density' of interaction will multiply the possibilities of dissolving prior barriers of space and opening new grounds for interaction and mutual recognition. The existing discourse enables to create spaces for the inclusive process, where the alternative approaches towards Muslim way of life attains recognition and legitimacy among a larger population. If not so, the domination of any one interpretation can no more have an uncritical acceptance within the community. The creation of a 'new space' will lead to accelerated possibility of creating a more vibrant public sphere effectively addressing contemporary problems.

These contestations need to be channeled to a particular direction so as to initiate among the members a more effective and productive dialogue, which will help the community in the long run. Efforts are needed to canalize the debate on some of the practical issues of the community, which need immediate attention. For instance, the recent CDS study (see Zachariah, 2002) shows that if the Gulf labour migrants – mostly consisting of Muslims – are not equipped to meet the developments of gulf labour markets, it will seriously affect their economic and developmental prospects. As mentioned earlier, lack of higher technical education skills will be the greatest hurdle for the migrants in coming times.[26]

As mentioned earlier, material prosperity has not led to inculcation of motivation towards higher education or professional qualifications. Thus, it is noted that the economic achievement of the community is not conducive to the social-cultural development of the community. For instance, the Mujahid group within the community, who started the reformatory measures long back and in the areas of their presence they have had a strong impact on the educational development. They are making use of the Gulf money for developmental activities. This can be seen in contrast to other sections, which even after improvement in the economic conditions have not made sufficient efforts to invest in education. In fact, they use large amounts of funds in religious and other socio-cultural activities. Hoever, the Mujahid group lacks support from the larger community because of lack of free and open public space. The moderate section has been unable to create an environment suited for proper intervention on the internal dynamics of the society. As a matter of fact, it is noted by scholars that the Muslims have been only able to achieve basic literacy and lag behind in higher education. The governmental and the private efforts have not helped the community in any substantial manner (see Salim, 1998). Thus within the community there is less enthusiasm towards engaging in serious dialogue on non-religious issues. It must be understood that an expanding public sphere is no guarantee for better prospects of the community. However, possible creation of a vibrant pubic sphere is necessary for creating a new path for cultural changes in everyday life. It can be expected that in near future, with evolution of an open social sphere congenial for innovative strategies, there will be more enthusiasm towards facing the challenges of the community successfully, without compromising the socio-religious identity of the community. However, it should be mentioned here though there is not yet been any real rapprochement, for the common interest the community has been able to unite especially in political terms.

To conclude, there are two major reminders for any kind of future research in the community. First, the modernization process will continue to play a key role in stimulating and influencing the social attitude and behaviour of the community. Global reaction to western cultural domination and hegemonisation has its manifest and latent impact on attributing cultural meanings to their practices and beliefs. The reaction to this hegemonic redefinition of cultural life may vary from time to time. The assertion of religiosity in recent time is a manifestation of the reaction of the community within the social milieu they are located. Various exogenous and endogenous factors have dialectic interaction determining the basic nature of strategies evolved. At present, these factors contribute unconsciously towards the intensification of cultural and religious contestations. The theory, that consciousness of the community did not more outside basic tenets and principle of Islam is asserted. International migration has led to economic transformation and in turn resulting in changing the attritudeand expectations of the community affecting the entire socio-cultural milieu. However, it should be mentioned that this phenomenon needs more attention for a better understanding of the cultural impact of Gulf migration on the community.

NOTES

1. See Nagel, J. 1994. 'Constructing Ethnicity: Creating and Recreating Ethnic identity and Culture': In *Social Problems*, 41:152-176, pp. 152.
2. The modernists generally regards that the modernization process would lead to disappearance of the traditional loyalties like religion, racism, caste system etc. There has been an upsurge in ethnic awareness in multicultural societies and groups are trying to rediscover their cultural roots. The recent ethnic conflicts show that the ethnicity asserts itself in even more concrete forms. Numerous studies have pointed out that economic and social development do not replace ethnocentric and communal feelings. There has been an upsurge in ethnic awareness and attempts to rediscover their cultural roots. For a detailed study on the response of Muslim to colonial dominance, see the work of Metcalf, 2002 on Deobandi movement.
3. It is pertinent to note here that scholars engaged in studying community relationships, especially the study of communalism, hardly appreciate the relevance of studying peaceful societies and how people of different of communities there relate themselves with the 'other' and engage in the process of constructing identity boundaries. In fact, analysis of the conflict and contestations within the community in a relatively peaceful society is equally important to gain a better understanding of the process of pressure group creation and negotiations related to socio-political issues concerning the community. The intra-community contestation is a manifestation of the active and critical self-analysis by the community in the process of construction and reconstruction of identity in religious terms. Other exogenous factors only play the role of ameliorating and intensifying the process. Also, in the era of globalization it is difficult to maintain that the south Indian states (like Kerala) are unaffected by socio-political tensions. Studies on communal/ethnic/sectarian conflict suggest that the scope for conflict has expanded from local to national and international dimensions, due to the expansion of communication technology and information revolution. Though it is true that communal political issues of north India have had relatively lesser impact on the Kerala society, this immunity has never been complete. Evidence of this fact is the sectarian debate on puritan and revivalist tendencies and the increasing relationship of Muslim leadership with the Arab World; increasing adherence to Arabic-Islamic symbolic culture and religious obligations.

   Gulf migration has influenced all aspect of Kerala's socio-economic life. It has contributed immensely towards rearranging of the social strcture of the Muslim community. Changing class composition and growth of the neo-rich, lack of psychic security, emerging leadership patterns along with the changing religious experiences and reorientation are crucial for understanding the emerging trends within the community. Many studies ignore this phenomenon, which remains a characteristic impact on the social and cultural life of the Muslim community.

4. The author attempts to deal with the influence of Gulf migration on the migrant and their social life. The paper addresses the following questions: Has Gulf migration influenced the understanding of socio-religious life in any manner. Does it in any way contribute towards new trends within the community? How do the Kerala Muslims come to terms with their association with the Gulf countries in terms of cultural meanings?
5. The existing studies among Kerala Muslims are based on the textual understanding of religion which brings out the fundamental principles of Islam, which do not reveal much about the actual influence of Islam in everyday life practices. There are lots of gaps in the study of the change in the Muslim community in Kerala. There are hardly any sociological works looking into the trends and dynamics of recent changes among Muslims in Kerala. Also, these studies fail to provide a comprehensive analytical understanding of the process of construction, and reconstruction of boundaries of the community in the changing socio-political scenario. Similarly, there are few studies which attempt to comprehend the changing trends in the cultural traditions of Kerala Muslims.
6. The early historical mosque architecture and the structure of house building is an excellent example of the culture milieu of harmonious blending of Arab and indigenous tradition. For further details, see K.J.John, 'The Muslim-Arabs and Mosque Architecture in Malabar': In Asghar Ali Engineer (ed) *Kerala Muslims: A Historical Perspective*, 1995, New Delhi, Ajanta Publications. Ahmad (1980) also observes that a dynamic society, constantly engages in the process of dialectic interaction with the native cultural tradition and shared experience along with the blending of Islamic belief and practice.
7. According to the 1991 Census the religious constitution of Indian population was: Hindus 82 per cent, Muslims 12.12 per cent and Christians 2.34 per cent, Sikhs 1.94 per cent, Buddhists 0.76 percent, Jains 0.40 per cent. Numerically, Muslims constitute the most predominant minority in India. In 1961 Census Kerala stands as the fourth largest state in India with the largest number of Muslim population following Kashmir, Assam, and West Bengal. In the 1991 Census, the district wise population of Muslims of Kerala is as follows: Malappuram 63.93 per cent, Calicut 30.62 per cent, Cannanore 24.3 per cent, Palghat21.27 per cent, Qulon 21.27 per cent, Trichur 12.83

per cent, Ernakulam 13.69 per cent, Trivandram 12.33 per cent, Aleepey 12.01 per cent, Waynad 6.85 percent, Idukki 6.06 per cent and Kottayam 3.48 per cent. Two-third of the Muslims are concentrated in northern Kerala, that is around 67 per cent of the total population. In 1981, the population composition of north Kerala was as follows: Hindus 56.3 per cent Muslims 34.3 per cent and Christians 9 per cent respectively, as compared to south Kerala, that is 57.5 per cent, 10.5 per cent and 32.0 per cent. In north Kerala, only Malappuramdistrict Muslims outnumber both Hindus and Christians. Other than Kashmir and Lakshadeep only Malappuram has the highest percentage of Muslim population among districts in India.

8. See Kunju 1989, also Zaynud-Din and Shaykh, 1942, *'Tuhfat Ul-Mujahidin'*, Translated by Muhamed Husayn Nainar. Madras: University of Madras.
9. See, S.M. Mohamed Koya, 'Educational and Social Progress of the Mappilas', Symposium on History Conference, Mysore, 1985.
10. Gulf countries undertook a massive infrastructural reconstruction and in a relatively short period of time were able to transform into most technologically advanced nations of the world. Foreign labour was central to this transformation. Since 1970s there has been a large-scale out-migration from Asian countries, particularly India and Pakistan to the Middle East. By 1980, 69.8 per cent of the workforce in the region was foreigners. Among these Asians constituted around one-third of the foreign workforce in the Gulf countries. Indians and Pakistanis account for more than 18 per cent. According to B.A.Praksh (1998) in the same year there are 2.8 million Indians in Middle East and in 1990-1991 it was 1.5 to 1.7 million. 95% of the emigrant's countries of destination, were Saudi Arabia, United Arab Emirates (consisting of Abu Dhabi, Dubai, The Small Emirate of Sharja and The Village States of Ras-Al-Khaimah, Umma-Al-Quaiwain, Ajman, Fujairah). Baharin, Kuwait, Qatar and Oman. A large section has immigrate especially to Saudi Arabia, U.A.E. Emigration from India to gulf countries take place mainly from seven states: Kerala, Andhra Pradesh, Gujarat, Goa, Maharashtra, Tamil Nadu.
11. Within Kerala, Mallapuram district has the highest rate of emigration, which is followed by Pathanamthita, Trissure and Kozhikode in the year 1998. For a detailed account of the economic profile of migration along with the effects on the sending country, see the following:

    Gulati I.S., and A. Modi, 1983. "Remittance of Indian Migrants to the Middle East: An Assessment with Special Reference to Migrants from Kerala State." Working Paper 182, Centre For Development Studies, Trivandrum, Kerala. P58. Gopinathan Nair P.R. 1986, "India", in Godfrey Guntilleke(ed), 'Migration of the Asian Workers to the Arab

World, Japan, The United Nations University. Gopinathan Nair, 1989. "Incidence, Impact and Implications of Migration to the Middle East from kerala." In Amjad Rashid, ed., To the Gulf and Back, New Delhi: ILO(ARTEP) 343. Gopinathan Nair P.R. 1991, 'Asian Migration to the Arab World: Kerala (India)' in Godfrey Guntilleke(ed), Migration to the Arab World: Experience of Return Migrants, The United Nations University, Hong Kong. Sekhar, T.V., 1997, Migration and Social Change, New Delhi, Rawat Publications. Prakash B.A., (ed) 1998, "Gulf Migration and its Economic Impact: The Kerala Experience." Economic and Political Weekly, Dec. 12. Zacharia K.C., B.A. Prakash, S. Irudaya Rajan, 2001, 'Kerala Emigrants in the UAE: Issues, Problems and Prospects,' CDS, Kerala University and Govt. of Kerla.

12. Women are going to the Gulf countries in very small numbers, as many incidents of misuse have been reported by the various foreign departments.
13. For statistics and further details see Sekher, 1997 also see Zacharia, Mathew, and Rajan, 1999.
14. See Myron Weiner, "International Migration and Development' in Population and Development Review 8, March 1982 p.13.
15. Thus they are in no way a brain drain to the sending country, as the migration of the unskilled human labour in turn bring remittance is an added advantage rather than a human resource loss. From the national point of view, migration of a few million persons does not perceptibly affect the labour situation in India since unemployment is severe and the population growth rate is high.
16. It is to be noted that there is hardly any study on the socio-political influence of the large number of the immigrants from the Asian countries on the of the Gulf society. The understanding of the behaviour and change in the nature of the return migrants is incomplete without studies in this dimension. There is serious complaints of Arab countries discriminating against Indians on the ground of nationality. There also exist wage differences between East Asian and South Asian migrants (for details see Nair, 1986). Nair observes that Indians face distress and contempt from the host-country nationals. Indians are known to be the "ABCs" of the Gulf- i.e., Ayahs, Barbers, And Cooks".
17. The Kerala state is not able to provide equal salary to the return migrants. In the Gulf even the menial job is accepted owing to the distance from the home place and the five digit salary for a menial job is unthinkable for a low educated semi-skilled labourer working in Kerala. The war between Iraq and Kuwait had a strong impact on the small state in India. The entire state was facing economic crisis as it was difficult to rehabilitate the huge number of return migrants.

The gulf crisis of 1990 created havoc in the state. The massive inflow of the return migrants gave an opportunity for the state to actually witness the real state of the economy and how deeply it is dependent on the gulf economy. The domestic income of the state was affected. The migration and the remittance has not changed the economy as a whole, though has contributed towards economic growth through the inflow of foreign exchange, and reducing unemployment.

18. The interesting issue is that there is little effort on part of the natives to create their own civil society organizations to support their cause in any substantial way. There is a lack of such organization which can function as pressure group and influence the foreign policies of the state.

19. Gulf migration being a male phenomenon, the women folk spend the better part of their family life in the absence of their husband. Separation from family for long periods affect the social structure, especially family system. In case of joint and extended family the elder male member is the main decision-maker. In most families it is the elder male members who play the social role in the absence of husband. The women are passive members whose only engagement is their presence at the site of decision-making. Female folk in general have a low status in the social life and it is difficult to maintain that the male folk have faith on their wife to give the full responsibility in the hands of the female folk. The women also feel more convenient to take decision discussing with the male members as they themselves are not confident of their capacity to understand the dealings of the outside world.

    But in most cases, the wife in the family takes responsibility for shopping, looking after children's education, which can be seen as a temporary structural adjustment. The acting head of the family reattribute all the responsibility to the male member the moment he returns. The female, in fact, do not feel empowered and free to take decisions. Every member will have their own bias and interpretation imbued with their own interest. Even in the physical absence of the male migrant he is very much the head. The mother-n-law has the claim that she knows her son best and she knows the best way he would have liked to take a certain course of action.

20. Most of the literature on international migrants and immigrants focuses on the impact of immigration on receiving societies, particularly to the developed countries. Since short term migration is generally undertaken for economic reasons, most studies have tended to focus on the economic aspects of short ter-migration. The studies focus primarily on the economic consequences of the migration that are framed within the neo-classical tradition. According

to this perspective, the economy is an autonomous realm largely unaffected by the social and culture context.

21. In the general diasporas studies the scholars observe that the migrant settlers have an imaginative and nostalgic narrative of their home, which most of the time is outdated or unrealistic. But in case of the Kerala migrants to middle east the case is different, as the migrants though physically are in a different territory, they are imaginarily still in their hometown. Their close interaction is being reinforced by the constant interaction with close relatives and friends through various means of communication. The increased number of STD/ISD phone-booths, newspapers and magazines availability, big budget entertainment and cultural programmes organized by the well-known TV channels and cinema artists in the Malayali populated areas of the Gulf countries. And most importantly, the influence of media especially the TV channels (like Asianet, Kilari, Surya, India Vision) with vide inter-action viewership is widely linking Malayalies globally. A migrant Malyali is equally aware of all the socio political events of the home place. So the effect of migration on the religious attitude is not formed by the non presence of the migrant in their home place.
22. See article by gardner, Katy and Filippo, Osella, A, 2003, 'Migration Modernity and Social Transformation in South Asia: An Overview', In *Contribution to Indian Sociology*, N.S.37, 1&2 pp-v-xviii.
23. In recent years scholars such as Geertz, Metcalf and Robinson have tried to analyse this trend from more flexible categorization. Metcalf in her book "Moral Conduct and Authority: The Place of *Adab* in South Asian Islam"(1984), attempts to put forward a new approach towards the understanding of Muslim culture.
24. In Islam realization of human being comes through the cultivation of *Aqal* and the consequent disciplining of the *Nafs*. This process of controlling the *Nafs* through the mediation of *Aqal* is considered as the 'greater *jihad*', as it tries to win upon one's own life through a constant every day spiritual battle targeted against the evil thoughts inside human beings, see Metcalf 1984.
25. In Islamic history it has been noticed that when the religion or cultural tradition was in trouble, there is an increased degree of focus on the dissemination of etiquettes. Robinson's essay "Ulama of Farangi Mahal"(1984) and Metcalf writing on Behisti Zewer(2002) shows that religions and political leaders use etiquettes as text of right conduct and disseminate on the basis of guarding the tradition and Muslim identity. Women are considered as the main carriers of the moral value and social role and responsibility is determined by the socio political situation. Metcalf's book "Perfecting Women"(2002) provide a

detailed account of the obligation of the women in both private and public life. Any attempt to combat with the observance of un-Islamic practice has tendency of focusing on women. Deobandi ulama, started taking interest in the Islamic practice has tendency of focusing on women. Deobandi ulama, started taking interest in the Islamic education of women, since women were the prime practitioners of the host of the rituals and customs. Thus, emphasis on the changing value orientation and motivation towards etiquettes will reflect upon the mental make up of Muslims.

26. In term of the educational level of the community, the low level of aspiration towards education can be attributed towards this gulf phenomenon. Though the performance of the community can not be addressed in isolation with the historical and political issues of the community the aversion towards English education has led to the low esteem towards higher or professional education.

BIBLIOGRAPHY/REFERENCES

Ahmad, Imtiaz, (1981), 'Modernization and Social Change among Muslims in India', New Delhi, Manohar Publication.

Ali, Mohammed (1985), 'The Development of Education among the Mappilas of Malabar 1800 to 1965', New Delhi, Nunes Publishers.

Appadurai, Arujun, (1996), 'Modernity at Large: Cultural Dimensions of Globalization', Minneapolis, University of Minneapolis Press.

Barth, Fredrik (ed.), (1996), 'Ethnic Groups and Boundaries: The Social Organization of Cultural Difference', George Allen and Lonwin, London, Oslo Universities Forlaget.

Bourdeu, Pierre, (1987), 'Legitimization and Structured Interests in Weber's Sociology of Religion', in 'From Max Weber. Rationality and Modernity ' edited by Samwhimster and Scott lash, Allen and Unwin London (translated by Chris Tumer).

Eickelman, Dale, (1999), 'The Coming Transformation of the Muslim World' in Middle East Review of International Affairs Vol.3, No.3, Sept.

Gardner, Katy and Filippo Osella, (2003), 'Migration, Modernity and Social Transformation in South Asia: An overview', In Contribution to Indian Sociology, N.S. 37, 1&2, Pv-Xxviii.

Geertz, Clifford, (1960), 'Religion of Java', Glencope 111.

Gulati, Leela, 1983, 'In the Absence of their Men: Impact of Male Migration on Women', New Delhi: Sage Publication.

Habermas, Jurgen, (1989), 'The Structural Transformation of the Public Sphere: An Inquiry into a Category of Bourgeois Society, Trans by

Tomas Burger with the Assistance of Frederic Lawrence. Cambridge. MA.

Hasting, Donnan, 2002, 'Interpreting Islam', New Delhi, Vistaar Publications.

Hirschkind, Charles, (2000), 'Passionate Preaching Aural Sensibility and the Islamic Revival in Cairo', in Michael Lambek (ed.), A. Reader in the Anthropology of Religion, Polity press.

Koya, Mohamed S.M., (1983), 'Mappilas of Malabar', Kerala, Sandhya Publication.

Kunji, Muhammad P.K., (1982), 'Muslimigalum Kerala Sanskaravum', Kerala Sahitya Akadami, TRISHUR.

Kunju, Abrahim A.P., (1989), 'Mappila Muslims of Kerala: Their History and Culture', Sandhya Publication.

Kunien, A. Prema, (2002), 'Kaleidoscopic Ethnicity: International Immigration and the Reconstruction of Community Identities in India', London, Rutgers University Press.

Metcalf, Babra Daly, (2002), 'Islamic Revival in British India Deoband, 1860-1900', New Delhi, Indian Paper Back. Oxford University Press.

Miller, Roland. E., (1976), 'Mappila Muslims of Kerala: A Study in Islamic Trends', Madras, Orient Longman.

Pandey, Gyanendra (ed.), (1993), 'Hindus and Others: Question of Identity in India Today', New Delhi, Viking Publication.

Panikkar, K.N., (2001), 'Against Lord and State: Religion and Pesant Uprisings in Malabar 1836-1921', New Delhi, Oxford University Press.

Salim, Abdul, A., (1999), 'Educational Development at Micro Level: Case Study of Two Villages in Kerala'. Tiruvanantapuram, CDS Publication.

Samad, M. Abdul, (1998), 'Islam in Kerala: Group and Movements in 20th Century', Kottayam. Laurel Publications.

Schneider D.M. and Kathleen Gough (ed), 1962, Matrilineal Kinship, Berkley And Los Angeles.

Singh, Yogendra, (1999), ' Modernization of Indian Tradition', New Delhi, Rawat Publications.

Wilson, Brayan, R, (1996), 'Religion in Secular Society', Wonder, C.A. Walts and Company.

Zachariah, K.C., et al. (eds.), (2002), 'Kerala's Gulf Connection', Kerala, Centre for Development Studies.

SUBSISTENCE, ECOLOGY AND SOCIAL ORGANIZATION AMONG THE HUNZAKUT: A HIGH-MOUNTAIN PEOPLE IN THE KARAKORAMS

M.H. Sidky

Introduction: Hunza and Its People

The Hunzakut, the people of Hunza, live in the western Karakoram mountains (now part of northern Pakistan), in what has been called one of the most formidable upland regions on earth. To survive in their harsh high mountain environment, Hunzakut farmers operate a subsistence economy that combines the cultivation of cereal crops, vegetables and fruit trees, with animal husbandry and transhumant pastoralism. Traditionally, agro-pastoral production, based on a range of complementary plant and animal species, and coordinated through rituals, has been closely linked to ecological circumstances. This paper examines Hunza's traditional production strategies, the social arrangements and land-use pattern associated with them and their implications for household and village organisation. The data upon which this article is based were gathered during field research in Hunza during 1990 and 1991.

The former princely state of Hunza is located in an area where the Hindu Kush, Karakoram and Himalayan ranges converge to produce a vast network of glaciers, peaks and isolated valleys. This is the most massive concentration of mountains to be found anywhere on earth. Hanza's territory is roughly 7,900 km^2, bordering Afghanistan and China to the north, Kashmir to the east, and Pakistani Panjab to the south. Hunza is populated by an agglomeration of ethnic groups, whose ethnolinguistic diversity and economic self-sufficiency are the consequence of centuries of geographic isolation.

For centuries Hunza was an independent principality headed by a hereditary autocratic ruler, the Mir (Biddulph 1880:23; Schomberg 1935: 43, 116; Knight 1893:330). During the 19th century Hunza was among the more important of the self-ruled "princely states" of this far northwestern part of the British empire (cf. Stanley 1969: 229; Barth 1956: 79-86). By the mid-19th century political events occurring outside. Hunza were to bring significant changes to the tiny mountain kingdom. The British, then involved in the so-called "Great Game" with Russia (c. Keay, 1979), invaded Hunza in 1891 and made it a part of the Gilgit. Agency, within Jammu and Kashmir State (Leitner 1889; Durand 1900; Nevill 1912). Thereafter, Hunza's political and socio-economic status remained relatively unchanged until the British withdrawal from India in 1947. Shortly after the partition of the subcontinent into India and Pakistan, and the subsequent dispute over Kashmir, the Mir of Hunza proclaimed allegiance to Pakistan.

For the first two-and-a-half decades of Pakistani rule (from 1947 to 1974), the Mir retained full internal administrative powers. But this autonomy was ended in 1974 when the Bhutto regime abolished the privileges of the princely states. Hunza state was now brought under the direct administration of Islamabad, and became a sub-division of the Northern Areas District.

Hunza's isolation from the rest of Pakistan, however, was not breached until 1978. In this year, the 1,284 km long Karakoram Highway was completed. A joint Sino-Pakistani venture, the highway links, via the Hunza valley, the ancient Silk Road oasis of Kashgar in Xinjian with the twin cities of Islamabad-Rawalpindi in Pakistan. Since the late 1970s the pace of change has escalated significantly, with the arrival of Panjabi truckers and an influx of European mountaineers and tourists. Despite these new circumstances, however, much of Hunza's traditional culture is still intact, although acculturation processes are clearly at work.

Four ethnolinguistic groups are represented in Hunza. The first are Hunzakut, "the people of Hunza". (They are also called Burosho, an ethnonym I do not use here because it also refers to the dominant population of the neighbouring former state of Nagar). The Hunzakut live in the central portion of the Hunza valley, from Murtazabad to Nazimabad, and were the dominant ethnic group in the former princely state. Their language, Burushaski, is a linguistic anomaly. It seem not to be related to the Indo-European languages spoken in India, Pakistan and Afganistan, nor to the Sino-Tibetan linguistic groups found in northeastern Xinjian and Ladakh (Morgenstierne 1935: vii-xxx; Lorimer 1935: xxi-lxiii; Berger 1985:37).

The second group are the Shin, who inhabit the lower part of the Hunza valley, roughly from the village Nomal to the village Hini. Their language, Shina belongs to the so-called Dardic group of Indo-Aryan languages, and is spoken throughout the Gilgit region (Jettmar 1961:81).

The third ethnic group are the Wakhi, immigrants from Afganistan and former vessals of the Mirs of Hunza. They occupy an area stretching from Gulmit to Pasu. Their language, known as Wakhi, belongs to the East-Indian Pamir languages and is spoken in upper Huza and the Pamir area of Afghanistan (Buddruss 1985: 27-29).

During the 18th and 19th centuries, three Mirs of Hunza-Silim (1790-1824), Ghazanfar (1824-1865) and Ghazan Khan (1865-1886) – compelled the Hunzakut to colonise both the upper and lower altitude areas to the north and south. Consequently, Hunzakut villages are to be found in all three of the above mentioned zones.

The fourth and smallest ethnic group of Hunza are the Bericho, a small caste-like community of blacksmiths and musicians. They live mostly in their own segregated village of Berishal (Mominabad); a few scattered Bericho households are also found in some of the Burusho villages in central Hunza. Their language, Domaaki, is thought to be related to the Indo-Aryan languages in Kashmir (Lorimer 1939: 1-19).

The total population of Hunza is 32,300, distributed among 52 villages (cf. Kreutzmann 1986:99; Charles 1985:19-26). The Hunzakut, who make up the largest segment of the population (roughly 58.7%) comprise 2,606 of a total of 4,441 households in Hunza. The Shin constitute approximately 20.3% of the population and occupy about 900 households; the Wakhi 19.1%, distributed through 850 households, and the Bericho, roughly 1.91%, in 85 households.

Households, comprising anywhere from 8 to 10 people, are the primary units of production. Villages, which constitute discrete local communities are located on the glacially-formed Pleistocene terraces above the precipitous river flood valley walls. These villages usually consist of clusters of 50 to 100 houses, built in close proximity to one another, with the village's fields and orchards nearby.

The Environment and Production Strategies

Hunzakut farmers have had to adapt to the special climatic and geophysical conditions of their high-mountain environment. Hunza has a dry continental climate, but the considerable variations according to include altitude, aspect and localized relief. Average temperatures range from -12 degrees Celsius in January to 35 degrees Celsius in July.

This trans-Himalayan region is unaffected by monsoon rains, annual precipitation is only about 130 mm (Goudie et al. 1984: 37) and insufficient for dry farming. The Hunza River, which slices through the Karakoram range, runs nearly a hundred metres below the arable lands and, therefore, is unusuable for irrigation purposes. Precipitation in the form of snowfall, approximately 2000 mm a year, however, occurs at altitudes above 6000 m, feeding the glaciers which, in turn serve as the altitudes source of irrigation water for the populated valleys below. Agriculture is totally dependent on the seasonal glacial melt-waters channeled into the valley by means of a complex man-made irrigation network.

Physical and biotic variations along the Hunza valley, which are caused by the interaction of latitude, altitude, aspect and localized relief have significant implications for human subsistence. Agricultural productivity varies inversely with increasing altitude (cf. Guillet 1983:563; Groetzbach 1988:25). As one travels from Gilgit (1,454 m), the administrative centre of the Nothern Areas, to the Khunjerab Pass (4,733 m), some 275 km to the north, one moves through a continuum of double-to single-cropping zones.

In the lower double-cropping zone (up to 2,000 m), where the Shine are the demographically-dominant group, the principal cultivated crops are wheat, maize and barley. Domesticated animals include goats, sheep, cattle, donkeys and horses. In the upper double-cropping zone (roughly 2,000 m to 2,300 m), inhabited entirely by the Burusho, wheat and barley are the principal cultigens. Livestock here comprises mostly sheep, goats and cattle. A elevations of 2,400 m and higher one enters the single-cropping zone, where the Wakhi constitute the predominant population. Here wheat and barley are cultivated as the primary crops, and livestock include yaks in addition to sheep and goats.

In order to survive, each Hunzakut household must have access to sufficient amounts of arable land, pasture and alpine forests (both for timber and fuel). To be able to exploit such diverse resources the Hunzakut combine the cultivation of cereal crops, vegetables and fruit trees, with animal husbandry. Their dependence on a multiple resource base represents an adaptation that minimizes risks from perturbation affecting any one resource cluster (cf. Thomas 1979:154).

The way natural resources are exploited (i.e., the tools and techniques used for the production or procurement of food and other essential materials under the given ecological conditions), along with the relationships which the producers establish between themselves to facilitate the optimal utilization of their available resources, comprise distinct "production strategies" (cf. Terray 1972:99-107). Each strategy entails different social arrangements, as well as different land-use patterns (cf. Ellen 1986: 123, 278: Netting 1977: 73-74).

Production strategies influence the socio-economic organisation of society through their effects on the "social relations of production", i.e., the size, composition and structure of the productive units and the patterns of land use. Production strategies, which represent the interconnection between economic and ecological processes, are central to our understanding of the material basis of any social formation. Ascertaining this interconnection requires investigation of the techniques of production employed for the exploitation of various resources, the requisite labour arrangements associated with these techniques and the significance of each in the overall subsistence pattern of the population.

The socio-economic arrangements which derive from the complex interaction of human populations and high-mountain environments have been well described for such diverse areas as the Andes, the European Alps and the Himalayas (Netting 1972, 1976; Rhoades and Thompson 1975; Groetlzbach 1988; Troll 1972). With the exception of Kreutzman's (1986, 1988) short articles and Muller-Stellrecht's (1984) brief paper, Hunza has received little or no attention.

Food Crop Production

In Hunza intensive cereal and vegetable farming as well as arboriculture are only feasible in the lower zones of the valley (2,000 m to 2,300 m). For the most part, farming here is possible only because the Hunzakut have made significant modifications to the natural landscape. Two paramount problems confront the Hunzakut farmer: the lack of level land and of water for irrigation.

In order to solve the first problem, farmers have constructed spectacular terraces that cling to mountain sides like colossal staircases. In this way they have been able to convert steep slopes into level fields. The farmer first selects a suitable spot for his field, marks out the desire parameters and, starting with the higher part of the slope, begins to dig the site. As he excavates his terrace, the Hunzakut farmer separates the boulders, rocks and other debris from the soil. The rocks and boulders go into the retaining wall, which depending on the angle of the original slope, can be up to 100 metres high. Smaller field stones are used as fill, on top of which the farmer deposits the sifted soil.

These terraces not only facilitate watering and manuring but also serve to capture and preserve heat, moderating the effects of the naturally cold temperatures by receiving sunlight at a higher angle than can unmodified slopes. Terraced fields also permit the soil to retain water for longer periods, thus further alleviating the cold temperatures (cf. Price 1981: 397). Terracing allows the cultivation of crops at higher elevations than would be possible on natural slopes. In central Hunza the farmers are able to double crop up to an elevation of 2,300 m, well above the maximum double-cropping altitudes elsewhere in the region (cf. Whiteman 1988:65).

Hunzakut farmers have resolved their second problem, the lack of water, by creating a complex irrigation network that delivers water to the fields from the glaciers high above the valley. The irrigation channels are several kilometes long and cling precariously to sheer cliff faces as they wind down to the villages in the lower zones. These channels, an engineering marvel, were constructed without the use of metal tools of modern survey equipment. Indeed, Hunza's irrigation network was once famous throughout Central Asia (cf. Schomberg 1935:112-113). The construction of these channels was possible only through the combine labour of entire communities, mobilized by the state.

The irrigation system is shared by several villages and is under communal management. Ensuring the operation and maintenance of the hydraulic works requires the cooperation, not only of all the households in a single village, but of many neighbouring village communities. Each village is responsible for the upkeep and annual cleaning of its own sections of the total system; all communities relying on the system supply additional labour to repair obstructions and breaks as they occur. Water allocation is based on a complex system of distribution jointly supervised by a "water monitoring committee", comprising two to three individuals (elected by the village leadership), the village leaders themselves, a *chawkidar* (watchman) who guards the channel heads, and the individual farmers. Such rigorous control is needed to ensure the equitable distribution of water and to safeguard the terraces themselves. The imprudent application of water by one farmer can easily undermine the stability of the whole network of terraces, stacked one atop another over an entire slope.

All agricultural lands in the lower zones are privately owned. This is because they represent modifications of the original landscape for the purpose of intensifying crop production. Such modifications have been achieved only through heavy investment of labour, not only to build terraces, but also containing walls, conduits and pathways.

A typical Hunzakut household owns a total of one hectare of land, divided into locationally separate fields, orchards and irrigated pastures at different elevations. Such a dispersed landholding pattern is the result of Hunza's traditional land tenure system. In the former Hunza state all lands ultimately belonged to the Mir. Households were permitted to develop pieces of the "royal estate", add them to their freeholds and benefit from them so long as they fulfilled the various tenancy requirement and obligation attached to each particular piece of land. The intricate set of obligations and duties connected with land enabled the Hunza state to function without the use of currency. Those who found the venture unprofitable could relinquish their right to the property, passing it on to another household.

Just as Hunzakut dependence on a multiple resource base minimizes risks from perturbations affecting any one resource cluster, the fragmentation of landholding over different ecozones provides the farmer with a certain degree of protection against production failures, which may thus be confined to one particular locality (cf. Price 1981; 411-12).

Arable lands in central Hunza, although very scarce, are highly productive; relatively smaller tracts can meet the agricultural needs of the average family. The optimal utilization of these small, privately-owned parcels of land is achieved primarily through the household's own labour household input. Relationships of mutual assistance among neighbours permit one to call upon others should it face labour shortages. (In recent years rich Hunzakut families have also begun to hnire men from Skardu, in Baltistan, to lay down mature for them. The labourers are paid 60 rupess a day, plus food, tea, and housing). The household divides its labour according to sex and age. The men prepare the fields, irrigate the soil before and after sowing and plant the crops. Women weed and manure. All able-bodied members of the household jointly reap, winnow and thresh the crops. Neighbours often help one another prepare fields and harvest crops. Such inter-household aid at critical times during the agricultural cycle not only alleviates the labour shortages of particular productive units, but also reinforces household interdependency and village solidarity.

Hunzakut farmers cultivate a variety of crops suited to specific microzones and complementing each other in terms of tolerance, maturation rates and yields. All cereal crop require the application of substantial amounts of manure, for which the farmers rely upon their livestock. Hunzakut farmers make optimal use of their short growing season with a regimen of double-cropping that requires enormous labour inputs and careful scheduling.

In the past all phases of agricultural production (as also pastoral production, see below) were coordinated through a series of elaborate rituals presided over by the Mir himself. The stage regard such coordination as crucial, since any delay could residue yields and so decrease the surplus which it expropriated in the form of taxes.

The agricultural year was initiated through the *Bopfau,* or seed scattering ritual, held in early February. The actual date of the ceremony was decided by the Mir, in consultation with his court officials and village elders. The decision was based on the particular seasonal climatic conditions, especially the amount of glacial melt-water flowing in the channels which had been opened late-January. The ceremony began with an elder of the Diramitting clan, Hunza's ritual initiators, and an *akhund* (religious divine), who combined the function of religious teacher and oracle, praying for fertility and abundance in the coming year. The next stage of the ritual involved the ceremonial ploughing of the land by the Mir, Wazir and Gushpur (crown-prince). The proceedings concluded with the Mir ritually scattering the first barley seed on the sacred *mamutsha* field in Altit village. (I could not discover from Hunzakut informants the origins of the use of a particular field at Altit village, although they trace the custom back to the time of "Alexander the Great". I note that the word *mamu* means "breast" in Burushaski. Possibly this ceremony represents the survival of an ancient pre-Islamic fertility rite). No Hunzakut was permitted to sow his crops until the Mir had cast the *Bopfau* seeds.

The first barley harvest was also marked by ritual. This was the *Gigani* ceremony held in June. The ritual began with the Mir inspecting his own barley fields to see whether the crops were ready for harvesting. He then conferred with the elders, court officials and an *akhund*. The later consulted astrological texts and set the precise date for the harvest, which village officials announced to the people. Before they began actually cutting the crops, about ten days after *Ginani*, Hunzakut households slaughtered a goat or sheep and ate its flesh during a thanks giving feast called *Piakemar*. After the first of the Mir's barley crops were harvested, people could begin work on their fields. In the past, no one was permitted to harvest their crops until the *Ginani* was held.

Besides the opening of the sowing season and the harvest of the barley, the timing of other crucial phase of the agricultural year, such as the sowing of succeeding crops and manuring of the fields, were also set by the state. The end of the agricultural year was ritualized by the *Thumushelling* festival, a nocturnal torch-lighting ceremony, celebrated at the Winter Solstice. Following this were the six weeks of high winter when no agricultural work was possible and when the people occupied themselves playing music, telling tales, drinking wine and dancing. The winter rest period was ended with the *Apitso* dance held in Baltit, over which the Mir presided and in which headmen and dignitaries from all the villages participated.

In the past the Hunzakut placed great emphasis on these rituals. Failure to perform a ceremony on time, and according to correct procedures, Huzakut believed, would usher in a period of sadness and misfortune. Today, however, the ritual calendar is no longer followed. With it has gone the precise state-manatement and coordination of agricultural production. As one Hunzakut farmer said to me, "who has time for the old ceremonies anymore?". Nevertheless, Hunzakut farmers still plant many of their traditional crops and follow roughly the same timetable as in the past.

Barley (*Hordeum vulgare* L.) and wheat (*Triticum compactum*) are the principal cultivations. Barley, which is sown in February and harvested in June, matures faster than wheat and so affords the farmer sufficient time to plant a second crop, such as millet. Wheat, the Hunzakut's preferred grain, is sown both in spring and winter. Usually local wheat varieties are used because they give high straw yields (crucial for the maintenance of livestock) and because they do not require inputs of pesticides and chemical fertilizers. Spring wheat is sown in early March and harvested in late July. Winter wheat is planted in November on roughly half the farmer's fields (depending on the amount of manure available); it will be ready for harvesting in late July of the following year. This winter wheat crop has a higher yield, but is susceptible to crop disease. Fields not planted to winter wheat are left fallow to receive the following springs' barley crop. The sowing of winter wheat marks the end of the agricultural work season.

Hunzakut farmers sow two kinds of millet (*Setaria italica* L. and *Panicum milieaceum*). Both are fast-maturing grains and are sown at the same time in fields cleared of barley. Both millets are ready for harvest in October. The Hunzakut favour *S. italica*, because it can be stored for long periods with spoiling. Its stems, however, are not palatable to livestock, *P. miliaceum*, on the other hand, is planted both for its food value and because its stalks make excellent animal fodder.

After the winter and spring wheat crops are harvested, in June and late July respectively, the fields are rapidly prepared to receive buckwheat. The Hunzakut farmers plant two varieties of this crop : sweet and bitter. The sweet *Fagopyrum esculentum* is preferred, because of flavour and also because its stalks can be used as animal fodder. On the other hand, it requires an abundance of sunlight and is susceptible to frost. Sweet buckwheat requires at least two more weeks to mature than the bitter variety; and hence it is planted in the fields vacated by winter wheat. This crop is ready for harvest in late November. Bitter *Fagopyrum tataricum* is less desirable because the plant cannot be used as fodder. Moreover, its grain is acceptable for consumption only when mixed, in equivalent proportions, with wheat or barley and milled into flour. But bitter buck wheat matures faster, is harder and more resistant to frost than is *Fagopyrum esculentum*. It is grown, therefore, as a hedge against early frost (what would damage the sweet variety) and is planted after the spring wheat is harvested in late November.

Hunzakut grow potatoes, both for sale as seed to Panjabi farmers and for domestic consumption. Each household sets aside about 2.5% of its total arable land for potato cultivation (Whiteman 1985: 101). This crop is ideally suited to local conditions and yields of as much as 50 tons per hectare have been reported. In comparison with even the best cereal crop, potatoes provide up to three times the calories per hectare; moreover, they require no threshing, winnowing or milling. On the negative side, however, potatoes have little value as animal fodder, which seems to be the reason why Hunzakut farmers do not allocate more land for their cultivation.

Other cultigens, mostly vegetable sidecrops, include, onions, radishes, carrots, lentils, peas, broad beans and cucumbers. All vegetable crops are brought in by mid-October.

Alfalfa (Lucerne) is grown as fodder on privately-owned irrigated pastures. These grass fields are located on slopes adjoining cultivated areas, where water is available but is insufficient for cereal production. Alfalfa is able to tolerate longer periods without water than can be annual crops; it is therefore well suited to water-deficient fields (cf. Whiteman 1988: 65). Alfalfa is cut three times during the agricultural cycle, in June, August, and September, and is dried and stored for winter fodder.

Aside from cereal production, the Hunzakut utilize lower zones for growing fruit trees. Arboriculture, a non-labour-intensive production strategy, is a vital subsidiary economic activity, because fruit (a nutritious and storable food) forms an important part of the Hunzakut diet. Orchards are planted on privately-owned lands; they depend upon irrigation, but are watered only after the cereal and vegetable crops, that always receive top priority.

Orchards provide fruits of various kinds, such as apricots, apples, pears, peaches and mulberries. Hunzakut farmers also grow grapes, but due to land scarcity, few households can afford the luxury of a vineyard. Instead, grape vines are planted in the orchards and allowed to grow up the fruit trees. Apricots and mulberries ripen in late July and early August. Young boys climb up the trees and shake the branches, while women and smaller children stand below with stretched out blankets, held at the four corners, to catch the fruit. As soon as the apricots are gathered, they are split open, stoned (kernels are squeezed for cooking oil) and set out on rooftops to dry in the sun. Mulberries, which require no preparation other than cleaning, are put out to dry at the same time. Apples, peaches and pears mature in late September or early October. These are eaten fresh, although are sometimes dried. Grapes are picked in October and are used for wine-making.

In addition to fruit, orchards provide the Hunzakut with precious timber and fodder. Whenever the Hunzakut farmer plants a new orchard, for additional economic benefits, he usually intersperses poplar and willow among the fruit tree saplings. Consequently, many orchards provide poplar and willow leaves for fodder, branches for firewood and trunks (which make excellent beams) for house construction. Poplar and willow trees are also planted along the southern boundaries of fields. Their placement is stringently regulated by communal rules designed to protect crops from deleterious shading which at this altitude can decrease air temperatures by up to 10 degrees Celsius (Whiteman 1988:75).

The various production strategies related to agriculture, horticulture, and arboriculture just described enable Hunzakut farmers to make a living in an otherwise extraordinarily harsh, resource-scarce natural environment. It is true that the soil is fertile and the system of terraces and hydraulic works sophisticated, but the growing season is short and arable land limited. Consequently, the Hunzakut's subsistence economy seldom provides more than small amounts of surplus grain or other foodstuffs. In the past, what surplus there was had to be turned over to the state as taxes. Consequently, the Hunzakut farmers had to produce sufficient food for his own use as well as for state taxes. Many Hunzakut farmers were barely able to meet the nutritional and caloric needs of their own households and partial famine was common every year from spring until the first barley crops were harvested in June (cf. Clark 1956:84).

One way for the Hunzakut households to ameliorate food shortages, as well as to protect themselves against annual yield fluctuations, is through careful hoarding, storage and management of domestic food supplies. It falls upon the senior female of the household to carefully ration the family's food supplies so as to make both ends meet until the much awaited barley harvested in June. A poor manageress could easily find herself divorced.

In terms of labour organization, the Hunzakut farmers exploit the lower zones, as we have observed, by allocating their labour in two forms. First, household units are used to work privately-owned farms and orchards. Second, larger intra-village and inter-village cooperative units are organized in order to maintain the agricultural infrastructure (terraced slopes and hydraulic networks) upon which Hunza's agriculture depends. We may conclude, therefore, that the Hunzakut household is economically self-sufficient (able to sustain its members on the produce of its own lands), but the total agricultural enterprise depends upon group cooperation and mutual assistance among neighbours and between villages.

Our discussion thus far has focused on Hunza's traditional self-sufficient economy, based on the exploitation of multiple resource clusters spread over different altitudinal zones. Since the abolishment of the mirdom, and the opening of the Karakoram Highway, Hunza's traditional self-sufficient subsistence has been subjected to significant forces of change. For the Hindu Kush and contiguous regions as a whole, Allan (1984: 202-206; 1986: 185-190) has argued that the new government-built roads, which have made formerly-isolated communities accessible to motor vehicles, have drastically and irreversible altered traditional land-used patterns. In Hunza the new and easy accessibility to the Panjabi plains has resulted in an increased out-migration, a new focus on cash-cropping and increasing reliance on lowland markets and governmental institutions (cf. Dani et al. 1987:26-27, 32; Kreutzmann 1988: 105).

The new conditions are transforming Hunza's traditional production strategies, alfalfa and other cash crops are now being planted in fields formerly used for wheat, as the latter is increasingly imported from the Panjab at government subsidized prices. Also, because modern transportation has made fruit a readily marketable commodity, fruit trees (which require little labour and protect tenure) are being planted on prime agricultural land (cf. Dani et al.1987:28). Such interference with the traditional agricultural economy, which provides not only human but also animal foodstuffs, has important implications for livestock husbandry.

Animal Husbandry

Each Hunzakut household keeps about eight to ten head each of goats and sheep. It may also own one or two cows and a bullock. Most domestic animals in Hunza are unimproved local species that tend to be small in body build. They are considered suboptimal by economic development personnel, but attempts to introduce improved stock have yet to prove successful (cf. AKRSP 1989:62). Traditional Hunzakut animal husbandry practices (the retention of old animals, the absence of breeding schemes and use of agricultural residues as fodder) mitigate against the introduction of improved breeds, which cannot be maintained by such traditional methods.

The household's cows provide milk, but in insufficient quantities to make a significant dietary contribution. Cows are more useful for threshing barley and wheat (millet and buckwheat are threshed by hand) than they are dairying. Lashing a team of two to five cows together by their muzzles, the farmer drives them across the grain that he has piled on a circular, earthen threshing floor constructed on the edge of his field. As the animals trample the harvested crops, their hooves separate the husk from the grain, which is then ready for winnowing.

Hunzakut farmers use their oxen for ploughing. They fasten a yoke over the necks of a pair of beasts and harness them to a metal-tipped wooden plough. The farmer derives the team lengthwise over his field to produce parallel grooves. Ploughing is strenuous work for both man and animal, and tilling a one-hectare plot can take up to a week or ten days.

Goats are the main dairying animals. They also provide hair, hides, and meat. Sheep supply a limited quantity of milk, but are useful mostly for their wool, hides and meat.

The Hunzakut eat the flesh of their domestic animals, but only on rare occasions, such as during the barley harvest. This is a time when household members, still relatively weak from their protein-deficient diet during later winter or early spring, must exert a considerable amount of extra energy. Meat is also eaten in mid-winter, when fodder supplies dwindle and it is difficult to keep all the stock alive.

Caloric and nutritional contributions aside, the Hunzakut's livestock play vital role in their agricultural enterprise. This is because animal manure, from 25 up to 40 tones per hectare of land (Whiteman 1985: 31), is vital for maintaining sufficient levels of soil nitrogen necessary for the fertilization of food crops (cf. Frissel 1977). In effect, farming would be impossible. The dung produced by cattle accumulates in the stalls and is used during the sowing of crops in spring and summer.

Equally important as crop fertilizer is the goat and sheep manure produced on the upland pastures. Although it is less abundant than cattle dung, Hunzakut farmers regard the manure from goats, and especially from sheep, as the finest of all fertilizers, far superior to the expensive chemicals introduced by Pakistani development agencies during the 1970s. As a matter of fact, laboratory analysis reveals that sheep dung not only has more nitrogen, calcium, and potassium than cattle dung but also causes more rapid bacterial action and humus formation (Price 1981: 425).

The shepherds gather the precious goat and sheep dung in the upland pastures, taking it from inside the corrals where the animals are confined at night (to prevent attacks by snow leopards). They dry the dung on the roofs of their huts, periodically bringing it down to the villages. They do not collect the dung from outside the corrals, believing this is best left to fertilise the alpine grasslands. Dung produced by goats and sheep during the winter (when they are kept indoors in sheds) is allowed to accumulate, as is that from the cows and oxen throughout the year, are kept in the villages and stalled at night.

At first sight it seems strange that Hunzakut farmers apply the less favoured cattle manure to their principal cereal crops, and use the highly-regarded sheep and goat dung for their vegetable side crops. But the reason is simple. Sheep and goats produce relatively small amounts of dung as compared to cattle.

Pastoral Production Strategy

Unlike agriculture, which involves the intensive use of limited parcels of land, the Hunzakut's strategy for pastoral production entails extensive exploitation of a resource that is spread out both vertically and horizontally.

Pastures are productive only during the short summer season, but even then they cannot sustain intensive and prolonged grazing. This is because they constitute a fragile environment with thin and immature soils, limited biomass and slow rates of plant growth. Consequently, to prevent grassland degradation, shepherds move their flocks over the distances and successive levels (cf. Rhoades and Thompson 1975: 540). This strategy involves coordinated effort and mitigates against individual ownership of pasture lands.

All pastures are owned by patrilineages and are under collective management, thus facilitating the judicious allocation of labour. The community can entrust its animals to a small group of shepherds and so free the remainder of its working population for crucial agricultural activities in the lower production zones.

Communal pasture management also allows for the collective maintenance of mountain paths, corrals and shepherds' huts, tasks that require more labour than any individual household can provide on its own.

The annual transhumant cycle in Hunza begins in late May and ends in September. In the past the state organized all pastoral activities, as it did all agricultural events. The Wazir determined the time when the animals were to be assembled for the drive to the mountains, the itinerary for the move itself and the time for the flocks to return to the villages. The drive to the mountains, which was marked by rituals, had to be called *Odi*, in which all the Hunzakut villages participated, was held about a week before the flocks were sent to the mountains. The date for *Odi* was set by the Wazir and announced by village officials. After this, a resident herdsman of the ritual-initiating Diramitting clan visited each house in his village and milked its goats. These animals, thin from the their winter stall-feeding, provide very little milk at this time. Usually only one to two gourds of milk (about 8 litres) could be obtained from the whole village. The resident herdsman took whatever milk he was able to draw to the Wazir's house in Baltit. Here it was processed into cheese, before being taken to the Mir's palace to be blessed. After receiving the cheese brought to him by each village's Diramitting herdsman, the Mir would take a bite and bless the remainder. This ritual act inaugurated the pastoral season.

Following the Mir's blessing of the cheese, people could take their livestock to the upland pastures. Those who failed to follow the state's schedule were deemed to have committed a ritual offence and were fined a sheep or goat. As was the case with the agricultural festivals described earlier, the *Odi* ceremony is now defunct. Decisions pertaining to the opening and closing of pastures are made by village leaders and the coordination of former times has completely disappeared.

Central Hunza's principal pastures are located at altitudes between 3,300 m and 4,200 m, well above the limits of agriculture. Most pastures are within a day's walk from the villages, but the drive is no easy task. It often involves vertical distances of 1,500 m to 2,000 m, and requires negotiating incredibly narrow and steep footpaths which ascend through dark, constricted and sometimes treacherous ravines. These trails eventually lead to spacious meadows, but the terrain is still fairly rough and vegetation comprises patches of grass interspersed with shrubs. Willow scrub and recumbent juniper are found along the steeper inclines.

Traditionally the Hunzakut have regarded these upland pastures, and the mountains beyond, as sacred places, the hallowed domain of the *pari*. These are supernatural creatures thought capable of bringing good fortune and prosperity, but also as being able to harm, or even kill people, injure their livestock and blight their crops. Shepherds who behave improperly, neglect their flocks, or allow them to damage the fragile meadows are sure, so Hunzakut believe, to invoke the wrath of the *pari*. Likewise the *pari* are offended by the presene of women (believed to be impure because of their menstrual periods) and cattle (which, unlike goats and sheep, Hunzakut regard as impure animals). Similar belief found among the Dardic speaking populations to the south have received considerable attention (cf. Drew 1875: 428; Parks 1987: 647), but scholars have overlooked their presence among the Hunzakut. Jettmar (1961: 87) even denies their existence in Hunza.

Sheep and goats are pastured in meadows located between 3,300 m and 3,700 m, but the two species utilize different ecological niches. Goats are markably agile and can climb precipitous slopes in order to browse on scrubs and bushes found among the rocks. Sheep, on the other hand, unable to traverse precipitous slopes, stay in the lower, less steep areas, where they graze on grassy patches. Shepherds generally allow the goats to forage on their own for most of the day, but have to pay more attention to the sheep. The latter have a tendency to fall off steep ledges and cliffs;

they also feed in clusters and, unless moved on, can quickly damage the fragile pastures.

Cattle have traditionally had little part in the Hunzakut transchumant cycle. In the past, as a few elderly Hunzakut still recall, they were seldom taken to the mountains. In part this was because they were considered impure animals, as we have seen, offensive to the *pari*. This quasi-religious explanation, the origins of which are obscure, is no longer credible to most modern Hunzakut; nevertheless cattle are still infrequently taken to the pastures. This is because only a limited number of alpine meadows have footpaths wide enough to accommodate such large-sized beasts. Moreover, as no Hunzakut shepherd will take cattle under his charge, those who wish to take their animals to the upland meadows must drive them there themselves. On the pastures, the cattle, like sheep, remain in the gently-sloping areas. But thee is a price to pay for having these large bovines up here. This is because cattle compete with sheep and goats for the naturally sparse vegetation, which they consume in greater quantities than do the smaller ruminants. Moreover, cattle hooves easily tear up the thin, moist grass cover, thus further endangering the fragile alpine ecosystem.

Yaks play little or no part in the present-day economy of central Hunza. In 1991, there was only one herd of about 20 heard, all the property of a single household. These yaks were kept for the entire year on pastures near the snowline (4,500 m).

The sheep and goats remain on the pastures until after the final harvest of crops in the valleys below. Having the livestock well away from the lower zones during the growing season ensures the safety of the crops (cf. Rhoades and Thompson 1975: 539-540). But for the Hunzakut, driving the flocks to alpine pastures is more than a matter of simple crop protection. It is a strategy that enables them to convert otherwise unusable high-altitude biomass into high-protein, high-fat, dairy produce. Once the goats and sheep reach the pastures they rapidly gain weight (roughly 5 to 10 kgs in four months), and soon reach their peak lactation. Shepherds make cheese and butter daily, which they store in small pools of ice-cold glacial melt-water. Periodically they bring these dairy products down to the villages, where some of the cheese and butter is immediately eaten and the remainder stored. As these foods first become available just prior to the heavy agricultural labour associated with the first barley harvest, they are especially welcome supplements to the protein-deficient diet on which the Hunzakut have had to subsist from late winter or early spring.

In September the shepherds drive the animals back to the lower agricultural zones, where they are left to graze on the privately-owned irrigated-pastures, in orchards and on newly-harvested fields. By late October to early November, the animals will have devoured all the vegetation at these locations.

Thereafter, all livestock (goats, sheep, cows and oxen) are kept in stalls until spring. They are fed primarily from the stocks of straw and alfalfa produced during summer, but Hunzakut households also make great efforts to supplement this winter fodder with tree clippings (brought down from alpine forests) and leaves from poplar, willow and apricot trees, poplar bark for the goat and spoiled apricots (from their orchards). They also collect shrubs that grow along the irrigation channels in the lower zones. Nevertheless, animals still lose weight during the winter months and, ultimately, livestock-fodder imbalances must be rectified by slaughtering a few beasts during the *Thumushelling* festival.

Traditionally, the density of the Hunzakut livestock is regulated by the quantity of winter fodder (straw from cereals and alfalfa) most of which is grown on limited amounts of arable land. Herd density, in turn, determines the amount of manure available for farming and thus governs agricultural productivity (including the amount of fodder produced). If an enterprising farmer ventures to expand his animal herd without increasing his existing fodder supplies, which would mean obtaining more arable land, he puts his entire herd at risk. On the other hand, he must have a sufficient amount of manure to avoid jeopardizing his harvest. Herd density and agricultural production are thus intricately linked, so that a change in either would affect both. This homeostatic relationship serves to regulate the agro-pastoral production by keeping the crucial variables of manure and fodder within a range which does not disrupt the whole production system.

To sum up: Hunzakut animal husbandry involves the maintenance mainly on goats, sheep and cattle. The latter have traditionally served non-pastoral functions, as draught animals and as source of manure. Sheep and goats, on the other hand, are true pastoral animals that allow the Hunzakut to exploit upland grass resources. Sheep and goats provide dairy products, wool, hair, hides and meat. They also contribute modest amounts of high-quality dung which the Hunzakut use for vegetable farming. The traditional Hunzakut agricultural enterprise, as we have seen could not function without animal husbandry.

The Hunzakut pastoral strategy is based on the use of communally-owned pastures for the maintenance of privately-owned domestic animals. In terms of labour organisation, this strategy involves cooperative arrangements among households (and sometimes between villages) and facilitate the management of livestock and the protection of the alpine meadows.

The traditional Hunzakut husbandry practices that have been described here have been undergoing significant changes since the mid-1970s. Alterations in cropping and land-use patterns, discussed previously, are destabilizing the intricate relationship between livestock, herd density, amount of available manure and agricultural productivity that characterized the traditional Hunzakut agro-pastoral system. Moreover, increasing out-migration of able-bodied men, enticed away by high-paying jobs in the lowlands of Pakistan, has reduced the manpower available for animal husbandry. Furthermore, children, who once served as the household's shepherds, are now in schools for most of the day, thus further eroding the household's capacity to maintain large herds.

Many families, no longer having sufficient manpower to maintain their previous herding arrangements, frequently leave the care of their animals to women and old men, unable to make the difficult treks to many of the upland pastures. Consequently, the utilization of the highest and most distant alpine pastures is gradually decreasing, while those closer to the villages are becoming subjected to over-grazing and consequent degradation.

Gathering and Hunting

Besides agriculture and animal husbandry, the traditional Hunzakut economy has a significant gathering sector and a somewhat less important hunting component. Wood for construction and fuel is the major resource gathered from the alpine forests above the valley. Composed mainly of juniper (*Juniperus macropoda*) and cedar (*Cedrus deodara*), these forests are located at elevations of 3,000 m and above. Trees grow most abundantly on north-and west-facing slopes, which are generally moister than the south- and east-facing ones.

In the past, the exploitation of the upland forests was subject to strict rules. No trees could be felled without the permission of the Mir and the village council. Moreover, villages had to pay a modest tax based on the total weight of the wood collected from the forests. Normally, only tree branches were culled, leaving trunks intact to regenerate branches. Indicative of traditional Hunzakut conservation practices, some of the trees in the alpine forests are reputedly over a thousand years old (Bilham et al. 1982:599).Whenever it was necessary to fell entire trees, this was done selectively and at a frequency matching the rate of forest regrowth. The system ensured equitable distribution of wood among village households, while preserving the protective capacity of the forests.

Upland forests, besides providing timber, make a significant contribution to slope stability. Tree roots anchor soil and so deter erosion; they also assimilate water and hold back surface snowpack, thus protecting against calamitous flash floods and avalanches (Price 1981: 428). When tree-cover is removed, the temperature of the air near the ground decreases; this enhances frost penetration (needle-ice activity) and consequently, soil erosion (Price 1981:421-428; Little and Morren 1976:9).

Today, the Government of Pakistan has assumed ownership of Hunza's alpine forests, making traditional controls over the indiscriminate cutting of trees inoperative. However, Islamabad's administration is not fully enforceable in this still relatively-remote area (cf. Dani et al. 1987: 26-27, 32). Thus, while traditional conservation practices have disintegrated, but substitutes have not been instituted.

Aside from exploiting the wood resources of the alpine zones, the Hunzakut also hunt here. The principal large game animals include wild sheep (*Ovis poli*), urial (*Ovis orientalis*), markhor (*Capra falconeri*) and ibex (*Capra ibex*). These animals are killed for their meat, horns (as trophies and for knife handles) and hides (for shoes, gloves and other leather goods).

In traditional Hunzakut ideology, the *markhor* and the ibex are sacred animals, the property of the mountain spirits. To hunt them the *shikari* (hunter) has to observe certain ritual conditions so as not to evoke the wrath of the *pari*. He must first beseech these supernatural beings to appear to him in his dreams and grant him permission to kill one of their beasts. Simultaneously, he must improve them to reveal the locality where he might find the game. Without such supernatural assistance, Hunzakut believe, it is impossible to locate the wily caprids. Finally because he must enter the domain of the mountain spirits the hunter has to bathe and abstain from sex the night before the hunt.

These ritual restrictions may have once served as a conservation measure against unrestrained hunting. Over the last century, however the excessive slaughter accompanying the introduction of modern firearms has led to a sharp decline in ibex, *markhor* and wild sheep populations (cf. Akbar, 1974: 2; Schomberg 1935:56, 136; 1936: 59, 135; Rasul 1982:49050; ricciuti 1976:32). This in turn, has deprived carnivores, such as snow leopard (*Panthera uncial*) and lynx (*Felis lynx*), of their natural prey, forcing them to attack domestic livestock on the high pastures.

Although one frequently sees ibex and *markhor* horns adorning Hunzakut houses, hunting plays little part today in then Hunzakut economy. It has tended to become the avocation of a few intrepid individuals, who say that they find village life and Pakistani influences distasteful, and so prefer to spend their time in uninhabited upland regions.

Conclusion: Hunzakut Production Strategies and Socio-Economic Organization

This paper has focused on production strategies and their influences on the socio-economic organization of Hunzakut society. As we have seen, to survive in their resource-poor and harsh high-mountain environment, Hunzakut rely on several strategies: the cultivation of cereals, vegetables and fruit crops, animal husbandry and transhumant pastoralism, and the gathering of wild timber resources.

Hunzakut food crop production is intricately adjusted to ecological conditions through the use of cultigens suited to specific microzones and complementing each other in terms of tolerance, maturation rates and yields. Animal husbandry is similarly adapted to ecological circumstances, through management of herd size and composition, as well as the ability of the various species to utilize different ecological niches. Herd density and agricultural production possess a homoe static relationship that serves to regulate the Hunzakut agro-pastoral system by maintaining the crucial variables of manure and fodder within a range that does not disrupt the whole system.

Each Hunzakut production strategy entails different social arrangements, as well as different land-use patterns that have certain implications for the social organisation of Hunzakut households, villages and larger inter-village units. Households constitute the principal units of production, while villages, the hub of communal life, are formed by agglomerations of households. Members of various households in a village may belong to one of four exogamous patrilineal clans. Clan membership regulates marriage (and one clan has certain ritual prerogatives), but otherwise these descent categories play little part in the economic organisation of Hunzakut society.

Households enter into various arrangements for mutual aid and cooperation in order to exploit communally and privately managed resources. Households operate privately-owned farms and orchards, and frequently neighbouring households help each other with demanding tasks, such as preparing fields and harvesting crops. These practical economic relationships, cutting across descent lines, constitute the basis of village social organisation.

Village membership, along with associated rights and obligations, is based on residence rather than ties of common kinship or affinity. Villages, in turn, are integrated into larger social units through cooperative exchange networks necessary for the continued operation of the agricultural infrastructure. Similar cooperative arrangements among households, and between villages, are necessary for the optimal use of communally-owned pastures, the management of livestock in summer and the maintenance of mountain paths and shepherds' huts. Cooperative management also serves to conserve grassland resources.

The integration of villages, each one of which exploits a slightly different resource cluster, or niche, into geographically more inclusive inter-village units also provides a means of protection against environmental perturbations. If a particular community in the valley experiences a crop failure, or some other calamity, it is likely that others will remain unaffected, and so be able to provide it with assistance. The Hunzakut agro-pastoral enterprise as a whole, one may conclude, depends upon economic cooperation and mutual assistance among households and between villages, irrespective of descent group membership.

Acknowledgement

I am greatly indebted to Dr. Anthony R. Walker (Department of Anthropology, The Ohio State University) for his generous editorial assistance through earlier drafts of this paper.

REFERENCES

Akbar, Ali (1974), "Chitral Gol Sanctuary for Markhor". *Pakistan Journal of Forestry* 24 (3): 209-212.

AKRSP (1989), *The Aga Khan Rural Support Programme: Seventh Annual Review.* Gilgit: AKRSP.

Allan, Nigel J.R.(1984), "Ecological effects of land intensification in the central and eastern Hindukush". In E. Groetzbach (ed.) Beitrage zur Vergleichenden Kulturgeographie der Hochgebirge. Regensburg: Friedrich Pustet. pp. 193-212.

———(1986), "Accessibility and Altitudinal Zonation Models of Mountains." *Mountain Research and Development* 6: 185-194, 205-206.

Barth Fredrik (1956), *Indus and Swat Kihistan: An Ethnographic Survey.* Oslo: Forenede Trykkerier.

Berger, Hermann (1985), "A survey of Burushaski students". *Journal of Central Asia* 8 (1): 33-37.

Biddulph, J. (1880), *"Tribes of the Hindoo Kush.* Calcutta: Office of the Superintendent of Government Printing. (Reprinted 1971, Graz, Austria: Akademische Druck-u. Verlagsanstalt, K. Gratzl ed.)

Bilham, R. et al. (1984), "A preliminary Study of Ancient Trees in the Hunza valley and their Dendroclimatic Potential". In Keith Miller (ed.) Proceedings of the International Karakorum Project. 2 vols. London: Royal Geographic Society. pp. 599-606.

Buddruss, Georg (1985), "Linguistic Research in Gilgit and Hunza: Some Results and Perspectives." *Journal of Central Asia* 8(1): 27-32.

Charles, Christian (1985), La vallee de Hunza Karakorum. Doctoral thesis: Institut de Geographie. Universite De Grenoble.

Clark, John (1956), *Hunza: Lost Kingdom of the Himalayas.* New York : Funk and Wagnalls.

Dani, Anis A. et al. (1987), *Institutional Development for Local Management of Rural Resources.* Honolulu: East-West Environment and Policy Institute.

Drew, Frederic (1875), *The Jammoo and Kashmir Territories: A Geographical Account.* London: E. Standford. (Reprinted 1971, Delhi: Oriental Publishers).

Durand, A. (1900), *The Making of a Frontier.* London: John Murray.

Ellen, Roy (1986) *Environment, Subsistence and System: The Ecology of Small-Scale Social Formations.* Cambridge: Cambridge University Press.

Frissel, M.J. (1977), "Cycling Mineral Nutrients in Agricultural Ecosystems". *Agro-Ecosystems* 4: 17-25.

Goudie, A.S. et al.(1984), "The Geomorphology of the Hunza Valley, Karakoram Mountains, Pakistan". In Keith Miller (ed.) Proceedings of the International Marakorum Project. 2 vols. London: Royal Geographic Society. pp.359-410.

Groetzbach, Erwin (1988), "High Mountains as Human Habitat". In Nigel Allan et al. (eds.) Human Impact on Mountains. Totowa, New Jersey: Rowman and Littlefield. pp. 24-35.

Guillet, David (1983), "Toward a Cultural Ecology of Mountains: The Central Andes and the Himalayas Compared." *Current Anthropology* 24(5): 561-573.

Jettmar, Karl (1961), "Ethnological research in Dardistan 1958: Preliminary Report. *Proceedings of the American Philosophical Society* 105 (1): 79-97.

Keay, John (1979) *The Gilgit Game.* London: John Murrary.

Knight, E.F.(1893) *Where Three Empires Meet.* London: Longmans, Green, and Co.

Kreutzmann, Hermann J. (1986), "A Note on Yak Peeing in Hunza (Northern Areas of Pakistan)". *Production Pastorale et societe* 19: 99-106.

———(1988), "Oases of the Karakorum : Evolution of irrigation and social organisation in Hunza, North Pakistan." In Nigel Allan et al. (eds.) Totowa, New Jersey : Rowman and Littlefield. pp. 243-254.

Leitner, G.W. (1889), *Dardistan in 1866, 1886 and 1893: The Hunza and Nagyr Handbook.* Working (England): the Oriental University Institute.

Little, M.A. and G.E.B. Borren (1977) *Ecology, Energetics, and Human Variability.* Duburque: William Brown.

Lorimer, D.L.R. (1935) *The Burushski Language.* Vols. 1-3. Oslo: H. Aschenhoug & Co.

———(1939) *The Dumaki Language: Outlines of the Speech of the Doma, or Bericho of Hunza,* Nijmegen: Dekker & van de Vegt N.V.

Morgenstierne, G. (1935) "Preface". *In* The Burushaski Language. D.L. Lorimer. Vols. 1-3 Oslo: H. Aschenhoug & Co. pp. VII-XXX.

Muller-Stellrecht (1984), "The People of Hunza: Their Life in the High Mountain area of Pakistan." *Journal of Central Asia* 7 (2): 21-28.

Nevill, H.L.(1912) *Campaigns on the North-West Frontier.* Delhi: Neeraj Publishing House.

Netting, Robert, McC (1972), "Of men and meadows: Strategies of Alpine land use". *Anthropological Quarterly* 45 (3): 132-144.

———(1976), "What Alpine Peasants have in Common: Observations on Communal Tenure in a Swiss Village". *Human Ecology* 4(2): 135-146.

———(1977), *Cultural Ecology*. Menlo Park, California: Cummings Publishing Co.

Parks, Peter (1987), "Livestock Symbolism and Pastoral Ideology Among the Kafirs of the Hindu Kush." *Man* (N.S.) 22: 637-660.

Price, Larry W. (1981), *Mountains and Man: A Study of Process and Environment*. Los Angeles: University of California Press.

Rasul, Ghulam (1982) "The Himalayan ibex". *Pakistan Journal of Forestry* 32 (2): 46-51.

Rhoades, Robert and Stephen I. Thompson (1975), "Adaptive Strategies in Alpine Environments: Beyond Ecological Particularism". *American Ethnologist* 3(3): 535-551.

Ricciuti, E.R. (1976), "Mountains besieged." *International Wildlife* 6(6): 24-34.

Schomberg, R.C.F. (1935), *Between the Oxus and the Indus*. London : Martin Hopkinson Ltd.

———(1936), *Unknown Karakoram*. London: Martin Hopkinson Ltd.

Staley, John (1969), "Economy and Society in High Mountains of Pakistan". *Modern Asian Studies* (3): 225-243.

———(1982) *Words for My Brother*. Karachi: Oxford University Press.

Terray, Emmanuel (1972), *Marxism and "Primitive" Societies: Two Studies*. New York . Monthly Review Press.

Thomas, R. Brook (1979) "Effects of Change on High Mountain Human Adaptive Patterns." In Patrick J. Webber (ed.) High Altitude Geoecology. Boulder Co: Westview Press, pp. 139-188.

Troll, Carl (1972) *Geoecology of the High-Mountain Regions of Eurasia*. Wiesbaden: Franz Steiner.

Whiteman, Peter T.S. (1985) *Mountain Oases: A Technical Report of Agricultural Studies in Hunza, Ishkoman and Yasin Valleys of Gilgit District*. Rome: United Nations Food and Agricultural Organisation.

———(1988) "Mountain Agronomy in Ethopia, Nepal and Pakistan." In Nigel Allan et al. (eds.) Human Impact on Mountains. Totowa, New Jersey: Rowman and Littlefield. pp. 57-82.

INDEX